John Callow is Visiting Tutor in the History Department of the University of Suffolk and the Head of Education at the General Federation of Trade Unions. He has written widely on Early Modern witchcraft, politics and popular culture. His books include *Witchcraft & Magic in Sixteenth- and Seventeenth-Century Europe*, with Geoffrey Scarre; and *James II: King in Exile*. He has appeared on the BBC's *The One Show* to discuss the roots of Hallowe'en and the BBC Radio 4 documentary *It Must be Witchcraft*.

'*Embracing the Darkness* is a refreshing and original perspective on the history of witchcraft. It traces the transformation of the witch over the last 2,000 years from a figure of fear, terror and loathing in late antiquity, and of deadly stereotyping in the great witch-hunts of the early modern period, to one of sympathy – even admiration – in the resurgence of "pagan" witchcraft in recent times. The great virtue of *Embracing the Darkness* lies in its eschewing any simplistic, reductionist explanations of witchcraft in favour of a series of detailed, finely nuanced accounts that give the reader a much richer appreciation of the many ways that the witch has been constructed and imagined in Western culture. It's a terrific example of contextual scholarship.'

– **Philip C. Almond, Professor Emeritus of the Study of Religion, University of Queensland, author of *The Lancashire Witches* (I.B.Tauris, 2012) and *The Witches of Warboys* (I.B.Tauris, 2008)**

'A compelling treatment of the witch in culture, literature and art – with a strong social and political critique evident throughout. Callow shows a nuanced appreciation of pagan history, and indeed a sensibility, in Western Europe's understanding of witchcraft and magic.'

– **Christina Oakley Harrington, Founder and Director, Treadwell's Bookshop, London**

'Be warned: this is a dangerous, seductive book which contains the power both of metamorphosis and of time travel. Open at any page and step into the past as living, breathing history. With effortless and meticulous scholarship, a playful spirit and the style of a natural-born storyteller, John Callow taps 2,000 years of that most ubiquitous figure of the Western imagination – the terrifying, compelling archetype of the witch who has grown up with us from our most intimate individual childhood to our collective, publicly shared cultural and political unconscious. The author's genius is to explain the strange transformation of the witch from a female archetype of fear and hate to a modern-day sympathetic and aspirational figure and forerunner of feminism. He thereby gifts us startling, unexpected delights and "the freedom to dream of a new form of an old magic".'

– **Rachel Holmes, author of** *The Secret Life of*
Dr James Barry: Victorian England's Most Eminent Surgeon,
African Queen: The Real Life of the Hottentot Venus **and** *Eleanor Marx: A Life*

'This is one of the most fascinating books on witches and witchcraft that I've read for some time. Through a sharply discerning lens, separating cultural assumptions from historical fact, John Callow looks at the history of witches and the variety of ways in which they have been viewed. The result is a highly educational tour of an important but too often misunderstood part of our heritage. *Embracing the Darkness* may lead the reader through shadows, but is a most enlightening book.'

– **Gary Lachman, formerly bass guitarist with Blondie,**
author of *The Secret Teachers of the Western World* **and** *Turn off*
Your Mind: The Mystic Sixties and the Dark Side of the Age of Aquarius

'John Callow's cultural history of witchcraft is a vivid, compelling, bizarre and terrifying history of devils, witches, demonic seduction and witch-hunts – deeply researched, highly readable and strangely relevant for our own times.'

– **Simon Sebag Montefiore, author of** *The Romanovs*

Embracing the Darkness

A Cultural History
of Witchcraft

JOHN CALLOW

I.B. TAURIS
LONDON · NEW YORK

Published in 2018 by
I.B.Tauris & Co. Ltd
London • New York
www.ibtauris.com

ISBN: 978 1 84511 469 5
eISBN: 978 1 78672 261 4
ePDF: 978 1 78673 261 3

A full CIP record for this book is available from the British Library
A full CIP record is available from the Library of Congress

Library of Congress Catalog Card Number: available

Typeset by Riverside Publishing Solutions, Salisbury, UK
Printed and bound in Sweden by ScandBook AB

Contents

Illustrations

captured this dangerous essence. Sister Jeanne (played by Vanessa Redgrave) hangs – and is prepared to hang others – upon his every word (Private Collection).

24 **Urbain Grandier Confronts the Hooded Tribunal**, Oliver Reed's finest moment as an actor and the climax of *The Devils*, as the doomed Grandier tears apart the terror and the lies of the witch-hunters at Loudun. Detail from an American film poster, 1971 (Private Collection).

25 **The Witches' Sabbath**, an engraving by Michael Herr, 1620. The hollow hills, riotous dancing and feasting shown here, when taken out of context, could distort Isobel Gowdie's tales of night flight, 'elf bulls' and meetings with the 'king and queen' of the faerie, into something altogether darker and more threatening to the Kirk and the State (Author's Collection).

26 **'Credulity, Superstition & Fanaticism'**, by William Hogarth, 1762. The Anglican clergyman attempts to strike fear into his congregation by brandishing images of the broomstick-riding witch and the trident-carrying devil. However, his wig flies off to reveal the tonsure of a Catholic monk, while Mary Tofts – who was believed to have given birth to a litter of rabbits – and a 'Demoniak', who vomits forth pins and nails to order, are satirised. A bewildered Turk (no doubt a relation of Montesquieu's *Usbek* and *Rica*) peers in at the window (Author's Collection).

27 **Tam O' Shanter and the Witches**, as drawn by John Faed. Robert Burns' poem, written in 1790, is an Enlightenment satire against superstition and drunkenness. The account of the coven meeting in the ruined Kirk would seem to be based on the account of the trials of the witches of North Berwick. Yet, fear has turned to laughter, the devil has become a figure of fun – corpulently blowing upon the bagpipes – and the 'maiden' of the Coven is now both young and inviting (Author's Collection).

28 **Hansel and Gretel**, by Hermann Kaulbach, 1872. This illustration to the Grimms' *Nursery and Household Tales* emphasises the bestial nature and murderous cannibalism associated with the witch figure. If her femininity is negated and perverted, then Gretel's mixture of kindness and cunning, as pictured here, fulfils a feminine archetype (Author's Collection).

29 **'The Singing Ringing Tree'**. Despite the petulant commands of Princess 'Thousandbeauty', the little tree will neither sing nor ring, until her heart is true. Christel Bodenstein stars in the definitive DEFA fairy tale, released in East Germany in 1957 and brought to the BBC in 1964 (Author's Collection).

forest god, Potter's 'Herne' has lost his human aspect and stands at the gateways of life and death (whereabouts of the original unknown).

43 **Drawing Down the Moon – or Raising Hell?** Morgwyn of Ravenscar, the high priestess of the Coven – played by Rula Lenska – performs her art, in a still from *Robin of Sherwood* (HTV/Goldcrest/ITV).

A Note on Dating and Terminology

Every book needs to find its own voice and manner of expression. In dealing with a subject such as witchcraft, which is – in both its modern and ancient forms – the product of markedly different polytheistic societies, and which since the eighteenth century has been the product of successive counter-cultural strains, it seems somewhat out of place to make use of a system of dating that reflects only the claims of one particular, monotheistic, faith. It also suggests that we are dealing with grey areas of thought, rather than with single, absolute truths. Consequently, 'Common Era' (abbreviated to CE) and 'Before Common Era' (abbreviated to BCE) are preferred throughout to the traditional designations of 'Anno Domini/the year of our Lord' (AD) and 'Before Christ' (BC).

In a similar fashion, the term 'pagan' – lower case – is used to signify the cluster of beliefs held in Europe prior to the advent of Christianity, while 'Pagan' – in the upper case – is used as an inclusive term to refer to comparatively modern revivals, spanning a variety of pantheistic beliefs, polytheistic pantheons and ritual practices, that regard the divine as being immanent in both human beings and in nature. This reflects, and hopefully respects, the self-designation of contemporary practitioners of witchcraft, which has become common, if not quite standard, since the late 1980s. It also reflects the personal choice of the author who shies away from the term 'neo-pagan' on account of its roots in the distortion, and ultimate corruption, of folk culture in Nazi Germany.

As in modern usage, the New Year is taken as beginning on 1 January and not (as per the Julian, or Old Style Calendar) on 25 March.

Acknowledgements

Though the selection and interpretation of sources, together with any errors or omissions, within the text are exclusively my own responsibility, this book has been shaped by the advice and friendship of the following individuals and, simply, would not have been the same without them. Those you meet on the way make the journey worthwhile and suggest that the 'Republic of Letters', as both a concept and a practice, is still one of our most vibrant legacies from the seventeenth century and very far from being merely a thing of the past.

Beginnings are times of discovery, promise and excitement. Dr Geoffrey Scarre first set me on the road towards an academic career during my time at the University of Durham and, in the midst of a torrential downpour that sent hailstones bouncing off the tiles of his office roof – high up in the attic room of the Philosophy Department – he took me through his original copy of King James VI and I's *Daemonologie* as we discussed the phenomena of witchcraft and witch-belief. I was lucky to have come into contact with him and luckier still to benefit from his insights and friendship.

Professor Ronald Hutton is the linking thread running through so much of my own writing: a generous patron and a supremely gifted historian. His researches are central to any significant understanding of the genesis and development of the modern Pagan movement, and it is my firm belief that future generations of scholars and Pagans, alike, will be greatly in his debt.

It was Ronald who first introduced me to Christina Oakley Harrington, who has fashioned in Treadwell's, her London bookshop, a centre for esoteric studies, a haven for like minds, and a true successor to the literary salons that illuminated the intellectual and social life of eighteenth-century Europe. Her engagement with the emergent culture of modern Paganism has done much to shape and to guide this work.

Several of the chapters in this book formed the basis of lectures given, over the space of several years, for Treadwell's, the 'Moot with No Name', conferences of the Pagan Federation, the Manx Museum, at Douglas, and as part of the excellent, and innovative, BA undergraduate course run by Dr Louise Carter, on 'The Witch Hunt in East Anglia and Beyond', at the University of Suffolk. In Louise and Dr Harvey Osborne, the Head of the History Faculty at Suffolk, I have been blessed with the best and brightest of colleagues, and the firmest of friends.

Louise, together with Christina Oakley Harrington and Rebecca Dudley, was crucial in providing advice and editorial skill in knitting the book together, and getting it over 'the finishing line'.

Professor Jeffrey Richards of the University of Lancaster shared his unrivalled knowledge of Victorian popular culture in the reimaginings of witches. As generous as he is perceptive, Jeffrey – together with his colleagues, Professors Eric Evans and Michael Mullett – represented the finest expressions of the 'Golden Age' of the History Department at Lancaster, under the inspiration of the late Austin Woolrych. Individually and collectively, I personally owe them more than I could ever hope to repay.

To Caroline Oates, I owe my introduction to the wonderful collection of books and journals housed at the Warburg Institute of the University of London, and to the work of the Folklore Society. Our conversations about folk cultures and the nature of witchcraft started in the cafés bordering New Cross, during our time teaching at Goldsmiths College, and have been renewed at the Warburg, where Caroline is now based.

The library of the Museum of Witchcraft at Boscastle must be one of the most wonderful places to research any subject. The books, the resources and the artefacts are national treasures. I am very grateful to Simon Costin, the museum's director, for his unfailing help, efficiency and enthusiasm in granting me access to the materials there, for answering my research questions and for providing illustrations for this book. His colleagues at the Museum, Peter Hewitt, Joyce Froome and Hannah Fox, made my research trip to Boscastle as pleasant as it was highly productive.

Thanks are also due to Suzanne Vincent for the image of Ursula Kempe, in her collection, and to Louise Woods for supplying photocopies from her extensive collection of *Robin of Sherwood* memorabilia. I am also indebted to Yvonne Cresswell, Folklore Curator at the Manx Museum, for her insights into Manx customs and witch-beliefs, both ancient and extremely modern.

Alex Wright, my editor at I.B.Tauris, has believed in this book from the outset, and shown enormous patience and great forbearance with the stop–start nature of the project. He has been the model guide: enthusiastic and supportive, yet always thoughtful. Without him, it is fair to say, *Embracing the Darkness* could never have been realised.

The initial idea for this book came together in the garden of the 'Witch's House', an old inn that sits underneath the castle walls of Nuremberg, on a warm, late autumnal afternoon, as the oak leaves and the acorns were falling all around. Much has passed between that day and this. Yet, throughout, I have been fortunate in the constant love, support and inspiration of my father. Dad took me, as a small child, to see the Ince Blundell Hall statues preserved at Liverpool City Museum. There, in an atmospheric, dimmed room, was the pantheon arrayed in a semi-circle and the realisation, for the first time, that 'the eyes that gaze into yours at the bend of the road may be those of the goddess herself'.

'... however we may cry out for magic,
at heart we are afraid of pursuing life wholly under the sign of real magic'.

Antonin Artaud, *c*.1936

CHAPTER ONE

The Figure at the Window

I

As with all folk tales, where the solitary crone arrives at the door begging for our charity, or comes tapping at the windowpane, it is best to start at the very beginning. For such beginnings lie rooted in our collective childhood, where the figure of the witch was first released from the pages of a storybook, to be cast in shadows upon the bedroom wall, fashioned by the old tales of the fireside.

There can be few more immediate, universal or potentially terrifying figures in the Western imagination. Think, for a moment, of Walt Disney's rendering of her in *Snow White*, transformed from an alluring, eldritch beauty into a shuffling crone, carrying her basket of apples and proffering poison from the bony grasp of a gnarled and palsied hand. She is love and lust, youth and old age, the sexual moment laced with the knowledge of eventual, inexorable, decay and death. From the fairy tales, the advertiser's billboards, Hollywood cartoons and teen movies, she is instantly recognisable: the sharp, pointed hat, the arch black cat, and the knotted broomstick that never once swept a hearth but rather carried her over the land by night.

This archetype is rooted in Charles Perrault's creation of the character of Mother Goose, in order to give a more 'authentic' expression to his own retellings of folk tales. He already sensed, by the 1690s, that an older, more communal and agrarian culture was on the wane in the face of a new, possessive, individualist capitalism. In contrast to that which had gone before, it was both urban and urbane. It was left to his fictitious old woman, wrinkled and wrapped in the shawls of the peasantry, to defend one aspect of popular culture against condescension and oblivion. It is significant that a would-be courtier, such as Perrault, who wrote largely for a sophisticated, well-to-do audience, felt that he could not use his own voice to tell these stories. Within a few years, the figure of Mother Goose as the kindly matriarch – a repository of homespun wisdom – would be thoroughly confused and conflated with the images of those very witches whom Perrault had bid her create in order to entertain, educate and to inspire.[1]

Consequently, when we gaze at eighteenth-century prints designed to bring visions of already outmoded country customs and dress into the homes of inquisitive and increasingly affluent Londoners, these images strike us today not as reference works on costume or manners, but rather as portrayals of a witch; an anglicised reflection of Perrault's most popular and durable creation. Our attention is automatically drawn to the women's hooked noses, their sugar loaf hats, bowed backs and wide skirts. The stubby clay pipes clenched between toothless jaws appear unbecoming to their age and gender, and seem to signal other unknown aberrations in their conduct and the state of their souls. The birds that wheel above their heads, the herbs that grow beneath their feet and the rows of slates that border their gardens – leaning backwards, like a row of lazy and forgotten tombstones – seem to defy nature, rather than to record it.

Thus, 'Mother Damnable' – or 'Mother Redcap', as she was also known – was immortalised in an engraving of 1793, based on an earlier seventeenth-century print, as a filthy, wrinkled crone, crouching beside a cold hearth, surrounded by cinders, broken pitchers and snapped tobacco pipes. She is thoroughly degraded, and degrading and is to be feared on account of her poverty, rather than pitied. Her cottage, which in 1676 was on the outskirts of North London, is shown as having smashed windowpanes, while the witches' diabolical art is alluded to by the tattered print hanging on her wall, depicting two cats hanging upside down, and tied together by their scrawny tails. The artist, familiar with engravings of Baldung Grien's witchcraft scenes, has also included the pitcher of a weather witch but, unaware of its function in raising storms, has toppled it onto its side, so that the crudely rendered tempests simply and meaninglessly gush out on to the floorboards. The site of Old Mother Redcap's cottage, on waste ground, close to the crossroads, was still being pointed out to travellers in the eighteenth century. When it was rebuilt as a coaching inn, it carried the witch's name and continued to trade as a public house, until the 1970s.

When, in 1910, Bram Stoker came to consider witchcraft as a matter of simple imposture, he had little difficulty in constructing a vision of the 'well-known shrew of Kentish Town', who moved through and supposedly murdered – by use of poison and fire – her lovers at a prodigious rate. He thought that her 'ostensible occupation was as a teller of fortunes and a healer of odd diseases', and that her

> public appearances were usually attended by hounding and baiting by the rabble; and whenever anything went wrong in the neighbourhood the blame was, with overt violence of demeanour, attributed to her. She did not even receive any of the respect usually shown to a freeholder … Her only protector was that usual favourite of witches, a black cat, whose devotion to her and whose savage nature, accompanied by the public fear shown for an animal which was deemed her 'familiar', caused the mob to flee before its appearance.

As befitted the creator of *Dracula*, he thought to give her a suitably Gothic ending. 'When', he wrote,

> having been missed for some time, her house was entered she, attended only by her cat and with her crutch by her side, was found crouching beside the cold ashes of her extinct fire. In the teapot beside her was some liquid, seemingly brewed from herbs. Willing hands administered some of this to the black cat, whose hair, within a very short time, fell off. The cat forthwith died.

'Then,' he added, 'the clamour began.'²

The designation 'Mother Redcap' refers not to a particular individual but instead to a conventional portrayal of – and generic name for – witches on pub signs along the Great North Road to London. As Diane Purkiss noted, a play of that name was performed in 1597, conceivably based upon the recent trial of Alice Gooderidge. A little boy lost in Winsell Woods encountered 'a little old woman who had a grey gown with a black fringe', a broad brimmed hat, 'and three warts on her face'. She certainly conformed to the popular stereotype of the witch as, she conceded to her cross-examiners: 'Every boy doth call me witch.'³

Most likely 'Mother Redcap' was a composite figure, established as early as the 1590s in Staffordshire, with the name settling upon the later figure of 'Mother Damnable', when a coaching inn was established, in Kentish Town, in the 1700s. It is significant that James Caulfield, a London printer, writing in 1794, thought that her 'real name has not reached posterity.'⁴ He sourced a broadside verse, which he dated to 1676 and claimed had once been in the possession of Samuel Pepys, to accompany the engraved portrait of the witch of Kentish Town. 'Mother Damnable', we are told, was a

> monstrous thing
> Unmatched by Mackbeth's [*sic*] wayward womens ring,
> For cursing, scolding, fuming, flinging fire
> I'th face of madam, lord, knight, gent.

She is described as being little more than 'dry'd bones, in a Westphalian bag', who

> Through th' wrinkled weason [i.e. Reason] of her shapeless crag
> Sends forth such dismal shrieks, and uncouth noise,
> As fills the town with din, the street with boys;
> Which makes some think, this fierce she-dragon, fell,
> Can scarce be match'd by any this side [of] hell.

So not only did 'Mother Damnable' look like a witch, but she acted like one as well. Destructive and disruptive, she already appeared to be linked to the brewing trade, as the anonymous author of the broadside tells us that

> when but ruffled into the least pet
> Will cellar door key into pocket get.
> Then no more ale: and now the fray begins!
> 'Ware heads, wigs, hoods, scarfs, shoulders, sides and shins!

However, if she was indeed an innkeeper – or, more likely, the proprietor of a grog shop – her inn sign was not yet that of the 'Redcap' but of the shield depicted in the engraving, with the two executed cats:

> So fam'd, both far and near, is the renown
> Of Mother Damnable, of Kentish Town,
> Wherefore this symbol of the cats we'll give her,
> Because, so curst, a dog would not dwell with her.[5]

Bram Stoker's details about the cat seem to derive from the print, rather than from a trial record or another contemporary source. The same is true of his tale of the lover locked in an oven. It mattered little what 'Mother Damnable' or Alice Gooderidge really did or said: what mattered to their contemporaries was that they looked like witches, and that they were, therefore, expected to fit the role and play the part.

II

Similarly, if we chance upon a photograph, taken in the 1920s, of eight old women drinking tea outside their almshouses, we are likely to perceive a coven of witches rather than ladies receiving charity. It is a photograph in which the collection of symbols subverts the photographer's intended meaning and gives it a different meaning to today's eyes. We see a gathering of women at tea. There is a carefully tended lawn, cups on matching china saucers, a welcoming cottage door. There is a sense of accord and sisterhood among the women.

But the jarring elements point to witchcraft, to our eyes. The women are draped in dark cloaks; wear tall, conical hats that appear to be equally black. They give their attention and deference to one figure who seems more affluent, more poised than they. Her shoes are finer than the rest; sharply pointed, of patent leather, they gleam as they spike upwards from underneath the table. All eyes fix upon this woman, save for those of one old lady, whose gaze is directed straight down the camera lens. Two cups are left on the table, suggesting the absence of two more of the party, who have momentarily stepped away from the near side of the table in order to allow the photograph to be carefully posed. The table, itself, is otherwise swept clear of any of the normal accoutrements of a tea party – such as teapots, sugar bowls and plates of biscuits or sandwiches. Two books – one open and one firmly shut – are perched at either end of the heavy brocade cloth. All these elements lead our imaginations to weave a sinister purpose about the meeting, recasting the books as grimoires and the women, themselves, as witches.

This interpretation might just be possible if the photograph had no provenance. As it is, there is written source evidence, which demonstrates an entirely different context. The women are recipients of charity of Castle Rising, Norfolk, from the Order of the Holy and Undivided Trinity, founded by the Roman Catholic Church in 1610 to give support to poor, elderly, faithful women. The women were provided with food, a place to live and a respectable new suit of clothes. Their outfit acted as a uniform, identifying them with the Order and as recipients of the Church's charity. The cloaks and tall hats were practical, relatively cheap and thoroughly in keeping with the clothes worn by the wives of yeomen, countrymen, and even gentry, in the early years of the seventeenth century.[6] The uniform remained unaltered from generation to generation: the Order could afford to become more visible as sectarian tensions began to ease in the century after its creation, and it was economical to hand down garments which had only been worn for a year or two due to the advanced age of the recipients.

The uniform given to the devout women by the Order became more distinctive as fashions changed, and it was calculated to indicate their separateness and devotion. But even as early as the eighteenth century, the style of dress had come to imply precisely the opposite: social deviance and religious depravity. The persuasive power of the stereotype displaced any earlier interpretations of the dress of the poor women of Castle Rising. In one sense, therefore, the photograph, which recorded the eight women for posterity, also inadvertently made a mockery of the purpose of their lives.

Taken before the advent of colour photography, the black and white image deadens the impact of the sunshine on 'Founder's Day' and renders the cheerful bright red of their cloaks into the deepest black. The period costume itself not only reinforces tradition, as was intended, but also divorces the image from its own time. Aside from the knitted cardigan that protrudes from underneath one of the women's cloaks, and the modish shoes of the group's senior member, there is no effective evidence for conclusively dating the image. The fact that these old and socially conservative ladies have preserved the long hair of their youth, rather than opted for the angular bobs of the 1920s, removes another possible clue. Moreover, the wearing of antique mob caps by most of the women, underneath their hats, and the putting back their hair into tight buns, further adds to the sense of timelessness. It is this sense of a lack of historic context that renders the photograph so striking, intriguing and unworldly in the first place.

We do not know the year the picture was taken – almost certainly by a studio professional – but it was between 1920 and 1929. But we do know the day: 'Founder's Day', which falls upon 24 February. Since the seventeenth century, the Order in Castle Rising has celebrated this day the same way each year: the women make a procession through the village from the almshouses to church; they together hear mass; and then they share together a festive meal or drinks at the almshouse. Few events since the Repeal of the Penal Laws can have been so orderly and dignified. Like the witch-finders of Manningtree and Salem, the danger is that we see witches where none really exist.

III

The cases outlined above serve to highlight the dangers in attempting to recover particular cultural responses to the phenomenon of witchcraft. Cultural studies tend to be woven from intangibles on gossamer threads; it is well to remember that an experience or impression which was era-defining for one person will be irrelevant to another.[7] As a consequence, the themes brought together in the following chapters are constructed from an entirely personal viewpoint. They present both Classical pagans, accused peasant women, witchcraft persecutors, novelists, film makers, television writers, modern revivalist Wiccans and artists. Their case studies point to ways in which we have come to define, understand and relate to that thing we call witchcraft. Other examples could have just as well been chosen, but as Robin Briggs observed: 'It is simply not worth trying to write a "safe" book about witchcraft.'[8]

Of course, there are perils in a case-based approach to the construction of cultural values, not least in the question of perspective, as what we filter out of the picture is sometimes just as important as what we leave in. I can furnish the following example from experience. I can tell the reader that I grew up in Churchtown, the oldest part of Southport, where gingerbread-style houses, with low thatched roofs and wattle walls pushed back against the canopy of trees that marked the border of the Fleetwood-Hesketh estate. The village had its own green, parish church and eighteenth-century coaching inns that served as the local pubs. The squire could be seen at the local newsagents, settling his paper bill, and in his family pew for the major religious services that punctuated the Christian ritual year. My grandmother was on good terms with the old gypsy woman who lived at the end of the lane, and who could often be seen walking her little dog along a track-way lined with hedgerows that had, within living memory, been a thoroughfare for shrimper's carts making their way from the beach, through apple orchards to the village itself. It was not hard for a child to imagine the presence of a fairy tale witch within such a community, when her broomstick lay propped up for all to see, on sale, alongside its fellows, outside the door to Gorse & Son's ironmongers. If there was a broomstick, it followed – for a creative child – that there had to be a witch. The landscape of the Grimms was made tangible by the thatch and the woodsmoke at the bottom of the lane.

This is one vision of my Merseyside village in the 1970s. On one level, it is true. Nothing within it is inherently false; it accounts, in part at least, for my early love of folktales, make-believe and a sense of the past as a deep and almost tangible presence. However, a different filter would create a different image. Parts of the picture left out, when brought to the description, shift the image greatly. The place was hardly rural, and certainly neither homogeneous nor traditional in form. The village green with its circle of picturesque cottages had long been part of a major conurbation – a grey-suited commuter belt – that stretched practically unbroken, by the early 1970s, from Liverpool, in the south, to Preston, in the north. Red-brick terraces from the Railway Age hemmed in the little enclave of North Meols, and empty factory space bore sullen testament to the oil crisis and the coming recession. The gypsy woman did indeed live out the span of her life within the bounds of Little Churchgate, but my grandmother had grown up in Australia, the child of immigrants from Glasgow and Belfast, and had spent all of her married life in Polynesia and central Africa. As much as the first family of Nigerians who had recently settled in the village, my grandmother was only just becoming familiar with 'Englishness'. The fluidity in impermanence of my village's culture was epitomised by the fact that we had to endure, late at night, the local 'tough' repeatedly sounding his car horn which played the opening bars of *Dixieland*, in imitation of the rebels' car horn in the current hit American television show *The Dukes of Hazzard*. Even rebellion took its inspiration from abroad!

Such continuity, as there was, appeared to stem from the operation of chance and parsimony, rather than from common values. The gingerbread houses only survived because a former Lord Hesketh had been anything but an 'improving landlord' and had refused to sweep away thatch, wattle and daub, for the dourly utilitarian comforts of Victorian brick, tile and plumbing.[9] Some of these dwellings had become picturesque through the care and attention of their tenants, with baskets of flowers hanging outside and families of swallows nesting under their heavy eaves. These were calculated to draw admiring comments and elicit the rapid click of camera shutters from passing tourists on their way to the neighbouring tearooms or to the Botanical Gardens. But other cottages, neglected out on the rim of the estate, drew far less sympathetic gazes. One of the more tumbled-down cottages, with its overgrown garden, decaying fences and dark interior, was known as 'The Witch's House'. Its elderly occupant occasionally came off the worse from the attentions of gangs of youths and mean-spirited children. They rang at the bell on mischief night, or pitched stones against its soot-smeared windowpanes. The old, the powerless, the awkward and the just plain 'different' would ever seem to have been targeted. Fortunately, by the early 1970s, this persecution was confined to the young. But it had not always been so.

IV

At times of security, social cohesion and self-confidence, such beliefs are likely to be confined to the outer margins of society; but in times of crisis, the witch figure may once more be summoned up in order to misdirect genuine grievances, to remove an obstacle to power, or to face an otherwise unchallengeable enemy. Through previous centuries, almost any misfortune could be, and indeed often was, attributed to the hatred, spite and suffering that the witch visited upon humanity. She cast spells, caused farm tools to go blunt, or weapons to shatter and betray their masters in the heat of battle. She was said to cause mothers to miscarry, marriage beds to remain barren or husbands to become impotent. In the home, she might make the milk go sour or the butter refuse to churn. Out in the fields, she could cause livestock to sicken, crops to fail or fruit to wither upon the tree. Sailors might be lost at sea due to her raising of sudden storms, or whole states could fall on account of her visitation of plague and poverty. Villagers might fear their suspected witch neighbour on account of her 'evil eye', or small children be brought to sudden obedience by the threat of her tread upon the stair.

In folktales collected across eighteenth- and nineteenth-century Europe, she could appear, in turn, as the tempter, imprisoner and devourer of infants; or as the perverter and destroyer of young girls' dreams. In Austria, she might appear in the guise of the 'Kornmütter', naked, black and dishevelled, hiding in the midst of the corn, ready to strike out with red-hot fingers at the unsuspecting passer-by. In Finland, the whispers of her lying tongue might be caught in the expanse of the forest, amid the rustling of the trees.[10]

On one level, therefore, she might seem an almost universal figure, common across all ages and recognised independently within practically every culture. Yet satisfactory definitions, embracing every facet of the witch and her activities, are surprisingly hard to come by. The pioneering anthropologist, Edward Evans-Pritchard, sought to draw a distinction between the operations of witchcraft and sorcery. As the result of his fieldwork among the Azande tribe of the Sudan, between 1926 and 1930, he concluded that witchcraft was an innate, internal power that some people inherited, in exactly the same way that genetic factors – such as the colour of hair or eyes – were passed down from parents to their children. Witches were perceived to be mean, rude and grasping, and could cause harm, both consciously and unconsciously, by the merest glance or passing thought. Moreover, Azande witches could harm other human beings, their animals or their crops, without performing special rituals. Their conception of witchcraft required no interventions from either supernatural or preternatural beings in order to flourish. By way of contrast, sorcerers had no innate ability to cause occult harm. They sought to employ magical rites, such as the chanting of spells, or damaged something belonging to the victim – such as a piece of clothing, a strand of hair or nail clippings – in order to transfer misfortune to the victim. Therefore, while any Azande could become a sorcerer through application and learning, it was impossible to become a witch by anything except by birth.

There was little doubt in the mind of Evans-Pritchard that tribal society was under enormous economic, religious and political pressures and that the Azande were approaching their breaking point. Under colonial rule, their population had fallen from 2 million in 1870 to 750,000 by 1953. As a result, he noticed that witchcraft accusations tended to cluster together in areas of ambiguous social relationships, and where neighbours were denied the option of moving away from each other and thus diffusing the sources of their conflict. He also discerned that the Azande remained a clever, sceptical and innovative people. Under unprecedented strain, accusations of witchcraft multiplied rapidly; the tribe evolved a complex system of beliefs in oracles, divinations, magic and leechcraft in order both to detect and counteract the effects of witchcraft, and to bring the offenders to trial.[11]

It is not difficult to see why Evans-Pritchard's work was embraced by scholars seeking to account for the virulence of witch-belief in Europe. From the late 1940s through till the early 1990s, the guiding motifs of his studies – namely the differences between witchcraft and sorcery, and the function of misfortune in provoking accusations of the crime – dominated discussions of witchcraft in the British Isles. Keith Thomas and Alan Macfarlane, the two seminal scholars of their respective generations, embraced Evans-Pritchard's model to account for witch persecution in England in the sixteenth and seventeenth centuries.[12] By substituting the Protestant Reformation and the Elizabethan Poor Law for the introduction of Christianity and the impact of colonial taxation, they created a persuasive explanation for England.

However, while the importance of stresses within society remains crucial, the division between the witch and the sorcerer is increasingly seen as unhelpful. Trial records do not point to two distinct classes of offenders. In contrast, accusers and judges were uninterested in the *modus operandi* of the witches brought before them. Moreover, there was growing unease at equating twentieth-century tribal African culture to that of sixteenth- and seventeenth-century Europe. Furthermore, it emerged that the witch-beliefs of the Azande seemed to be exceptional among African tribes. Consequently, the Evans-Pritchard model has been less and less applied by scholars. It seems that modern French historians are justified in applying the one term – *sorcier* – to describe those charged with causing harm through occult means. In a similar fashion, over the course of this study, the term 'witch' will be used to embrace the practitioners of both sorcery and witchcraft. While it remains possible that in some parts of Europe a greater measure of distinction was drawn between witchcraft and sorcery at the popular level than is apparent from the surviving records, on the basis of the evidence available to us, it is of little practical use to the historian to hold the two terms sharply apart.

Occult forces did not only have to be enlisted for harmful ends. Known as 'cunning folk' in England and as *devins-guerisseurs* in France, 'white' witches existed within many communities across Europe, up until the advent of industrialisation. For the payment of a fee, they might endeavour to foretell the future, cure disease, identify enemies, nullify the curses of others, and help to locate buried treasure or lost and stolen property, through magical means. Even allowing for out-and-out charlatans, the deluded, and the deliberate air of mystique that many of these practitioners cultivated in order to drum up business, it seems that some of these 'cunning folk' really did believe that they could manipulate nature for their own benefit, and for that of their clients.[13] While 'black' witches inflict sickness and discord, 'white' witches do the opposite: they cure sick children and animals, and pinpoint the sources of local tensions. The problem, unfortunately, lay in deciding who fell into either category, for it seems that often one person's white witch was another person's black. While clients might confidently seek out a *guerisseuse* in a distant village and ask her for advice, those who lived in her immediate vicinity may have feared her powers, shunned her company and – if the opportunity arose – denounce her as a maleficent witch.

Usually, those who laid accusations of witchcraft believed themselves injured by a witch. They normally do so in order to identify servants of the Devil within their midst. Moreover, it seems that the idea of witchcraft as the manifestation of demonic power had considerably less of a grip on the popular mind, than on the learned. Recent examinations of court records show that the peoples of Mediaeval and Early Modern Europe were not particularly concerned with witchcraft as the work of the Devil. Rather, they envisaged the world as containing hidden forces into which intuitive or practised individuals could tap.

Theologians, rulers and judiciaries of the sixteenth and seventeenth centuries, by contrast, had become fascinated by the demonology, and saw the witch as a follower of the Devil. She was sworn to him in a signed pact, in a conspiracy to ruin souls.[14] The distinction between 'white' or 'black' witchcraft was irrelevant in light of the most important fact – the Devil was behind all magic. The witch was seen by these people as an agent of pure evil, an agent working to fulfil plans wrought deep inside the pits of Hell, and devoted to corrupting both human flesh and the immortal souls. As an ally and agent of the Devil, the witch figure could not be overlooked within the community as a nuisance or a mere oddity. The judiciary had to root her out ruthlessly. This demonological conception of the witch and her powers, when added to the idea of primary witchcraft, is distinctively European and is possible only within a Christian culture. In this book, the term 'witch' will inevitably often bear this extra demonological connotation.

Much ink could be, and indeed has been, spilled in attempting to characterise the witch in a definitive way. Yet, as we have seen already, perceptions are coloured by differences in social class, gender, ideology and religion.[15] The interpretive divide that separates the twenty-first-century historian from the seventeenth-century demonologist, is mirrored by the gulf that separates today's revivalist Pagan from the Christian fundamentalist. Furthermore, in dealing with our everyday assumptions, cultural influences and simple prejudices, we are limited by both the nature and the extent of the surviving evidence. This is often patchy: judicial records are partial; the voices of the victims lost or obscured; and documentary evidence scanty. It is small wonder that imagination and conjecture have often filled in gaps. And from that, wildly competing theories have arisen.

For some, she has been the surviving practitioner of an ancient fertility cult, driven underground by the imposition of Christianity from above, but continuing to function secretly among the peoples of Europe, as healer and visionary, right down to the present day. For others, she has been a political radical forerunner of the modern feminist movement. Yet others see her as a role model for the independent and sexually liberated woman of the 1970s and as a repository for knowledge about the female body, reproduction and the care of the natural environment. Some see her as a entheogenic pioneer of consciousness expansion with hallucinogenic drugs – the types of 'magic mushroom' that became commonly recognised in the free festivals of the late 1960s – or as an out-of-body experience akin to the visions sought by the shamans of Native American and Siberian tribes. Finally, for historians of the Enlightenment, the persecutions were a collective hysteria among the very sections of society who should have 'known better', with Voltaire, for example, blaming 'indolence, stupidity and superstition'.[16] After 1945, some chose to draw analogies between the Nazi death camps and the witch-hunts, culminating in the 1970s with the coining of the term 'gynocide' (the slaughter of the womb), and its employment by leading feminists to argue that witch-hunts were a concerted campaign to break the spirit and economic independence of women.[17]

The twentieth-century revived Pagan movement frames the witch as a being who is – and, it is alleged, was always in the past – completely free; who is intuitive rather than intellectual, who is untrammelled by either greed or sexual repression, and who is in tune with the ecology of the earth. For these Pagans, the rise of patriarchy replaced worship of goddesses with exclusively patriarchal male gods and led to the conversion of Europe to Christianity and thence to industrialisation. These alienated the individual from both themselves and their environment, but they see the Early Modern witch as an embattled survivor protecting a timeless Pagan tradition within an increasingly harsh and materialistic world. Her contemporary counterpart, the Wiccan priestess, sees herself as a successor fulfilling a role as the agent of positive change.[18]

Though comforting to their creators, each of the above visions of the witch is flawed, and the flaws are increasingly apparent as scholarship reveals more information. Three decades of intense scholarly work have shown that almost every previous assumption about the activities of the witch must be re-evaluated or discarded.

It is clearly not possible to generalise. Few characteristics hold true for the generality. Thus, English and Scottish witches worked with familiar spirits, who took animal form and did their bidding, but they are absent elsewhere in Europe. The Scottish witch Isobel Gowdie spoke of a structured coven of 12 people with a leader, but this was unusual. The witch was often poor and old, yet there were rich men accused as well: men such as Chancellor Haan and Mayor Junius, who we will discuss in the next chapter. Even their activities vary from place to place and case to case. Swedish witches took the shape of magpies, while in Spain and Italy they flew as owls. Some lured children into the forest; others vomited iron pins. Most witches were associated with the countryside but a significant minority were to be found in highly urbanised centres.

We now know there is no checklist or 'identity kit' by which to measure the characteristics of an individual witch. Helpfully, we can borrow the notion of a 'familial noun' from the work of Ludwig Wittgenstein. This permits us to conceive of an abstract notion like a 'game' or, in this case, a 'witch', not as a solid and exclusive totality but as a series of assumptions about the nature of a designation that bear a familial resemblance to the ideal.[19] Thus, no two members of a human family have exactly the same appearance, yet they have shared genetic characteristics, which permit those in the community about them to observe, at a glance, that they are closely related. What signifies this in the immediate family unit – red hair, freckles or a snub nose – may be accepted in wider society as constituting characteristics of behaviour or type. The peoples of Mediaeval and Early Modern Europe described the activities and attributes of witches in many different ways, yet they recognised a common resemblance in their behaviour. Consequently, it mattered little if an English witch brought sickness through creating a wax image and tortured it with pins, or if her German counterpart tormented her victim by physically straddling him, or the roof beams of his house. What did matter, however, was the common recognition of harm wrought in the community through magical means, and latterly, among the educated classes, that this harm was effected by the summoning of demonic powers. The initial chapters of this study aim to show how these two central ideas about witchcraft came to be so deeply, and uniquely, embedded in Western consciousness over the course of some 2,000 years, while later chapters attempt to clarify why these beliefs suddenly declined, in the late seventeenth and early eighteenth centuries, before being comprehensively refashioned over the last hundred or so years, with the rise of modern Paganism. The transformation of the witch from a figure who had occasioned fear and loathing for the best part of 2,000 years into one perceived as sympathetic – even aspirational – is one of the most radical and unexpected developments of modern Western culture. It is to this dramatic metamorphosis that this book primarily addresses itself. The arc of this book consequently follows the creation of the witch figure as archetype, through to its deadly and destructive stereotyping in the Early Modern period, and closes with an appreciation of the modern resurgence of interest in Pagan witchcraft.

The witches' remarkable revaluation was largely contingent upon values born out of the European Enlightenment. However counter-intuitive it may seem, rationalism, the scientific revolution, and a belief in human progress, brought with them a sense of tolerance and a marked mistrust of religion as a political or totalitarian force, and by so doing opened up the possibilities for new explorations of long-established cultural themes and for the freedom to dream of a new form of an old magic.[20] If modern Pagan witchcraft is, indeed, 'the only religion that England has ever given the world', then it is all the more remarkable for rescuing the witch from centuries of odium and for embracing the darkness that surrounds her; not through blind terror or simple superstition, as was formerly the case, but through a joyful – and perhaps even playful – form of engagement with the mysteries, and the realisation of the full potential of the human spirit.[21]

CHAPTER TWO

The Witch House of Bamberg

I

In the summer of 1627, Bishop Johann Georg II gave the city of Bamberg a present. Thanks to his wealth and influence, the orchard near the city walls was cleared, the ground levelled and the stream running through it dammed and channelled. Each day, carts brought in fresh loads of coloured roof slates, painted tiles, bottle glass panes and newly hewn stone to be set in place and finished on the site. Local artisans applied layers of plaster to the rising walls, while a figure of Justice, blindfolded and with her scales in hand, was lowered into place above elaborate door lintels. By August, the work was completed and Johann Georg could see the result of his personal piety and civic pride, as the Hexenhaus – the detention house for suspected witches – rose up to dominate the city's skyline. Two carved tablets – one in Latin, the language of officialdom and one in German, the language of the commonality – spelled out the purpose of the building, in a text chosen from the first chapter of the Book of Kings:

> This house ... shall be a byword ... Every one that passeth by it shall be astonished, and shall hiss; and they shall say, Why hath the Lord done thus unto this land, and to this house? And they shall answer, Because they forsook the Lord their God ... and have taken hold upon other gods, and have worshipped them, and served them: therefore hath the Lord brought upon them all this evil.[1]

The Baroque splendour of the building, and the care, attention and money that had been lavished upon it, sat uneasily with its stated civic purpose: the chastisement of the citizens of Bamberg and the construction of a highly visible symbol of state power wielded specifically in order to extirpate the crime of witchcraft.

Yet such a statement fitted perfectly well with the Prince Bishop's world view. Raised in the atmosphere of the Counter-Reformation; in the struggle for souls and for religious conformity, amid a shattered and bleeding Christendom, Johann Georg had made it his business to destroy the causes of Sin and to create about him an orderly, and godly state. At times, this manifested itself in attacks upon popular revels, poor manners and licentious conduct; at others, it focused upon the witch figure who similarly corroded the fabric of society and imperilled the salvation of its people. And Bamberg, it seemed, was extraordinarily rich in witches.

The first known trial of a witch in the area had been recorded in 1590, and, five years later, Margaretha Bohmerin was led to the stake after having admitted attending a Sabbat and having sexual intercourse with the Devil. In 1612–13, 15 people were arrested for witchcraft, while accusations gained credibility and snowballed in the years from 1616 to 1619, when more than 150 individuals were detained and subsequently tried for the crime.[2] The outbreak of the Thirty Years' War temporarily halted the prosecutions, as a more moderate faction held sway on the Prince Bishop's Council and withheld the necessary funds for witch-hunting on a large scale. However, in 1622, an alliance between the Catholic League, the Bavarian court and Friedrich Förner, the suffragan Bishop of Bamberg, had secured the succession of Johann Georg II as Prince Bishop, and effectively harnessed temporal and ecclesiastical power, on an unprecedented scale, in the pursuit of witches.

Förner, as Prince Johann Georg's patron and the general visitor of his churches, provided much of the intellectual framework for the subsequent trials and published 35 of his sermons on the subject, under the title of *The Splendid Armour of God*, in 1625. These were recommended for use in churches across Bamberg and quickly became established as readings, in both Latin and German, on Sabbaths and Saint's Days. In them, Förner postulated a grim duality – of good and evil – locked in a perpetual battle for the human soul, and of an acceleration in its pace and violence as the Day of Judgement grew ever nearer. The Devil 'loosed from hell' was a constant presence, seeking and plotting 'the ruin of mankind' in the limited time allowed to him 'before the world ends'. Amid such worsening conditions, Förner believed that, in their poverty and misery, the people of Bamberg were turning for succour not to the Roman Catholic Church, but to countless 'cunning women and little women-witches', who would lead the simple, the ill-effected and the plain weak-willed to certain damnation, were they not quickly and effectively controlled. In order to cauterise such running and grievous sores, he advised civil society to evoke the law. One would think nothing of bringing thieves and robbers to justice, and of classifying theirs as capital crimes. So, he reasoned, why should not the stealers of men's souls be brought before the courts, and be held similarly accountable for their far more serious offences? For such transgressions there was only one possible verdict, and as Förner was at pains to make clear: 'It is not I who says this; the divine law says it, out of God's own mouth. "Do not suffer witches to live". The law of the Church proclaims it, the Imperial law proclaims it ... what more do you want?'[3]

In 1626, the seasons turned upside down; in late spring the ragged peaks of the Jura mountains turned white overnight, freezing boats at their moorings, destroying the fields of rye and barley, stripping the trees of their leaves and killing the grapevines. Both the governed and the governors knew precisely whom to blame – and how to act. Writing in his diary, Johann Langhans, Lord Mayor of the nearby town of Zeil, recorded that on

> the 27th of May [1626], the grapevines all over Franconia, in both Bishoprics [of] Bamberg and Würzburg, were destroyed by frost, as well as the dear corn, which had faded already … everywhere around Zeil, everything was destroyed by frost, which has never happened in people's memory, and caused substantial price rises … Whereupon an intensive pleading and begging started among the common rabble [asking], why the authorities went on tolerating that the sorcerers and witches are damaging even the crops. Therefore, his princely highness [Johann Georg II] was alerted to punish such an evil, and therefore the witch persecutions started this year.[4]

The frost had settled upon the roofs of Bamberg two days earlier and, from the window of her convent cell, the nun Maria Anna Junius wrote likewise that on St Urban's Day, 25 May, 'a loud cry went up in the city … [and] people were frightened to death' as they awoke to find that an 'unnatural' night frost had killed off all of the fruit trees, rendered the ground 'as hard as stone' and put paid to the grain harvest. 'Our prince,' she noted ominously, 'is furious about this crime.'[5]

The half-starved peasants who roamed the countryside often blamed witch-craft for war, sickening cattle and crop failure. It was they who made the initial charges. But, unlike past cases, the Prince Bishop now joined in. He established a witch-finding commission of trained specialists to gather evidence and to co-ordinate prosecutions throughout his territories. The Hexen-Kommission, as it was known, was extremely well-paid and well-funded, and had little difficulty in drawing to it renowned academics. Dr Ernst Vasoldt, Dr Steiner and Dr Harsee took to their task with single-minded ruthlessness. Their hand was strengthened by the Prince Bishop's order of 28 October 1626, which stated that: 'No person may criticise or malign officials whose duties involve them in witch trials or witch executions … [or] interfere with officials carrying out [their] councillors orders, especially at occasions of executions of witches', under threat of flogging or banishment for life.[6] A culprit was quickly found. Local woman Katharina Merckhlerin confessed to the judiciary, in November 1626, that she had taken a leading role in a plot to bring down the state, through conjuring the frosts that laid waste to its food supply.

However, it did not stop with Katharina Merckhlerin. Investigations expanded to target the young as well as the old, the rich alongside the poor, the men as well as the women, and in particular the children. In Bamberg, children and adolescents are at the heart of the story, appearing prominently both as victims of witchcraft charges and as accusers. Bamberg's warehouses and wine cellars were haunted by juvenile street gangs, made up of the many homeless children drawn to the city from the rural hinterland. The authorities had been trying for more than a generation to deal with their unruly behaviour. Maria Anna Junius confided to her diary that the morals of the young had been corroded and that it was now commonplace to see children gambling and fighting in the squares and alleyways of an otherwise grand and glittering city. The crackdown upon juvenile delinquency was part of a wider programme by Johann Georg to reform the manners and the conduct of his people. He had already instituted harsher punishments for bigamists and prostitutes, and compelled couples suspected of premarital sex to wear straw hats, as a sign of penance and humiliation, on their wedding day. Youth crime was just part of it.

However, in a letter of 1631 Johann Georg entered into uncharted territory when he claimed that the cause of children's unruliness was witchcraft. He wrote: 'you can hear children tell in the street how they came to be seduced' by the Devil and his servants. Children appeared in significant numbers before the Hexen-Kommission and their testimony flowed thick and fast. One case is that of Andreas Foster, a five-year-old, who recounted how his grandmother – who had 'ugly hands, like a chimney sweep' and clubfeet – had doused him in cold water and re-baptised him, in the Devil's name, as 'Tree Branch'. It might just have easily have been the product of a scolding, prompted by a childish misdemeanour, but the memory of his drenching still rankled and a grudge had developed. He had been brought to the court, from the hamlet of Oberscheinfeld, on the evidence of a neighbour, who had heard the child boast of his night flights on pitchforks fashioned of silver and brass, to church towers where he would dance till dawn in the company of other witches.

Another suspect, a poor child of unrecorded name, bragged of breaking into the wine cellar of a monastery with his friends and managed to jumble a childish rhyme into an incantation by simply adding a reference to the Devil. After proffering his soul to the Devil, he claimed to the court that he soon found that he was able to fashion fleas from out of grease, and watched as his friends changed their shape from boys into field mice. He, too, said that he flew by night on a pitchfork to 'three different witches' dances' where there was raucous music and plentiful food. He told his interrogators that at these dances, held in a pasture outside the city walls, 'each witch-person had behind or beside him or her a light, which was stuck in the ground and burned a bright red. One of the fellows, the son of a well-known burgher was charged with the responsibility to keep the lights burning'. However, he was twice frustrated and drew rebukes from the dancers as two of the torches blew out because the witches had, through their actions, 'caused a fierce wind' to blow across the fields. Night flight, too, appeared to be attended by difficulty as, on one occasion, his friend toppled from his pitchfork while speeding over the River Main. 'As the poor fellow splashed in the water, he changed into a mouse and scurried over the water toward a row boat', from which – still in his rodent form – he then sculled safely to the shore. Such imaginings certainly enlivened the naïve and clumsy testimony of suspects.

This child informant began to realise how to act his part in the courtroom, the joy to be found in pleasing his interrogators by providing the 'right' answers, and the opportunity to settle old scores. Thus, he incriminated a burgher 'who, instead of doing an honest day's work, gossips like a washer woman'; a neighbour who worked weather magic, stopping hail storms by placing 'a saucer on top of a heap of dung'; and another woman who had allegedly assisted in his initiation into the dark arts but who, he had heard and laconically reported to the court, had since been executed for witchcraft.[7]

The above children were of humble backgrounds. But the child whose case would rock Bamberg to the core was not. Hans Morhaubt was the 14-year-old son of an affluent city burgomaster. Arrested in 1627, Hans was literate, well educated and seemingly in receipt of a generous allowance from his parents. His troubles began with a lost book. Several weeks prior, his Jesuit schoolmaster found him reading *The History of Doctor Johann Faustus* and duly reported him to the authorities. Now, the legend of Dr Faustus had been the stuff of folk tales for almost a century, with a fictional account of his life committed to paper sometime around 1580, and a German print edition of the *History*, surfacing in 1587 courtesy of a Protestant bookseller. The problem was partly subject matter, but the crux of the issue was more than that; Faustus was linked to Bamberg. In February 1520, The, then, Prince Bishop paid 10 Gulden to a real 'Dr Faustus, phil.' for casting his horoscope.[8] Stories about Faustus, both real and imagined, clung to Bamberg. The *History* – though transposing the action to Wittemberg – struck a chord with Bamberg's inhabitants in a manner that was particularly relevant and pronounced. So young Morhaubt had been reading a book on demonology, printed by a Protestant press, in a fiercely Roman Catholic territory, about Bamberg's most infamous sorcerer. And this, in the midst of a full-scale witch-hunt. Hans was duly brought for interrogation. Once there, he admitted far more. He claimed that after his teacher had seized his book, a succubus had appeared before him, in the guise of his mother's maid, Helena Ellin and promised to retrieve it for him provided that he, too, signed a demonic pact renouncing God.[9]

A closer look at Morhaubt's case reveals that the 'confessions', far from being spontaneous expressions of guilt, were coached, guided and cajoled in order to fit a narrative framework well rehearsed by the authorities and generally understood by the populace. Hans Morhaubt's demonic seduction and fall through corrupting literature was neither new to the witnesses and spectators in the court, nor unique to the boy. Friedrich Förner had devoted a great deal of time and effort, in both his preached and printed sermons, to warning parents about the dangerous effects of unregulated and unsupervised reading upon the minds and the morals of the young. Most interestingly, in his ninth sermon – published two years before Hans Morhaubt's arrest, and dedicated to another witch-burning prelate – he told of a boy who, having read *The History of Dr Faustus*, was approached by his own demon. Having abjured his faith and signed a pact with the Devil, the youth then flew off to nearby Nuremberg, where he visited death and famine upon the hapless citizens.[10] It seems that the city's juvenile delinquents were simply reworking themes and stories, in their confessions, that were already familiar to them and to their interrogators through the pulpit and frequent recapitulation in the schoolroom. The one reinforced the other.

In this manner, Förner's homily became reality once the unfortunate Morhaubt was observed reading a forbidden book in class. His copy of *Faustus* was seized and he was reported to the Hexen-Kommission. From then on, his own thoughts, motivations and persona were lost amid a wider interpretative narrative that had already been scripted by Förner's sermon. The trouble was that, in trying to fit his own circumstances to the example given to him in the ninth sermon – which Hans Morhaubt probably remembered from church and had been made to read at school – he set the scene of the most unforgivable crime: the selling of his soul, in his own home. The place of protection and comfort became a portal to Hell. His mother's maid – supportive, obedient – hid a rebellious force working against the order of both God and man, and charged with the Devil's preternatural powers.

The Morhaubt household was ripped apart by the testimony of young Hans, as first Helena, the maid, then his parents, their siblings and neighbours all fell under the gaze of the Hexen-Kommission. The precedents provided by Förner's sermons, allied to Dr Vasoldt's preoccupation with the role of conspiracy, detonated a chain reaction of accusation, confession and counter-accusation. A frenzy tore through the fabric of the city and recast poor women, marginal men and disaffected youth as merely symptoms of a far greater malaise embedded within Bamberg's leading families and even the Prince Bishop's council itself.

II

In such circumstances, everyone was a suspect. And indeed, one of the most decisive factors that enabled the spread of the trials in Bamberg was the collapse of the self-confidence of the elites. They looked among themselves, rather than to an external threat, for an enemy and were all too quick to find one. Perhaps this is a little surprising, given that the witchcraft trials are often viewed today as a means of scapegoating a recognisable *other* within society. Indeed, Hugh Trevor-Roper conceived of witch-hunting as a means of 'ideological struggle' by which both Protestant and Roman Catholic rulers 'had revived the dying witch-craze just as [the Reformation and Counter-Reformation] had revived so many other obsolescent habits of thought: biblical fundamentalism, theological history, [and] scholastic Aristoteleanism'." It is plausible enough to think of the rival religious creeds making use of the charge of witchcraft literally to demonise and, if necessary, to extirpate their rivals. The problem when applying such a thesis to Bamberg was that the Protestants had long since gone. There had been a period of relative toleration in the city, when the minority Protestant and dominant Roman Catholic factions existed side by side, under the rule of Prince Bishop Johann Philipp von Gebsattel (from 1599 to 1609).

Yet, those very traits that to modern sensibilities mark his reign as being progressive and benign – his worldliness, distrust of religious enthusiasm, appreciation of music, fine things and delight in pleasures – were the very same that would have made them seem contemptible and corrupt to a younger generation of ascetic churchmen raised in the spirit of the Tridentine reforms. As a consequence, his successor, Johann Gottfried von Aschhausen (who ruled from 1609 to 1622) wasted little time in rescinding the religious liberty granted to his Protestant citizens, began to close down their churches, and removed all of those Roman Catholic clergymen whom he deemed to be 'unreliable' or obstructive to his 'reforms' in church governance.

Key to this process was his emphasis upon the education of the young. He introduced the Jesuit Order to the principality to take charge of the schools and enforce religious conformity. A Jesuit College was founded in Bamberg, together with a high school, in 1611 and 1613 'basic' schools, as the Protestant population was first edged out of the professions and trades, and then out of the city, itself. The seemingly 'lax' government of Prince Bishop Johann Philipp was replaced by a far more rigorous administration, which was both centralised and single-minded. Indeed, its reforms appear to have been welcomed by the Roman Catholic majority and to have fitted in well with ideas of 'good governance' and the twin strands of political and theological renewal as understood and charted by the Counter-Reformation Church. With the state strengthened by an increasingly regularised system of taxation, a more effective judiciary and the beginnings of a recognisable bureaucracy in the councillors, clerks and burgomeisters who ran the day-to-day administration, the Prince Bishop had ample time and scope to refashion the morality and the thought processes of his subjects, and to come down hard upon any sign of dissent. Within this context, the daily lives, the thoughts, and public and private behaviour of Bamberg's citizens took on an importance for the authorities that had not existed before. The winning of 'hearts and minds' could not, unfortunately, be judged by empirical measures alone and so snapshots of opinion, chance remarks and signs of dissidence, or even diffidence, were eagerly seized upon by the government of the city state.

It was against this background of moral reform that the first large-scale witch-hunts were activated within Bamberg. However, while they may have been the products of confessional strife, their prime purpose was certainly not the extirpation of Protestant heresy: Protestants had already been banished from the territory. Furthermore, Bamberg had never been a Lutheran stronghold and seemed unlikely to be won over, now, to the Protestant cause. Johann Philipp's quiet but persistent attempts at conciliation had won many back to the Roman Catholic fold, while increasingly sophisticated print propaganda, honed since the meeting of the Council of Trent, appeared to have successfully appropriated the Protestants' own major weapon and turned it back against themselves, halting their tide and forcing it to ebb in many states. The Hexen-Kommission showed no interest in trying to sort Protestant witches from Roman Catholic ones, or to link a demonic plot with a wider Protestant conspiracy. Instead, the overwhelming majority of those brought to trial in Bamberg were, like their accusers, conventional and – on occasion – exceptionally devout Roman Catholics. Ironically, it may have even been the case that new Catholic converts, or the children of former Protestants – like Förner himself – took the lead in formulating the prosecutions as a means of emphasising their own religious orthodoxy and faithfulness to Rome. What is clear is that the elites who governed the city were steeped in the thought of the Counter-Reformation, took an increasingly pessimistic view of human nature and potential, and were prepared to commit themselves to a policy of stamping out heresy and moral deviance from their midst by any means necessary. In this light, Protestantism was simply one sure route to damnation, and witchcraft was another. While the Devil had no need to seduce Protestants as they had already been won to his cause, he still had a use for witchcraft in order to first subvert and then destroy the souls of godly Catholics. In this manner, the fires lit on Bamberg's execution grounds would help to purify the city and save far more souls from the eternal fires of Hell than they ever consigned to the midst of the burning pyres.

If those convicted of witchcraft in Bamberg, between 1623 and 1631 were not Protestants or recognisable 'outsiders', who were they? It was not the old, poor, marginal woman involved in 'healing' or fortune telling. Few unmarried girls, unattached women or elderly widows were arrested. Most were married women or women of marriageable age, capable of childbirth and child rearing. Infertility was not significant either. Nor, it seems, was the working of sympathetic magic or divination. Of those women convicted for the crime in Zeil, one of the epicentres of the trials outside the

city walls, only two were described as being 'wisewomen'. The high volume of surviving records does allow analysis. William Bradford Smith has estimated that women
accounted for 72.7 per cent of those accused, and that the proportion of men accused
grew by almost a third when compared with the earlier spate of trials, between 1616
and 1622.[12] So, gender and poverty did not frame the trials.

What did frame them, however, was kinship. Whole family units, together with
their neighbours and close friends, were brought in for questioning. No less than
17 households on the Lange Gasse, or 'Long Street' – Bamberg's main thoroughfare,
where the merchants and 'good people' lived – were targeted, while in Zeil even after
the town council was systematically purged – with seven of its members, including
the Lord Mayor, Johann Langhans, who had first recorded the untimely frost,
going to the flames as witches – 20 of their relatives were similarly convicted of the
crime and executed.[13]

The Hexenhaus took on an entirely different aspect at this time, as spiralling
numbers of suspects were now being brought to Bamberg. It was far more than a
purely functional building in which to hold those suspected of one very specific
crime. Rather, the Hexenhaus was a symbol of both Förner's educated vision and the
Prince Bishop's political will, manifested through bricks and mortar. And it was their
instrument. We know a good deal about the experience of prisoners from the cop-
perplate engraving of the Hexenhaus. Along both the upper and lower floors were
parallel rows of cells, permitting up to 26 prisoners to be held in isolation at any one
time. In stark contrast to these, the guardrooms and offices were well lit by large
windows, respectively at the front and rear of the building, and comfortably heated
by six gigantic and decoratively tiled stoves. An apse built out at the rear of the house
formed a two-storey chapel, which enabled the inmates to hear services throughout
the day and also, on occasion, to see the altar and its cross on their way to, and from,
interrogation. Thus, in reviewing his building plans, the Prince Bishop had not only
had an eye for ostentation, but also for what was savagely effective. The house was
designed not merely for detention, but for processing inmates, depriving and altering
their senses, cumulatively breaking their resolve and obtaining a confession from
them as the end result.

The compound was cut off from the surrounding buildings by a low wall; the cells
deprived the prisoner of human contact and provided a space for reflection between
bouts of torture, while the judges' chambers, on the ground floor, offered swift access
for questioning the accused and plentiful storage room for case notes. At the rear of
the compound, only a few yards across the courtyard and clearly visible from both
the judges' room and chapel, stood an imposing, half-timbered tower that had been
requisitioned to serve as the torture chamber. The stream was channelled underneath

its boards to serve as a plunge pool for immersing or swiftly ducking prisoners; elsewhere within its walls inmates were force-fed heavily salted-herrings, forced to kneel for hours on end on a 'prayer stool', splattered by red-hot sulphur or confined to a set of stocks fitted with iron barbs. Once the accused was broken, he or she was escorted back to the main building where a visit was made to the narrow 'confession room', on the upper floor, where the proof of guilt could be signed.

III

Miraculously, we have a last letter from one of the Hexenhaus inmates, which survives because it was smuggled out of its walls by a warder. From it, too, we learn a great deal about the experience of prisoners, as well as gaining an insight into the politics of this phase of the Bamberg witch-hunt. By 1628, it had claimed hundreds of victims and was beginning to transcend the established boundaries of class and gender. Indeed, Bamberg was becoming so noted for the zeal with which it rooted out its witches that Johann Georg was offering his advice to the neighbouring princes and was prepared, for a fee, to loan them the services of Dr Vasoldt.[14] The Bishop had gained a reputation for learned piety and good governance. Yet, lower down the social scale, not all of the judiciary were so sure about the wisdom of the hunt or the veracity of the confessions.

The Prince Bishop's own wealthy chancellor, Dr Georg Haan, was one. He remained in office despite the ascendancy of Förner's protégés after 1622 through ability, luck and his unquestioned loyalty to the Catholic League. He had powerful enemies, not least the suffragan Bishop himself. He began to hold up cases brought before the commission and to voice his doubts about the legality of the convictions that he was being asked to approve. Problematically, it had been Haan who had brought the earlier witch trials to a sudden end in 1622. He had been Chancellor then, and had stopped authorising payments to underwrite the trials. At the time it seemed sensible, for funds were needed for arming the state in light of the confessional wars but now it was a strike against him. Enemies could point to the rumour that his mother had been suspected as a witch, and in Poland, the Teutonic knights had actually burned his mother-in-law as a sorceress. Dr Vasoldt disliked him for personal reasons: he had supplanted the man's father as Chancellor.

Even worse, Förner hated him as a symbol and a leftover of all that had been worst under the former regime. In particular, the old Prince Bishop, Johann Philipp, gave the care of his two illegitimate daughters to Haan, who had to go to court repeatedly to defend their inheritance against the repeated claims of their brothers.

Thus, his name was linked with the former ruler's lustful vice and abuses associated with the old-style Roman Catholic Church. With hindsight, it is difficult to understand why Haan did not read the signals of danger. But perhaps reassured by the knowledge that he had not only weathered the earlier trials, but brought them to a successful halt, he remained at his post in Bamberg. Haan even led a 'moderate' faction on the council opposed to Förner and his acolytes. He publicly allied his faction to a sceptical attitude towards the crime, using the mounting number of witchcraft persecutions as something of a 'political football' to test the political temperature and to harness opposition to Förner's rival party. His high-risk strategy appeared to have succeeded.

Then, in 1627, Haan accepted the petitions of a group of Bamberg's 'injured' women, whose families had been torn apart by allegations. He appeared as the defender of justice and of all those wrongly accused, and maltreated, by the authorities. He accepted the responsibility of being their protector. Tragically, he made his petition on their behalf just as he was about to leave the city. While he was away on business in Speyer, more than four days' travel away, Förner and Vasoldt swooped. They arraigned his wife Catharina and daughter, Maria Ursula, for witchcraft. They managed to try them, convict them and have them burned on the pyre before Haan could return to Bamberg. When he did return, he himself was arrested with his son and the household servants, for witchcraft. He was tortured and confessed; likewise his son, who named several family friends, all prominent citizens.

Their neighbour, the Mayor of Bamberg Johannes Junius, was one of those named. His is the letter that gives us the account of what transpired inside the walls of the Hexenhaus. Junius was accused of having joined with Chancellor Haan 'at a witch gathering in the electoral council-room, where they ate and drank'; of joining in 'a witch dance' in the pine forest that stretched out beyond the city walls; and of desecrating the Host. Six witnesses gave evidence, each with differing conceptions of the witch gathering. Those in the elites described rich food and a political, as well as demonic, intent within the council chamber. The poor witnesses concentrated upon the wild dances in the woods, drawn from peasant life, and upon the desecration of the Holy Wafer, reflecting popular anti-Semitic prejudices. All, however, gave the bare minimum required of them by the tribunal of the Hexen-Kommission and their testimonies were notably free of personal hostility towards the man they accused. One, a day labourer implicated as a witch at the dance, admitted to Junius that she was not sure how she could have seen him in the tree-covered night.[15] The evidence so far was flimsy.

Then, however, Junius recorded that there 'came ... the executioner, and put the thumbscrews on me ... so that the blood ran out at the nails and everywhere'. He was stripped naked, his hands were bound and the Strappado applied, drawing him 'up in the torture'. 'Then,' he confided, 'I thought heaven and hell were at an end; eight times did they draw me up and let me fall again, so that I suffered horrible agony'. Again, Junius denied his guilt, but as he was dragged back across the compound, the executioner advised him:

> for God's sake to confess something, whether it be true or not. Invent something, for you cannot bear the torture which you shall suffer; and even if you bear it all, you shall still not escape, not even if you were a count, but one torture will follow another until you say you are a witch. Not before that will they let you go, as you may see by their trials, for one is just like another.[16]

Mayor Junius was left in no doubt his was a political accusation sanctioned from the very top. Georg Haan was led in to see him and told him that the Prince Bishop 'wanted to set such an example with me that people would be amazed. The executioners had been saying this the whole time and wanted to torture me again'. He decided to make a confession in order to escape further pain. Junius fashioned a story that he hoped would please his judges.

His confession shows elements of personal experience, combined with a knowledge of demonic practice drawn from chapbooks, folklore and possibly even from Förner's sermons. He began his tale with a low point in his life a few years earlier when he had lost a lawsuit and suffered from depression and debt. He was in the middle of a field, contemplating his woes, when a 'wild girl' appeared, presumably naked but for the matted hair that clung to her body. She asked him why he was so sad. He replied that he did not know, 'so she came closer' and transformed into a billy-goat. The creature seized his throat and revealed its true identity as the Devil. He was given the choice between death or abjuring his faith. Junius claimed that he had initially resisted and that, in crying out for God, he had managed to dispel the Devil before him. Yet he quickly reappeared, 'bringing two women and three men with him'. Junius 'was [told] to deny God and the heavenly host' and was baptised afresh by the Devil, with the women acting as his sponsors in his new faith. They gave him a gold ducat as a present, to cement the pact, but even this revealed the Devil's trickery and perversion, as 'it turned out [only] to be a shard' of broken pottery upon later examination.[17]

Junius had hoped that this confession would suffice, but his judges required much more of him. They expected confirmation of the original charges – woodland dances and political plots – and the names of other accomplices. Junius resisted the latter demand, to visit suffering upon other innocents. He was again threatened with torture and further disorientated by being taken from his cell, under guard and led around the town, street by street, from the market place to his former home in the Lange Gasse, across the bridges and up to the castle walls. Along the way he was encouraged to identify fellow 'witches' from among neighbours and passers-by. Junius relates in his letter to his daughter:

> I had to name a number of people [in the market], and then turned to the Lange Gasse. I recognised no one from there. But I had to name eight persons from there, then [to] Zinckenwert, another person and then onto the Upper Bridge and out to the George Gate on both sides. I said I didn't recognise anyone from there either. I was asked if I hadn't recognised someone from the castle, whoever it might be ... [but] I neither wanted nor could say anything more.

The Mayor's silence resulted in his return to the torture chamber of the Hexenhaus, where he was stretched upon the rack. His interrogators repeated the name of Dietmeyer – who they particularly wanted convicted – so 'I was forced to name him too'.

The Hexen-Kommission fixated on the idea of a canker hidden in Junius' respectable family life. Hoisted up on the Strappado once more, his accusers asked if the Devil had ever asked him to kill his own children. He was devoted to his daughters – Veronica in the town, and Anna Maria in the cloister. This is the charge that he fought with the greatest success. Despite being repeatedly raised, then dropped, he only admitted to causing a horse to die. This failed to satisfy the tribunal but when he also confessed to stealing the host from church, his interrogators 'left [him] in peace.'[18] The combination of his full confession, seeming repentance and exalted social status gained Mayor Junius a measure of clemency. In his file is a 'mercy note', which permitted him an honourable death by a blow from the headsman's sword.

In his last hours, on 24 July 1628, he bribed either the executioner or one of the gaolers to bring him paper and ink. He then wrote a last testimony, to his daughter, the nun Anna Maria. When we read it today, we find an exceptionally well-collected and composed account. It assuaged his need to preserve the shreds of his reputation for his daughters, but also his need to express his deep personal piety. It sickened him that he should have been tortured and abused upon Good Friday, in a mockery of the Passion. It outraged him that he was denied a priest or prior. He makes it clear that his confession was carefully weighed, in his conscience, precisely in terms of his own ultimate salvation.

Junius had feared a failure to confess would risk his entire family. This was reasonable, for the hunt took families. The entire Morhaubt family, who also lived on the Lang Gasse, was exterminated by 1629. Other wealthy families, such as the Orters and Merkleins, shared the same savage fate.[19] Chancellor Haan's case exemplifies this extraordinarily well. As related earlier, the Chancellor's wife and daughter had preceded him to the flames, then his son was executed. But the prosecutors had gone further, into his relations through marriage: his daughter-in-law Ursula Haan, and her parents – Georg and Anna Neudecker – were also tried as witches. Georg Neudecker was the wealthiest citizen of Bamberg, with a fortune of 100,000 Gulden. In 1628, he burned alongside his daughter. Then his wife was arrested as a witch and died in the Hexenhaus a year later. In 1630, his other daughter, Anna Barbara, tried escape from Bamberg together with her servants, but was taken on the road and executed.

Johannes Julius wrote to his daughter of the Hexenhaus, 'whoever comes to the house either must become a witch or be tortured for so long that he claims something pulled from his imagination'.[20] The image of the huddle of beaten and bleeding prisoners, begging forgiveness from their fellows for testifying against them, is strikingly modern. It could just as easily be drawn from the novels of Arthur Koestler and Franz Kafka, or from the real life prison diaries of Pastor Neimöller and Julius Fučik, during the Nazi terror. Yet, the case of Johannes Junius is not general but is specific to one age and to one particular, dominant culture and set of beliefs, located at the heart of Western Europe during Early Modernity.

Witchcraft was an overwhelmingly female phenomenon. This was just as true of Bamberg, as elsewhere. Yet, here we are presented with the narrative of a male witch, with the women accused of the crime, such as the Chancellor's wife and servants, appearing only as 'walk-on' parts when they directly intrude upon the Mayor's case and influence his ultimate fate. Moreover, we know that Junius's own wife was convicted of witchcraft and executed for the crime, a year before his own arrest. Yet the circumstances of her conviction, her thoughts, feelings and sufferings, even the manner in which her own trial laid the foundations for the fall of her husband – are all entirely unknown to us.[21] The voice of the woman was stilled as effectively by the denial of modes of self-expression, within that society, as by the flames of the bonfire and the stroke of the Headsman's sword.

Save for verbatim trial records, it is extremely rare to find preserved the opinions of those accused of witchcraft. In part, this gap in the primary evidence accounts for the numerous, and often widely conflicting, interpretations offered by historians, anthropologists, authors and artists, to account for the persecution. Conversely, the ideas of the ruling classes who legislated and judged – and likewise those of demonologists, who published treatises on the causes and detection of the crime – are relatively easy to recover. The mental processes of the poor, illiterate, elderly and inarticulate, are immeasurably harder to reconstruct and chart with any measure of

certainty. Their social superiors showed little interest in understanding them at the
time and, as we have seen from the proceedings at the Hexenhaus confessions, even
where they included autobiographical details, they were shaped by the immediate
needs and long-term prejudices of the accuser, and not by those of the accused.

Consequently, from fragmentary records it is, now, quite possible to create an
elaborate and surprisingly compelling, if entirely flawed, thesis about the nature
of the witch-hunt in Bamberg. If the letter from Junius to his daughter had not
survived, then it might be possible to hypothesise that the Mayor had confessed to
this crime through a combination of repression and sexual guilt. The liaison with
the 'Wild Girl' in the fields might simply be the internalisation of his past adultery.
Caught up in the sudden maelstrom of a witch-hunt, the Mayor might be held to
have sought to expiate his sin and to seek atonement. Thus, he buckled under questioning because of his guilt in another matter. We, of course, know that this was not
the case and that the existence of the letter makes plain the use of torture and the
manner in which Junius fabricated his confession in order to please his tormentors.
Yet such a counterfactual interpretation is included here in order to show just how
easy it is to interpret and inflate the existing evidence and unwittingly end up with an
entirely incorrect picture.

It is because he was far from the typical suspect in such cases of witchcraft that
his biography has survived. Had he been illiterate, pen and ink could not have benefited him. Had he not been wealthy, he would have been unable to bribe his guards to
smuggle his letter to safety. That he was a man also assisted his chances in both of the
above instances. However, even from the exceptional it is possible to glean the general:
the rhythms of life within the Hexenhaus; the patterns of questioning, alternated
with torture; and the driving need of the Hexen-Kommission for fresh confessions.

IV

Bamberg was not unique. Henri Boguet, a judge who had made his name trying
witches in the borderlands between France and Switzerland, wrote in 1602:

> Germany is almost entirely occupied with building fires for them. Switzerland
> has been compelled to wipe out many of her villages on their account. Travellers in
> Lorraine may see thousands and thousands of the stakes to which witches are bound.[22]

Successive waves of persecution washed over the Duchy of Luxembourg, then
under Spanish rule, in the period 1580–1600; the Pyrenees from 1580 to 1610; and in
Burgundy, Champagne and Languedoc, during the late 1630s. The Spanish Basque

country suffered in 1507, 1517 and throughout the 1520s, before undergoing one last ordeal in 1610. There were over 1,000 executions recorded in Lotharingia, 800 in Westphalia and more than 500 in Schaumburg-Lippe, while in the single heaviest judicial onslaught in Europe, the religious zeal of Archbishop Ferdinand of Bavaria accounted for approximately 2,000 deaths in his patrimony of Cologne. The Prince Bishoprics of Mainz, Trier and Würzburg joined in similar hunts as those practised in Bamberg and Cologne during the first three decades of the seventeenth century, while to prove that Roman Catholicism did not enjoy the sole monopoly on cruelty, the Lutheran Duke of Brunswick – Bishop Heinrich Julius of Halberstadt – directed a spate of trials across his territories, between 1590 and 1594. In the grip of the terror, his Duchy took on the aspect of a savage moonscape, with men and women broken on the wheel along the roadsides, and the local Chronicler recording that there were so many stakes set into the execution ground at Wolfenbüttel that, from a distance, it could be mistaken for 'a small wood'.[23]

Bamberg's witch-hunt, driven from above, carried on unabated even after the circle of suspects around Chancellor Haan was convicted. Whereas the elites in other territories tended to rein in new enquiries once the original threat had been neutralised, Bamberg's rulers kept on. With internal opposition crushed, the Prince Bishop and his Hexen-Kommission were free to continue arresting, trying and executing suspected witches. Förner wrote 'many prominent gentlemen and members of the Council, in particular some persons who had sat at table with the Bishop, were all executed and burned to ashes'.

Förner was, as he saw it, fulfilling his duty to God. To his contemporaries in the Catholic League, at the Bavarian court and on the Prince Bishop's council, he appeared as an implacable enemy of Sin; 'who worked beneficially for the diocese'. Posthumous tributes recalled a learned author, a 'prudent' politician; a man of truthful and eloquent speech, the most perfect integrity and religious zeal. He was the individual who, it was claimed, 'did more for the restoration of Catholicism in the diocese of Bamberg' than any other 'since the Council of Trent'.[24] It is this same combination of characteristics, which so firmly recommended Förner to the Counter-Reformation courts of Bavaria and Bamberg, in the seventeenth century and which so utterly appals and revolts us today. Yesterday's virtues and, in particular, the rigid adherence to intellectual principle and religious dogma, are today's chief vices. If tolerance was a virtue of the Renaissance and the Enlightenment, then intolerance was a virtue in the Reformation and the Counter-Reformation of the sixteenth and early seventeenth centuries.

The one surviving portrait of Friedrich Förner shows vulpine features – high forehead, bright eyes and smiling rosy lips. However much it invites us now to read into it cruelty, superciliousness and intellectual arrogance, his contemporaries would have seen an exemplary son of the church, clad in the symbols of his holy office; his dark biretta, silken casque and bejewelled crucifix. It has become common to associate witch-hunting with anti-intellectualism, a lack of education, irrationality and blind hate: Förner possessed none of these traits. He was the product of the greatest schools and universities that Southern Germany had to offer; a natural administrator, with a love for the order and seemliness to be found through the collection and collation of official documents. His study was littered with books, drawn in equal measure from his own library and that of the Jesuit college. Alongside Augustine, Gregory the Great and the other fathers of the church, he knew of Machiavelli as well as Bede, and Luther alongside Loyola. Integral to Förner's view of historical processes as the manifestations of divine will, were his demonological textbooks and, particularly, those by Jean Bodin, Nicholas Remy, Peter Binsfeld and Martin Del Rio. These writers, far from being credulous or mired in superstition, had constructed an internally coherent and complex rationale for witch-belief. This system was rooted partly in the Bible, partly in the patristic writings, and partly in the works of Classical antiquity. Förner owned a witchcraft handbook by Martin Del Rio, a learned Spanish Jesuit jurist, one passage of which is worth exploring in more depth as it shows this point particularly well. Del Rio outlines the demonic pact which gives the witch magical power. The reality and efficacy of the demonic pact is

proved by the authority of the Church Fathers. Saint Cyprian says that magicians have a treaty with an evil spirit. Gratian recalls the words of Saint Augustine, firstly: 'All arts of this kind, either of frivolous or harmful superstition, come from a certain established plague-bearing association, like a pact of faithless and deceitful friendship, between individuals and evil spirits'. Secondly, it is proved by Imperial decree: 'Many people use magical arts to disturb the elements. They do not hesitate to undermine the life of children and they dare to summon the spirits of the dead and expose them to the air, so that someone may destroy his enemies by means of their wicked arts' ... Thirdly, one should believe the decree of the Articles of the School of Paris, which runs ... 'We maintain that there is an implicit pact in all superstitious observation whose effect one may not reasonably expect to come from God or from nature'. Fourthly, reason persuades us of this pact, for many wicked people wish it and the evil spirit desires it. As the prophet Isaiah tells us, they say: 'We have severed the treaty with death and we have made a pact with Hell'.[25]

For men such as Del Rio and Förner, then, there was no possibility of doubting the pact or witchcraft. It was attested in the core texts of Christianity. Scripture, canon law and the Imperial Legal Codes simply could not be wrong.

Förner believed demonology had been practised at the courts of the Pharaohs. It was brought back to the twin kingdoms of Israel and Judea by the Israelites after their flight from Egypt, as recounted in the Book of Exodus, and reinvigorated through the demon worship and black magic wrought by Simon Magus at the time of the Apostles. All heresy, Förner argued, ultimately traced its way back to Simon Magus, who had sought the deaths of Saints Peter and Paul, and who had attempted to destroy the one true Church of Rome with the help of the Devil. Every generation was destined to re-fight this battle, with Roman Catholicism threatened successively by the Waldensians, the Lollards, the Hussites and now, by the Lutherans and Calvinists. False prophets set the stage for the destruction of kingdoms, and Förner determined that the litmus test to distinguish between religious veracity and falsehood was the abject failure of Protestant divination and the success of Roman Catholic churchmen in witnessing miracles and in exorcising demons.[26] In this light, the appearance of witches, when all other forms of heresy had already been exterminated, was a symbol of success rather than of failure. The destruction of whole tiers of Bamberg's society should, by this logic, have served as a beacon to all other godly princes to enter into a final phase of struggle against the Devil.

Mayor Junius' interrogation, torture and confession in the Hexenhaus, seen through the eyes of suffragan Bishop Förner, is fully justified. Torture was far from being inhuman, for the suspected witch did not appear to feel any pain. Together with the uncovering of the witch's mark, it is proof of the union through demonic pact. However, the decisive factor for the witch-hunters was the apparent revelation that confession was made freely, and without torture, due to the ministrations of confessors and members of the Hexen-Kommission itself.[27] Few processes can have been so couched in reassurance and self-justification, than that by which the persecutor took on the aspect of a victim, and the defenceless victim of torture was seen as possessing supernatural resilience and limitless powers to threaten his or her accusers. It was an insidious inversion of reality, but all the more effective for that. It was this iron logic that drove forward the trials in Bamberg.

V

As no halt from the council chamber could be seen, many citizens fled to neighbouring territories of Nuremberg, Ingolstadt and Franconia and even further to Bohemia, Hungary and Rome. There, at least, they might stand a chance of safety and more effectively petition on behalf of themselves or their loved ones, incarcerated in the Hexenhaus. It was this external pressure, coupled with new outbreaks of disease and the approach of the Swedish army that finally ended the witch-hunt in Bamberg.

The sheer volume of petitions reaching the Imperial Court of Justice in Regensburg attracted the attention of legal experts and Emperor alike. Emperor Ferdinand II determined to bring Johann Georg to heel, as he now represented a threat to the unity of the Catholic cause. The Emperor had been enraged by the 'judicial murder' of Chancellor Haan and his family but the last straw for Ferdinand was the arrest and trial of the daughter of a prominent Nuremberg family, Dorothea Flockhin. Dorothea was the wife of an exiled member of Bamberg's ruling council. She was young, rich and extremely well connected – and she was pregnant. Her plight elicited the sympathy of the Capuchin monks of Nuremberg, and then that of the courts of Vienna and Rome. As a result, the Jesuit Order began to distance itself from Johann Georg, cold-shouldering his envoys to the Diet at Regensberg.

Then the Emperor's own Court of Justice intervened directly. The Emperor fired off a series of increasingly strongly worded letters between October 1628 and April 1630, mandating Johann Georg to dispense with his 'irregular inquisition'. He was to halt the use of torture; review procedures in relation to the arrest of women; and release Dorothea Flockhin immediately. Johann Georg replied belligerently: 'I have only instituted such trials to increase and further the honour of God and the salvation of many imperilled souls.'[28] The Prince Bishop ignored the Emperor's command to stop making new arrests and, in an act of breathtaking defiance, had Dorothea Flockhin dragged away from the arms of her newborn baby and beheaded before the couriers carrying the Papal and Imperial reprieves could arrive to save her.

Flockhin's death forced Emperor Ferdinand's hand, and he overhauled Bamberg's judiciary in June 1631. The Prince Bishop was obliged to replace the head of his witch-finding Kommission, together with many of its members and outside experts. More significantly still, the Emperor decreed that imperial law and the criminal legislation of 1532 – known as the Carolina Code – was to operate throughout the Empire, without exception. This overruled Johann Georg's own legal system, which he had applied in Bamberg territories. Until then, he had maintained that his own legal system was necessary because witchcraft was such an exceptional crime, and so difficult to detect. His local legal system permitted the frequent use of torture and trials in secret. A further integral element of the Bamberg legal system was the confiscation of all the goods and property of those convicted of witchcraft. It was part of the trial process and the penalty for the crime itself. Of course, the seizure of wealth provided a strong motive to target the richest citizens – such as Chancellor Haan, Georg Neudecker and Mayor Junius. In contrast, the Carolina Code distinguished between different types of magic, did not automatically demand the death penalty for witchcraft and restricted the use of torture. Trials were a matter of public record and the confiscation of goods did not automatically accompany a conviction.[29] Once the Empire imposed its standardised legal code, subject to imperial scrutiny, Bamberg's witch-hunt at last began to stall. The death of Förner in 1630 also contributed to this process. However, the Prince Bishop clung onto the notion of both reforming and validating his state through the fires of inquisition. New arrests and executions continued.

It would take the complete collapse of Johann Georg II's administration and the utter ruin of his state before the hunt could be brought to a final halt. In February 1631, the Swedish army was advancing upon the suburbs of Bamberg while, from within the walls, the Emperor's agent, Dr Anton Winter, was attempting to wrest control of the Hexen-Kommission from the Prince Bishop and to press the necessity of an unconditional surrender. There were insufficient troops to defend the city's impressive walls, as all the funding had been expended on witch-hunting. As the Swedes prepared to take the citadel, the remaining members of the Hexen-Kommission sought refuge in a nearby fortress. The Prince Bishop fled, in his coach, to his family's estates in Carinthia. With the city's government in ruins, it was the Emperor's representative, Dr Winter, who surrendered the keys of the castle to the Swedes. The Swedish occupation lasted little over a month but it destroyed the Hexen-Kommission's control over the city's judiciary. In September 1631, the last ten inmates of the Hexenhaus were released from custody.

The Prince Bishop had further problems. Amid his political collapse, his health too, collapsed. And his land was in crisis. The crops had failed and starvation was gripping farm and city. The execution of more than 600 suspected witches had done nothing to restore the harvest or to return the seasons to their proper order. The invading armies left disease, as well as destruction, in their wake. When fresh Swedish scouts approached Bamberg in 1633, they reported to Marshal Horn and his generals that there were unburied bodies – the victims of plague and famine – littering the city streets. The Swedish soldiers who marched into the stronghold barely noticed the deserted Hexenhaus. Certainly, as they tethered their horses, or pulled scarves over their faces to shut out the stench of the dead, none of the cavalrymen would have remarked upon the empty execution ground. None would have spared a thought for the ashes of Johannes Junius, Chancellor Haan or young Hans Morhaubt, whose dust would have been whipped up by a sudden wind or trampled under hoof and foot.

CHAPTER THREE

The Widow, the Fish and the Enchanted Goatskins

I

The Mediaeval craftsman is anonymous. He is a worker. However gifted he is, he will never be revered for his individual insight or genius. His art and labour will add lustre to the Church or to his courtly patrons, but not to his own biography. By chance his work survives pestilence and poverty, the Thirty Years' War, the depredations of Napoleonic looters and the bombs that obliterated Hitler's Leipzig. Yet, his name does not. Posterity, and the later academic requirements of gallery cataloguers, designate him as 'the Master of the Lower Rhine' (or *Niederrheinischer*) but all those clues to personality and motivation to be found in diaries, diocesan account books or letters are entirely absent. This is frustrating for the historian and the art historian alike, and leads to the artist's work being largely ignored in the textbooks.[1] As a result, it does not easily bear multiple readings, or fit a fashionable paradigm. Perhaps, more damagingly, within modern Western society – which celebrates the individual over the mass, and often links artistic merit and financial worth to a colourful life story – there is something disturbing about an image that appears to stand alone without exegesis or lengthy provenance.

Yet, towards the close of the fifteenth century, the 'Master of the Lower Rhine' began work on an oil painting depicting 'Love Magic' (or *Der Liebeszauber*), which is familiar today to students, teachers and Pagans through its use as the cover illustration of the Penguin edition of Keith Thomas' seminal study of *Religion and the Decline of Magic*, and as a misattributed plate in Tania Luhrmann's *Persuasions of the Witch's Craft*.[2] It appears to show a witch, naked but for her fashionably pointed shoes and gauze drape, working a charm before a roaring hearth. She is clearly a woman of substance, at home in a light and airy chamber, at the top of a house easily recognisable to the burgermeisters of Cologne, Dortmund or Munster. Her room is richly furnished, complete with a pet bird and a lapdog curled up at her feet, lying on a velvet cushion. A golden dish, a bolt of silk and a spray of peacock feathers decorate the sideboard, while the doors of a normally locked and bolted cupboard swing open to reveal shelves full of costly jugs and bowls. The witch is young and shapely, with pert breasts and long, flowing, golden hair. By the standards of her own, or any time, she would be considered beautiful and is certainly confident of her own sexuality and allure. She is pictured in the act of sprinkling drops of molten wax from a phial onto a stylised human or animal heart, which is kept in an ornately gilded box. A young man, in the background of the painting, looks on, unobserved, from an open doorway as the ritual is performed. Freshly picked flowers are scattered across the floorboards and they, too, would seem to be integral to the spell. There can, therefore, be little doubt that the artist is intent upon depicting the practices of a witch, in working love magic.

Surprisingly, witchcraft scholars have rarely made the painting a subject of critical examination.[3] The man in the background may be the lover she has brought, through her art, to her door. He may be an inquisitive servant – a 'peeping Tom'. We may be seeing evidence of late fifteenth- and early sixteenth-century witchcraft, as it was practised – before its demonisation – linking powerful magic with the naked human form. Conversely, we may be seeing no more than a study in eroticism commissioned for the private pleasures of a rich patron.

However, when taken as a whole, the painting can be viewed as one of the founding documents of European witchcraft. Without it, the worthy Christian women of Castle Rising might not have been conflated with demonic witches; and Bishop Förner would not have been able to trace his list of authorities from antiquity through the Church Fathers to the Neo-Platonists of the Renaissance, in order to 'prove' the existence of the witch. Furthermore, modern-day Pagans have chosen to celebrate the painting as proof-positive that ritual magic was still being worked in the nude – or 'skyclad' – during the High Middle Ages.[4] Yet, as with most things, the truth is a little more complex. This is an image of the working of magic fashioned for the elite, devoid of both pejorative comment or explicitly Judeo-Christian content; it is illustrative of practices and a particular narrative that now appear lost. Yet, if such an enigma exists it does so as the result of modern scholarly preoccupation with the period of the witch trials and with the persecutory texts that fanned the flames of the pyre. The subtlety of literary and artistic device, of biting satire and rational scepticism, are often assumed to be purely modern developments, while the witch as object of – rather than as barrier to – passion, tends to be sidelined and left as the preserve of today's Pagans and the champions and polemicists of the feminist movement. Indeed, so powerful is the paradigm of the ragged, reviled, crone – outlined in our introductory chapter – that the image of Circe and Medea, the Classical archetypes so familiar to artists such as Dürer, Baldung Grien and the anonymous 'Master of the Lower Rhine', have largely faded from our consciousness. Yet, it was not always so and it would seem that the painting of 'Love Magic' owes far more to the world of Classical, than Mediaeval, Rome.

II

The absence of a single, dominant and persecuting religious creed, of the type evidenced in the Prince Bishopric of Bamberg, did not always ensure that the worker of magic would go unnoticed by the law. Thus, during the Proconsulship of Claudius Maximus between 155–8 CE, Lucius Apuleius – sometime philosopher, poet, rhetorician and priest of Isis – was in big trouble.

Taken ill at Oea (modern-day Tripoli) Lucius Apuleius had met and married Aemilia Pudentilla, a wealthy widow some years his senior. In the minds of her two full-grown sons, her brothers-in-law and the father-in-law of her elder son, the unexpected match signified a massive shift in the control, and future distribution, of her property and estates. Consequently, her sons – Sicinius Pontianus and Sicinius Pudens – who had initially befriended Apuleius during his time in North Africa, now became concerned about their inheritance. Pontianus' father-in-law (Herrenius Rufinus) saw his dynastic plans thwarted and Pudentilla's former brothers-in-law also had very serious axes to grind against the 'new man' on the scene. Sicinius Clarus – stamped for posterity by Apuleius as 'a boorish and decrepit old man' – had once been scorned by Pudentilla, who had rejected his advances, and refused to countenance a socially convenient marriage to him. This snub also reflected upon the elder brother-in-law, Sicinius Aemilianus, who had favoured the match as a means to keep Pudentilla's wealth within the family circle, and who had been, until the arrival of Apuleius, the head of the clan. Aemilianus, therefore, initiated a plan to strike against Apuleius before the cuckoo could settle too far, and too comfortably, down into the nest.

The young philosopher was, after all, a foreigner with strange habits and interests, who kept irregular hours and refused to dress according to established custom. Moreover, he made little secret of his interest in magic and was regularly seen carrying piles of scrolls and other tightly wrapped and half-hidden objects about with him. Most disturbing of all, Lucius was an intellectual, and he had already run through most of his own fortune in the pursuit of travel and study. It was incomprehensible that Pudentilla should love this stranger of 'Greek eloquence and … barbarian birth.'[5] He must have bewitched her into loving him, in order to gain her fortune. Aemilianus knew the court at Sabrata, 60 miles west of Tripoli on the coast, would see that too.

However, just as the case was coming to trial, Pudentilla's elder son, Pontianus, suddenly died. For several days his enemies went around the market place accusing Apuleius of the 'practice of the black art and with the murder of [his] step-son' but the case was dropped before the first session of the court.[6] What remained, however, was damaging enough. The author and philosopher stood trial for what was, effectively, fraud, accomplished by the means of witchcraft. Though the indictment and the prosecution case have not survived, we can reconstruct most of the charges brought against Apuleius from his defence against them.

He had, it was alleged, blended secret magical powders; kept 'a mysterious object in his house which he worships with veneration'; caused a young slave by the name of Thallus to collapse in his presence; bought large quantities of fish from the quayside, in order to manufacture his love potions; and determined to compel Pudentilla, who had never before thought of marriage, 'to be mine by the exercise of the black art; that I alone had found to outrage the virgin purity of her widowhood by incantations and love philtres'.[7] For good measure, his accusers heaped on subsidiary accusations, of a more or less serious nature, in the hope that if they threw enough mud then at least some of it might be sure to stick. Among these charges were allegations that Apuleius was an unnaturally 'handsome philosopher'; dressed badly; had grown his hair long; was mean despite his access to wealth; and had written 'frivolous verses of an erotic character'.[8]

Such a barrage of hatred might have sunk a lesser man. However, even though Apuleius was given only five days to prepare his defence, several factors worked in his favour. First, he was well connected. He had money of his own, came from an important family, and had counted at least two future proconsuls of North Africa as his friends and patrons.[9] In this light, his frequent nods towards the person and wisdom of Claudius Maximus – who tried the case – might have been not merely the signs of deference, or simple rhetorical flourishes, but pointed reminders about their own relationship and Apuleius' own status within the Roman colonies. Second, and perhaps more important still, was the refusal of Roman courts to employ torture in obtaining confessions for magic. The absence of the threat of torture permitted Apuleius a greater freedom to reason with the court, and to mock his accusers.[10]

Apuleius was a skilled debater, a natural raconteur possessed with a great sense of comic timing. He was highly intelligent and had made the mysteries of religion and magic his lifelong study. As they glowered across at him in the courtroom, Aemilianus, Rufinus and Clarus must surely have begun to suspect that they had picked upon the wrong man.

Apuleius ridiculed the charges one by one. 'Do you really think,' he asked his accusers, 'to prove your charge of magic by such arguments as these; the fall of a wretched boy, my marriage to my wife, my purchases of fish?' The boy, Thallus, was, he contended, not bewitched but a sufferer of epilepsy, who had fitted frequently and been examined by doctors long before he had ever come to Tunis.[11] He had married Pudentilla 'for love and not for money' and his love had been freely reciprocated, rather than coerced by the administration of potions. Because of this, he explained: 'This marriage of ours caused frightful annoyance to Aemilianus. Hence springs all the anger, frenzy and raving madness that he has shown in the conduct of this accusation.'

With regard to the charge that he 'had sought to purchase certain kinds of fish from some fishermen,' he told the court that they might have as easily been bought for a dinner party, rather than for use in a spell: 'for who ever heard of fish being scaled and boned for dark purposes of magic?'[12] And it was here that Apuleius hit his comic stride, teasing his foes mercilessly. 'Did you infer,' he asked,

> that the fish were wanted for evil purposes because I paid to get them? I presume,
> if I had wanted them for a dinner party, I should have got them for nothing ...
> Or is there something mysterious in fish and fish alone, hidden from sorcerers?[13]

In a less free-spirited age, concerned with the prohibition of all forms of magic, his flippancy might have been dangerous and his next gambit almost certainly fatal. For Apuleius went on to lecture his accusers about their 'empty, ridiculous and childish fictions' and to point out exactly how it was thought love potions actually *were* made, and how they accused him of using entirely the wrong ingredients. Had the trial centred on the acquisition of magical learning, rather than the purposes to which magic could be put, then, at this point, Apuleius would surely have signed his own death warrant. As it was, he began to enjoy himself, to play to the gallery, to win over the crowd in the courthouse, and to establish his authority over his opponents.

'What use for the kindling of love,' he asked of them, 'is an unfeeling chilly creature like a fish, or indeed anything else drawn from the sea?' Rather, if he had really wanted to brew a love potion, he would have taken his cue from Virgil and looked for 'very different things ... for this purpose'. Soft, garlanded flowers, rich herbs, multicoloured threads and 'clay to be hardened' and 'wax to be melted in the fire' were needed for such a charm, but his accusers attributed

> far different instruments to magicians, charms not to be torn from new-born
> foreheads, but to be cut from scaly backs; not to be plucked from the fields of earth,
> but to be drawn up from the deep fields of [the] ocean; not to be mowed with sickles,
> but to be caught on hooks.[14]

Thus, he concluded, ridiculing them, that when Virgil writes of 'the black art ... [and] mentions poison, you produce an entrée; [when] he mentions herbs and shoots, you talk of scales and bones; [when] he crops the meadow, you search the waves.'[15]

Here, Apuleius is reminding the court, comprising the elite of Roman society in North Africa, just who is the educated gentleman, and who is not. Why, he asks, are there 'such general charges as the uninstructed are in the habit of levelling at philosophers?'[16] If only they had read their Virgil, as they should, they would never have made so many elementary mistakes. His accusers, he tells the court, are merely betraying their ignorance, and with it their utter duplicity and perjury in bringing the original charges.

Apuleius went even further in his defence. He provided a justification for the type of magic he was practising. He began by explaining that the

whole of Aemilianus' calumnious accusation was centred on the charge of magic [and that] I should therefore like to ask his most learned advocates how, precisely, they would define a magician? If what I read in a large number of authors be true, namely, that magician is the Persian word for priest, what is there criminal in being a priest and having due knowledge, science, and skill in all ceremonial law, sacrificial duties, and the binding rules of religion?

This magic, he suggests, 'is no other than the worship of the gods [and] ... is an art acceptable to the immortal gods, full of all knowledge of worship and of prayer, [being] full of piety and wisdom in things divine'. If this is truly the case, and if Plato was right in asserting that 'magical charms are merely beautiful words', Apuleius asked the court, 'why should I be forbidden to learn the fair words of Zalmoxis or the priestly lore of Zoroaster?'[17]

Having clarified his practice of the magical arts and firmly rooted it within accepted religious observance, Apuleius now distinguished it from malign sorcery. 'Now this magic', he told the court,

of which you accuse me is ... a crime in the eyes of law, and was forbidden in the Twelve Tables because in some incredible manner crops had been charmed away from one field to another. It is then as mysterious an art as it is loathly and horrible; it needs as a rule night-watches and concealing darkness, solitude absolute and murmured incantations, to hear which few free men are admitted.

By way of contrast, he was now being accused of practising his magic in broad daylight, in front not only of his stepson, Pudens, but also some 15 household slaves, whose very presence – he felt – would have automatically rendered any such spell void, on account of their lowly, unlearned status.[18]

Witchcraft charges were, Apuleius contended, used as an insidious 'handle' with which to ensnare the accused. There was no way of stilling accusations of that nature once they had been made, or of giving a 'right' answer to the prosecutor. For, if

> any man who is charged with sorcery [is asked] ... Have you breathed silent prayers to heaven in some temple? [Then] you are a sorcerer! Else tell us what you asked for? Or take the contrary line. You uttered no prayer in some temple! You are a sorcerer! Else why did you not ask the gods for something? The same argument will be used if you have made some votive dedication, or offered sacrifice or carried sprigs of some sacred plant.

Thus, the rules of witch prosecution – that were to become so depressingly familiar to thousands of largely nameless victims over the next 1,500 years – were stripped bare in a North African courtroom. Perhaps more remarkable still, Apuleius also provided the judiciary with a graphic description of the spread and intensity of a witch-hunt, that could sudden flare up, spread like wildfire and then die down again.

Apuleius' trial speech, together with the evidence for his later career, indicate strongly that he was acquitted of all the charges. Indeed, in his careful preservation, and later copying, of his defence, we can detect his pride in having won the day. Yet, there is palpable irony in the fact that Apuleius was arraigned in the first place: he clearly had been practising magic, had spent years enthralled by it, and made absolutely no attempt to hide the fact. Magic, in his eyes, was an integral – particularly specialised and exhilarating – part of his religious observance. Moreover, Apuleius had created his own particular portrayals of the witch in his novel, *The Transformation of Lucius Apuleius of Madaura* – later shortened by St Augustine, to *The Golden Ass*.[19] The plot follows the protagonist, a fictional Lucius, who undergoes a transformation into an ass and has adventures on his way to an initiation into a mystery cult of the goddess Isis. It is deemed the first novel of the Western canon. The hero's encounters with witchcraft provide not only some of the most richly comical passages in the novel, but also account for the disastrous transformation of the handsome young nobleman. Lucius is repeatedly warned to be on his guard against witchcraft, and against the terrible fates accorded to anyone who either fell under the spell of a witch, or through their own sense of hubris felt that they could play around with magic. The novel relates that the witch Meroe turns an old innkeeper into a frog; fixes rams' horns onto the head of a lawyer who attempted to prosecute her and condemns an unfriendly woman to perpetual pregnancy. Worse still, she turned her unfaithful lover into a beaver, an animal which 'bites off its own testicles.'[20] Of course, Apuleius is having fun here, but he is harnessing these fears to stretch them out to the logical, and comical, conclusions.

Meroe is able to

> pull down the heavens or uplift the earth; to petrify the running stream or dissolve the rocky mountain; to raise the spectral dead or hurl the gods from their thrones; to quench the bright stars or illuminate the dark Land of Shadows.

These are grand claims, suggesting that witches might operate in successful opposition to the gods. However, this was not always the case. While citing one (nameless) witch as only being 'able to exert a certain pressure on the gods' in order to effect her spells, Apuleius introduces a witch – Pamphile – who can (and does) harness her power from obedient ghosts, puts pressure upon the stars and 'blackmails the gods.'[21] It is through Pamphile – whose name translates as the 'lover of everybody' – that we gain the fullest insight into the workings of Classical witchcraft.

Pamphile is old, vengeful and consumed by her desires. Having fallen in love, or at any rate lusted after, a youth from Boeotia, she determines to use 'all her best sorceries to seduce him'. Working her magic in secret, she climbs up to a cockerel's coop, perched up high on top of her house, 'open to all the four winds, with a particularly wide view of the eastern sky' and begins her incantations. Unobserved, Fotis – her servant girl – notes her practices. The witch, she tells Lucius,

> had everything ready there for her deadly rites: all sorts of aromatic incense, metal plaques engraved with secret signs, beaks and claws of ill-omened birds, various bits of corpse-flesh – in one place she had arranged the noses and fingers of crucified men, in another the nails that had been driven through their palms and ankles, with bits of flesh still sticking to them – also little bladders full of life-blood saved from the men she had murdered and the skulls of criminals who had been thrown to the wild beasts in the amphitheatre. She began to repeat certain charms over the still warm and quivering entrails of some animal or other, dipping them in turn into jars of spring-water, cow's milk, mountain honey and mead. Then she plaited the hair I had given her, tied it into peculiar knots and threw it with a great deal of incense on her charcoal fire. The power of this charm is irresistible – backed you must understand, by the blind violence of the gods who have been invoked: the smell of the hair smoking and crackling on the fire compels its owner to come to the place from which he is being summoned.[22]

However, the spell spectacularly miscarries. Unable to secure a lock of the Boeotian's hair and terrified of her mistress' displeasure, Fotis had substituted bristles from a goatskin thinking that the difference would never matter or be noticed. This reveals her complete lack of understanding for the principles behind sympathetic magic and the importance of the right ingredients. Thus, instead of bewitching the handsome young man, it is the goatskins which are enchanted. The Boeotian goes on his way unharmed, while the goatskins come to life, 'magically endowed with human ... senses and understanding,' their desire to love and possess Pamphile enflamed and their members engorged by lust. Dashing through the town, trotting upright on their plucked legs, they sought out the witch's house and began hammering upon the gate, in order to force themselves upon the witch.[23]

However, neither Pamphile nor Lucius – who seduces Fotis in order to learn the secrets of the old witch – are prepared to heed the warning signs, or to abandon their magical designs.

Witchcraft works but not for the good of either the practitioner or of wider humanity. It would seem to rebound with terrible, if often humorous, consequences for all concerned. Both the witch and the nobleman should, by now, have known better but Pamphile continues to pursue the Boeotian and Lucius continues to spy upon her works.[24] As a consequence, Pamphile now decides to transform herself into an owl to fly in at her beloved's window and seduce him in his sleep. Once again, at twilight, she clambers up to her workshop in the cockerel's coop and begins to work on her magical transformation, as Lucius looks on from behind a partition. The witch first undresses before opening a cabinet and taking out a little box containing an ointment, that Apuleius tells us 'she worked about with her fingers and then smeared all over her body to the crown of her head. After this she muttered a long charm to her lamp, and shook herself'. Then she assumes the form of an owl, or *strix*. These creatures, who flew silently by night, had been described by Ovid's *Fasti* as beings turned 'from crones to birds'. Ovid wrote: 'They are said to gorge on milk-fed flesh with their beaks/And to cram their throats with gulps of blood'. 'Their particular pleasure was to snatch infants from their cradles'.[25] Lucius, however, did not wish to become an owl in order to peck out the eyes of infants, but rather so that he could glide over the roof tops and learn, for himself, how to work transformative magic. He returns to Fotis – despite her track record of ruining spells – and begs her to help him change into an owl. Unfortunately, Fotis – true to form – mixes up the two little boxes in the witch's cabinet and gives Lucius an ointment that transforms him, not into an owl as he had hoped, but into a jackass. To make matters even worse, she had not thought to fashion the chains of rose garlands that would have acted as an antidote. Misfortune follows misfortune, as Lucius – as an ass – is carried off in a bandit raid.

The rest of the tale is devoted to Lucius' various degradations as a beast of burden. All of his luck fails him for, as Apuleius makes clear, 'no one can prosper, however wise he may be, if Fortune should rule otherwise'. Fate cannot be cancelled or modified in any way, and Fortune – personified here as a goddess – is frequently reviled for her cruelty and spitefulness.[26] Indeed, Robert Graves, as the first modern translator of the work, appears justified in stressing Apuleius' belief that bad luck is catching. Lucius ruined his own luck by debasing himself, first by sleeping with a slave girl, and second by dabbling in witchcraft.[27] As with the contagious bad luck, almost all of the ass's masters and mistresses are ruined by coming into contact with him. The bandits begin to lose men in their raids and are then caught and slaughtered by Tlepolemus, the bridegroom of a girl they had held for ransom; Tlepolemus and his wife are destroyed through the actions of a rival suitor for the girl's hand; and a kindly, but poor, market-gardener is ruined by her greed and by the bullying of a professional soldier. As Lucius passes from owner to owner, Apuleius is able to vent his scorn for those people, practices and professions for which he had absolutely no time. Lawyers and gangs of travelling eunuch priests come in for particular censure; and Tlepolemus and his young bride are shown as fatally jeopardising their happiness through breaking their promises to look after the ass.

It is the novel's one Christian character in the book who Apuleius singles out for his particular contempt.[28] The miller's wife – we never know her name – was, claims Lucius,

> the wickedest woman I met in all of my travels … There was no single vice which she did not possess: her heart was a regular cesspool into which every sort of filthy sewer emptied. She was malicious, cruel, spiteful, lecherous, drunken, selfish, obstinate, as mean in her petty thefts as she was wasteful in her grand orgies, and an enemy of all that was honest and clean.

He finds her mill to be worked by half-starved, mange-ridden animals, driven to turn the wheel, both day and night, by curses and savage beatings, while her slaves – who made up the human part of her workforce – are treated no better. They are barely clad, shackled, scarred by the marks of 'old floggings', and with her owner's stamp branded onto their foreheads. These terrified precursors of H.G. Wells' Morlocks, stripped of all dignity and scarcely recognisable as human, toil ceaselessly to provide for her pleasure: 'their eyelids caked with the smoke of baking ovens, their eyes so bleary and inflamed that they could hardly see out of them.'[29] When she takes a young lover, the little ass who often lay awake in his stall groans in 'secret pity' for her long-suffering husband. When her affair is exposed and she is divorced, the woman takes her revenge by hiring the services of a local witch. Skilled in love magic and necromancy, the witch summons up the shade of a woman who had been the victim of violence, and drives the ex-husband, a poor miller, to hang himself from the rafters of his own bedroom. Apuleius is keen to show the upstanding morality of the pagan miller, who keeps the image of the Corn goddess in his workplace, in contrast to the hypocrisy and immorality of his ex-wife. The latter is even prepared to sanction murder to achieve her wicked ends.[30] Yet her wickedness, double standards and extreme willingness to take 'refuge in the magical arts with which women of her sort usually defend themselves', appear to Apuleius to stem from her rejection of the gods and her embracing of Christianity. The root of her canker was her

> professed perfect scorn for the Immortals and [rejection of] all true religion in favour of a fantastic and blasphemous cult of an 'Only God'. In [whose] honour she practised various absurd ceremonies which gave her the excuse of getting drunk quite early in the day [through the partaking of the host] and playing the whore at all hours.[31]

When the miller's savage wife is brought to trial for the murder of her husband, Apuleius has her convicted and crucified as a common criminal along the highway, perhaps in a parody of the sufferings of Jesus on the cross. However, for her there would be neither resurrection nor redemption.

Apuleius, like most educated Roman citizens, saw Christianity as a socially divisive and dangerous movement. It threatened to dissolve the bonds of morality and class that held the fabric of the Empire together, so it was to be dismissed or despised. Yet, it was a cult like no other within the Roman world; in terms of its insistence upon a monopoly of truth, its insularity, extreme unwillingness to compromise with the rest of Imperial society, and highly developed institutional structure, it simply could not be ignored. As a consequence, pagan philosophers such as Marcus Aurelius' tutor, Fronto, and Lucian of Samosata, alleged that Christians were a dangerous, disruptive and unnecessarily secretive band of fanatics, who had rejected mainstream culture in favour of the worship of an obscure miracle-worker, or magician, from Galilee. Christians refused to participate fully in the spiritual and social life of the Empire, holding themselves as a people apart, and shunning those cultural events – such as civic processions, the Games and theatre performances – that brought other disparate religious and ethnic groupings together in common endeavour and helped to create a more harmonious civic society.[32]

Apuleius was clearly alarmed by the sudden spread of the 'new cult' of Christianity across Egypt and North Africa and sought to combat what he felt were its destructively anti-social tendencies. Indeed, it is possible – though by no means certain – that his later prosecution at Sabrata was motivated, in part, by score-settling on behalf of the local Christian community. *The Golden Ass*, despite its recourse to jokes and sexual humour, is an avowedly religious text. The beauty and piety of the work are often overlooked in favour of the knock-about comedy. Indeed, one modern critic has written of the religious passages contained within the novel, that: 'Apuleius is content merely to tack on at the end a piece of solemn pageantry as a ballast to off-set the prevailing levity of the preceding ten books.' Yet, this is to entirely miss the purpose of Apuleius' writing.[33] For, it was the genius of the Classical world, and of Apuleius in particular as an author, that what was held to be sacred could also be amusing, playful, provocative and joyous. In this manner, the tale of Cupid and Psyche could sit alongside that of the goatskins, without seeming – to a Classical audience, at least – in any way incongruous.[34]

Apuleius' novel is also a devotional work, chronicling the fall and subsequent redemption of Lucius himself. Once transformed into the ass, he has become the low-est of the low. However, while he had played around with the 'wrong sort' of magic, Lucius had not sought to use it for evil purposes, and this enables him to win back the sympathies of the gods. Unlike St Augustine's Christianity, Classical paganism permitted – and encouraged – a free will that applied both to mortals and to the actions of gods.

After unmasking the adultery of the miller's wife, Lucius the ass is taken into service in the household of an honest magistrate, and something of his humanity is restored to him. Finally, he prays in his desperation to the goddess Isis. She comes to him in a vision as a 'dazzling full moon was rising from the sea'. For it is, we are told, 'at this secret hour that the Moon-goddess, sole sovereign of mankind, is possessed of her greatest power and majesty'. Lucius' vision of the goddess rising from the waves is worth recalling in some detail as it not only reveals something of the Classical idea of the divine, but also allows us to see – at the outset of this book – the manner in which modern-day Pagans have built upon such imagery in their conception of the Mother Goddess. Thus, Apuleius writes that:

> Her long thick hair fell in tapering ringlets ... and was crowned with an intricate chaplet in which was woven every kind of flower. Just above her brow shone a round disc, like a mirror, or like the bright face of the moon, which told me who she was. Vipers rising from the left-hand and right-hand partings of her hair supported this disc, with ears of corn bristling beside them. Her many-coloured robe was of the finest linen; part was glistening white, part crocus-yellow, part glowing red and along the entire hem a woven bordure of flowers and fruit clung swaying in the breeze. But what caught and held my eye more than anything else was the deep black lustre of her mantle ... part of it hung in innumerable folds, the tasselled fringe quivering. It was embroidered with glittering stars on the hem and everywhere else, and in the middle beamed a full and fiery moon.

Apuleius then has her reveal herself and something of her universal nature to the sleeping Lucius, proclaiming that:

I am Nature, the universal Mother, mistress of all the elements ... sovereign of all things spiritual, queen of the dead, queen also of the immortals, the single manifestation of all gods and goddesses that are. My nod governs the shining heights of Heaven, the wholesome sea-breezes, the lamentable silences of the world below. Though I am worshipped in many aspects, known by countless names, and propitiated with all manner of different rites, yet the whole round earth venerates me ... the Athenians ... call me Cecropian Artemis; for the islanders of Cyprus I am Paphian Aphrodite; for the archers of Crete I am Dictynna ... for the Eleusinians their ancient Mother of the Corn. Some know me as Juno, some as Bellona of the Battles; others as Hecate ... and the Egyptians who excel in ancient learning and worship me with ceremonies proper to my godhead, call me by my true name, namely Queen Isis.[35]

This is the moment to which the whole novel has been building: it is its climax. Humbled and moved by the goddess's glory and wisdom, Lucius promises to devote his life to her service, joins a religious procession held in Corinth, and nibbles at a rose garland offered to him by the High Priest of Isis. Just as Odysseus was saved from Circe's enchantment by eating sprigs of moly, so Lucius breaks the spell of witchcraft by eating the blooms of another plant. However, the garland has now come to symbolise far more than a simple antidote to the witch's ointment, rather a 'crown of victory over cruel Fortune, bestowed on me by the Goddess.'[36] The whole moral purpose behind the novel now becomes clear, as Apuleius has the high priest tell Lucius that:

Neither your noble blood and rank nor your education sufficed to keep you from falling a slave to pleasure; youthful follies ran away with you. Your luckless curiosity earned you a sinister punishment. But blind Fortune after tossing you maliciously about from peril to peril has somehow, without thinking what she was doing, landed you here in religious felicity.[37]

Now devoted to the service of Isis, Lucius holds true to his vows, is eventually initiated into the mysteries of her cult, and goes on to have a rewarding and felicitous spiritual life in first Corinth, and then Rome.

It seems likely that Apuleius was, himself, a follower of Isis but it is by no means certain that his account of the fictional Lucius' religious experiences, as recorded in Book 11 of *The Golden Ass*, was in any way autobiographical. He had, after all, been reworking a series of themes from earlier works, including the Milesian tales and the now lost *Metamorphosis* of Loukios of Patras, in an attempt to translate the idiom from a Greek to a Roman setting. It is further argued that it was actually Asclepius, the god of healing, as opposed to Isis, who emerges from his other extant, original writings as Apuleius' tutelary deity.[38] However, the change of tempo and profound religiosity of the final book do seem suggestive of a particular sense of engagement with – and devotion to – the cult of Isis. Yet, within a specifically pagan context this does not signify, as Keith Bradley has convincingly argued, a religious disjuncture or 'conversion' narrative underpinning the novel's ending. The fictional Lucius is 're-formed' – through his journey from man to ass, ass to man – emerging with a heightened spiritual awareness, rather than a sense of being 'converted' to another faith. He does not reject his prior religious conceptions and allegiances, rather, he adds to them. Classical paganism did not seek converts, it did not prose-lytise and its understanding of polytheism was both highly nuanced and intrinsically tolerant of differences of religious expression. Indeed, Apuleius had Isis acknowledge her different forms – as Aphrodite, Artemis and Athene, among others – and while she bargains with Lucius in order to secure his devotion, she does not seek to make him repudiate his other gods, to achieve exclusivity of worship, or dominance over other deities in the pantheon.[39] Difference was to be celebrated, rather than to be feared, and within this schema Isis might happily co-exist alongside Asclepius, within the author's devotional life.

Both Apuleius, as a political actor, and the novel, as literature, were part of a pagan rearguard action against the Christianity encroaching upon North Africa at that time. Apuleius became something of a hero of the pagan resistance movement: he emerged as a major figure for Hellenic scholars, anxious to celebrate and sustain their traditions at a time when their world view, and the Imperial institutions that had always sustained them, were dissolving. Apuleius' bust appeared upon monuments of the late pagan revival and it would seem that *The Golden Ass* was repeatedly copied as a means of propagating devotion to Isis.[40] As Christianity transformed itself from an underground to a state religion in the fourth century CE, paganism still appeared capable of rallying its forces and regaining lost ground. Staunchly pagan communi-ties continued to flourish in the British Isles – though largely outside of the urban centres, where official scrutiny and doctrinal discipline were more difficult to enforce. They similarly flourished in Apuleius' adoptive homeland in North Africa: pagans often forcefully protected temple complexes and statues of the old gods when bands of monks and Christian-led soldiers came to tear them down. Against this back-ground, we can see *The Golden Ass* as a counterpoint to another, very different, reli-gious journey: the *Confessions* of St Augustine of Hippo, itself an explicit conversion narrative written by another African and near contemporary of Apuleius.

The pagan religious revival was hampered by its own, inherent, social and spiritual conservatism. The strength of Roman paganism had always lain in its ability to appropriate the local gods and goddesses of its subject peoples, permitting these to grow and develop alongside the Empire's existing pantheon. The diffuse and hetero-geneous pagan revivalists of the fourth century CE retreated into a highly traditional-ist celebration of the core pantheon of Greco-Roman gods – such as Jupiter, Apollo, Minerva or Mars – that reflected a comfortable nostalgia for the former grandeur of the Empire. Had they instead promoted the vibrant Eastern mystery cults, they might have been able to rival the powerful devotional experiences and rigid doctrinal certainties offered by Christianity.[41]

Apuleius' account of devotion to a Mother Goddess, operating in duality with a male deity (here Osiris) might have provided a clear blueprint for modern-day Pagan mysteries. His advocacy of 'perfect chastity' sits ill at ease with today's Paganism, with its celebration of sexual union, but in fact pagan 'chastity' simply meant continence and monogamous propriety.[42] Far more difficult is the exclusivity of the ancient mystery cult. To be initiated, one had to pay, and to pay heavily. The Roman Empire's poor, uneducated and slave-bound could never hope to be favoured by, or even to understand, Isis. Amid squalor and injustice, and by the apparent hopeless-ness of their condition ordained by gods who appeared cruel, patrician and remote, it was little wonder that Apuleius' contemporaries turned in ever greater numbers to Christianity, which embraced the poor and the weak, offering inclusive religious practice and a more egalitarian society. We might recall that Apuleius was himself a slave-owner and that the court case in Sabratha revolved, in part, about the division of 400 or more Sub-Saharan slaves.[43]

More practically, pagan cults did not write down liturgy. Terrible penalties were to be exacted upon anyone who divulged the secrets of initiation and the core truths of the individual cults, including the 'hidden' names of the deities. Hence, when Apuleius came to write of the most momentous moment of his character's life – when he was fully initiated into the service of the goddess Isis in her sanctuary at Corinth – he could only inform his readership that:

> I approached the very gates of death and set one foot on [the goddess of death] Prosperine's threshold, yet was permitted to return, rapt through all the elements. At midnight I saw the sun shining as if it were noon; I entered the presence of the gods of the underworld and the gods of the upper-world, stood near and worshipped them.[44]

Clearly he experienced a life-changing religious ecstasy during the overnight ceremony. But today's witches need to have details with which to recreate it, even approximately. Who else was involved? Were narcotics imbibed? Was music played? Were the dangers literal or purely metaphorical? Apuleius is acutely aware of the gaps in his account. He tells only 'as much as I lawfully record for the uninitiated', adding that 'now you have heard what happened, but I fear you are still none the wiser'.

The pagan mysteries were unable to proselytise and were extremely exclusive in terms of both the gender and class of their adherents, and the Mystery religions were never intended to harness the faith of the masses. Yet this was precisely what Christianity did. St Augustine taunted the dwindling pagan communities of North Africa: 'let them laugh at our Scriptures; let them laugh as much as they can, while, day by day, they see themselves thinner and fewer, either through death or conversion.' St Jerome, similarly, caught the essence of the difference between paganism and Christianity, when he sniffed that no one was prepared to die on account of Apuleius' religious vision and his working of miracles.[45] Pagans, it seemed, had none of the attributes – or the savage appetite – of the religious fanatic.

Moreover, once Christianity had achieved the status of *the* official faith of the Imperial family, after 313 CE, it was incredibly difficult for the heterogeneous pagan cults to pose an effective counterargument. They had no doctrine or tradition of resistance. They lacked both central organisation and discipline, and now money. Speaking of costs, Christian philanthropists gave to help the poor. Even their staunchest critics, gave them grudging respect for this. The pagan revivalist Emperor Julian noted of Christianity: 'It is generosity toward non-members, care for the graves of the dead, and pretended holiness of life that have specially fostered the growth.'[46] They condemned sacrifice, a core pagan religious activity, as a costly destruction of valuable livestock.[47] Christians showed a far greater respect for individual life and a far less callous approach to the sufferings of animals. Modern Paganism – which is often extremely antagonistic to the consequences of the rise of the Christian Church – is, in this sense at least, a product of this profound theological and moral sea change. A love of nature rather than its fearful propitiation, the respect for life and for animal rights, are all enshrined at the core of Gardnerian witchcraft. These come from Christianity. In 363 CE, Christian soldiers joked that there would be scarcely a live bull left in the Empire, after Julian's mass sacrifices for victory in his Persia campaign. Their senses, just like ours today, recoil from the thought of the smoke of the pyres, the stench of the spluttering animal fat, and the piles of carcasses turning to dust under the eyes of a remorseless, burning Sun God.[48]

Historians are divided as to when and how the vitality drained away from Rome's traditional gods. Though a violent mob, backed by Imperial spears, destroyed the temple of the god Serapis at Alexandria, in 392 CE, the neighbouring temple complex dedicated to Dionysus had already been converted into use as a church without a fight. There is no evidence that pagans died in significant numbers for their faith, though we know the pagan philosopher, Libanius, petitioned the aggressively

Christian Emperor Theodosius I for redress against the gangs of monks who attacked pagan temples with 'wooden beams, stones and iron tools' and threatened the priests. The exception proving the norm is Hypatia, who taught mathematics and philosophy at the academies of Athens and Alexandria. Targeted for censure by Bishop Cyril of Alexandria on account of her popularity as a teacher, in 415 CE she was cornered by a mob – enflamed by his monks – branded as a sorceress, and torn limb from limb. Her mutilated body was 'scattered through the city'.[49] She has been recently recast for a new generation as both feminist icon and suspected witch, in the 2009 movie *Agora* (which saw Rachel Weisz deliver an outstanding performance).[50] Though Hypatia's achievements are exaggerated, the film stands out as the only major cinematic representation of Classical paganism, which is considered, and sympathetic. It is a world away from the posturing masculine-Christianity of the 'sword and scandals' epics of the 1950s–60s, typified by *Ben Hur*, *Quo Vadis* and *The Robe*. Yet, as Mary R. Lefkowitz has recently argued, Hypatia probably did not die primarily as a result of her adherence to pagan religion.[51] The historical Hypatia was butchered as the result of high politics, intellectual jealousy and the implicit misogyny of both Bishop Cyril and the crowd.

Hypatia's savage fate could not inspire pagan martyrs, because there was no such tradition in Classical paganism. It was pantheistic and therefore pluralist and thus, ultimately, tolerant in nature. Unlike Christianity, it did not possess a totalitarian view of the possession of 'truth'. To die in the promise of eternal life spent in paradise was one thing; to voluntarily leave the world for a realm of desolate shadows was quite another. Martyrdom, in this sense, has a resonance with the Peoples of the Book – Judaism, Christianity and Islam – that it lacked for the pagan. As a result of its failure to rally fighters, Classical paganism was totally extinguished. The pagan cults closed down one by one, over the course of the fourth and fifth centuries. One can imagine them like tea lights, or so many brightly coloured lanterns, left out on a summer's lawn flickering-out amid the encroaching darkness of night.

The pagan gods even lost their dignity. Today, when we think of the gods and goddesses of the Classical Age, we do not do so within the framework of 'comparative religions' but rather as the characters of the 'myths and legends' of Ancient Greece and Rome. They are the stuff of children's stories and not of serious theological debate. There can be no greater condescension, and no greater symbol of the victory of Christianity. Thus, when contemplating the literature of the pagan past, the Christian polemicist Lactantius dismissed the 'magician' Apuleius and his work, and indeed all imaginative fiction, declaring that to 'invent all that you present is to be a fool and a liar, rather than a poet'.[52] The sacred groves became overgrown by weeds, the altars were cleared and re-dedicated: and the poetry stopped.

III

We move forward to the Renaissance. Apuleius' novel *The Golden Ass* survived; indeed, it was *the* only Classical novel to survive in its entirety to this era. Apuleius had been a devotee of Isis and had woven his tale about the goddess. What better work to spearhead a resurgence of Classical, pagan literature, religion and philosophy? In the Renaissance, *The Golden Ass* was one of the first books to be printed and translated into the vernacular. It owed its survival, in part at least, to Apuleius' role in the pagan resistance of the fourth century CE, where he was a sort of hero. Also, pagans appropriated one of Christianity's major weapons – the book, as opposed to the papyrus, scroll or wax tablet – in order to disseminate core pagan texts. Foremost among these was *The Golden Ass*, which was copied in North Africa from scrolls into the new codex form and spread along the trade routes from Libya to Constantinople, Rome and Southern Gaul, before the schools of copyists collapsed completely after the mid-sixth century CE. This enabled the freshly copied man-uscripts to escape the great destruction of 'magical books' ordered by Emperor Honorius in the West, and Emperor Arcadius in the East, in 409 CE.

It also brought *The Golden Ass* to an audience that included Christians as well as pagans. Lactantius (who lived c.240–c.320 CE) was disturbed by Apuleius' post-humous fame and by the widespread belief that his magical healing abilities rivalled those of Jesus. Similarly, Eusebius of Caesarea (c.260–340 CE) was at pains to distin-guish the root source of those seemingly conflicting forms of magic and to make it plain that the miracles worked by Jesus had an entirely different source of power to those claimed for Apuleius.[53] However, it was St Augustine of Hippo (354–430 CE) who launched the most telling attacks upon Apuleius and all his works. Augustine, a fellow North African who had been educated in Apuleius' home town of Madaura, not only attacked what Apuleius had written but also his medium: the novel. 'There is no point in striving,' Augustine wrote in his *City of God*, 'as Apuleius strives, to justify the poetical fictions and buffooneries of the theatre.'[54] Furthermore, Apuleius' 'marvellous doings' were, he said, accomplished by demonic, as opposed to divine forces. Though these demons 'can also do similar things to Angels', this was 'not in truth but in appearance, not through wisdom but deceit.'[55] His, then, was very much a demon-haunted world.

Yet, Apuleius in a rhetorical flourish, which has survived in a fragmentary part as *The God of Socrates*, had already provided a contrary, pagan, view of those same beings. Apuleius had delivered his speech, possibly the second of two on the same theme, in order to bolster his own reputation within the Socratic school of literature, to stress his own intellectual credentials, and to exhort his listeners to adopt a philosophical form of life. His demons – or 'daemons' as he preferred to style them – had already been outlined in Socrates' own teachings, and were simply mediators between the gods and men. In Apuleius' view

> they are capable, in the same manner as we are, of suffering all the mitigations on incitements of souls; so as to be stimulated by anger, made to incline to pity, allured by gifts, appeased by prayers, exasperated by contumely, soothed by honours, and changed by all other things, in the same way that we are … Thus, from dreams, predictions and oracles, we have for the most part found from them that the divinities have been indignant, if anything in their sacred rites has been neglected through indolence or pride.

They were 'in their genus animals, in their species rational, in their mind passive, in body aerial and in time perpetual'.[56]

However, Apuleius chose to follow his own definition with a statement which not only reveals a little more about the characteristics of pagan religious observance but which also makes a case for a wider pagan sense of toleration. 'It is requisite,' he thought,

> to believe in the different observances of religions, and the various supplications enjoyed in sacred rites. There are, likewise, some among this number of Gods who rejoice in victims, of ceremonies or rites, which are nocturnal or diurnal, obvious or occult, joyful or doleful. Thus, the Egyptian deities are almost all of them delighted with lamentations, the Grecian for the most part with choirs, but the Barbarian with the sound produced by cymbals, drums and pipes. In like manner, other things pertaining to sacred rites differ by a great variety, according to different regions; as, for instance, the crowds of sacred processions, the arcane of mysteries, the offices of priests, the compliances of those that sacrifice; and further still, the effigies of the Gods, and the spoil dedicated to them, the religions and situations of temples, and the variety of blood and colour in victims.[57]

Both Classical paganism and the Roman State had been, up until 312 CE at least, broadly tolerant of new deities and promoted forms of worship that aimed to deny no one their faith in a particular, favoured deity. The local god or goddess was not repudiated or overthrown, but was instead synchronised within a wider pantheon of deities, drawn from across the Empire, who all exhibited common characteristics. Thus, as Apuleius clearly understood and taught, Minerva – just like Isis or Hecate – could have many homelands, faces and aspects of divinity. The trouble was that Christianity was an exclusive religion prepared to challenge the right of older religions even to exist.

Plato and the pagan philosophers believed in *daimones* who could manifest themselves through a dog or a mumbling old beggar, but they could not ascribe evil to one particular divinity, let alone to a collection of gods. There was no polarisation between rival camps among the immortals and no sense that one god was a 'good' god, while another one comprised pure 'evil'. The gods were, simply, the gods. War, sickness and death could be invoked through the angering of a deity, but they could also be caused by pure chance or 'blind' fortune. Ill luck was precisely that – as Lucius the ass had discovered to his cost – and it could not be attributed to the sheer malice of just one spirit. Thus, both dog and beggar were held to be innocent of ill-intent. The *daimone* worked through them and brought them to ruin, but it was not necessarily the product of their own misdeeds or their implicit badness. For Christians the 'god of this world' was the Devil.[58] The world was a battleground divided between the forces of good and evil, where demons were always waiting to tempt. Demons were, according to Augustine, 'a race of deceitful and malicious spirits, who come into the souls of men' and are 'deceitful, full of contrivances, capable of assuming all forms'. Such spirits, he continued, 'only desire … to do harm'. Their purpose is 'to entangle wretched souls in the deceptive worship of many and false gods and to turn them aside from the true worship of the true God'.[59] Apuleius was, thus, in the eyes of St Augustine, one of 'those pretended and deceitful mediators' deceived by the demons.[60]

Many exorcists were plying their trade in Rome by the sixth century CE. As Ramsay MacMullen has noted: 'the manhandling of demons – humiliating them, making them howl, beg for mercy, tell their secrets, and depart in a hurry – served a purpose quite essential to the Christian definition of monotheism.'[61] The downside of publicly driving demons out of troubled individuals was that the line between the afflicted (to be pitied) and the demon (to be despised) was often blurred. Consequently, with Christianity it became possible for the first time to demonise an individual. Furthermore, the insistence of Christian philosophy that it was superior to the Greek necessitated the defence of a single 'correct' belief. All other faiths were to be treated with the greatest antipathy and suspicion, and those who followed them were condemned to eternal damnation. Little wonder, then, that St Augustine felt that, had Apuleius been tried before a panel of Christian judges, then he would surely – and justly – have been convicted on the charges of working harmful magic, consulting with demons, and practising witchcraft.[62]

Attitudes towards magic, divination and astrology similarly hardened across the newly Christianised empire. If Lucan had been unsure about where sorcerers gained their powers, the Christian Fathers were in no doubt at all that it was channelled through demons and stemmed from Satan himself. The old pagan distinction between workers of 'good' and 'bad' magic no longer applied, as all such practitioners of the art were ultimately held to be in league with *Misokalos* – 'He who hates the Good' – or the Devil. Thus, according to Lactantius:

> The whole art and powers of the sorcerer consists in the conjuring up of fallen angels [i.e. demons]. They respond at once to such a call and darken the man's mind ... these forlorn and lost souls wander through the length and breadth of the world, consoling themselves for their downfall by encompassing the downfall of others. They fill the universe with their traps, lies, and deceptions; they invade our privacy, going from door to door.[63]

As a consequence, the sorcerer was now key to their intercession in human affairs, and divination was now being deemed dangerous, with many practices that had previously been part of religion now treated as magic. The Emperor Constantius II (reigned 337–61 CE) heard that remote Egyptian oracles were storing old petitions – piles of 'papers and parchments' recording lists of individual 'desires'. So he despatched his feared chief of the secret police, Paul 'the Chain', to get to the heart of matters. Paul conducted trials and created such a climate of fear that it was said that

> if anyone wore on his neck an amulet against the quartan ague or any other complaint, or was accused by the testimony of the evil – disposed of passing by a grave in the evening, on the ground that he was a dealer in poisons, or a gatherer of the horrors of tombs and the vain illusions of the ghosts that walk there, he was condemned to capital punishment and so perished.

Torture was used to extract confessions.

Other examples survive too. Parnasius, a former prefect of Egypt, and 'a man of simple character' was put on trial for his life because, it was said, he had once obtained office having 'dreamt that many shadowy figures in tragic garb escorted him' and helped him on his way. Demetrius Cythras, 'a philosopher of advanced years', was charged with offering sacrifice 'several times' at the shrines of the god Besa. He was put to the rack, but his repeated refusal to deviate from his original defence, that he had sacrificed 'from early youth for the purpose of propitiating the deity, not of trying to reach a higher station by his investigations', saved his life. His interrogators were finally convinced that he possessed no threat to the State and he was permitted to return to his home city of Alexandria, and a form of internal exile.[64] We have no way of knowing the numbers of those caught up in the persecutions, or their demographics. Marcellinus, a pagan army officer, concerns himself only with the elite but does tell us that 'men were brought in from almost the whole world, noble and obscure alike; and some ... were bowed down with the weight of chains, others wasted away from the agony of imprisonment'. Marcellinus repeatedly refers to 'men', but the absence of women among his case studies does not necessarily mean that they were excluded from prosecution as witches.[65]

Certainly the charges of looting graveyards and necromancy would have been familiar to anyone conversant with Classical notions of witchcraft, but the broadening of the association to try people for sacrificing to the gods was new and cut at the very foundations of Roman paganism. Apuleius, revelling in his learning and attempts to communicate directly with the divine, had been lucky not to have lived through this period or to have encountered the judiciary as directed by Paul 'the Chain'. As it was, he was permitted to go on his way to Carthage, with his magical books, threadbare cloak and matted locks, escaping both the later hatred of his fellow countryman, St Augustine, and the rage of the Christian mob in Tripoli.[66]

IV

St Augustine of Hippo hated Apuleius' religious pluralism and conception of Socratic philosophy, but he acknowledged him as a source of knowledge on demonology. Indeed, he devoted the whole of Book IX of *The City of God* to first examining and then pulling apart his ideas. For him, Jesus and not the *daemons*, was the true – and, indeed, the only – real mediator between a singular god and man.[67] In his view, 'a demon is [one] who deceives', and 'these animals of air … only have reason so that they may be capable of wretchedness, and passions so that they may in fact be wretched, and eternity so that their wretchedness can have no end'. They are creatures who delight in obscenity – particularly in obscene laughter – and in 'turbulent and degraded passions', and 'are beings who are not blessed but wretched.'[68]

Augustine laid the foundation for demonological witch theory in a few short passages written specifically to confute Apuleius: 'Apuleius is at great pains,' St Augustine begins

> to persuade us that the demons are situated midway between gods and men to serve in some way as messengers and go-betweens, to carry our petitions to the gods and to convey to us the gods' assistance. We must realise that they are in reality spirits whose only desire is to do harm, who are completely alien from any kind of justice, swollen with arrogance, livid with envy, and full of crafty deception. They do indeed dwell in the air, because they have been cast down from the upper heights of heaven as a reward for their irremediable transgression and condemned to inhabit this region as a kind of prison appropriate to their nature … the demons clearly hold sway over many men, who are unworthy to participate in the true religion, and they treat them

as prisoners and subjects; and they have persuaded the greater part of them to accept the demons as gods, by means of impressive but deceitful miracles, whether miracles of action or of prediction.[69]

Apuleius was, of course, foremost among those willing dupes who made offerings 'to those birds of prey, the fallen angels' but had he been a little more reflexive, Augustine might also have considered that 'the sing-song voice of a child in a nearby house' that proved crucial to his own conversion narrative, could have equally been directed by demons as by the angels of God.[70] From the first, therefore, the line between ecstatic religious vision and demonic possession was very finely drawn in the Christian canon.

Augustine's thoughts on demons informed the core theorists behind the European witch trials, such as Jean Bodin, Martin Del Rio and the authors of the *Malleus Maleficarum*.[71] Del Rio – whose work had so influenced Bishop Förner at the Bamberg trials – used Apuleius to 'prove' the existence of *striges* and the night flights of witches; he cites Augustine to introduce the idea of specific demonic pact, as all magical arts and divinations 'either of frivolous or harmful superstition, came from a plague-bearing association, like a pact of faithless and deceitful friendship, between individuals and evil spirits'.[72] Kramer and Sprenger, in the *Malleus Maleficarum*, quoted *The City of God* as means to link instances of witchcraft with outrages inflicted by demons: 'For Augustine says "Fire and air are subordinate to demons to the extent that this is permitted to them by God"'.[73] Thus, through the agency of the demonic pact, the activities of two entirely separate figures – the witch (as seen in *The Golden Ass*) and the demon (as envisaged in both *The God Socrates* and *The City of God*) – were effectively joined together in the Early Modern period. It was this new concept of the witches' working of harmful magic, or *maleficia*, through the aid of demons which made possible the witch trials of the sixteenth and seventeenth centuries.

Perversely, then, Apuleius' writings survived because of theologians' need to engage with Augustine on demons and because he offered them a much-needed Classical source which proved the existence of the witch and the efficacy of magic. Unsurprisingly, a large apocryphal literature grew up around Apuleius in the Middle Ages. Apuleius' works were re-copied in the Carolingian revival of the eighth and ninth centuries and redistributed throughout an empire that consciously strove to be the successor to Rome. In the eleventh century CE, the monastery at Monte Casino, a repository for key Classical texts, contained Apuleius' *Apologia*, *Metamorphoses* and *The Golden Ass*. The papal library at Avignon also held a manuscript of *The Golden Ass* among its treasures. One of the most popular manuscripts on herbal lore in

Mediaeval Europe was ascribed to his name.[74] Both Boccaccio and Chaucer were familiar with Apuleius as a writer of fiction.[75] Apuleius was brought to a wider English audience by Humphrey, Duke of Gloucester, the younger brother of King Henry V. He was a bibliophile whose agents scoured the Italian city states for Classical and Humanist texts. He sought after, and by 1440 had obtained, a copy of *The Golden Ass*.[76] Though access to the manuscript appears to have been restricted to a narrow circle of academics and churchmen, it survived Duke Humphrey, stored safely away in the Oxford University library that came to bear his name.[77]

It was the papal librarian in Rome who, in 1467, first prepared the manuscript of *The Golden Ass* for publication. De Bussi dedicated his work to Cardinal Bessarion, patron and protector of Humanist writers, the author of books on Plato, and the founder of a Neo-Platonist Academy.[78] The appearance in print of *The Golden Ass*, in Rome in 1469, was calculated by de Bussi to revitalise the Neo-Platonist movement, but its subject matter and novel form ensured its popular success. Further editions followed, with publication in Vincenza in 1488, Venice in 1493 and Milan in 1497. Such was its fame that a commentary upon the text had been written by 1500 and there were at least eight more printed editions of the book between 1519 and 1549, with a German translation appearing in 1538.[79]

V

Copies of the book were moved along the main arteries of trade into Northern Europe well before the 1490s. Sometime in that decade, a painter we know only as the 'Master of the Lower Rhine', began his commission – a painting of a naked woman doing a love spell for his patron in the Munster region. This witchcraft painting survives to this day and is usually called *Der Liebeszauber*. It was intended to delight and to titillate behind closed patrician doors. The subject matter precluded the display of the painting in a church, guildhall or public space. Its opulence and sexual licence re-enforce the illicit subject. Such frissons made the image highly desirable at a time when private consumption, or identity, of any kind were rare, hard won and ruinously expensive, subject at any moment to reversion and to being drowned out by the voices of the crowd and the wider community, under the gaze of God. This is precisely what fate had in store for both the painting's original owner and for the craftsman who laid down the colours on the panel and gave the witch her form. Their names and their stories are lost to us. Within a generation this world would be overturned, as the print made the witch an image that could be mass produced and mass circulated, and so become instantly recognisable.

The anonymous German craftsman – and presumably his wealthy patron – seem to have read, or at least heard read to them, Apuleius' *Golden Ass*. The parallels become remarkable when the painting is set alongside Apuleius' text and, in particular, the accounts of Pamphile's magical practices in Books Two and Three. The action takes place at the top of a bourgeois home; the spell is worked in the nude save for the exception of the girl's fashionable slippers, which taper suggestively to exaggerated, phallic points; and the scene is witnessed by a youth, who is captured in the moment of crossing the threshold of her chamber, taking in every one of the witch's actions. The peacock plumes and little bird, sitting patiently, perched atop a bowl of sweets, seem to hint at the possibility of physical transformation and night flight. Only the open casket and the enlarged red heart kept within, sit askance with the text. Yet even here, it might be argued that the symbol indicates the subject of the painting, giving external, visual representation to the fact that it is a love charm being worked. The witch, admittedly, does not resemble the aged and ungainly Pamphile, but the subject might be the young servant, Fotis, captured in the misdirection of her spell. Such a reading would allow for the comic and the erotic elements in the painting, and sideline the malefic. In any case, if this is a transmission of a literary tale to a visual medium, the action is necessarily compressed into a single scene. It is suggested that we are being shown Lucius observing an act of witchcraft.

Admittedly, the decisive provenance for the subject of the painting – the texts once worked into the scrolls that frame the witch's figure – are now either irreparably lost or were never actually finished in the original composition. However, even without them, there is more than enough to link the painting with Apuleius' vision of witchcraft. If this is correct, then Apuleius' image of the witch had made its way into the visual culture of Northern Europe at the turn of the fifteenth century, a culture to which we now turn.

CHAPTER FOUR

A Nightmare Given Form

I

On the night of Wednesday to Thursday, 30–1 May 1525, Albrecht Dürer awoke, blanched and trembling, from a terrible dream. In his sleep he had seen a great pillar of water falling from the heavens to strike the fields outside Nuremberg 'with terrific force and tremendous noise'. Upon impact, the deluge 'broke up and drowned the whole land'. Dürer later wrote, 'I was so sore afraid that when I awoke … for a long while I could not recover myself'. When he awoke properly in the morning he felt compelled to take out his watercolours and to attempt to record his nightmare exactly 'as I saw it'.[1]

The artist's vision of this apocalyptic dream survives. It looks eerily reminiscent of a spreading mushroom cloud, but to a burgher of Nuremberg it was clearly the second biblical flood, when the wrath of God would cause the sun to go out, rains to lash the earth, and the stars to fall from the heavens. The sick and prematurely aged Dürer saw around him all the signs: the Reformations shattering religious unity; the then new disease of syphilis ravaging the population; armies marauding the land; and bands of wandering peasants attacking the communities. Unsurprisingly, Dürer, who had been haunted throughout his life with a sense of mortality, was overcome by melancholia. He gave figurative form to his depression in one of his greatest engravings, and used his art to fashion two of the most potent, innovative and enduring images of witchcraft in the Western World.

For Dürer, the key to artistry was the ability to be the one who 'pours out new things, which had never before been in the mind of any other man', and it was precisely in this vein that he approached all that appeared unusual, exciting or unnatural. Thus, he sought out, among others, the bones of St Ursula, the Giant of Antwerp, the 'great fish' (or whale) washed ashore on the coast of Zealand, and the 'man who was 93 years old and still strong and healthy', who would later became his model for his *St Jerome*, seated in his study. In a similar fashion, he drew the head of a deer with monstrous antlers, and painted a freakish, bearded child.[2] He had his horoscope cast, noted the fall of 'blood rain' upon the streets of Nuremberg, and wondered at the stone or meteor, which fell to earth just beyond the gates of the city.

He embraced Renaissance Humanism, loved nothing more than technological innovation and new means of production, and was the first European artist to truly appreciate the aesthetic value of Native American art. He was also a man of deep Christian spirituality, for whom the age of divinely inspired miracles – and demonic interventions – was not yet past. On a single surviving page torn from his common-place book of 1503, he recorded:

> The most wonderful thing I ever saw ... when crosses fell upon many persons [from the sky], and especially on children rather than on older people ... [One] had fallen into Eyrer's maid's shift, as she was sitting in the house ... She was so troubled about it that she wept and cried aloud, for she feared she must die because of it.[3]

We know nothing more of the incident, or of what these crosses were made, or looked like, though Dürer does seem to link the event to the passage of a comet through the night sky, which he noted, with laconic brevity, on the same page. For the artist, the wind-driven crosses, fluttering down to earth, were a wonder, conveying a reassuring message of God's power and love; for his neighbour's maid, such unexplained phenomena were deeply disturbing and seemed to signify that she had been selected, by the Almighty, for an early death.

Dürer relished what he termed his 'dreamwork', the composition of fantastical scenes, and from the outset of his career possessed a firm grasp of those topics and themes that were capable of seizing the imagination of the public, and of generating revenue through the sale of his prints. The advent of the printing press, in the mid-fifteenth century, had opened up entirely new audiences, in terms of both social composition and geographical location, for the marketing of images. Religious scenes, once viewed largely within communal settings such as churches, wayside shrines or processions to mark saints' days, might now be privately owned, not just by the elites and churchmen but also by artisans and tradesmen, and be brought into the domestic environment. Where, once, shared experience of a unique, almost magical, rendering of a biblical scene had been the norm for the overwhelming majority of Europe's population, individual responses to modestly priced, mass-produced, works of devotional art were now not only possible, but eagerly sought.

In 1492, the 21-year-old Dürer purchased his own printing press. For a young man, who had only just finished his apprenticeship, it was a bold move. Yet it demonstrated his determination, from the very outset, to control every aspect of the manner in which his art was conceived, produced and distributed. So that his work might not be pirated, he created his own trademark – conjoining the 'A' and the 'D' of his initials – which he used after the late 1490s. Unlike his predecessors,

Dürer was determined to be known and recognised.[4] Moreover, by licensing the right to sell his prints to agents throughout Germany and the Low Countries, his brand name and style were firmly established and maintained. By having his wife and other retailers sell the works at markets and fairs, he was able to enjoy a symbiotic relationship with his customers. Their faces and forms are reflected in his early engravings of market traders, fashionable young men, buxom cooks and pear-shaped townswomen. He understood the public appetite for 'wonders', as well for religious scenes and images reflecting the contents of the latest newsletters. In an age where literacy was still limited, and culture was largely rooted in the visual and the oral, a well-chosen picture assisted greatly in the retelling of a popular and commercially marketable news story.

II

The very first of Dürer's engravings to carry a date was his study of *The Four Witches*. Printed in 1497, it represents one of the seminal, and easily one of the most widely disseminated, images of the practice of witchcraft in European art. We have no clue as to why the artist should be so keen to signify the date of this work, and it has even been suggested that the picture does not actually represent witches at all but rather the Three Graces, joined by a fourth figure from antiquity, sometimes held to be Discord. Yet, while noting this possible alternative reading, Dürer's first great biographer, Joachim von Sandrart, writing in 1675, was quite clear when he wrote of the artist's engraving of: 'three or four naked women, which some take to be the Three Graces. I, however, take them to be witches because ... a death's head, a thighbone, a Hell-mouth and the spectre of the Devil are shown in it.'[5] Modern writers and picture researchers concur, as the image has been widely reproduced in order to illustrate the figures of witches, most notably as the cover of John Updike's novel, *The Witches of Eastwick*, and as with *Der Liebeszauber*, it has been taken as providing evidence of a long-standing tradition of women working their magic 'skyclad', or naked, as an expression of equality, sisterhood and democracy.[6]

The picture does, indeed, show four women, naked save for their headdresses, standing in a hallway, on the threshold of two doorways: one arched, one oblong. A grotesque, dragon-like Devil starts up from the floor of the adjoining chamber, his jaws open in full cry and his body shrouded in sparks, flame and sulphur. A spear, or stave, is gripped in his clawed fist. As he appears below ground level, and at the corner of the door, the women are oblivious to his presence: but there can be little doubt that their eventual fate is to be seized by him and cast down into the fires.

They have entered the hall through the arch, but are destined to leave through an entirely different, and darker, portal that serves as the gateway to another realm: in this case, one that will lead them straight to Hell. One of the women, wearing a myrtle wreath, has her back to the viewer, while her hair streams out behind her, pulled out of her topknot and caught by a breeze. The faces of the other three can be clearly discerned, and each of them has their hair covered. The left-hand figure, the eldest and seemingly highest-ranking of the group, sports the elegant veiled headdress of a prosperous merchant's wife, while the figure in the background wears the turban and coif normally associated with a respectable matron. The right-hand figure, the youngest present, has her hair partially covered and knotted by a long scarf that wraps around her body, concealing her own genitalia and those of her companion, and trailing out behind her onto the floor.

So far, it is clear that the women are of different ages and classes, with the two appearing on the left-hand side of the picture being wealthier to those on the right. Dürer has borrowed the fashions, worn by the witches, from his earlier studies of the women of Nuremberg. The rich headdress sported by the senior partner in the crime is taken from an earlier engraving by the artist, *The Young Couple Threatened by Death*, but there is nothing whatsoever in that work to suggest that this coiffure is associated with anything, save high fashion. Indeed, it is the girl's paramour who is leading her down a path of discovery to sex, in the earlier work, and by extension in Dürer's mind, condemning her to sin and the ravages of the ageing process.

Similarly, the artist's sketch of *The Women's Bathhouse*, made in 1496, contains elements that were to be adapted and re-used, 12 months later, in his *Four Witches*. The setting is a dark-panelled steam room, where six women – including a grotesque – are in the process of combing their hair, and scrubbing themselves or each other. All have taken off their clothes in order to bathe but even amid the steam, are either in the process of combing their hair, or are wearing caps or veils. Their nudity, the heat and the low-ceilinged room, all echo the composition of *The Four Witches*. Even the presence of two small children, a boy and a girl, at their feet, seems to prefigure some of the thinking behind Dürer's later work, for the little boy offers up an apple to his mother, in a reversal and reminder of Eve's temptation of the first man. Once again, the link is made between sensuality, pride in appearance and the inevitability of decay and death occasioned by all such sin. Indeed, the fact that the young, high-status woman in the foreground regards the viewer with an inviting glance, while captured in the act of scrubbing the back of a chronically obese, and seemingly bald or shaven-headed, crone displays the artist's concern to show us the inversion of social norms and the physical results of licentiousness. The bathhouse is certainly a place where the necessity for nudity encourages a form of egalitarianism:

yet the retention of headgear would seem to demonstrate that, even here, the wives of Nuremberg's burghers were acutely concerned to emphasise their relative social status. The theme of the unobserved Devil found in *The Four Witches* is also invoked by the presence of a voyeuristic man, a heavily bearded 'peeping Tom', pulling back the shutters from the street, and similarly unnoticed by the women, in order to gratify his lust. In this case, the man is there to introduce the element of humour reflected in Dürer's companion piece, *The Men's Bathhouse*, also of 1496, where a hooked tap strategically placed in front of a bather's genitals comically evokes the form of the phallus it is obscuring.[7] Whereas the men are pictured actively talking, drinking and playing musical instruments, their female counterparts are passive, mute and concerned only with beautifying themselves. When we think about witchcraft, and Early Modern attitudes towards women, it is significant that it is the fall of the woman through lust – rather than necessarily that of the man – that is occasioned in each case through sex. The artist suggests that vanity results in sin, and sin leads directly to death and the Devil. Therefore, the link between *The Women's Bathhouse* – with its themes of nudity, pride and temptation – and *The Four Witches* may be far closer than has often been thought. It is certainly more than a matter of just borrowing stock figures or poses, and adapting them to suit a new subject.

In purely practical terms, in *The Women's Bathhouse*, Dürer used the arch of the back and the facial features of the woman handed the apple for the senior of his witches, while the figure of the licentious girl in the foreground of his sketch is used as the model for the youngest witch. All that is altered is their social status. Significantly, Dürer has chosen to swap their headdresses. The young girl now becomes the petitioner, rather than the social superior, of the older woman by the time the two figures are transposed into *The Four Witches*.[8] Thus, he utilised the faces, fashions and frames of the women who were his neighbours in Nuremberg for his *Four Witches*. They are not stereotypes, or crudely distorted images of femininity. Rather, the four women he has chosen are full-figured, with broad hips, curvaceous thighs and full breasts. Their faces are ordinary, even plain, and are not distorted in any way by traces of hatred or anger. They are not old, but in the prime of life, and – though naked – there is, at least to the modern observer, no sense of eroticism or pressing beauty inherent in either their appearance or actions. Rather than archetypes of lustful or aged women, they are, in one sense, perfectly representative of the ordinary women of Nuremberg. As such, their very normality and homeliness would prove far more dangerous to generations of women suspected of witchcraft, than the later highly sexualised depictions of the witch as wanton or crone.

In showing the witch naked, Dürer was breaking with artistic and demonological convention. The most notable exception to this trend possibly known to Dürer, himself, was, of course, *Der Liebeszauber*, which was probably painted only a few years earlier, during the same decade as *The Four Witches* was engraved. Though the setting is markedly different, there are other themes besides the witches' nudity that are held in common: namely, the sense of illicit discovery and the act of being spied upon, as evidenced by the positioning of Lucius in *Der Liebeszauber*, the 'peeping Tom' in Dürer's bathhouse scene, and the unobserved Devil in *The Four Witches*.

As a young man, Dürer had travelled throughout the Rhineland area, in 1490–4, visiting Basle, Colmar and Strasbourg in the Upper reaches of the river and pushing as far as Cologne in the Lower. However, while it seems unlikely that he reached Utrecht, Haarlem and Leyden on this trip – as has sometimes been suggested – it is not beyond the bounds of possibility that the traffic on the Rhine brought him news, or sight, of *Der Liebeszauber* and its anonymous creator.[9] It was certainly the case that at Mainz and Frankfurt, Dürer became acquainted with the work of the 'Master of the Housebook' and there is no reason why examples of the art of the 'Master of the Lower Rhine' should not have followed the same trade routes, from roughly the same geographical sources.[10]

Even if he did not encounter *Der Liebeszauber* directly at this time, there is good evidence that he was familiar with the transformation of Lucius and the scenes of witchcraft described by Apuleius in *The Golden Ass*. Conrad Celtis, once labelled as the 'arch-Humanist' of the Northern Renaissance, was a frequent visitor to Nuremburg. Furthermore, Celtis held the works of Apuleius in particular esteem and produced a printed version of Apuleius' *De Mundo* in 1497, just as Dürer was working on *The Four Witches*. He lectured on Apuleius at the University of Vienna and drew censure from the Dominican Order for his love of the Classical, pagan past. A friend warned, 'in the farthest corner of Germany it has been reported that you have published a certain book [i.e. Apuleius' *De Mundo*] in which you have worshipped, venerated and adored Phoebus, Mercury, and Apollo.'[11]

This criticism resurfaced, again, in 1502, when Celtis presented a collection of his published works to Sister Charitas, a nun at the Convent of St Clara in Nuremberg; oddly, his life of St Roswitha was parcelled up with his erotic love poetry, the *Amores*. Charitas was enraged, not on account of the erotic poetry but rather by his use of pagan sources, rooted in his studies of Apuleius. 'Out of singular friendship,' she wrote, 'I admonish your worship [i.e. Celtis] to abandon the evil fables of Diana, Venus, Jupiter, and of other damned pagans.' This exchange is significant not only for demonstrating the animus with which many educated members of the religious orders viewed Classical literature, but also because of who Sister Charitas was. Born into one of Nuremburg's wealthiest patrician families – the Pirckheimers – she had been a neighbour and childhood playmate of Dürer's. Through this web of friendships and business relationships, Dürer knew Celtis. Celtis chose Dürer to illustrate both his *Amores* and the second edition of his work on Nuremberg's patron saint.[12] Dürer likely knew of *The Golden Ass* through his acquaintance with Celtis. The work, would have reinforced for him both the theme of witchcraft and also the image of the naked witch, as pioneered in *Der Liebeszauber*. Thus, when considering the ritual nudity in Dürer's *The Four Witches*, we have to be aware that he, too, might well have been looking back upon Classical models of witchcraft.

Turning to the nudity itself, in the engraving a close examination reveals that it does not convey equality among the women. Rather, it emphasises the differences between them. The two women to the left of the composition, those whose headdress and garland appear to mark them out as being of high social status, are standing on a raised ledge, and are looking down upon the other two, who wear more humble headscarves. A clear hierarchy would appear to be in place, with two of the women as supplicants, petitioners or junior partners and the other two as their superiors in terms of wealth, status and magical skill.

The presence of a human skull at the feet of the dominant pair, and a human thighbone behind those of their junior partners, makes it clear that something dark and objectionable is about to occur. At least three of the four women appear to be doing something with their right hands – either holding an object or each other's outstretched hands – and have formed a circle, which can turn clockwise about a central axis marked by the skull below and the globe suspended above. Cast in the form of a fruit – possibly a pomegranate, as a symbol of fertility, but certainly not a mandrake root as has previously been suggested – the globe bears not only the date of the composition but also the mysterious initials 'O.G.H'. Dürer left nothing among his voluminous papers to suggest what these letters signified, but later writers have attempted to provide answers, suggesting – among others – that they might mean: 'O Gott Hute' (May God Forbid); 'Origio Generis Humani' (Origin of the Human Race); and 'Obsidium Generis Humani' (Enemy of the Human Race).[13] With the exception of the second suggestion, which seems to be out of all context with the image shown, each is probably as good as the other, as from this distance we can never know for sure.

Moritz Thausing, writing in 1882, suggested that both the scene and its coded motto were inspired by the publication of the *Malleus Maleficarum*, while later authorities sought to identify it with one particular case study. This is an episode set in Strasbourg involving three women who visited a pregnant woman who was magically paralysed. One of the three was a witch who enacted the curse by touching the woman's womb.[14] Dürer has certainly shown four women, and three of them could be touching the belly of the woman in the myrtle garland. However, there are several discrepancies. The *Malleus Maleficarum* relates that only one of the witches reached out to touch the victim while her two accomplices urged mercy. Moreover, even allowing artistic licence in this regard, the scene is clearly not set in a bedroom, let alone in an inn. The woman wearing the myrtle crown does not look paralysed; she does not look beset by her fellows; nor is she the central dramatic figure. The composition does not ask for sympathy for any one woman at the expense of another.

It has also been argued that Dürer was inspired to draw witches because the *Malleus Maleficarum* sparked the persecution of witches in Nuremberg. Dürer's godfather, the printer Anton Koberger, certainly printed editions of the book in Nuremberg, in 1494 and 1496; the artist would surely have known of its existence and the debate it produced.[15] However, it is one thing to seize upon a theme that is currently popular, and quite another to be aware of the implications, or even of the basic theories, that generated public interest in the first place.

The *Malleus* was written in Latin and Dürer had at best a smattering of the language. It was a complicated, convoluted work, one which he could not have hoped to have studied in any great detail for himself. Nor did the work seem to take root in Nuremberg, in terms of hunting witches. Though popular enough to warrant two editions within two years of each other, Nuremberg was not gripped by a 'witch mania' during the artist's lifetime. In fact, the city council sought to define itself against other Imperial cities, such as Cologne and Bamberg, that instigated and directed large-scale witch-hunts.

Nuremberg's trial records, such as they are, have much to do with 'natural magic', love charms and disputes between neighbours. In 1471, the municipal court banished a woman for sorcery, on grounds of theft and poisoning, and another for love magic in 1474, while in 1477 a man was apprehended for 'knowledge of his parents' magical theft of a neighbour's milk'. In a far more sinister twist, in 1486, two women were tried for 'taking potentially magical pieces of clothing from people executed on the wheel', in order to practise *maleficia* or necromancy.[16] However, the penalties handed down in each of these cases remained surprisingly light and this sense of moderation was to continue into the sixteenth century. The city council opposed the Dominican Order's drive towards persecution and refused to accept the intellectual and judicial foundations for witch-hunting as laid down by the *Malleus Maleficarum*. Consequently, it is hard to envisage Dürer being inspired by Heinrich Kramer and Jakob Sprenger for his image of the witch.

Instead, Dürer's vision of *The Four Witches* was, I suggest, formed far closer to home, in the library of his closest friend, Willibald Pirckheimer – incidentally, the brother of the aforementioned Sister Charitas. Though he had been raised alongside

Dürer, Pirckheimer was the son of a native patrician rather than an immigrant craftsman, and became a political and military leader of Nuremburg. He had travelled widely and spent seven years in Italy, where he had studied law and the humanities at the universities of Padua and Pavia. Pirckheimer raised and led a regiment during the Swiss wars, fathered a prodigious number of illegitimate children, and was an avid collector of Classical texts. Possessing knowledge of Greek that was still rare in the West, he boasted in 1504 that he owned a copy of every book ever printed in that language, in Italy.[17] Conrad Celtis was his houseguest in 1501 and 1502, and referred to his home on Nuremberg's market square as the 'scriptorium or poet refuge'.[18] Pirckheimer and Dürer together frequented the clubroom at the Nuremberg Chamber of Commerce – or Waaghaus. There, in an atmosphere of financial well-being and relative intellectual freedom, the two friends often discussed the latest developments in philosophy and religion. Both men embraced the 'new learning', or Humanism, championed by Erasmus and Celtis. They eagerly looked forward to the next discovery of forgotten Classical texts or artefacts, and enjoyed a truly mutual friendship, their interests and talents complementing one another. Dürer would find Pirckheimer rare artefacts and works of art for his collection, produced the bookplates that stamped ownership on his vast library of books, and worked to illuminate the margins of Pirckheimer's personal copies of ancient texts and devotional tracts.

In return, Pirckheimer lent Dürer translations of the works of Classical authors, and also suggested cryptic or unusual subjects for his friend's prints.[19] We know that Dürer was introduced to the Roman poet Lucan through his friend's library, and moreover adapted some of the poet's themes in his graphic work. Most relevant here, he would almost certainly have read – or have heard read by Pirckheimer – Lucan's poem *Civil War*, which contains vivid portrayals of necromancy wrought by the witch Erictho. In the same way as Dürer encountered the witch Erictho in Lucan's *Civil War*, he came to know another famous Classical witch in Theocritus' *Idylls*. We know this because he illustrated Pirckheimer's copy.

Idylls is a cycle of poems set in Alexandria in the third century BCE. One is labelled *The Witches*. It concerns the lady Simaetha, who has been abandoned by her lover, a young athlete called Delphis. Her unrequited lust causes her hair to start to fall out, her skin to become jaundiced, and her body to wither. Determined to win the athlete's love, she visits every witch's house in the area and 'pestered the homes of spell-chanting hags'. Finally, however, it is her slave girl, Thestylis, who accomplishes the magic. Then, having gained her lover through magic, Simaetha must perform another spell to keep him. With Thestylis, she gathers together kitchen ingredients – bran, barley and bay leaves – and uses them in conjunction with exotic poisons – the herb, coltsfoot and the ground-up bones and blood of a lizard – and makes the charm. This spell debases the normally accepted conception of the domestic hearth, and corrupts familiar, life-giving, grains: the poisons of the wild outdoors are brought into the home where normally they have no place. The resulting paste is to be smeared upon the athlete's door before dawn. It must first, however, be imbued with a magic that only the gods can bestow, so they prepare a libation for the Goddess Hecate and offer up prayers under a full moon. Fringes lost from the athlete's cloak are thrown into a roaring fire. 'Fine red wool' is bound around Simaetha's cup in order that she might 'bind my unkind lover to me' and wax is melted in a flame to seal the charm.

This ritual is not what we see in Dürer's *Four Witches*. However, it certainly does echo the practice of the witch in *Der Liebeszauber*, with her flaming hearth, and offers proof that Dürer was familiar with the idea that witchcraft was associated with love magic.[20] The equation of female sexual passion to physical decay was reflected strongly in Dürer's art. Also, Simaetha's incantation, 'Magic wheel, draw my lover to me' links to the fact that Dürer's understanding of witchcraft involved a magic circle – though probably the original writer was referring to the whirring circular disc which was being spun.

Dürer drew firm conclusions about the nature of witchcraft from his reading of Theocritus and other Classical sources, which he then put to good use in his depiction of *The Four Witches*. He appears to have seen witchcraft as primarily associated with love magic, and viewed it as primarily a female preserve, the product of a profoundly troubling outpouring of women's desire, and saw its inevitable consequences in decay, death and eternal damnation. Significantly, this view of witchcraft is not confined to a narrow group of professional practitioners. Rather, it can be utilised by ordinary women if they could acquire a modest source of arcane knowledge from a professional witch. The fear is that this knowledge, and the power it gave over men, was there to be shared among groups and – literally among circles of magic-working – women. Magic could be used to the detriment of a society that was otherwise, in all aspects, male-dominated.

With this in mind, we can view *The Four Witches* as portraying the ritual working of love magic. In this reading, two or even three of the women are townswomen, and they are coming before a professional witch who is denoted by her rich headdress. They have come to consult her and acquire her power and magical skills for their own, ultimately diabolical, purposes. The ease of their art, and their familiarity with one another is what makes the scene feel threatening for the fifteenth-century viewer. The witch really is the enemy within: by turns, ordinary, alluring and destructive.

Literary sources do not account for the whole story. Dürer's urban audience was also steeped in a highly visual culture, in which Classical aesthetics were increasingly fashionable. Dürer had travelled to Italy for the first time in 1494. He went to visit Pirckheimer at his studies in Pavia, but also to immerse himself in both the work of his Italian contemporaries and the world of antiquity. His emphasis shifted away from the religious and courtly themes of Germanic art and towards that of pagan mythology, as exemplified by the paintings and prints of Andrea Mantegna. During that one year, he produced three engravings – *The Battle of the Sea Gods*, *The Bacchanal with Silenus* and *The Bacchanal by the Vat* – which were directly based upon the works of the Italian master. With these new sources of inspiration came the attempt to reintegrate Classical form with subject matter.[21] Thus, Dürer began to attempt to show the heroes, gods and goddesses of antiquity as they might have appeared to the eyes of the Greeks and Romans, rather than to the citizens of late fifteenth-century Nuremberg. It may just be that *The Four Witches* is a hybrid image, conceived within this framework.

Scholars, magistrates and mobs in the late fifteenth and early sixteenth centuries paid little or no attention to the nudity of witches. The working of magic was not associated with the abandonment of clothing. What nudity did denote, however, was pagan antiquity, particularly pagan gods and goddesses.[22] By making his witches naked, Dürer indicated that the scene of *The Four Witches* was both rooted in the Classical past and showed an inversion of normal modes of conduct. It also, incidentally, allowed him to sell erotic prints to the popular market without arousing censure, or more importantly censorship. He was, after all, telling a moral tale equating magic with damnation.[23]

It is clear that three of the four women are taken directly from Classical versions of *The Three Graces*. Yet, Dürer has a fourth figure present even though he had to shoe-horn her awkwardly into the otherwise familiar composition. I suggest that the woman on the right has just stepped in through the archway, bringing with her a friend for support, and that she is beseeching the two dominant figures, on the left of the print, to share with her their knowledge of magic and to enact a ritual for her benefit. The forming of a circle, and the conjoining of their hands, are key to the artist's conception of magical practice. Yet how far this is rooted in anything more than Dürer's imagination and his acquaintance with Classical witchcraft texts is highly debatable. What does seem clear, however, is that for both the artist and his audience, *The Four Witches* evoked a world of temptations and erotic dreams, inspired by the Greco-Roman past, rather than the grim reality of the present: a late fifteenth century, with its claustrophobic courtrooms, informers and suspicions of demonic magic as the catalyst for all bitter civil discord. It is, therefore, far more plausibly viewed as an image of poetic fantasy, representing the dark but fascinating side of Classical literature, than as the product of the handbooks of witch-hunters or of first-hand knowledge of an actual crime.

III

In this engraving, Dürer created one of the most enduring images of witchcraft. He returned to the theme less than a decade later to produce quite a different image of a *Witch Riding Backwards on a Goat*. For every stereotype – devalued through inappropriate and overuse – there must be an archetype, and Dürer's conception of the old, barren witch, with her sagging breasts and face distorted by hate, is precisely that. Our view of the elderly, haggard and frightening witch, flying by night, is so familiar that it is hard to conceive of a time when the image was fresh and challenging. Dürer's witch is, therefore, our witch. It proved to be so potent and terrifying that it came to dominate all others and became fixed in the European imagination over the next 500 years.

The artist shows us a vision of a naked crone, riding bareback and astride a leaping – or flying – goat, while fire and hailstones plunge down towards the earth. In her right hand she cradles a distaff, seemingly stabbing its point deep into her crotch, while she wraps her left fist firmly around the goat's horn. The self-abasement of the witch is all too evident. With one hand she pleasures herself with an instrument normally associated with a woman's domestic work, while the other massages the base of the phallus-like horn. At the same moment, she is masturbating both the female sex organ (her own) and the male (the goat's bone). It is far more evident here, than in the engraving of *The Four Witches*, that it is fertility and the sexual act that are being attacked by the witch; and artificially stimulated, perverted or thwarted. Yet, this sense of distemper and inversion goes much further. The witch is riding backwards, her bristling hair streams out behind her contrary to the direction of the breeze, and Dürer's own monogram at the foot of the engraving is reproduced back to front. Given Dürer's pride in his mastery of the techniques of engraving, it is extremely unlikely that he would have unwittingly made such an elementary error during the production of the plate. Even if he had, it is unthinkable – knowing the rigid control he exercised over the quality and marketing of his images – that he would have permitted sub-standard work to be sold under his name. This mirror image of reality is intentional and integral. Thus, even the artist's trademark has been bewitched, and twisted, by the power of the crone. It bows, bends and inverts itself before her might.[24] The witch has mastered the power of sex, but in the process has also stripped herself of her own female sexuality. Her face is masculine, her breasts are shrunken and her physique is muscular, powerful and taut. Un-sexed, yet sexual, violent and unpredictable, she flies over the earth, lashing it with tempests of fire and rain.

This witch is unambiguous. A female has appropriated the signs of male dominance and sexuality, and the symbols of feminine labour and virtue have been visually corrupted. However, Dürer also shows her as a figure who has been disgraced. In Early Modern Europe, cuckolded husbands and spiteful wives could be made to ride backwards through a baying crowd as a form of punishment. Moreover, the idea of rough justice applied through the inversion of customs – with the rich riding a horse forward with honour, and the poor and despised tied backwards onto a donkey, or a lamed animal, that would limp along the road to a chorus of insults – was another symbol of disgrace.[25] Yet, its component parts make far more sense than the whole. In totality it is strange, incongruous and problematic. We have already described the terrifying top half of the composition, but the bottom half seems altogether benign. It has cavorting Putti, carrying staves, a globe and an exotic, pot-bound tree. Two stand, while one bows down offering up his stave to his receptive companion. They seem oblivious to the witch and the goat, vaulting over them. Zika has tried to equate the figure of the witch with Aphrodite Pandemos, the earthly Venus, who was associated with lust and the night. In such a reading it is plausible, but hardly certain, that the four Putti represent her winged attendants. The goddess' flaming torch has simply been replaced by a distaff in order to set her within a recognisably Germanic, early sixteenth-century context, while both she and her counterpart, the witch, sit astride goats, she always faces forward rather than back.[26] However, the problem remains that the Putti appear thoroughly disengaged from, even inimical to, the main focus of the action. Most commentators have preferred to ignore their existence entirely.

The curious physiognomy of the goat has also been consistently overlooked. Its genitals are obscured by the wings of one of the Putti – and are, in any case, indicated by its large horns – while its rear half is arched and curiously elongated. Its hind legs and tail are not shown at all. Once again, Zika offers an explanation that is entirely cogent and, to the mind of this writer, simply the best interpretation of the image that has been presented to date: the goat represents the astrological symbol Capricorn, a sign associated with the malign aspects of the god Saturn. Capricorn is depicted elsewhere by Dürer, along with other late Mediaeval and Renaissance artists, as half-goat and half-fish or serpent.[27] The curve of the goat's back, in the engraving of the witch, is strangely denuded of hair and seems to be narrowing to a point beyond the borders of the engraving, blurred by the artist to indicate the high speed at which it is travelling through the air. As such, it is possible that we are seeing a representation of the star sign and that the Putti serve to mask the awkwardness of its form.

The *Witch Riding Backwards on a Goat* is, like *The Four Witches*, a work best interpreted as a composite scene, combining both local and Classical themes. Thus, the idea that witches flew upon goats was already being expressed in German popular culture in the early fifteenth century, and pictures of both male and female witches riding wolves and fantastical animals appeared in Molitor's illustrated edition of *De Laniis* from 1490–1, but the combination of this motif with the nudity associated with a Classical sorceress – or possibly a goddess – was new. Similarly, the association of the witch figure with astrological forces, and the juxtaposition of Italianate Putti with an old German countrywoman, reflects less the state of ideas of demonology at the turn of the sixteenth century, and more a fresh development in the portrayal of the witch. Dürer had a sense of playfulness, even of humour, that signalled the flourishing of Humanism in his world at that moment. The meaning of an image is, after all, created not just by the artist but also by the beholder. The subtlety of metaphors might easily be lost in the market place, where in-jokes and intellectual arguments might be taken simply at face value. This is seemingly what happened to the *Witch Riding Backwards on a Goat*.

The date of the *Witch Riding Backwards on a Goat* is unknown, but can be placed between 1500 and 1507. Given the care that the artist took to ascribe a particular date to his earlier *Four Witches*, this is surprising. It may well be that *The Four Witches* was, indeed, linked to some now forgotten *cause célèbre* or that, working three years before 1500, Dürer was caught up in the millennial angst that shaped his fifteen woodcuts of 1498, illustrating the *Apocalypse* for a book printed by his godfather. However, it seems it was rooted in no one incident but rather it expressed widespread fears about social tensions, the ending of the world and the coming of the kingdom of Heaven.

The *Witch Riding Backwards on a Goat* clearly had power and appeal. It was mass-marketed through the medium of print, and within just a few years it came to represent not an allegory of sorcery, but evidence of its reality, shape and form. It presented fear, topicality and an insight into a forbidden world of danger and sex, and so it offered much to the entrepreneur who owned a printing press and was not afraid to break Dürer's hold on that which we now call copyright. Copyists and lesser-known artists pirated Dürer's work in great number, but their inferior renditions stripped the image of its ambiguity.[28] Dürer's *Witch Riding Backwards on a Goat* may have been the inspiration for Albrecht Altdorfer's 1506 *Witches Riding Animals Through the Air*, or else the two works were the product of common anxieties. Altdorfer's work neatly compresses the subject matter of both Dürer's *The Four Witches* and *Witch Riding Backwards on a Goat,* ironing out discrepancies in the conflicting portrayals of the witch and her magic to forge a coherent, and plausible whole. In the foreground, four witches form a magical circle around a central point, governed by an ornate phial or casket. The central witch invokes the charm: she straddles a wooden rake, her femininity sublimated through her muscular physicality and the violence of her movements. She simulates sex (with the rake) and summons up the Devil through a left arm flung wide. At her feet lies a skull. She and the acolyte both wear garlands in their hair, while the elderly witch has flung her hair loose. All three are semi-naked. The fourth wears the simple coif and dress of a housewife. A purse and set of keys hang from a string belt at her waist. Her costume grounds the scene in everyday existence and suggests the presence of an outlandish enemy that lurks on the fringes of domesticity. To underscore the point, a row of houses sits on the crest of a hill, beyond the tendrils of the forest. A host of other witches straddling airborne goats are rising from the glade. The witches travel to and from their meeting on flying goats, borne upwards by the power of noxious gases and clouds of smoke. They indulge in ritual practice with a circle scribed in the earth. The witches carry symbols of female labour: the hoe, the rake and the distaff. One fellates the horn of a particularly knowing and self-satisfied goat.

Altdorfer's narrative is far more explicit than Dürer's, and different in focus. It shows unequivocally harmful magic worked at night in the woods, magic to destabilise the life of the household. These witches are intent on doing harm and causing death, a fact indicated by the skull on the ground and the casket from which they draw their ingredients. The idea of the witch as one practising love magic is gone, replaced by the witch as practitioner of *maleficium*. The beauty of the practitioner in *Der Liebeszauber,* and the comely sisterhood of Dürer's *Four Witches* is no more.

The portrayal of female lust is now realised through portraying rakes and distaffs as dildos. Before, the witch had used her magic to induce the love of a man; it was an unnatural recourse to secure a natural end. Now, the man is quite literally removed from the picture and the de-feminised witch simply pleasures herself. An unnatural instrument – the corrupted domestic object – is used for auto-eroticism, an unnatural act. Likewise, all suggestion of Classical mythology, or sense that one of these women might represent a goddess, has been removed. The setting of the farmstead, on the borders of a Teutonic forest, gives the scene a contemporary resonance that Dürer's images of high arches, stone vestibules and mischievous Putti lacked. These are German women, in a German landscape, engaged upon the working of real magic.

IV

This sense of disquiet was re-enforced, over the course of the next century, by a succession of images that built upon Dürer's archetypes. Niklaus Manuel Deutsch combined the artist's flying witch with Dürer's depiction of *Fortune*, in 1513, to create a vision of mayhem, personified by the female form rushing over the face of the land and bringing with it the twin spectres of war and death. Seated upon a globe, his own witch clutches at an hourglass in one hand, and the skull of a fallen soldier – or *Landsknecht* – distinguished by its extravagantly feathered military cap, in the other. A smoking philtre balances on her fleshy knee, and she is naked save for the ornate strings of little chains that criss-cross her limbs and fasten over her distended stomach.[29] Urs Graf, himself a former soldier, took these images even further, delighting in portrayals of *Landsknechts* led to death by prostitutes and devils. A grinning camp-follower, or sutleress, stares out at the viewer in one print, while a barefoot soldier hangs from a tree above, his eyes pecked out by the birds. In another work, two fashionably dressed young women are beating and kicking a lustful monk; one flails at him with a heavy set of keys, while he – poor-box still in his hand – tries to push his head deep into her groin. In a third print, a satyr or devil throws an offering of gold to a statue of a pagan god, while stepping on the body of a lover he has just slain. The dead man's naked partner seems none too concerned by the turn of events, and leaves arm-in-arm with the satyr, who is distinguished by an oversized shard of bone, or horn, jutting up – erect – from his skull.[30] His women are imbibed with danger, sometimes deformed, and always intent upon the ruin of man. His undoubted misogyny and love of violence were reflected, though often with far less intensity, by a series of other artists who attempted to explore and appropriate Dürer's images of the witch.

In this manner, the concept of the flying witch became gender-specific: the naked figure of a woman became divorced from its origins in antiquity and increasingly held to be synonymous with the practice of harmful magic; and the nature of that magic, itself, altered from seeking to win love to seeking to destroy lives. Thus, an illustration for Abraham Saur's *A Short True Warning* (against witchcraft), published in Frankfurt in 1582, showed a hag, naked save for her billowing coif, holding a pitchfork upright, while an entirely naked witch ploughed across the night sky, clinging on to the horns of a flying ram with grim intent. A woodcut by Hans Weiditz, dating from the early years of the sixteenth century, shows four witches, again arranged in a circle, brewing up storms. Once again, three of the four are naked and the housewife, who is not, carries a pitchfork from which a discarded item of clothing is streaming in imitation of a knight's banner. Both animal and human skulls lie at their feet.[31] By the time that Lucas Cranach 'the Elder', court painter to Frederick 'the Wise' of Saxony, came to paint his study of *Melancholy*, in 1528, the naked riding woman had become firmly established as an artistic convention signifying witchcraft and social dislocation. He retains Dürer's curious device of the four playful Putti, from the *Witch Riding Backwards on a Goat*, but his attempt to visualise a mood or feeling (in this case depression) which was increasingly identified with – and personified by – an attractive young woman, was very far removed from Dürer's own study of *Melancholia I*, which had been published some 14 years before.[32]

Dürer had conceived of a psychological study, with *Melancholia* portrayed as an angel, surrounded by all the symbols of human creativity and endeavour – mathematical problems, the tools of the artist, the architect, the soldier and the master craftsman – yet being bored by them all.[33] It is certainly not a commentary upon the strength of external, demonic powers to sap the willpower of the individual. This is precisely what *Melancholy* becomes in the hands of Cranach. His painting shows an unmarried woman at a laden dining table. She shows no interest in the bounty before her, preferring instead to whittle away at a stick with a small knife. As Dale Hoak has pointed out, in Germanic tradition it was thought necessary for a witch to peel away bark from a twig when she was swearing herself to the Devil.[34] Cranach peoples the background with a cluster of naked witches. Some wave military banners, evoking war, while others rise on the backs of goats and wild animals. Four witches – two mounted, two on foot – cavort around a flame. Apples hang from the branch, echoing the sin of Eve. Women's premarital idleness leads to devilish mischief and disaster.

The woman's streaming hair hints at her sexuality and self-expression. Where Dürer's free-haired witch evokes sorceresses of antiquity whose locks bristle on end, Cranach's witch is a local sight: a German girl of good family in the early years of the sixteenth century. Without the hand of a father to curb, or a husband to satisfy, her passions, she is left to turn in on herself and is free, in the midst of her depression and yearnings, to contemplate selling her soul to the Devil. Female sexual knowledge and experience, as symbolised by the apple, is just as dangerous, in Cranach's eyes, for his male friends and neighbours, as it was for Adam, the first of the species.

If we accept that Dürer's view of *Melancholia* is an exercise in Humanistic rhetoric, then we should see his witch as conceived in the same manner. Certainly his famous engraving of *The Knight, Death and the Devil*, printed just a year before *Melancholia I* in 1513, can be seen within the Humanist tradition.[35] The image has consistently been seen as a call for reform from within the Catholic Church, and linked with both the Humanism of Erasmus and the writings of the young Martin Luther.

Dürer certainly read both Erasmus and Luther. In particular, Erasmus's *Handbook of the Christian Soldier*, published in 1504, deeply influenced Dürer.[36] *The Knight, Death and the Devil* is a heavily researched case, showing Dürer's practice of marrying literary and visual sources, in a theme infused by Humanism, costumed and set within the realities of sixteenth-century Germany, inspired by Classical archetypes.

However, the worlds of politics and religion were rapidly changing, and 1525–6 saw local protests, which quickly escalated to a full-scale rising and a Peasants' War across Germany. The combination of a de facto class war and the Reformation served to split apart communities and divide friends. The convivial world of the Waaghaus, with its learned debates, had come to an end. The Humanist project faded. Dürer and his most talented pupil, Hans Baldung Grien, split away from the moderate Humanists (including Pirckheimer) to join the new Lutheran Churches. Despite their political and religious differences, Dürer and Pirckheimer never lost their respect for one another, nor their friendship. After Dürer's death, Pirckheimer could only watch in dismay as his widow sold off his possessions at less than their market value and dispersed, or destroyed, his correspondence. He had few doubts that the search for the platonic ideal – the creative ability to define new images and archetypes – had never deserted his friend Dürer, but the world around them was being distorted by the horrors of war and the suppression of revolution.

V

The witch as envisaged by Dürer was not a reimagining but a fresh creation. The trouble was that his image was so powerful it became pervasive, and thus eclipsed all other versions of the subject. Dürer created the archetype of the young naked witch working love spells, and of the withered yet still sexually active hag flying by night, that would become general and accepted as representing actual practice. The anxiety of the age, which found powerful expression in Dürer's terrifying nightmare of an apocalyptic deluge on the eve of the Peasants' War, could just as easily turn inwards to focus upon those unfortunates at the very margins of society, who might be held to account for every ill and malaise. Unwittingly, Dürer had helped make this possible and gave witch-belief, especially among the elites, far greater credibility and respectability.

Yet, as Willibald Pirckheimer contemplated what had been lost amid the ruin of the artist's personal archives, he did not dwell upon such matters or evil dreams but recalled better times and unrealisable hopes. Dürer had once written that: 'often in my sleep … I behold great works of art and beautiful things, the like whereof never appear to me awake, but as soon as I awake even the remembrance of them leaves me', and Pirckheimer would recall that Dürer 'told us how sometimes in his dreams he seemed to live among things so beautiful that if such only really existed he would be the happiest of men'.[37] Dürer's witches should properly be considered among these 'dream works'. However, one man's dream may constitute another's worst nightmare. And this is precisely what transpired.

CHAPTER FIVE

The Brutalised Witch

I

To the English imagination of the eighteenth and early nineteenth centuries, the seventeenth-century Italian painter Salvator Rosa symbolised all that was to be admired in a creative genius. Rosa had been a champion of artistic autonomy, a painter and poet of extraordinary merit and proficiency, an Italian patriot and heroic forerunner of the Risorgimento. His life story was romantic, too: he had been raised by bandits and had fought in Masaniello's libertarian revolt. Moreover, he had been an implacable foe of the irrationalism of the Roman Catholic Church and the Office of the Holy Inquisition.[1] Horace Walpole had admired him greatly, and herein lay the roots of his emergence as an idol of Romantic Neo-Classicism. The mainstream English public was introduced to Rosa after Walpole's lifetime, in 1824, through a seminal two-volume biography by Lady Morgan. The book was received by the English reading classes with great fanfare and won enormous popular – if not critical – acclaim.[2] Lady Morgan's biography spawned a spate of popular novels celebrating Rosa's boyhood, and Rosa's landscapes suddenly became collectable and sold for high sums, to then adorn the walls of more than a hundred country houses and galleries. His style and subject matter were emulated by aspiring watercolourists and engravers. The very use of Rosa's name was enough for an aspiring Gothic novelist, such as Ann Radcliffe in the *Mysteries of Udolpho*, to set an otherworldly scene, darken the tone and to signify impending doom.

In Rosa's paintings, the well-to-do found wild, untamed nature, characterised by precipices, caverns and dark forest, such as they had seen on their travels around Europe on their grand tours. At home, they could recreate such scenes in their parks and estates, building follies, caverns and ruined hermitages that cried out to be populated by a cast of brigands, *condiatorre*, anchorites, fallen deities and half-crazed witches. Rosa's images were sometimes used as models for these. In a grotto at Stourhead, Wiltshire, for example, the statue of a River God – his hair and beard matted and verdigrised to resemble water reeds – sat atop the source of a spring, ready to surprise or enchant, the unwary visitor to the gardens. The god is directly based upon Rosa's painting of the *God of the Tiber*.

The problem was, of course, that fashions change and Rosa's curious afterlife as an inspiration to the Romantic movement had little to say to the age of the steam engine, still less to that of mass production, Fordism, the microchip and the fibre-optic. Ruskin dismissed his art as uncouth and brutal, while his figure – unlike those of his contemporary rivals, Claude Lorrain and Nicolas Poussin – was omitted from the pantheon of great artists that ornamented the base of the Albert Memorial, commissioned in 1862 and opened a decade later. Worse still, as the art historians of the twentieth century were to discover, there was little or no truth to any of the exciting biographical details that had attached themselves to him.[3]

The historical Salvator Rosa was the son of a builder, born in a suburb of Naples in 1615, and destined, like his brother before him, for holy orders. As a novice, he was taught Latin grammar and rhetoric, acquiring the love for Classical texts and philosophy that would do much to shape his later artistic output. However, he soon chafed at the discipline and privations of monasticism and left his Order, picking up the rudiments of painting from his grandfather and his uncle – who specialised in small devotional pictures – and being apprenticed to his future brother-in-law, Francesco Francanzano, a noted painter of battle scenes. Describing himself as an artist from the age of 16 onwards, Rosa left Naples aged 20, settled in Rome and then went on to pursue his career in Florence in the 1640s. There he worked at the court of the Medici, and though he bitterly criticised its corruption, he sold his work to the Florentine elite. He founded his own literary circle and took retreats at the Tuscan villa of his friend and confidant, Giulio Maffei. It was during this period that Rosa produced a series of remarkable canvasses dealing with the theme of witchcraft.

These witchcraft paintings shocked and entranced the spectator in roughly equal measure. They raised excited comment when the paintings were first unveiled in Florence and Rome. By the eighteenth century, Horace Walpole was marvelling at the artist's unparalleled ability to express the deadly and the macabre, praising 'his masterly management of horror and distress' and the Victorian art critic John Ruskin also reacted strongly, though negatively, declaring the paintings to epitomise the 'dragon breath of evil'.[4] In spite of their great impact, Rosa's witch images have been dismissed by more recent scholars as a disagreeable or irrelevant aberration in his otherwise enlightened career. One wrote that the witchcraft paintings 'do not seem to reflect Rosa's philosophical leanings – they have no message'. Moreover, his interest has been seen as peculiar to the short period 1646–7. It is also said that no one believed in witches in Rosa's day: 'witches and witch-hunts became a folk memory rather than a present terror' so they were thus simply 'morbid imaginings'. Nor is Rosa thought to have known much about the subject: he possessed no 'deep knowledge of the ... arguments surrounding witchcraft and its persecution'.[5]

Rather, the 'witches were like macabre special effects from a self-parodying horror film, the spectres in which are intended to give a shock that then turns to nervous laughter'.[6] Rosa has now been cast as a cynic, a knowing satirist, a dealer in burlesques.

His depictions of witchcraft are, however, far deeper, more serious and long lasting than the assessment given so far. The engagement has been shown to be far from brief.[7] Rather than being a peripheral interest, Rosa's examination of witchcraft and ritual expanded to embrace ten major canvasses and a full-length poem. Furthermore, the production of these works has increasingly been seen to reflect his own personal tastes and preoccupations, rather than the brief, or passing interest, of an exacting patron. In fact, Rosa's conception of witchcraft was an integral part of his mission as an artist. It was undoubtedly an essential component of his pursuit of Classicism, but more than that; it was part of his attempt to reform the citizens and rulers of the Italian city states, who had traduced their noble heritage in their pursuit of money, office and power.

II

The witchcraft paintings began with *The Temptation of St Anthony*, painted most likely for Cardinal Giancarlo de Medici, shortly before Rosa left his service in 1646, and continued with a seminal study depicting a Witches' Sabbath that was sold to one of the artist's friends in 1646. A set of four *tondi* followed, probably painted in 1647 and catalogued collectively as *Divinations*. There was also a canvas known as *Incantations and Witchcraft* that was bought by the Marchese Corsini in 1655, and two studies of lone witches working their art, dated anywhere between 1643 and 1656. A later work, depicting *Saul and the Witch of Endor*, painted in 1668, stands outside this series in terms of its chronology, and brings the trajectory of the paintings full circle, as only the first and the last of Rosa's works are connected with themes of biblical, as opposed to Classical, witchcraft.

In the first work, *The Temptation of St Anthony*, a relatively standard subject among religious artists of the sixteenth and seventeenth centuries is transformed into something altogether different and more terrifying, as the figure of the central demon – all sinew and putrefying, corrupted flesh – becomes the focal point of the painting, rather than the fate and the appropriate Christian response of the tormented man. An internal conflict becomes, in Rosa's hands, an external physical threat. As the fiend advances, flanked by two lesser demons and two furies – or witch-like figures who urge him on – the hermit collapses at the mouth of his cave, crushing his prayer book under his fall. The simple wooden cross flailed out in an arc by the stricken saint seems to have stopped the demon in its tracks, but it is by no means certain that it has sufficient power to prevent him from pouncing upon the stricken man. It is St Anthony's mortal life, as opposed to his immortal soul, which seems to be at stake here. The Christian message is in danger of being submerged beneath the terror of the instant, while the artist establishes, from the first, his trademark reimagining of a demon as an abomination of nature. The creature is formed from a composite of animal skeletons – part bird, part oxen – with a swishing, rat-like tail and a man's emaciated torso. Its gender, in line with much demonological thought at the time, is neuter. The theatrical triumphs over the theological, and it is clear that Rosa was more concerned with unsettling his audience than with providing an uplifting homily. The will of the individual, and by extension the human spirit, was hereby asserting itself after its long negation under Western Christendom.

The painting proved a commercial success and Rosa began four more studies of witchcraft and ritual that represented the workings of magic at the key points of the day: sunrise, noon, evening and night. In the first of the cycle, a young witch skewers the tongue of a flapping toad, while *striges*, dragons and flying fish rise up to disfigure an Arcadian landscape. In the second, at noon, a crone squeezes the lifeblood out of a human heart, while a strix looks on; acolytes present her with human skulls and dissect a dragon corpse. In the third, the nightfall scene, lightning cleaves a tree and an hourglass-bearing skeleton hovers, as a group of witches cast a magic circle to melt a wax figurine. In the final canvas, a group of knights halt among the ruins of a Classical temple as a necromancer breaks open the cave mouth to Hell.

These four paintings originally hung on the ground floor of the Niccolini palace in Florence, in a room themed around 'Philosophy and Poetry'. For both the Marchese Filippo Niccolini, who commissioned the paintings and for Rosa, himself, witchcraft was a legitimate line of philosophical enquiry and a subject which had firm roots within the poetics of Classical civilisation. It has been suggested that the circular form of the paintings was consciously chosen to reflect the magical circles woven by the witches.[8] Clearly, different forms of magic were to be practised at different times of the day and by very different types of sorcerer. The painting for daybreak shows, for the only time in Rosa's work, a beautiful young witch – clad in aristocratic finery, like Circe – surrounded by her familiars. Even in the act of maiming an animal, at the height of her ritual, she is strangely impassive, appearing as the tool, rather than the true mistress, of her demons. Rosa had already painted a scene depicting *Latona and the Frogs*, in which a band of hapless peasants had been transformed into frogs by the goddess, whom they had angered, and it seems plausible that the artist is reworking several established themes rooted in Classical, as opposed to contemporary witch-beliefs. The noonday scene, despite its Italianate landscape is, by way of immediate contrast, influenced by the Northern tradition of Altdorfer, Cranach and Baldung Grien and shows a group of naked, aged witches working under the direction of their superior, who is herself caught in the moment of dismounting from her strix-like steed, broomstick in hand. In the evening scene, it is again a group of wizened, naked and partially clad crones who attempt to manipulate nature's laws through the use of charms, mirrors, a crystal ball, a scattering of coins, a tattered paper inscribed with a pentagram and a book of spells. The plumb line swinging above their heads seems to hint at the inversion and corruption of learning through rough, untutored hands, while the hourglass raised by the demon both suggests that they are racing to complete their task before dawn and that the hour will come when they will be judged. In the final scene, it is a male sorcerer – clad in a rich ceremonial gown – who invokes a demon before a makeshift altar and a burning brazier. His poor barefoot assistants bow their heads to the creatures welling up from the pits of Hell. Two knights wait on the edge of the moonlit glade. It has often been suggested that they have unwittingly stumbled upon the horrific scene, but nothing suggests surprise or revulsion. Rather, the demons seem to have been raised for their benefit, as both riders crane forward over their saddles as if to see whether the demons are ready to do their bidding. This sorcerer appears happy, for a fee, to open the gates to Hell for his wealthy patrons. Here, Rosa is clearly distinguishing High Magic from Low. The raising of demons is not gender-specific, but it certainly is governed by age, wealth and social class. The goddess, or Classical enchantress, is youthful and wealthy and, as a consequence, has far more in common with the learned necromancer than her ragged and aged sisters. Rich people work their magic when it is most efficacious at the polar opposites of the day, while the poor and excluded work at the margins, when and where they can. In this way, the unnatural order reflects the social inequalities Rosa knew all too well.

The next painting in the series, *The Witches' Sabbath* – now in the National Gallery, London – provides the fullest exposition of Rosa's conception of witchcraft and remains one of – if not *the* – most striking representations of witch-beliefs in the history of Western art. All of the components of the witches' rites are depicted: cannibalism, the worship of bestial deities, the conjuration of spirits and the sacrifice of children in order to propitiate the demons summoned to the night-time gatherings. The witches are old, ugly and obscene, performing their frenzied rites in a shattered and scarred landscape, under leaden skies and storm-blasted trees. In an inversion of the accepted social order, the knight bows the knee to the crone, so that she can dub him with a broomstick, while his sword is purloined by a beggar and used to skewer a freshly dripping human heart. Debased and dishonoured, the knight's hands clutch at a taper and a torch, which he uses to ignite a circle of candles and to offer up the sacrifice of the rabbit that waits unsuspectingly at its centre. As a young initiate is beckoned into action by a sturdy old hag, a skeleton is propped up in its coffin so that its lifeless fingers can be guided in the writing of a charm, or the directions to a treasure horde, by a tattered peasant couple. Nearby, nail parings are being taken from the toenails of a hanging man, while another witch attempts either to fumigate, or to revive, the body with the vapours emanating from a sulphurous vessel. In the foreground, a young woman attempts to catch the image of her future lover in the reflection of a wax doll in a hand-mirror, while her friend looks on in amazement and, oblivious to all, a corpulent old woman grinds out the essence of human bones with a mortar and pestle. Slumped and stupefied, she drips fluids from a human heart into her bowl, while clutching a bone in her fist, dragging it across her fleshy thigh in an action that speaks of a sexual debasement stripped of any last vestige of pleasure. Around her are scattered coiled ropes, playing cards, iron nails, a charm pinned to the ground, roots and herbs torn from the earth, bay leaves and a glass phial containing a discoloured liquid that is probably urine or bile.

To the right of the painting, slouching toads and creatures newly risen from Hell are offered the life of a child, while a giant skeletal bird presides over all, inclining its razor-sharp beak towards the infant. The creatures lope forward, ridden by hags whose naked breasts hang low and pendulous. The witch who proffers the tightly swaddled infant up for sacrifice, has hitched up her skirts to reveal that she has purloined a pair of men's riding boots. This signifies her rejection of her own femininity but also, more practically, allows her to maintain her grip on the scaly and oscillating sides of the monster. For its part, the creature on which she rides opens up its cavernous maw – resembling a flap of dead skin rather than a recognisable mouth – to swallow up the impassive, or simply drugged, child. Only a streak of light across the hillside hints at the urgency of their tasks, and the promise that, with the coming dawn, order will once more be restored to the landscape.

This is not so much one painting, depicting a single instance of witchcraft, but a composite, which intends to reveal every major practice of *maleficia* associated with the witches' Sabbat. As such, it can be read from left to right, as not one but three separate images, each with its own particular focus. The narrative begins with the summoning of spirits and the re-animation of the dead, moves on to the preparation of spells and potions and reaches a crescendo of horror in the appearance of the demons and their propitiation through the sacrifice of a human child. It also serves as a compendium of all the different forms of spell – for love magic, divination, the raising of demons and necromancy – and use of every magical artefact – the nails, wax mummets, chords and simmering brews – of which Rosa had knowledge. He holds nothing back and piles vision after vision of wickedness and vice into every square inch of his panel. It is a painting that revels in the occult, in its true sense, delighting in layers of hidden meaning and forbidden knowledge. The purpose and identity of the mysterious figure on the left of the canvas, shrouded from head to toe in white robes, garlanded with laurels and cradling a flimsy brazier of lighted tapers in her – or possibly his – lap, has never been adequately explained. Cybelline prophetess, or shade from the underworld, her presence serves both to unsettle and to provoke the curiosity of the viewer. When confronted with the image for the first time, a party of modern-day witches and New Age practitioners responded to the painting with something approaching reverence, as though it was a text-book for their craft.[9] The reaction of Rosa's contemporaries could hardly have been less profound.

III

The next major witchcraft canvas is known as *Incantations and Magic* or *Scene of Witchcraft*. At the time of its commission, the Marchese Bartolommeo Corsini described it as 'a beautiful painting of spells and witchcraft'. Recently, it has been the subject of reassessment in light of the discovery of a 1655 account book, which relates that Corsini paid 60 *scudi* for the small canvas.[10] This changes the chronology and places it after *The Witches' Sabbath*, putting it instead at the climax of his artistic vision, a reworking of established motifs. Corsini almost certainly knew of Rosa's earlier paintings of witchcraft and desired his own variant to hang in his palace in Rome: Corsini was related by marriage to the owner of the four *tondi*, and had strong contacts with the salons of Florence.

The image Rosa produced for him reveals a coven at work on their charms. The central group has gathered the personal belongings of a man that they wish to destroy. Aided by arcane texts, old nails, a saw blade, odd bones and a bird corpse, they have summoned a collection of demons from beyond the gates of Hell. A cockerel-headed skeleton pecks at a witch's back, while the malformed bird embryos and a giant, bony insect hover above the coven. As the central witches shake brooms, tapers and a thyrsus in the summoning spell, the acolytes on the periphery are caught between fear and ecstasy. Save for a buxom initiate, all the witches conform to the, now well-established, stereotype of the 'wizened old crone'. Significantly, this was not Rosa's original vision. Preparatory sketches reveal his original central figure was a full-breasted young priestess, assisted by a tonsured monk. In the final version, however, the witch has become a crone helped by a kneeling woman, and so Rosa's social commentary and anti-clericalism has disappeared.[11] Moreover, in the sketches,

Rosa marries the Classical symbol of thyrsus staff with the Mediaeval witch broom – but this study is much muted in the finished piece. On this occasion, it seems, the artist practised a form of self-censorship, perhaps with a view to warding off the unwelcome attention of the Inquisition in Rome.

Conceivably painted around the same time are two studies known respectively as *Witch* and *Witch Preparing the Cup of Immortality*, representing individual witches. With these works the argument that Rosa used witches as satire clearly breaks down. Rosa was certainly aware of his friend Lorenzo Lippi's poem mocking over-blown witchcraft epics: in the latter, a witch saunters through a garden where the trees are hung with gibbets, the walls of a grotto are papered with folds of human flesh, and statues are decorated with the severed heads of executed criminals. However, the resemblance is insufficient to sustain the idea that Rosa was reproducing these motifs in his paintings. It has also been suggested that Rosa's art and, in particular, *The Witches' Sabbath*, *Magic and Incantations* and the *Witch Preparing the Cup of Immortality*, were direct responses to the first book of Horace's 8th Satire. The poet certainly evokes themes common to both Classical witchcraft and Rosa's paintings. In the Satire, the witches Canidia and Sagana gather 'bones and deadly plants' from a burial ground atop one of the Seven Hills of Rome, scraping away the earth with their fingernails and trickling the blood of a black lamb they have just torn apart, 'into the trench, from where they meant to summon the spirits of the dead to answer their questions'. As in Rosa's canvasses, the hags melt wax mummets and use 'a woollen doll ... larger so as to dominate and punish the smaller [wax image]. The latter stood in an attitude of supplication as if expecting a slave's death.'[12] Furthermore, the witches go on to practise a form of magic that echoes Rosa's own verse, whereby they 'stealthily buried a wolf's beard along with the fang of a spotted snake, [as] the flame flared up the wax image melted' and 'the spirits sounded mournful and shrill as they answered Sagana's questions.'[13] So far so good, but the denouement of the piece – and the satire upon which it turns – concerns the reaction of a worn wooden statue of the god of vegetation, Priapus, to their horrors and impieties committed under cover of the 'high tombs'. Enraged, the god lets rip an involuntary fart 'which split my fig-wood buttocks' and sends the witches tumbling back down the hill in terror, with Canidia dropping her false teeth and Sagana losing her 'high wig' in the process. All their malevolence has availed them little, as they are held up as shrieking hysterics and objects of general derision, whose occult powers and deviancy can be dispelled by a lesser obscenity; a sudden flatulent gust of hot air.

Now, if we are to assume – and it is a big *if* – that the paintings of Salvator Rosa were conceived as withering satires on witch-belief, in the spirit of Horace, then we are forced to concede that he was an extremely leaden and clumsy commentator, almost entirely without humour. His images simply do not reflect the spirit of Horace's verse and seem to revel in the efficacy of the witches' practices, rather than to mock their futility and delusion. As Rosa was renowned in his lifetime as an accomplished comic actor and, by posterity, as one of the greatest post-Renaissance artists in Italy, the proposition that he was simply attempting to recreate the *Satires*, albeit in a different medium, does not seem to carry much weight. Where Rosa's work does intersect with Horace's is in their shared sources of inspiration from Greco-Roman witchcraft.

The Classical witch was thought to work through a commonly recognised mixture of curses, poisons and spells – evidenced not only by legal proceedings and the archaeological record, but also by the great poetics that underpinned Greek and Roman society. She might well be a ridiculous figure but she was a present, and at times extremely potent, force in the literature that was required reading for any gentleman who hoped to take his place in the Agora, or the Forum. As Circe, Medea, Erictho or Pamphile, the witch stood as a savage muse to the poetry of the Classical age and as the template upon which all subsequent variations of the witch figure, in the West, would be based.

Salvator Rosa knew this just as surely as Albrecht Dürer. But Rosa turned to Lucan's witch for his inspiration. Lucan's Erictho was crooked and misshapen in both body and mind; a degenerate with a gaunt and decayed face 'unknown to cloudless sky', and framed by 'matted, uncombed hair'. Delighting in the perversion of funerary rites, she was adept at raiding graveyards and deathbeds, stealing the still 'smoking ashes of the young' and 'blazing bones' from the middle of the pyre; immersing herself in the ashes of deceased as they waft up to the skies; plucking 'from young men's faces the bloom of the cheek/and from a dying boy [cutting] off a lock of hair with her left hand'. With Lucan, the witch had for the first – but by no means the last – time, become the enemy of humanity, to whom: 'Every human death is to her advantage'. Along the highway, she prises the corpses of criminals from their crosses, gnawing at their flesh, stealing the iron nails that held them in place, and draining off the 'black and putrid liquid' trickling through already stiffened limbs. If dead bodies are not available, then this witch would not scruple at murder, slitting the throat of the unwary traveller; or at infanticide, sacrificing foetuses 'on burning altars' should her 'funeral feast' demand 'still quivering organs.'[14] In Erictho – child slayer, grave robber and cannibal – we have, therefore, the archetype for the terrifying behaviour of the witch who so powerfully unsettled the imagination of late Mediaeval and Early Modern Europe. This is the woman who tramples and scorches 'the seeds of fertile corn/and with her breath corrupts the breezes not fatal before' knowing neither restraint nor anything of received morality. 'She does not pray to gods above nor with suppliant chant/ask help of heaven,' Lucan tells us. Rather it is her particular 'joy' to defile the altars of the gods; 'funeral flames with incense she has stolen from the kindled pyre.'[15] It is no large step of the imagination to replace the Classical pantheon with the notion of single Christian God, to use Lucan's poem as a sourcebook in the detection of witchcraft, and to transpose the witch's *modus operandi* from the first century CE to the sixteenth. In fact, this is precisely what many later demonologists, including Remy, Bodin and de Lancre, did, without ever really considering either the enormous cultural differences involved, or the nature of the literature itself.

Consequently, in the space of Book 6, of his *Civil War* – effectively some 410 lines of poetry, written during the reign of the Emperor Nero – Lucan succeeds in defining speech and behaviour of the witch figure that would come to dominate practically every major discussion of her malign influence, and now definitively maligned character, in the West for most of the next 2,000 years. Later developments, as we shall see, were very much variations upon an established theme. Where Circe had been a goddess, and Medea the daughter of a king, Erictho was a wretchedly poor woman, living in a stolen tomb, rather than a fabulous palace. Moreover, whereas both Circe and Medea had retained their essential humanity, as respectively successful and rejected lovers – who lived, breathed and felt as did other women – Erictho is a bundle of dirty rags, a creature of vice, who is completely divested of all sense of decency and worth. Thoroughly dehumanised, the only emotion she is capable of is blind hatred for the world, and for every creature within it.

Therefore, it was Lucan's witch, discovered among the rocks and crags of Thessaly with hundreds of her fellows, or found on her own, squatting upon a rock, in the midst of deserted fields and rifled graves – 'trying out words unknown ... shaping a spell for novel purposes' – that seems to have lent herself, perfectly, to Rosa's artistic conception. She can alter nature, cloud the sun, 'drench everywhere with rains', and raise tempests out at sea even when there were no winds. Furthermore, she is adept at love magic, making 'austere old men blaze with illicit flames' and drawing the unmarried to them 'by magic whirling of the twisted thread'. For the witch, Lucan writes in words amplified and yet rendered more crude and harsh by Rosa, 'the snake unfolds/his chilly circles and stretches out on frosty field and vipers' knots are wrenched apart and joined again.'[16] A satirical view of witchcraft is not being offered here – no matter what other points Lucan may have been choosing to make about the collapse of Republican virtue and politics – and the absence of humour from Rosa's paintings, in keeping with the view of witches taken in the *Civil War*, becomes all the more clear when we return to his single-figure studies.

The *Witch Preparing the Cup of Immortality*, painted c.1646–9, was conceived very much according to the Classical tradition. In the midst of her frenzied invocation, she thrashes a burning thyrsus branch overhead while offering up a glass bottle from which a small demonic figure rises. Crouched over a mirror, human bones, a torn parchment and a scattering of coins, her naked breasts sag and her belly is distended. Her grey, cropped hair is swept across her low forehead, while her features are more masculine than feminine. A few hardy stumps – all that remain of her teeth – are bared, as she shrieks out the words of her spell. Drugged, or already dead, an infant lies swaddled behind her, the sacrifice which will empower her invocation. In tone, and in terms of the magical apparatus which litters the floor of her cave, the painting is of a piece with the practices revealed by Rosa in his *The Witches' Sabbath*, while the figure of the witch echoes the attitude and physiognomy of the leading hag in *Incantations and Magic*. The same would seem to be true of his study of the *Witch* in the Capitoline Gallery, painted possibly as much as a decade later. In terms of its composition, it bears a certain resemblance to the depiction of the mysterious veiled figure to the left of the canvas in *The Witches' Sabbath*, with the wreath on the witch's brow and the magic circle of lighted candles at her feet, again in evidence. The inversion of conventional learning seems to be important: her gnarled, unshod toes clawing at the single sheet of parchment on the ground and her untutored fingers ponderously tracing out the letters and symbols in a spell book that she seems singularly ill-equipped to understand. Aged, heavily muscled and half-naked, the witch is once more defined by her pendulous breasts and ambiguous gender. Her masculine features, knitted together in a frown and a look of deep stupidity, give lie to any notion that this is a satire. Rather, we are being shown a peasant woman in the act of raising demons who scarcely realises what she is meddling with, or capable of achieving. Its companion piece, hung alongside it since 1750 – and probably long before that date – depicts a pikeman huddled against a mountainside before an uncertain dawn. If the two were intended by Rosa, from the start, to hang as pendants then their dramatic meaning is clear. The witch is raising the malignant spirits that will send the soldier to his death in the forthcoming battle.[17] While the earlier witchcraft paintings were meant to revel in their discovery of the occult and to preclude a straightforward interpretation, the Capitoline *Witch* is a study in the human tragedy that underpins *maleficia*. Demonic magic is destined both to rob a brave soldier of his mortal life and to destroy the immortal soul of the witch. The realisation of impending doom, written into the pikeman's gaze, and the witch's incomprehension of her own fate, lend the dual composition its poignancy. However, the reasons behind the soldier's destruction, the cause in which he serves, and the identity of the individuals who have employed the witch to seal his doom, are not shown. The power of the witch as a motif in art and literature lies in her mystery. If Rosa revealed everything to his audience, then the essential ingredients of fear, wonder and the danger of looking upon that which God and nature intended to be hidden would surely be lost.

When he returned to the subject one last time, in 1668, after more than 20 years since his first variation upon the theme, Rosa once again chose to imbue a story from the *Book of Kings* with a Classical, as opposed to a Judaic or even a recognisably Christian theme. Rather than attempting to reveal differences in culture and the understanding of witchcraft between the Judeo-Christian and Greco-Roman civilisations, he simply reworked several of his characteristic witchcraft motifs, already familiar to his audience through the earlier series of paintings. Thus, the cowering figure of King Saul is shown prostrating himself before the shade of the prophet Samuel, while the Witch of Endor lights her phial, and the by now stock figures of flailing skeletons, rotting ox heads and a winged strix, rise up from among the piles of bones stacked up in the corners of the witch's charnel house. Samuel, clutching his robes to him, with his solemn demeanour and toga-like shroud, has the aspect of a Roman senator, or Greek philosopher, as opposed to a Hebrew prophet. Portrayed in the same armour worn by his figurative studies of Alexander the Great, even King Saul is co-opted into the Classical rather than the Judeo-Christian world, while once again, the witch figure is defined by the masculinity and coarseness of her features and by the withering of her breasts. Amid this charnel house scene, the spirit of Samuel retains his composure and dignity in order to deliver his message directly to the witch, while Saul has lost all trace of his martial bearing or regality. Through his dealings with the Witch of Endor he has debased himself and thrown away his right to rule. Completed less than five years before the painter's death, *Saul and the Witch of Endor* serves as a coda and demonstrates that the symbols and drama of witchcraft remained part of the artist's repertoire throughout his career and were not abandoned, or downgraded in importance, once he had moved from Florence to Rome.

IV

Having considered the whole series of Rosa's witchcraft paintings, it is now worth considering the nature of his inspiration. Cabinet paintings of occult night-time scenes were very popular in Naples during the artist's youth, and a heightened interest in magic and witchcraft was maintained through the form of literature and the visual arts promoted by his own circle. He was certainly influenced by the studies of animal skeletons published by Filippo Napoletano, in 1620–1. Napoletano owned a museum of 'curiosities', which included shells and fossilised animals, as well as collections of bones and medical specimens. Napoletano was also fascinated by the occult, although sadly none of his own paintings on that theme have survived. For him, scientific enquiry had a moral dimension, but in seeking to understand the mystery of life, humanity also had to reckon with the even more powerful presence of death. The motto, printed on the frontispiece of his anatomical collection, asked the question, why: 'Deceitful Death, uncertain of your hour, why nevertheless are you given the charge of the hours?', echoed Rosa's own markedly pessimistic philosophical thoughts, and further recommended the studies to him. The anatomical studies were used as the primary reference work for Rosa's own paintings of skeletal animals and, in particular, that of the emaciated demon in *The Temptation of St Anthony*; the flapping corpse-birds rising to dominate the coven of witches in *Incantations and Magic*; and the razor-billed fiend that stares at the child sacrifice with hollowed-out eyes in *The Witches' Sabbath*. Such skeletal figures, closely based upon Napoletano's studies of anatomy and possibly, also, upon that artist's own lost images of witchcraft, appear in almost all of Rosa's subsequent witchcraft paintings, as a form of stock set-dressing.[18]

As subject matter, witchcraft was more usually associated with artists in Germany and the Low Countries than those in the Italian princely states. Furthermore, the comparatively infrequent and relatively mild nature of Italian witch trials suggests that Rosa would have had little first-hand experience of the crime. For both reasons, his interest in the witch is remarkable[19] He was clearly influenced by Dürer, whom he lionised and whose prints he copied and collected.[20] Yet, developments in the way that the witch had been viewed, in the years following the publication of Dürer's work, ensured that the image coarsened, lost the multiple layers of meaning previously attached to it, and became increasingly associated with malice, violence and carnality. In little more than the space of the century that separated Dürer from Rosa, the witch had been debased – even brutalised. The process of the debasement was assisted by Altdorfer and Cranach (discussed above) but it originated in the very workshop of Albrecht Dürer, not from the old master himself but from his friend and former pupil, Hans Baldung Grien.

Hans Baldung Grien was a man set apart in more ways than one. While most of his fellow apprentices hailed from solid artisan backgrounds, Grien came from a wealthy Swabian family. His father rose to the position of attorney for the Bishop of Strasbourg; one of his uncles became physician to Emperor Maximilian I; and his brother became Professor of Law at the University of Freiburg and later, an Imperial Councillor at the city of Speyer. After an initial apprenticeship with an unknown master in his native Swabia, he was articled to Dürer in 1503 and employed in his workshop for almost four years. During that time he was afforded considerable autonomy. A quick learner and an effective manager, he wholeheartedly adopted Dürer's graphical style, and distinguished himself as a painter, print-maker, and stained-glass window designer.[21] Striking out on his own, he completed a series of church altarpieces in Halle, before returning to Strasbourg in 1509 where he purchased citizenship and married a rich merchant's daughter. Wealthy and well connected, Baldung Grien moved to Freiburg, between 1512 and 1517, where he was so well remunerated for painting the high altarpiece of the cathedral that he was able to convert the payments to provide a lifelong annuity for himself and his wife. Though he continued to accept commissions from both Protestant and Roman Catholic princes, he was an early supporter of the Reformation and, in 1521, produced a famous woodcut of Martin Luther, his tonsured crown radiated by a nimbus of heavenly light and surmounted by a dove, conferring God's grace. In terms of hagiography, its success lay in deploying a conservative religious image in order to advance a revolutionary cause – an iconographic cleverness Baldung Grien deployed also in his works on witchcraft. Returning to Strasbourg, he and his wife forged a successful business partnership in the 1520s, dealing in loans and property. By 1533 he was a leading guild officer and by his death in 1545, a town councillor.[22]

Sadly, Baldung Grien left few writings and no surviving letters, making it difficult to establish a clear picture of his character and interests.[23] Yet, what is apparent is his threefold obsession with sex, death and violence, seen across all of his corpus, and not least in his witchcraft works. Between 1510 and 1544, he produced nine studies of witchcraft and *maleficia* that appeared to endorse and follow on from Dürer. However, in reality they debase and brutalise his master's conception and form. Baldung Grien's images of witchcraft show the detailed workings of harmful magic, with his witches primarily depicted as being engaged in raising tempests and hailstorms in order to visit death upon men and cattle. They are also exclusively female, and witches are always nude. There was harmful magic shown in art depicting witchcraft before Baldung Grien, but in his works it is separated from its Classical origins and forcefully grafted onto the forests and rocky outcrops of Germania.

Nowhere is this more apparent than in his 1513 woodcut *The Three Fates*. The Classical goddesses who respectively spun, measured and cut the lifelines of every man, woman and child, have been recast as the denizens of a German forest, propping themselves up against the roots of moss-covered trees and stumps in order to practise their rites. The women are of different ages; the youngest spins the yarn and offers the distaff to a plump, bonneted matron, who measures the length of twine to be cut by a hatchet-faced old hag who severs it with a heavy pair of shears. A child playing at their feet plucks a flower as easily, and as thoughtlessly, as they conspire to end a life. The distaff juts up like a phallus, and the strings of rotten vegetation dripping from the branches and the bark of the tree suggests casual indifference to the sufferings of mankind.[24]

Three years earlier his *Witches' Sabbath* had brought together the idea of the fully demonised Judeo-Christian witch and the earlier, Classical witch to devastating effect. This was one of the earliest prints issued by Baldung Grien from his independent studio in Strasbourg, and it is also the first to carry both the date and the artist's own 'G' monogram. In this, he would seem to be consciously echoing Dürer's *Four Witches*, revisiting the theme and appropriating the commercial branding of his erstwhile master, in order to declare his own artistic maturity and independence. It would seem that the witch had become a standard subject for German artists and the successful reimagining of her form was something that every aspiring master would have to attempt if he wished to be taken seriously by his peers. Thus, in publishing *The Witches' Sabbath*, in 1510, Baldung Grien was announcing his arrival upon the cultural scene. Moreover, in producing the woodcut as a chiaroscuro, he was not only evoking a sketch of Albrecht Altdorfer's that he had probably seen in Dürer's workshop but was also endeavouring to break new ground. The witch, just like the technology behind the dissemination of her image, was the signifier of all that was new, fresh and, above all, challenging.

Recently, a number of art historians have attempted to link Baldung Grien's interest in witchcraft to the Dominican Johann Geiler von Kayserberg, whose sermons the artist may well have heard or known in their published form, *Die Emeis* ('The Ant Colony'). It has even been suggested that his images of witchcraft were conceived as attempts to illustrate its texts.[25] This approach sees Baldung Grien within a Humanist, and largely sceptical, tradition.[26] Such scholars posit that his paintings thus make 'fun of witchcraft and the obsessive belief in witches.'[27] But this is to misunderstand Geiler. He believed that night flight was delusional but devil-prompted, writing that witches

> ride back and forth and nevertheless stay in one place, but they believe they are riding, for the devil is capable of making an apparition in their minds that is a fantasy, which they interpret in no other way than they ride everywhere ... the influence of witches or of the sorcerer is not really the cause of the work which comes to pass ... the devil does it and not they.

Consequently,

> what the witches do is merely a sign and not the true cause. Consider an example, then you will understand: A Witch wants to make a storm or hail. She takes a broom and plunges it into a stream and, with the broom, throws some water backwards over her head, and then the hail comes. Throwing water behind oneself and speaking

the word, that doesn't make any hail. But the devil, when he sees and hears the signs, rides up to the skies and the winds, and he makes the storm.[28]

Geiler's theory of witchcraft actually reinforces rather than denies the efficacy of the demonic pact. He believes in the interior process of the witch as petitioner, in the Devil's use of delusion and in a sympathetic magic dependent upon demonic agency. Furthermore, Geiler preached that witches were indeed present within the community and they should be punished with death. He cannot accurately be cast as a 'liberal' in the modern sense, as has been suggested nor can he be properly seen as the reason state-sponsored witch trials did not penetrate Strasbourg.

However, the greatest single stumbling block to the argument that links the expression of witchcraft through Geiler's words to Baldung Grien's art, was the fact that while the artist was commissioned to illustrate no less than six of the theologian's books of sermons, between 1510 and 1522, in 1513 he was passed over for the job of illustrating 'The Ant Colony'. As he was the foremost illustrator of witchcraft in his home city of Strasbourg, it is improbable that he would have been overlooked for the commission if his vision echoed Geiler's. His approach was different, and simpler. Where Dürer's *Melancholia I* and *The Knight, Death and the Devil* seem to illustrate internal, philosophical malaises, Baldung Grien's work never suggests such complexities. *The Witches' Sabbath* was largely a means of making money. After his first flush of success, he gained few major contracts for paintings, so he concentrated upon mass-producing woodcuts, experimenting with chiaroscuro as a means of printing cheaply and effectively in colour. *The Witches' Sabbath* was the first and most startling result of this endeavour. It was also a way to stake his claim to artistic vision: an exposition of, rather than a counterblast to, the belief in witches.

V

The Witches' Sabbath assails our senses, packing vivid occultist detail and riotous imagery into every grain and corner of the fabric of the page. No space is left empty, as dying trees, cooking pots, goats, fires, bones and a stolen cardinal's hat jostle for space. At the centre of the action, three witches – one young, one middle-aged and one elderly – are quite literally brewing up a storm. Their power is reinforced by three long roasting spits, laid across each other to form a triangle, in which the dominant, middle-aged witch crouches. All are naked, and their very bodies defy nature, their hair streaming against the direction of the wind. Above the group, a witch traverses the night sky, mounted backwards on a goat, carrying a long spit, which holds a cooking pot containing a noxious stew made up from animal bones, while behind them is a fifth sister. A cat whose tail protrudes between his own and the lead witch's rump suggests both the Devil and the witch's own dehumanisation. She, too, is a mere creature, an animal. The storms of fire and hail that fly out of the cooking pot, cradled between her thighs, could as easily be discharged from her genitals in a demonic spasm of lubricants, bodily fluids and menstrual blood. Her elderly companion throws up her tattered shawl to reveal barren breasts, holding up a dish filled with the corpses of baby birds. Above another cooking pot, three suggestively phallic sausages sizzle over the spit, while a depilatory brush stands upright among the stones and carcasses.[29]

There is nothing of cynicism or ridicule evident; rather, it looks to be an image about masculine anxieties over death, disaster and sexual potency. In all, the witches are intent upon activating the lust of women and establishing the female as the dominant sexual partner. As Charles Zika has pointed out, the title commonly ascribed to the print is something of a misnomer.[30] We are not witnessing a 'Black Sabbath', with the parodying of Christian rites; this image is all about female, as opposed to demonic power. The witches are harnessing, or more accurately, perverting, the elements – in this case castration or unsexing – as indicated by the sausages. The spell's victim is being blasted skywards, legs flailing and mouth open in mid-scream. The cod-Hebraic script engraved upon the pot, may be bringing in an anti-Semitic strand, linking the demonised Jew with the demonised witch.[31] Certainly, his altarpieces and crucifixions are populated with unflattering caricatures of Jewish people that are wholly absent from his master, Dürer's work. If we want an illustrated companion to Kramer, Sprenger, Bodin, Remy, de Lancre and Del Rio, we could do no better than to look to Baldung Grien.

During his stay in Freiburg in 1514, Baldung Grien drew two more images, both also known as *The Witches' Sabbath*. These follow a similar conception. In both, he uses the same triangular formation, and for the ritual he again uses cooking spits and human bones. In the sketch, now preserved in the Louvre, one of the witches fellates herself with a skewer on which the three drooping sausages, or severed penises, are pinned. A vomiting cat is echoed by the witch's streaming anus or vulva. The two main witches pull at a cord or necklace, decorated with dice and shrunken heads, that effectively link death with chance. A hag pats one of the fat and drooping penises, her mouth a toothless cavern of lust. In the sketch kept in the Albertina Gallery in Vienna, the main features are repeated, right down to the bones, the cats and the scrappily written incantations. However, this time, a flying crone appears to be pushing the youngest witch out of the apex of the triangle. Her two companions indulge in mutual masturbation, an act apparently central to the spell. One is intently rubbing her fingers in between her thighs; while her friend appears to have achieved a state of ecstasy by fellating the forked end of the turning spit and, at the moment of climax, throwing her cooking pot upwards.

The difference between these two images and that produced four years earlier was that – as far as we know – these were intended for private consumption. They never seem to have made it as far as being cut as wood blocks in his own studio, though they were well enough known for Urs Graf to see them and to copy them for himself. They may have been intended as smutty in-jokes passed between friends or, more likely, as an elite and highly accomplished, exercise in producing pornography that was intended to stimulate anger and fear as the secret mechanism for unlocking auto-erotic pleasure. The guilt often associated with masturbation may also have found an unnatural partner in the alienated figure of the witch. A forbidden practice lent itself to thoughts of forbidden arts and pleasures.

This may well have been the case with the 1513–14 New Year's card that Baldung Grien sent to the canon or choirmaster at Freiburg cathedral.[32] Three witches are positioned at each corner of a triangle, again for weather magic. This time, however, the pornographic and misogynist content dominates. The nearest witch to us is seen from behind, bent double and in a pose of surprised supplication towards the other two, who straddle her. The crone touches her rump while casting her eyes lasciviously over her form. The younger witch mounts her back with one foot while stimulating her own clitoris with one hand and raising the storm-raising pot with her right. The two dominant witches may intend to masturbate or urinate over their submissive sister, so the flaming vessel may simply be a chamber pot.[33] Whichever it was, it is safe to say Baldung Grien's priestly friend had more on his mind than his religious vows. All three Freiburg sketches are ribald pornography, but even so, there is no playfulness about their art, nor does the artist indicate any cynicism about the efficacy of witch spells. Rather, the sketches link female lust with moral deviancy and murder. They only reinforce the conclusion that Baldung Grien saw a woman's charms and reproductive power as ruinously polluting. This is a world away from Dürer's notion that it was lust and the act of consensual sex that speeded up the ageing process and occasioned death. The flight of time and the transience of all human emotions is less significant, in Grien's eyes, than the moment of the realisation of lust. That the act of love is also so degraded and brutalised, and that the fault for this seems to lie squarely with the female form and character, makes violence towards women – whether verbal, physical or sexual – far more acceptable than it was before.

The Reformation, if not providing the rationale behind the 'witchcraze' certainly did alter the way art was owned and viewed.[34] Private, secular patrons increasingly wished for smaller, more intimate scenes, with which to decorate their homes, salons or cabinets. From the 1520s, Baldung Grien produced a series of such allegorical nudes, sometimes identified with the witch figure or with melancholia. These permitted him to explore themes of female hygiene, sexual curiosity and self-awareness, in a fairly salacious manner. In several 1515 panels, probably painted for the so-called 'Nudities Room' at the court of the Margrave Christoph I of Baden in Basle, young women angle convex mirrors to view either their breasts or genitals.[35] In a surviving copy of his *Women's Bath with a Mirror*, preserved at Karlsruhe, he depicts three women emerging after their ablutions to view themselves in a convex mirror. As in the case of Dürer's *Women's Bathhouse* and the anonymous *Der Liebeszauber*, they are being covertly watched, this time by a plump matriarch. The youngest dusts her pubic hair with a depilatory brush – echoing the print of 1510 – while her companion looks into the mirror, to pin up her hair. The third, and old, woman clips a sliver of gold from the rim of the dish upon which the mirror sits. She may be engaged in a theft and malfeasance that goes ignored because of the girls' preoccupation with their own appearance. Female beauty is masking deeper corruption.

His *Weather Witches*, also known as the *Two Witches*, painted in Strasbourg in 1523, was probably commissioned by Christoph I of Baden. Two witches are naked, the younger staring out invitingly. She draws back a veil to reveal a companion squatting on a goat and holding up a jar containing an imprisoned dragon or homunculus. At the back, a child lifts up a lighted brazier which ignites the storm clouds to blot out the sun. Thus, the allure of the young witch masks the destructive and demonic aims of the group. The most recent scholarly treatment of the work has tried to reposition it as 'witch-tolerant' on account of the presence of a goat, who, rather than flying, is firmly pinioned under the leading witch. The improbability of flight on the back of such a skinny little creature has been attributed to Geiler's sermons about the delusory nature of witchcraft.[36] Moreover, it is proposed that it conveys anxiety about the outbreak of syphilis at the court of the Margrave of Baden, rather than about witches.[37] In the eyes of the present author, this is unlikely. It is too obtuse and nuanced a meaning for cabinet painting, and moreover one which clearly follows a depiction of witchcraft common to all of Baldung Grien's work on the subject.

Two full decades would pass before he would revisit the subject of witchcraft. *The Bewitched Stable Groom* was published as a woodcut print in 1544, just a few months before his death. In Baldung Grien's last major work, an unfortunate groom lies unconscious at the threshold of a stable, victim to the elderly witch leering in at the window. It is unclear whether he has been floored by the stallion or by the witch – or by her bewitchment of the animal. It is probable, however, that we are meant to assume that the groom has just received a sharp kick from the hind legs of the horse and has lost his senses, which allows the witch to steal in to set fire to the roof beams. A preparatory chalk drawing for the prostrate groom survives, and shows that he was originally to have dropped a broad gentleman's hat, rather than the tools of his trade; also, that his clothing was cheapened in the final print.[38] Attempts have been made to link his features with portraits of Baldung Grien in middle age. While one bearded man may look much like another, the shield on the wall bearing the unicorn crest of the Baldung family is more definitive. Whether or not the witch is a product of his unconscious dream, it seems reasonable to venture that Baldung Grien intended to focus attention upon a malaise – whether physical or psychological – under which he was himself labouring. Academics have tended to focus upon his fears regarding impotence, and the challenge to patriarchy, given the prominence of the fallen man's codpiece. It certainly suggests that, despite outward show, all was not well within the artist's household. The distempers popularly associated with witchcraft had visited themselves upon the once supremely self-confident portrayer of witches. Moreover, when we look at both the horse and the stable, we can perceive similarities with treatises on the *Taming of the Passions* that Baldung Grien would have known and did indeed seek to illustrate. His own series of woodcuts, published in 1536 and based upon these themes, depict wild horses fighting and tearing at each other in the woods. Once again, it is the outpouring of animal anger rather than its sublimation through the operation of human reason that interests the artist. Furthermore, it has been argued that the woodcut took Varro's satire *Eumenides*, which explored the nature of anger and madness, as its point of departure. There are certainly similarities between the image and the text. Varro, in the first surviving fragment of his writings, declares that 'nor will the groom who exercises the horses ever lead out a wild Damacrine colt since the groom is insane from the very disturbance of disease'. In a second fragment, the author envisages the 'third of the Furies, Infamy, standing striving in the crowd with loose flowing breast, uncut hair, soiled garb [and] severe mien.'[39] It is conceivable that Baldung Grien's witch is based upon this Fury, who embodies the spirit of punishment, afflicting the mind and causing insanity. In the eyes of the stoics, whom he had once tried so hard to emulate, madness was seen as the result of a simple failure of man to contain his emotions. It is, therefore, significant that in *The Bewitched Stable Groom*, rather than breaking the passionate stallion, the untamed horse has finally broken his master. Instead of promoting a rationalistic, Humanistic project, Baldung Grien – like his horse – kicks against it. He asserts that his own lust and violence, and those of men in general, cannot ultimately be bridled. Therefore, his witch embodies an anger born out of sexual desire, folly and a violence stemming from fear.

VI

Baldung Grien did not have a sceptical, rationalist position on witchcraft; on the contrary, his works were vital to the spread of witch-belief. It seems clear that his witch is the one that became Rosa's witch. Baldung Grien's, and not Dürer's image of the witch was the one that became the standard one. Just as demonologists built their work upon that of previous authorities, and new academic treatises re-enforced without justifying the impression of that which had gone before, so too did the work of artists creating layer upon layer of imagery that stressed the physical reality and developing stereotype of the witch. Thus, by the time that Rosa came to paint his canvasses, the witch had been fashioned – and refashioned – by a large number of painters, of printers and engravers, located primarily in Germany and the Low Countries. The Dutch Republic, in particular, possessed two things required in order to reinvigorate the market for witchcraft paintings. First, it was characterised by an exceptionally open and tolerant society, by seventeenth-century standards, in which occult themes could be explored and discussed in an atmosphere of relative openness; and second, it had an affluent mercantile class, capable of affording and commissioning artworks to hang at home for their private enjoyment. As a consequence, a number of leading Dutch artists – such as Jacques de Gheyn II (1565–1629), David Teniers the Younger (1610–90) and David Ryckaert III (1616–61) – produced many works of witches and witchcraft.

Rosa's skeletal and decaying demons, and monstrous carnivorous toads, take their conception directly from the works of de Gheyn and Ryckaert. In particular, the anthropomorphic canvasses which were the speciality of Cornelis Saftleven (1607–81) provided scores of tumbling, winged demons, crooked fiends and razor-billed birds, which on the one hand harked back to the biblical visions of Hieronymus Bosch and, on the other prefigured the more secularised nightmares of Salvator Rosa. In part, they were intended as allegory, or as a simple satire offered as social comment at the time of the Thirty Years' War, when much of Europe appeared to be unravelling. Thus, in a canvas of 1629, which pre-empts George Orwell's corrosive dystopias, an army of animals carrying banners and clubs appears to have taken over a farm.[40] In a later canvas, catalogued somewhat misleadingly as *The Witches' Sabbath*, three stout witches – one riding a white goat and bearing distaff – charge into a cave mouth, frightening away a demonic host. In the background, three more witches inscribe a magical circle in the sand, in order to raise storms. One of them raises a bony, naked arse towards the demons in flatulent defiance.[41]

These witches are fully in charge of the situation; the mistresses of the demons rather than their slaves. Yet, the image when taken as a whole appears to be a compound of different styles and messages regarding witchcraft. The storm-raising coven owes its inspiration to Grien and Urs Graf, while the butterfly wings and reptilian scales of the demons are more than a little indebted to the sketch books of Jacques de Gheyn II. The coarseness of the women's peasant features echoes the studies of Teniers the Younger, with the flattened nose, sunken mouth and deadpan stare of the witch riding the goat seeming to be taken directly from Teniers', much-copied, canvas of *The Witch* painted in the 1630s.[42] However, where Saftleven does depart from his peers is in his refusal to offer an explicit value judgement about the crime of witchcraft. There is no sense in *The Witches' Sabbath* that damnation is the sure-fire price that these women will pay in the next life for their transgressions in this; and, in fact, in banishing the ghouls and demons to the margins, they might even be performing a peculiar form of service to humanity. The artist has removed himself from the action and is acting as an observer rather than as a strict commentator upon events.

Saftleven's most original contribution to the genre, and the work that most clearly caught Rosa's interest and influenced his art, was *The Witches' Tavern*. Surprisingly, considering its quality and importance, this painting has largely failed to register on the academic radar. It is not catalogued in the only modern reference work on the artist, and is not discussed or illustrated in Jane P. Davidson's otherwise comprehensive study of *The Witch in Northern Art*. Such an omission is unjustified, as this canvas reveals a detailed and striking portrayal of the working of magic in a purely domestic setting. The dice, tumblers, scattered playing cards and abandoned sword familiar to us through Rosa's *The Witches' Sabbath* are in evidence, and a hand of power burns brightly above the chimney breast, as a familiar reads a grimoire to his demonic companions, and a naked devil stretches out, curling his talons and warming his feet on the blazing fire. The purpose of the spells that have just been cast is revealed by the presence of two witches, swirling above on their broomsticks, one disappearing into, and one emerging from, the chimney. The message? Hearth and home are not safe from the witch who finds the weak points in a building; she can steal into the very heart of the family.

VII

It is precisely this array of magical artefacts that formed for Rosa the tools of the witch's trade. Like Saftleven, Rosa was an innovator in that he sketched in oils directly from nature. He did so not to better observe the rhythms of the countryside, but to improve his handling of paint. Thus, Rosa's landscapes, despite their Arcadian grandeur, are harshly alien places. This is only accentuated when a witch is added to the scene. We may well ask if Rosa painted these scenes to order, but this was emphatically not the case. We know that it was Rosa himself who chose these themes, and was firm about his right to choose his subject matter.[43] He had repeatedly refused to be tied to one single patron. His stubborn individualism would later endear him to the Victorian *literati*, but in reality hit Rosa hard in the pocket and compelled him to market his wares creatively. Thus he turned his studio into a show-room where wealthy clients might visit (but not haggle), and he made a point of putting his works into big public exhibitions twice a year. He worked to stay in the public eye and to create a climate of celebrity and controversy around himself.

In 1646, Carlo de' Rossi paid him 15 doubloons in order to produce a canvas from his workshop. Rosa had determined that the subject should be *The Witches' Sabbath* but in later years, he wished to buy it back. It was his own conception and passion that had fuelled the project, and with the passage of time he regretted that he had ever let another possess it or permitted its setting to be restaged. He ruefully esti-mated that its value had risen tenfold, on account of the aura that Rossi had created about it, hiding it behind a silk curtain at his house in Rome and only revealing it, at suitably dramatic moments and with all due ceremony, to close friends and visiting dignitaries.[44] If the paintings stood alone, then dismissive conjectures might still be justified: we could argue that the painter had intended them to shock and nothing more. However, Rosa was also the author of a poem called *La Strega* (*The Witch*) that was composed in Florence, between 1646 and 1647, and later set to music.[45] Phyllis, a spurned lover, is drawn on through the woods by the Goddess Aphrodite. Calling out into the night, she begs spirits to grant her redress against the 'indifferent lover' who has ruined her life. Like Medea long before, she utters her baleful curse:

I'm attempting magical methods,
blasphemous notes,
different herbs, and knots,
whatever can stop the celestial wheels,
magic circle,
icy waves,
various fishes,
chemical water,
black balms,
mixed dust,
mystical stones,
snakes and noctules,
putrid blood,
flabby bowels,

dry mummies,
bones and small worms,
fumigation,
that blackens,
horrible voices,
that frighten,
cloudy lymph,
that poisons,
fetid drops,
that infect,
that darken,
that freeze,
that rot,
that slay,
that win
the Stygian waves.[46]

The final verse, excluded from Cesti's score, brings Phyllis to the very gates of Hell, where she works her charm:

I will make a black ghost
burn a cypress, a myrtle,
and while, a little at a time,
I will melt his image made of wax,
with a mysterious fire
I will make his real image die,
and while the fake one is burning, the real one is also.
Perhaps in this way, this deceived beauty
with magic vigour
will extinguish for me the cruel one that still lives,
will revive for me the dead hope.
Because the cruel one doesn't hear me,
because he doesn't value my tears,
deceit, deceit,
dishonour, dishonour
incantation, incantation,
and the one who didn't move the sky, move Acheron.[47]

It is worth emphasising that 'the evil one' is the lover, not the Devil. It attests to psychological, rather than preternatural, tension. There is no recognisably Christian element in the entire work; its themes are taken from Classical paganism, and it is the power of Strygian Hell that is able to disgorge its fiery rivers against the lover. And just as in Rosa's canvasses, it is desire and love that motivate the witch's curse, not a desire to ruin crops, men and cattle. Thus Phyllis's incantation accurately reflects many of the charms allegedly recited by witches, according to Northern Italian court records. Margarita Chiappona was one such, to cite but a single example. She was brought before a judge in Modena, where she confessed that she had prayed to St Martha to send

> branches of fire and flame ... through the veins of the heart, of the head, of the lungs, through the marrow of the bones, the flesh of the legs, with such love that it beats and scourges, so that for my love he should suffer incessantly ... For love of me, take away from him drink, food, sleep, [and] power that he might walk, nor have relations with any woman, until he should come to me to satisfy all my desire and do all that which I will ask of him.

Another example is the woman we know just as Barbara who told the Venetian Inquisition, in 1627, that she had made a spell for reconciliation with her former lover, Alvise Foscari, in which she had used snakes, burning brands, sharpened swords, and a heart wrenched from a living body.[48] Living in such a world, Rosa's *maleficia* was prompted by lovelorn desperation rather than the wiles of the Devil.

Exploring these themes, even through oil paint and verse, did however carry risk. Rembrandt's teacher, Jacob Isaacsz, had been censured by the Roman Inquisition in 1608 for painting an image of a group of 'dancing witches' and selling it in a stall next to the church of Santa Maria della Carità, though his Jewish lineage may have played a part in his persecution. The Dutch artist, Jacob van Swanenbergh was brought before the Inquisition in Naples on the charge that he had exhibited a witchcraft scene. When cross-examined, he wisely chose to play dumb and testified that his works were mere copies of compositions by other artists, which had been commissioned for the household of the Viceroy of Naples. He had no notion of the symbolism he painted, knew nothing about the activities of witches, and had never had cause to know one, personally. Even so, it was with some difficulty that he was eventually released from prison and his paintings were lost, or more likely destroyed by the Inquisition. Significant for us, however, was the description of the themes of his canvasses, which match those beloved of Rosa. There were paintings of witches brandishing torches, sitting astride demons, skeletons and dragons, and stealing babies from the cradle (that clearly influenced Rosa) alongside other motifs drawn from the Northern Renaissance – witches flying through the air and emerging from the chimney pots of houses – that were absent from his art. It would seem that Rosa consciously rejected some elements present in Germanic portrayals of witchcraft – Cranach's night flights, in particular – in favour of those attested to in Italian trials. He conversely rejected the Southern paradigm of the witch as the beautiful Circe, in favour of the Northern vision of the haggard crone – such as Erictho – to be found in the works of Baldung Grien. Furthermore, the last-ditch defence used by van Swanenbergh before the Inquisition – that he painted witches merely as 'jokes' to amuse and to show folly – suggests that the dismissal of witchcraft paintings as knowing satire was a means of devaluing them, then as well as now.[49]

Where van Swanenbergh and Isaacsz were fortunate, however, was in the nature of the Inquisition in the Italian city states. The centralisation of its powers in Naples, Venice and Rome ensured that limits were placed on the use of torture and coercion in order to extract confessions, and shifted the focus of trials away from learned conceptions of *maleficia* and back towards popular beliefs in magic being employed for divination and treasure seeking. This almost certainly saved the lives of the two artists and permitted them to return to their professions. However, even if Rosa's witchcraft paintings did not directly lead him into the path of the Inquisition, then his unconventional lifestyle eventually did. In 1655, at approximately the time he was working on his single-figure study of the *Witch*, an anonymous informer told the Roman Inquisition that he was living with his mistress, Lucrezia. Fearing the repercussions, Rosa packed Lucrezia and their son off to Naples to stay with his family, unaware that the plague had once more broken out there. The child died and Rosa, in his grief, wrote that all of his hardships came 'from being afraid of running into some misfortune in prison or into some damned cuckold of a spy from the Holy Office'.[50] He quietly retreated from further examination of the occult. It might be that by the early 1650s he had exhausted all he had to say on the subject, or it could be that he found it too dangerous a subject to continue to pursue in the public arena.

What cannot be doubted was that Rosa's view of witchcraft was undoubtedly his own: driven by fear, by a knowledge of human passion, and by the hatreds born out of a hopeless, unrequited, love. It reflected trends that were well documented in the records of the Italian law courts of the time, and was neither credulous nor irrational, nor to be intended as a simple satire. The belief in the magical arts did not merely survive into the Early Modern period, but was consciously revived as part of the Humanist movement. It was, therefore, not surprising that educated and enquiring Italians, such as Rosa, were prepared to countenance the efficacy of its practice in both Classical and contemporary cultures. We know that Rosa was familiar with hermetic writings and did not fear inversion of societal norms and of the established social order. Instead, he rejoiced at Masaniello's revolution in Naples, though he preferred to cheer it on from a safe distance, rather than actually participating in the struggle. It was corruption itself that was Rosa's main target, and it seemed to him that there was no greater corruption in society than that of witchcraft. Although he shared with Francisco Goya a common sense of purpose to educate and to censure 'human errors and vices', that is where the similarity between these two great illustrators of magical rites begins and ends. Unlike Goya, Rosa was convinced of the efficacy of the emotions and base desires that underpinned the crime of witchcraft. We should make no mistake that the claws of Rosa's strix-like owls really were intended to tear, to torture and to kill.

CHAPTER SIX

Little Sister Jeanne of the Angels

I

Balthazar de Monconys, servant of the king, stopped at Loudon in order to admire the sights. For, although by 1645, the city had lost its protective ring of Mediaeval walls, along with much of its former prosperity, it still retained considerable charm for the sightseer and more than a little notoriety for the curious. Tales of demonic possession of the nuns at the Ursuline Convent, of their public exorcisms; of the pact made between the Jesuit priest, Urbain Grandier and the Devil; his trial; sensational confession and subsequent execution, had been the subject of more than 50 books and pamphlets, between 1634 and 1638.[1] Miracles had been performed, the voice of the Devil heard, and demons cast out. Cardinal Richelieu, King Louis XIII, the senior members of government, church and royal family had followed the case almost day by day, delighting in the seemingly watertight proofs that an age of miracles had not yet passed.

The possession had centred upon Sister Jeanne des Anges, the Mother Superior of the Convent, who had achieved the status of a celebrity following the 'banishment' of her demons: Leviathan, Aman, Iscaron, Balam, Asmodaeus and Behemoth. She had proven her fortitude, become associated with the working of miracles – particularly through helping women, including the queen, through difficult child births – and had been marked by a stigmata on her left hand, which recorded the 'sacred names' of *IESUS, MARIA, JOSEPH* and *F.D. SALLES*. She had toured France to great acclaim in 1638, been received at the Royal Court and had shown her hand 'sculpted by the Devil' to crowds of thousands – straining it in the process, so that it had to be placed upon a little cushion, in order that she might display her wounds more easily from her window, as they passed. The Princess de Condé had lauded her sanctity – treating her as a living holy relic – and Queen Anne had held her hand 'more than an hour, admiring the thing that had never been seen since the beginnings of the Church'.[2] The king had vouched that his own faith had been greatly strengthened by the sight, while Cardinal Richelieu – though, perhaps, more measured – considered her scars to be 'admirable'.

The Convent at Loudun was re-endowed by new and plentiful benefactors, and the rich and gifted daughters of noblemen clamoured to take the veil and devote their lives to the service of God, under the spiritual direction of Sister Jeanne. Pilgrims flocked to the city and the Mother Superior's autobiography became a bestseller; serving to keep the memory of her sufferings and eventual triumph alive. Dictated in 1642, the book enabled the faithful to read of her deliverance from the clutches of the Devil, of the appearance of her 'good angel' – who still confided in her – and of St Joseph, who appeared to her in a vision to touch her and to heal her pain.

Sister Jeanne had delighted in her unexpected fame. Yet, by the time Balthazar de Monconys came to call upon her, on the morning of 8 May 1645, her career seemed to be stalling. There were no new miracles, the streams of would-be acolytes and hopeful petitioners had turned into a sorry trickle, and her own claims to sanctity now scarcely seemed strong enough to secure her mention in the official church histories, let alone to gain her eventual beatification.

Alone in her cell, in the dead watches of night, she was becoming used to the idea that, after all, there might not be a 'St Jeanne of Loudun' to sit upon the right-hand side of the Lord until Judgement Day. There were some who already whispered that the priest, Grandier, had been falsely accused. More troublingly, it could not be denied that one of her exorcists, Father Tranquille, had lost his mind and that another, Father Barré, had been exposed as a fraud and sent to jail. For his own part, de Monconys – as a professional lawyer, a habitual traveller and a man of letters – was interested enough to seek her out and to ask to examine her hand. A decade after her original possession, the hunch-backed nun appeared older than her 40 years, and expressed surprise when the visitor to her cell suddenly ran his nail up the length of her exposed arm and 'with a light touch ... removed the leg of the M [for *MARIA*]'. While the Mother Superior spluttered her indignation and, for once, was lost for words, the courtier took his leave of her and swept out of the convent, satisfied with what he had come to see.[3]

II

There can be little doubt that Sister Jeanne was a deeply troubled, and troubling, individual. The daughter of an aristocrat, she had ruined her life chances by dislocating her shoulder in childhood, in an effort to prevent a fall, that ensured 'that ever after her body was somewhat twisted, with one shoulder higher than the other'.[4] Her disability was seen, even by her, as a 'disgrace' and she was packed off, as little more than an infant, to be raised in a succession of convents. She suffered from 'fainting spells' as a child and adolescent, and entered the Ursuline Order as a novice, at Poitiers, in 1622, at the age of 17. The Ursulines were a relatively new Order, founded in 1592–4, with a remit to establish themselves in often harsh and seemingly unprofitable areas, and Sister Jeanne seems to have set her heart upon joining the Convent at Loudun, upon its creation in 1625–7. Significantly, she was sufficiently reflexive to record the manner in which she was prepared to mirror the wishes or beliefs of her superiors, moulding herself, her behaviour and character, in order that she might be 'capable of surpassing the others in all sorts of company.'[5]

The case of witchcraft at Loudun began with the visions of a young nun, Sister Marthe, one of the girls who boarded and received her education at the convent. In the early hours of 22 September 1632, an apparition – or, as Pierre Barré already styled it, an 'evil spirit' – appeared before Sister Marthe

> in the form of a man of the Church, cloaked in a large coat and soutane, holding in his hand a book covered with white parchment; and holding it open, showed her two pictures, and after having conversed with her somewhat of said book, attempted to force her to take it. The which she refused, saying that she would never receive a book save from her Mother Superior, and the said spectre fell silent and remained awhile weeping at the foot of her bed.[6]

Sister Marthe thought that it might be a soul rotting in purgatory and thought to pray for it, running to tell her Mother Superior of the encounter, in clear terror. At this point, Sister Jeanne now sought to own the experience of the younger nun, explaining that she had heard the spectre begging her to say prayers for its soul. Then, two days later

> during the hour from six to seven of the evening, in the refectory, there appeared another spectre in the form of a globe, all black, that went and threw Sister Marthe violently to the ground, and said prioress [i.e. Jeanne] onto a chair, taking each one by the shoulders; at the same time two other nuns felt their legs struck, where red contusions the size of testons [a small coin] remained for eight days.[7]

Within 48 hours, the vision had shifted from that of a suffering Christian soul – the staple of late Mediaeval and Early Modern ghost stories – to that of a malignant spirit, and with its attack upon the group of nuns while they ate, it was Sister Jeanne who was singled out for the most vicious attack. Thereafter, Sister Marthe fades from view, doing little to shape or drive the narratives of possession. Indeed, she was the last of the eight nuns to be exorcised and then of only a single demon, whereas four of the others had between two and four demons, and Sister Jeanne and Claire de

Saint-Jean, a lay member and niece to Cardinal Richelieu, were both held to be possessed of seven demons.[8]

The Mother Superior, who might ordinarily have been expected to take her House in hand and restore order, effectively set the tone for the alleged possessions, by intensifying hysteria. Thus, Father Barré and Father Mignon recorded that the nuns

> told us that for the entire rest of the month there had not been one night without great agitation, damage and terror. And even when they did not see anything, they often heard voices calling out to one another. Some were punched with fists, some slapped, some felt themselves being prompted to immoderate and involuntary laughter.[9]

Yet, the catalyst for action and the calling-in of outside authorities, once again came from Sister Jeanne, who felt that an invisible hand had pushed 'three thorns of a hawthorn' into her own palm.

She determined to burn the thorns in the presence of the leading Capuchin father in the city, but sadly this proved to offer no remedy.[10] On 5 October 1632, the first attempt to exorcise the nuns took place, accompanied by screams not held to be their own, obscene laughter, and growls signifying the presence within the women of the 'Enemy of God' and 'the wicked one'. Then, we are told, having been commanded to leave Sister Jeanne, 'after much violence, vexation, howling, gnashing of teeth, of which two back ones were broken, he [i.e. the demon] finally left [the] said prioress in great peace'. There the story should have ended, as Sister Jeanne 'declared that she was cured of a strong suffering of spirit and great beating of the heart, and thought she was perfectly cured'. However, despite sleeping well, she and 'the other exorcised nuns showed a great repugnance at holy communion, and when they were ordered to get ready for it, the devils began their vexation, agitation and benumbling'. Exorcism begat further – largely futile – exorcism, with the sufferings of the nuns turning into an increasingly public spectacle.

Thomas Killigrew – the future English Royalist, playwright and diplomat – penned a graphic account of Sister Jeanne convulsing during a church service. 'As she lay on her back', he wrote:

> she bent her waist like a tumbler and went so, showing herself with her heels, on her bare shaven head, all about the chapel after the friar. And many other strange, unnatural postures, beyond anything that I ever saw, or could believe possible for any man or woman to do. Nor was this a sudden motion and away; but a continuous thing, which she did for above an hour together; and yet not out of breath nor hot with the motions she used.[11]

Throughout the exorcism, her tongue lolled out, 'swollen' wrote Killigrew, 'to an incredible bigness and never within her mouth from the first falling into her fit; I never saw her for a moment to contract it'. At the climax of the rite, Father Surin called upon Balaam, her demon, to venerate the sacrament held out before him, and Sister Jeanne screamed out the single word 'Joseph!' in a shriek 'that you would have thought had torn her to pieces'. After this, the priest ran to see if they could discern the appearance of a mark or stigmata signalling the intercession of the saint. Killigrew and his lord and employer, Walter Montagu, rushed to do the same and saw on her left arm, as her sleeves were rolled up, 'a colour rise, a little ruddy, and run for the length of an inch along her vein, and in that a great many red specks, which made a distinct word; and it was the same she spake "Joseph."'[12]

The nun's ordeal – enacted before a large, curious and excitable crowd – moved the spectators in very different ways. For Walter Montagu, an earl's son on his way to Rome, it provided a clear testament of faith, of the inherent truth of Catholicism and of the daily battle fought for souls between God and the Devil, Catholic and Protestant. It speeded his conversion and confirmed him in his resolve to take holy orders. For his young travelling companion, Thomas Killigrew, it represented a tawdry sham, which 'in all of his [i.e. the demon's] actions, I saw little above nature or a tumbler's expression'. When invited to reach out to embrace one of the nuns, who had supposedly undergone this miraculous physical transformation, he 'only felt firm flesh, strong arms and legs held out stiff. But others affirm, that felt it, that she was all stiff and heavy as iron'. Faith, or perhaps credulous belief, held the key and Killigrew stomped off in search of a local inn, pausing just long enough to confide that there were more, and greater, liars than himself at large in the world.[13]

III

Devils, of course, were not thought to have sufficient powers to enter a convent, or any house of God, through their own volition. They – rather like the vampires of nineteenth-century Gothic fiction – had to be invited in. In this case, Sister Jeanne believed that three demons had breached the walls of the convent by hiding themselves away, amid the petals of three sprigs of fresh musk roses. Returning from her duties, Jeanne had chanced upon the fallen stems on the convent stairs and, thinking that one of the sisters had dropped them by mistake, gathered them up and paused to smell their fragrance. Carried on the scent of the roses, she believed that the three highly sexualised demons, Asmodee, Iscaaron and Balaam, had entered her body through the breath of her nostrils and then began to wreak havoc upon her mind and soul. The effect was, seemingly, instantaneous, as once she had placed some of the flowers beside the crucifix in her oratory and tucked the others into the rope belt at her waist, she began to tremble 'and was seized with love for Grandier throughout the period for prayers, being unable to apply her mind to anything other than the picture in her mind of the person of Grandier'.[14] It does not take a great deal of historical imagination to picture the distraction and conflict of Sister Jeanne at her breviary, with the heavy perfume of the flowers mixing with, or perhaps overriding the incense from the church, the delicacy of the petals contrasting with the coarse cloth of her habit, and the thorns of the roses at her belt needling into her thighs as she knelt. The exquisite itch: part pain, part forbidden pleasure, waiting and yearning to be scratched.

What is, perhaps, more difficult to conceive is why Sister Jeanne should have focused her thoughts and passions upon the figure of Urbain Grandier. Father Grandier was a rising star in the Jesuit Order who had served, for almost 15 years, as the parish priest of Loudun, and had, in that time, established himself as a significant figure in the city's political, cultural, and religious life.[15] As a member of an enclosed Order, Sister Jeanne would have never seen or met him, and there is little hard evidence to suggest that they had had any correspondence with each other on even the most mundane aspect of administration or ecclesiastical affairs. It is possible that word might have reached the Mother Superior of the rumours of Grandier's scandalous relationships with local women, through the grille in the convent wall. However, it is just as plausible that she would have known of Grandier's reputation as a man of great intelligence and considerable influence, and become attracted to the notion of him as a man of power: a far greater aphrodisiac than any physical lust could ever be on its own. Whatever the case, the demons lodged inside her began to chatter their obscenities, incessantly, and Sister Jeanne began to feel that she was losing control over her body and her mind. One demon in particular, Asmodee, 'continually operated within me, as much in imagination as in the mind, which he filled with unseemly things. Modesty,' the nun attested, 'prevents me from describing the details, for they are inappropriate'.[16] This sense of what was, and was not, appropriate for her audience to hear, to an extent coloured both her confessions during her exorcisms and her later autobiographical writings. She appears to have consciously tailored her accounts in order to navigate the treacherous line, to be trod during any witch trial, between innocent victim and demonic agent. Consequently, when she admitted to her lust for Grandier, Sister Jeanne was careful to check and to qualify her statements, negating her own agency in the final analysis and attesting to the continued influence of God upon her tortured soul. Thus, she could write of Grandier that, although 'I could not see him, I burned for love of him,' she was careful to emphasise that 'when he presented himself to me and wanted to seduce me, our good God gave me a great aversion. Then all my feelings changed, I hated him more than the devil.'[17]

Grandier, himself, did not seem unduly worried when the first accusations emerged, on 11–12 October 1632. He was no stranger to legal wrangles and attempts to defame his character and had earned the enmity of Cardinal Richelieu's followers by speaking out in favour of regionalism, and the autonomy of Loudun against the pull towards the centralisation of the French state. However, most damagingly of all, he had broken his friendship with the powerful Trincant family after fathering, and then abandoning, an illegitimate child with Philippe, the daughter of the house. The Trincants and their numerous clients had sought to dominate the politics of Loudun, and their undying hatred for the priest was not to be taken lightly. Yet, Grandier appears to have shrugged this off, too. Having defended himself ably in front of his clerical accusers at Poitiers and having cleared his name – for the moment at least – over his affair with Philippe Trincant, Grandier seems to have overestimated his ability to contain these new charges. After all, they stemmed from a woman he did not know and seemed too outrageous to ever be taken seriously. If the matter was entrusted to a civil investigation, as opposed to a church court, as Grandier had expected, then they would most likely have simply been brushed aside.

Once the decision was made to grant full authority to the ecclesiastical courts, and the exorcisms – carried out under the supervision of the newly arrived Father Barré – increasingly taking on the aspect of a public attraction, capable of drawing great crowds, Grandier found himself the subject of considerable attention, and popular suspicion. This said, he pursued a clear and level-headed plan which aimed at the removal of the three main exorcists, who were all either found to be the friends or clients of his political rivals, and to isolate the nuns from one another in other religious houses, in order that their testimonies might not cross-fertilise, through suggestion or the operation of collective hysteria. The separation of Sister Jeanne and the lay sister, Claire de Sazilly, who were judged to be the worst affected, resulted in a respite from fresh charges and controversy until late November 1632.

At this juncture, it was Sister Jeanne who once again seized the initiative and moved to regain control over the tenor and tempo of events. As she fell sick, her spasms and her projection of demonic voices took on the aspect of deathbed confessions, bringing her exorcists and attendants as close as any mortal could be to the embodiment of evil and providing a chilling insight into what it was like to be tortured by the spirits of the damned. Naturally enough, her brush with death and the sense that she was being torn apart by the depredations of her seven resident and contesting demons – who fought for control of her frail and pain-wracked body – helped garner sympathy for her plight. The expert testimony of Gaspard Joubert, a doctor of medicine, and his team of colleagues, summoned to attend the ailing Mother Superior and her nuns, showed no hesitation in finding that the possessions were more imagined than real. Joubert concluded that the nuns had been in the habit of dosing themselves with fomented liqueurs, which had served to increase their strength as well as lessening their inhibitions. He presented a dossier of evidence that should have served to close the case in December 1632, and demonstrated that the professional classes of Early Modern France were neither gullible nor entirely culpable when it came to questions of identifying witches in their midst.[18] What was lacking at Loudun, as elsewhere, was the political will to act upon their findings.

The triumph of the statecraft of the Cardinal's supporters and servants, in demolishing the city's castle and protective walls over the course of the following year, provided the tangible expression of the victory of national over local government, and confirmed the ascendancy of the Trincant family within the dramatically reshaped polity of Loudun. With his own supporters either having died, or retired from the fray – unprepared and ill-equipped to face a showdown with Richelieu – Grandier suddenly found himself isolated and thrown back upon his own resources. By May 1633, the Trincants had formulated and forwarded a new set of denunciations concerning the conduct of the Jesuit priest, which began to filter through to the Royal Court in Paris. Almost certainly as a result of Loudun's renewed occult celebrity, the old Prince de Condé paid a visit to the stricken convent and was convinced of the veracity of the possessions when he witnessed, with his own eyes, Sister Jeanne, Sister Agnes and the lay member, Claire de Sazilly, fall into a convulsive frenzy during holy communion. For Condé, and an increasing number of courtiers, churchmen and local citizens alike, it was clear that the possessions had to stem from a pernicious and predatory evil embedded within the society at Loudun. Every line of enquiry, garbled demonic confession, and inchoate expression of pain that issued forth from the nuns now seemed to lead back to just one source: Grandier. Once this was added to Richelieu's priorities – namely, the removal of a troublesome, independently minded priest, who had shown friendship and understanding to Protestants, who had stood in the way of the royal will – the fate of the charismatic Jesuit was effectively sealed.

Arrested on 7 December 1633, Grandier was whisked away from the city to the dungeons of a castle at Angers, in order to remove any chance that his friends in Loudun might attempt a rescue or threaten public order. The final acts of the legal drama, where it touched upon Grandier, were therefore closely choreographed. Regular public exorcisms and interrogations of the 'demons' who spoke through the mouths of the nuns, dominated the court proceedings, while Sister Jeanne – channelling the spirit Asmodee – contrived to spew out a paper containing the 'actual' demonic pact signed by Grandier alongside the contents of her stomach lining, at the height of her exorcism, held on 28 April 1634. Such a *coup de theatre*, coupled with the disclosure of written 'evidence', which seemed to confirm the reality of Grandier's demonic pact, understandably gripped the courtroom and focused public opinion upon the south-western city. The document still survives, though after the passage of almost 400 years it appears remarkably unsullied, considering its dramatic interjection into the courtroom and the affairs of man.[19] Nevertheless, in an age when relics and miracles were being tested, reviled or celebrated as never before, it offered a tangible link with their negation and parody by the Devil. No less miraculous than a phial of the Virgin's tears or a nail from the True Cross; the codicil that sold Grandier's soul to the Devil for eternity appeared to prove the presence of an imminent God, and the eternal dualistic struggle – enacted through a form of holy war – between His angels and the demonic hordes anxious to snatch and murder souls. The net could have been thrown even wider, as Sister Jeanne accused Madeleine de Brou – who may well have been another of Grandier's lovers in the city – of being a witch. However, unlike Grandier, Madeleine came from a powerful local, who exerted considerable influence and called in a large number of favours in order to secure her rapid release.

In the event, Grandier appears to have handled himself remarkably well before his accusers but the refusal of the king to countenance any sort of appeal to a higher judiciary, and the court's ready recourse to torture in order to gain a confession, acted to seal his fate.[20] The drawing of his fingernails was followed by the repeated breaking of his shin bones, as all his eloquence was finally submerged beneath his roars of pain and by the methodical, rhythmic fall of the hammer blows of his jailers. Whenever a confession upon a particular point was not forthcoming, his judges, the team of exorcists and a Capuchin friar began to give word to the crowds that thronged the courtroom and spilled from its doors into the marketplace, that the accused had to be a sorcerer, as he felt no pain. By then, of course, Grandier was drifting in and out of consciousness, yet he still managed to retain his composure through the last act: his ritualised humiliation on the way to the scaffold. He was forced to run a gauntlet through the gloating Trincant clan, and to endure a bungled execution amid the flames, cat-calls and fury of his enemies and judicial tormentors. At the last moment, stung by the heat and smoke, a flock of pigeons flushed from the their roosts in the portico of the church, scribed an arc across the square and fluttered for a moment above the fire and the remains of what had once been a man. Some of those in the crowd envisaged them as winged demons, come to steal away Grandier's perjured soul to feed an even greater fire beyond the gates of Hell.[21] Others saw doves, reflecting the purity and innocence of their former priest, unjustly condemned, with every beat of their snow-white wings. As with most cases of witchcraft, one's prejudice or predisposition not only informed but also shaped one's perception and recapitulation of reality, itself.

IV

Grandier's death did not provide the expected release for the torments of the nuns. Nor did it serve to shift public attention away from the afflicted city. Rather, it magnified it. Following the execution, between 18 August and 31 December 1634, no less than 21 tracts were printed describing and commenting upon the witchcraft case, as opposed to just three published in the year before the priest's death.[22] The exorcisms continued apace, with Father Surin and a fresh team of Jesuit priests brought in to Loudun to examine the afflicted nuns, just before Christmas 1634. Yet, the audience for the exorcisms had shifted. While tourists still flocked to the performative drawing-out of demons, the city folk began to stay away. Their fears had been allayed and their bloodlust satiated by Grandier's death, and their feelings seemed to turn to embarrassment and then, to boredom.

Father Surin contributed greatly to the personal fame of Sister Jeanne, amplifying the miraculous tale of her battle with the demons, and overlaying her sufferings with a sense of mysticism and purpose that dignified her afflictions. Her attempted suicide was quickly forgotten and her encounters with the saints were accentuated.[23] Thus, the process was ongoing, with Surin making it known that Behemoth – the last of Sister Jeanne's 'seven demons' – had begged to be freed by an exorcism performed, expressly, by his own hands.

With Behemoth gone, and the stigmata appearing upon the Mother Superior's hand, a five-month pilgrimage, initially presided over by Surin, was decided upon. The woman who had once embraced vows of seclusion, and pledged never to step outside the walls of her convent, now toured through France and Savoy, stopping to converse with the rich, the famous and the powerful at Paris, Tours, Nevers, Lyons, Moulins and Grenoble. The trouble, for Sister Jeanne, was that celebrity faded. Returned to her convent, Sister Jeanne began work upon her memoirs, urged the editing and publication of Surin's, as yet unfinished, accounts of the possessions and promoted her own views of the angelic and demonic visitations that continued to trouble her sleep. The ghosts of nuns – her long-dead companions – were said to appear before her in her cell and told of their experiences in purgatory. Themes from the initial disturbances in the convent were reworked and revisited. In the main, though, her taste for devils and rumours of witchcraft had given way to a sense of the power of the divine and the drama that attended the miraculous. This reflected a wider shift in the preoccupations of theologians and elite society, but her miracles – unlike her possessions – were far less newsworthy and were eclipsed in 1656 by the cure of Pascal's niece by the Holy Thorn, preserved by the Jansenists at Port Royal.[24] The visitors to Loudun fell away; without its walls, the city shrank to the status of a provincial backwater and the convent itself fell out of fashion and onto increasingly hard times, being closed down in 1772.

What Jeanne was oblivious to – but which was probably not lost upon Surin – was the manner in which her life and reputation, together with that of Grandier, was no longer her own or within her capacity to shape. Instead, the reality or the fraud surrounding the demonic possessions at Loudun became the test-bed for theology and demonological theory, to be fiercely contested initially between Catholic and Protestant, and later between fundamentalist and rationalist, over the next 200 years. It was a litmus test for belief, or disbelief. As a consequence of its wider implications for both believers and free thinkers, and for the wider societal values, polarised between the fight for dominance between clerical and secular values, which they respectively celebrated or decried, the witchcraft trial and the exorcisms of Loudun remained a live issue and were never completely forgotten.

The interpretative battle lines had been drawn between the account of the Reverend Father Tranquille, published shortly after Grandier's execution, which attested to the validity of the priest's conviction and the veracity of the exorcisms, and the works of the Abbé d'Aubignac, printed in 1637, and Nicolas Aubin, published in 1693 but probably formulated much earlier, which argued that, while demonic possession could take place, the reports in this case were entirely fraudulent.[25] Though Tranquille established a formidable position of Catholic orthodoxy regarding the operation of witchcraft at Loudun; d'Aubignac was a Roman Catholic priest who had witnessed the exorcisms first hand, while Aubin was a Protestant who had grown up in the city and had known Grandier and many of the main actors at the trial. Consequently, no one denomination had a monopoly upon one side, or other, of the argument. However, in many respects, it was Nicolas Aubin's polemic that has proved the most durable and, in many respects, the most gripping.

Driven out of France by the Edict of Nantes, Aubin wrote his *Histoire des Diables de Loudun* as a political and religious exile in Amsterdam, and conceived of the possessions as part of a wider campaign, on the part of Richelieu's church and state, to destroy the Huguenots. In this he was probably correct, but he almost certainly overstates the extent to which Sister Jeanne and the other nuns were calculating or even conscious participants in anything resembling a plot.[26] Only one author has mounted a credible defence of Sister Jeanne on theological grounds, which takes issue with the earlier editing and presentation of her spiritual autobiography, and seeks to move beyond her image as either an irrational liar or a perjured criminal.[27] That this attempt at revisionism has largely failed to carry academic and public opinion with it, even in Jeanne's homeland, would seem to result from the fact that two of France's most popular and brilliant writers had already produced grand, patriotic narratives that had excoriated the crippled nun.

Jules Michelet and Alexandre Dumas virtually recast the entire history of France for both national and international audiences and, in the course of their long and incredibly prolific careers, fastened their respective gazes upon Loudun, producing popular accounts of the witchcraft trial that made good use of Aubin's descriptions of Grandier and his critique of the court proceedings.[28] Both wrote from a secular viewpoint, critical of clericalism and supportive of a vision of the French Revolution that emphasised individual and collective freedoms, together with a belief in the progressive force of history. Michelet, from his vantage point as the nation's historian, and Dumas as France's premier novelist, had both made it their business to harvest previously overlooked source materials to present new stories, with which to entertain, educate and illuminate the present. Published in Paris, in 1839–40, Dumas' collection of crime stories was the work of a young man, anxious for success and the attendant financial stability, who had not yet found success with d'Artagnan and *The Three Musketeers* and whose earlier work, short stories centring on the legacy of the Revolutionary and Napoleonic Wars, had failed to sell and had mired him in a sea of unresolved debt. The salacious mix of passion, transgression and violence contained within the covers of the serialised editions of his *Crimes Célèbres* was calculated to grab public attention and to break him out of his financial impasse. In this, they succeeded admirably. However, it also had an unexpected result in bringing the forgotten figure of Urbain Grandier to a whole new, bourgeois and nationalist audience in the nineteenth century. Dumas' historical imagination built on the bare bones of the legal case, focusing not upon the possession of the nuns – whose exorcisms appeared too obscene, distasteful and outlandish for his readership – but rather on the personality and politics of their priestly victim. This served to give his retelling of the trial an immediacy, an economy and a focused sense of tragedy that the earlier accounts had tended to lack. Moreover, in Grandier he recognised a character who combined brilliance with arrogance, and fallibility with personal kindness, who was a delight for the pen of any author. Dumas was not interested in fashioning a morality tale, or in seeking to whiten Grandier's character. What interested him, and what he had a real feel for, was the brutal workings of the *realpolitik*, for evoking the grandeur and essential otherness of a past age, and a sense of darkness and danger which might spill over to animate his own times. Dumas' gift for tight plot lines permitted him to construct a clear and coherent tale from an extremely heterogeneous collection of sources.

Through this lens, Dumas perceived the possessions to be trickery and delusion, contrived at by human beings rather than spirits, in order to settle old scores and effect dramatic and bloody political change.[29] The exorcisms had the tinge of a 'dark' or 'disgusting comedy', rather than being tests of faith and revelations of the divine will. The ignorance and spite of Sister Jeanne were stressed; Dumas has her tell her investigators that a demon had entered her body no less than four times, taking each time the form of a different animal: a cat, a dog, a stag and a billy-goat.[30] Until torture was brought to bear, 'no trick had succeeded, never before had the demons been bunglers'.[31] The court procedure was fundamentally flawed as the 'long succession of violent and irregular breaches of law procedure, the repeated denials of [Grandier's] claim to justice, [and] the refusal to let his witness appear, or listen to his defence', made conviction a foregone conclusion in Dumas' eyes.[32] As a result, in the summing-up of the trial, he cannot help but feel that in contrast to the other cases he has described: 'This time it was not the man who was executed who was guilty, but the executioners.'[33]

Accordingly, his quest for atonement and justice expresses itself through a preoccupation with an examination of the fates of those who brought the priest down, and how an avenging nemesis might be seen to have overtaken them all. Consequently, the exorcists fall into depression brought about by their collective guilt and perish in pain and misery, lamenting their role in Grandier's fall. Their perjured judgements had, for Dumas, brought about the withdrawal of God's favour and resulted in their certain damnation. One of his torturers, in true Gothic fashion, is haunted by Grandier's ghost and dies shouting his name in the dark; while de Laubardemont, the royal commissioner, sees his sins repaid by the destruction of his son, who was hanged at the crossroads as a common criminal. Reason, as understood and projected by Dumas, needed a sense of restorative justice, just as surely as faith. Yet, now the roles were reversed with the priest (rather than the nun) speaking to – and for – the sympathies of a new age.

Jules Michelet, writing in 1862, put Grandier's case at the heart of his discussion of *La Sorcière*, or *The Witch*. Writing quickly and stridently, with the mendicant Orders in mind, he was prepared to go even further than Dumas in his retelling – projecting thoughts onto long-dead characters, and weaving together scenes and actions that were extrapolations, rather than evidences, from the original sources. He wrote with passion, verve and a powerful overarching commitment to the values of the European Enlightenment.[34] Thus, his Grandier was a libertine priest, caught up in a net of deceit spun by 'the jealous Monk and the maniac nun'.[35] He is 'a debauchee, a sorcerer, a demon, a free thinker, who at church' bent one knee only and not two, 'a man who laughed at rules and regulations, and granted dispensations contrary to the Bishop's prerogatives'.[36] With feet of clay, Grandier is brought down by the 'cunning and calumny' of the nuns and by Richelieu's bribes. The priest is

> dragged to churches to confront the mad women ... [and there] he finds a band of furious Bacchanals whom the condemned apothecary was busy intoxicating with his potions, throwing them into such paroxysms of rage that on one occasion Grandier came near to perishing under their nails.

Michelet thought

> the absurdity of these scenes increased *pari passu* with the odiousness. The scraps of Latin that were whispered in [the nuns'] ears they pronounced all wrong. The public said scornfully that the devils had not passed their Fourth Standard [Grade at school]. The Capuchins, not in the least disconcerted, replied that if the demons were weak in Latin, they spoke Troquois to perfection and very fine Double Dutch.

And yet, this 'ignoble farce, when seen from a distance of 60 leagues, from Saint-Germain or the Louvre, appeared something miraculous, terrifying, and appalling'.[37]

In contrast to much of the rest of the book, the image of the witch is re-gendered, and transposed to Grandier, while the nuns are – as we have already seen – pictured as being as irrational and neurotic as they are spoiled and predatory. However, it is not their corruption but that of the monastic Orders, which is Michelet's real target. In a sense, his problem is that – in variance with the rest of his book on the nature of the witch – he could not find a sympathetic female figure in Loudun, on whom to project his thesis. In essence, therefore, this is a story of witchcraft without a witch. Apparently, unaware of Madeleine de Brou – who might have fitted his archetype – Michelet makes Grandier, by way of default, emblematic of all those treated unjustly and ultimately destroyed by a church that was bridled by few restraints and driven by the solipsisms, credulity and cruelty of monastic thought.

V

If Dumas and Michelet had created a vision of Grandier and the possessions at Loudun that fitted the mindset of the nineteenth century, then it was Aldous Huxley who recast them for the twentieth century, in light of the rise of totalitarian regimes across Europe. Huxley's work straddled the fields of historical research, theology and psychology. As he later wrote to the dramatist John Whiting, he had 'exaggerated nothing' in his account of the possessions, exorcisms and trial procedure at Loudun. It would be misleading to describe his famous retelling of *The Devils of Loudun* as simple 'faction' or, worse still, to dismiss it as mere fiction. It was the product of considerable primary research, at a time when many of the key sources were still difficult to obtain, and bears the hallmarks of his quest for veracity, shot through with real artistry and the touch of true creative genius. Unlike Dumas, he had come to *The Devils of Loudun* as a well-established author whose dystopian projection of a *Brave New World* on to Fordist modes of production had been in print for more than 20 years. Yet somewhat surprisingly, whereas both *Crimes Célèbres* and *La Sorcière* were instant successes, *The Devils of Loudun* was a slow and disappointing seller. Reviewers baulked at the subject matter and, though noting his attention to original sources and period detail, they thoroughly resented his descriptions of plagues, putrefaction and the cycle of sexual repression and sadism. Furthermore, his pithy use of modern metaphors and willingness to parallel the governmental techniques of Richelieu with those employed during the Nazi terror, or the show trials of the 1930s in the Soviet Union, seemed for some to over-step the barrier between respectable – if dry – historicism and polemical social satire. Where else might one find the verses of Walt Whitman, and the teachings of the Bodhisattva and Zen Buddhism discussed alongside, and used to illuminate, the struggles between Cartesian, Jansenist and Jesuit in seventeenth-century France?[38]

The rituals accompanying the exorcisms were for Huxley circuses or vaudevillian turns, orchestrated by the vengeful Trincants and presided over by a cynical and debased priestly class. Thus, 'Surin was one of those frail, nervous beings in whom the sexual impulse is powerful almost to frenzy', and Huxley leaves the reader in no doubt that 'he died a virgin, burned the greater part of his literary productions and was content to be not merely not famous, but ... positively infamous'.[39] Barré, meanwhile, 'was one of those negative Christians to whom the devil is incomparably more real and more interesting than God. He saw the print of cloven hoofs in everything'.[40] We do not encounter Sister Jeanne until almost a third of the way through the book, and then it is as an individual crippled not so much by her medical deformity but rather by its impact upon her own psyche. 'Disliking and consequently disliked', Huxley writes, 'she lived in a defensive shell, issuing forth only to attack her enemies – and everybody, *a priori*, was an enemy – with sudden sarcasms or strange outbursts of jeering laughter'.[41] For Huxley, it was her contact with the intelligent, thoughtful and attractive Madeleine de Brou, at the grille in the convent wall, which activates the 'Envy modulated into hatred and contempt' that is eventually displaced onto the person of Grandier. For Madeleine has the qualities and the freedoms that the Mother Superior desires, and an actual relationship with the man for whom she longs.[42]

'Soeur Jeanne', he continued,

> had tried to free herself from her servitude to the erotic images she had conjured up: but the only freedom she could achieve was freedom to be the self she abhorred. There was nothing for it but to slide down again into the dungeon of her addiction.[43]

Thus, the exorcisms and purgings, intended as a holy rite, become twisted, on Sister Jeanne's side to become a form of masochistic masturbation, and on Barré's into a form of sexual violation and abuse. 'Exhibited to the rabble', Huxley sees her becoming

> a less than personal creature fit only to be bawled at, manipulated, sent by reiterated suggestion into fits and finally subjected, against what remained of her will and in spite of the remnants of her modesty, to the outrage of a forcible colonic irrigation. Barré had treated her to an experience that was the equivalent, more or less, of a rape in a public lavatory.[44]

Despite the fact that Dumas had successfully dramatised his work for the stage in 1850, Huxley was quick to appreciate that any attempt to visualise his own work, in the theatre or cinema, would be problematic. It would risk outraging public opinion and the attentions of the censor, who in the 1950s–60s still enjoyed sweeping powers. Yet, if he baulked at the idea of a production of *The Devils of Loudun*, Sir Peter Hall – at the English National Theatre – was prepared to pursue the project, in an attempt to reinvigorate the career of his friend and colleague, John Whiting. Consequently, Hall commissioned the dramatist, who was known to have a predilection for Huxley's work, to write a play based upon the novel. Huxley would seem to have been generous in terms of offering his help and advice but still thought fit to urge caution upon Whiting, as when: 'Dramatised and well directed and acted they [i.e. the scenes of exorcism and torture] may be almost more than many people can take.'[45] Whiting may well have taken the hint, as his play *The Devils*, which premiered at London's Aldwych Theatre on 20 February 1961, focused largely upon Grandier's interior struggle – between his reason and physical passion – as opposed to the very public torments of Sister Jeanne. In doing so, Whiting fundamentally altered the character of the priest and the nature of the political imperatives that combined to destroy him.

Whiting's anti-hero is far more deeply troubled, self-doubting and self-loathing, than Aubin's archetype. His melancholia, his preoccupation with the metaphysical, and willingness to rush to accept and embrace death put him at odds with the interpretations offered by Dumas and Michelet, and also with the profoundly modern and materialist version of Grandier that transferred from stage to screen with Ken Russell and Oliver Reed.[46] Laubardemont, the inquisitor – recast as a professional soldier and servant of the state – is invested with dignity and a gift for perception and reflexivity that the original had so singularly lacked in life. Ultimately, though, it is Sister Jeanne – played with chaste dignity as opposed to simple sexual frenzy, by Dorothy Tutin – who is allowed to provide the coda to the tale, lamenting in the wake of her attempted suicide that she now wonders if it is

> only in the very depths that one finds God? Look at me. First, I wanted to come to Him in innocence. It was not enough. Then there was lying and playacting. The guilt, the humiliation. It was not enough. There were the antics done for the dirty eyes of priests. The squalor. It was not enough. Down, down further.[47]

VI

Sister Jeanne's abject humiliation and eventual transcendence was being captured on celluloid – at roughly the same time as Whiting's play debuted in London – by the Polish new wave director, Jerzy Kawalerowicz, in his film *Matka Joanna od Aniolow/ Mother Joan of the Angels*. The screenplay was closely modelled not upon Huxley, but upon another novel by Jaroslaw Iwaszkiewicz, that had been published at the height of World War II. The characters and the setting were transposed, in both the book and the film, from the France of Cardinal Richelieu to the Poland of the great days of its Commonwealth, in the seventeenth century. Accordingly, while Sister Jeanne or Joan remains virtually unchanged, Grandier transforms to Garniec, Surin becomes Suryn and Loudun doubles as the Eastern European city of Ludyn. In the largest change, the figure of Richelieu was replaced by Queen Marysienka, as the focus for court intrigue. Set after the witchcraft trial, both works chronicle the nature of the unfolding relationship between Sister Jeanne/Joan and Father Surin/Suryn.[48] At the time that the film version was made, *Mother Joan* was seen as an allegory for the Polish people, torn between the official Communism and dour rationalism of Gomulka's regime, and the traditional brand of militant ultra-Catholicism, which embraced religious ecstasies and an aggressive brand of nationalism. In 2001, Kawalerowicz explained to an interviewer that it was, instead

> a film against dogma ... It is a love story about a man and a woman who wear church clothes and whose religion does not allow them to love each other. They often talk about and teach about love – how to love God, how to love each other – and

yet they cannot have the love of a man and a woman because of their religion. This dogma is itself inhuman. The devils that possess these characters are the external manifestations of their repressed love. The devils are like sins, opposite to their human nature. It is like the devils give the man and the woman an excuse for their human love. Because of that excuse, they are able to love.[49]

It is an uncompromisingly bleak film, starkly shot in black and white. It is undeniably a film about totalitarianism: but a totalitarianism of belief, as opposed to politics, that stems from all-embracing, self-imposed theological constraints. Consequently, the blasted lunar-like landscape in which the convent sits; its echoing spaces and sudden confines, all contribute to a sense of barrenness, spoil and alienation. Even the inn, around which several sub-plots develop, is a draughty and inhospitable place. Between the convent and the outside world stands the charred remains of the pyre upon which Grandier/Garniec was burned before our own story began: a disfigured spindle jutting up to the heavens. The witch has been burned, but the devils have not vanished with the flames. The absence of a soundtrack, save for the plainchant of the cloisters; the brutal clarity of the black and white filmstock – which contrasts Father Suryn's robes with those of the nuns – the reliance upon dialogue – that is often delivered straight down the camera lens – and the absence of fast-paced action, creates a sense of separation and a lyricism. This is captured in the flight of birds, in the disciplined solemnity and the profound silence of the nuns, or in the swinging of scores of bleached habits, drying in the laundry room, which can swiftly turn to a haunting, or profoundly unsettling, imagery.

The shock value of the film stems not from the physical and sexual degradation of the sisters but from the unpredictability of their sudden shifts from seemliness, to complete breakdown. Yet in their madness they attain a sense of individuality. One young nun spins round and around like a whirling toy; the sisters recoil from holy water as though it were sulphuric acid; they strike contorted poses during mass, and choreograph swirling dances which see them move like a flock of startled doves, flapping and flailing against invisible nets and snares of their own devising. Father Suryn, a consumptive and a flagellant, cannot either effect or abjure his own desires, and as a consequence spirals into a cycle of madness and senseless murder. Sister Malgorzata attempts to break free and to embrace the world, but is shamed by the reproachful gaze of Suryn as she dances in the tavern. Betrayed by her lover, the local squire, she returns utterly broken to the seclusion of the convent and the arms of Mother Joan. Yet Joan, who is incapable of suitably expressing or realising her passions, is left no less bereft. Neither the consummation of desire, nor its utter abrogation, are seen to hold the answer to their inner torments. The window on the convent closes to on the women, offering them no hope in their despair and solitude, and at last even the church bells are silenced to their ears as the screen becomes a void.

VII

Yet, if *Mother Joan of the Angels* received critical acclaim, garnering the prestigious Jury Prize at the 1961 Cannes Film Festival, and served to consolidate Kawalerowicz's reputation at the head of the Kadr studios in Warsaw, winning him international fame beyond the confines of the Iron Curtain, then, Ken Russell's attempt to film the same story, a decade later in the West, all but ruined his career and resulted in a groundswell of censorship and prurient scorn that contrasted, ironically, with the reception of Sister Jeanne's story in the East.[50] In part, this was not surprising. Kawalerowicz had opted to use Iwaszkiewicz's measured and atmospheric novel as his source material; whereas Russell attempted to film a script based upon the more earthy and calculatedly shocking Huxley novel and Whiting play, which used graphic depictions of Sister Jeanne's exorcisms, her obsessive masturbation and an orgy scene in which the nuns attempt to rape a figure of Christ in a cathedral. The *New York Times* lamented that Russell seemed to know no limits and 'will stop at no outrage in pursuit of effect for effect's sake', while the *Los Angeles Times* thought it 'a degenerate and despicable piece of art'. Stanley Kauffman described the film as a 'swirling multi-coloured puddle' and concluded, savagely, that it made him 'glad that both Huxley and Whiting are dead, so that they are spared this farrago of witless exhibitionism'.[51] Billy Graham ranted against the film on one side of the Atlantic, while his acolytes, right-wing British evangelists organised against it on the other. If this was not bad enough, then Russell found himself deserted by his natural allies among the socially liberal intelligentsia and arts world, such as George Melly – who reviewed the film for the *Observer* – and Alexander Walker, in the *Evening Standard*. More predictably, Mary Whitehouse decreed that *The Devils* was 'offensive, obscene, repugnant and likely to injure the moral standards of society', and organised prayer meetings and rallies around screenings of the film, in an attempt to have it banned.[52]

Far more damaging were the attitudes of the movie studios and the cuts demanded by the censor before *The Devils* even made it onto the screen. Shocked by the tenor of the script, United Artists had dropped the project during production, and although MGM had picked it up, it is clear from the studio's subsequent reticence to re-release the movie on home video, or more recently on the increasingly popular 'director's cut' DVD format, that it had serious reservations about *The Devils* and would really have preferred Russell's work to have been quietly forgotten about.[53] The director was lucky to have evaded criminal charges for blasphemy at the hands of Whitehouse and her fearful cohorts, and while John Trevelyan – the enlightened secretary of the Board of British Film Censors – tried to defend the picture as best he could, he was unable to pass *The Devils* in its entirety. The 'rape of Christ' scene had to be cut before a certificate was granted, together with a now lost scene of Father Mignon abusing himself on top of the church roof. In the USA, *The Devils* was only cleared for release after some 23 cuts and changes had been made.

Yet, the furore surrounding the film seems surprising given the context of cinema in the early 1970s. At the same time as *The Devils* premiered, *A Clockwork Orange* and *The Exorcist* were enjoying significant box office success. Both films were permitted eventual acceptance into the mainstream and achieved considerable impact upon wider popular culture in a manner that was denied to *The Devils*. Bart Simpson, boy bands and Britney Spears have all referenced Coppola's vision of Alex and his 'Droogs', in adopting asymmetric eye make-up, bowler hats and white overalls, while there is scarcely a lonely and alienated teenager on either side of the Atlantic who has not dabbled with a Ouija board in their bedroom, while *The Exorcist* plays on late night TV or the DVD.[54] Therefore, we might ask ourselves, what makes *The Devils* – and its portrayal of demonic possession – so troublesome, transgressive and unpalatably different?

In part, the answer lies in the respective attitudes towards authority, the church and the efficacy and nature of exorcism, itself. Demonic possession and charges of witchcraft are, for Russell, no more than a politically motivated sham. For Friedkin in *The Exorcist*, they are a reality and one which can be successfully combatted by the very priests that Russell – and by extension, Huxley – so bitterly decried. The violence and the obscenities depicted in *The Devils* are used to highlight a miscarriage of justice and the viciousness of human nature; those shown in *The Exorcist* – though claiming their inspiration from a supposed case of possession of a young girl in 1949 – provide justification for the exorcist's art and fall more naturally into a horror genre that postulates a view of traditional Christian duality, which pits good against evil, and sees the former reassuringly triumph. By way of contrast, *The Devils* has no room for the miraculous and an imminent God, and no trust in elites and traditional power structures. Organised religion is a sham. Ultimately, we make our own hell, or heaven, upon earth and it is this realisation that makes the film so profoundly subversive.

For his own part, Ken Russell thought that:

> *The Devils* is a harsh film – but it is a harsh subject. I wish the people who were horrified and appalled by it had read the book [i.e. Huxley's *The Devils of Loudun*], because the bare facts are far more horrible than anything in the film.[55]

THE SONG
OF THE
Whip-poor-Will.

Even-tide drooped like a veil,
Over misty Hill and Dale.
Th' old witch passed us on the path
That climbed the tangled Hill;
We laughed for she was strange and old,
Then her eyes gleamed green and cold,
Like a serpent's in its wrath;
While sang the Whip-poor-Will.
  "Whip-poor-Will,
    Whip-poor-Will;"
The strange witch bird that silent flits
Thro' the dusk, or crouching sits,
And sings its song of omen ill,
  "Whip-poor-Will,
    Whip-poor-Will."

Bleak the winds of Winter blow,
Bringing ice, and frost, and snow.
That look the old witch gave to me,
It made me deathly chill.
At dead of night I see her gloat,
And hear that bird its lonely note,
In fancy still that look I see,
And hear the Whip-poor-Will.
  "Whip-poor-Will,
    Whip-poor-Will;"
That witches' bird that silent flits,
Thro' the dusk, or crouching sits,
And sings its song of omen ill,
  "Whip-poor-Will,
    Whip-poor-Will."

H Pyle

1. 'The Song of the Whip-poor-Will', from *The Illustrated London News*, 16 October 1880. The engraver has captured the essence of the witch as an 'ill-wisher', whose presence in the village community creates discord, fear and suspicion among her younger, and more affluent, neighbours (Author's Collection).

2. Mother Goose as Witch Woman, an illustration for *Old Nursery Rhymes*, a children's book
by Arthur Rackham, 1912. An elfin child is spellbound by her tales, while his playmates watch
with a mixture of trepidation and fear (Private Collection).

3. Mother Damnable of Kentish Town, *c*.1676. The Witch as poisoner, diviner and wanton destitute (Author's Collection).

4. 'The Witches' Tea Party', or in reality, members of the Order of the Holy and Undivided Trinity, on 'Founder's Day', Castle Rising, Norfolk, in the 1920s. Appearances, and our assumptions, can be deceiving (Library of Congress).

5. The Witch as the Stuff of Nightmares, a late nineteenth-century print by St Grocholski (Author's Collection).

6. North Meols: The Witch Made Tangible by Thatch and Woodsmoke, *c*.1965–6 (Author's Collection).

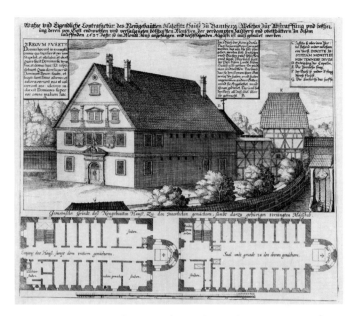

7. The Witch House of Bamberg (Museen der Stadt Bamberg, Inv. No. 1171).

8. Franconia, a mid-seventeenth-century map, showing the pocket state of Bamberg in the context of its neighbouring territories (Author's Collection).

9. The Witch Bishop, Johann Georg Fuchs von Dornheim, Prince Bishop of Bamberg, by Michiel van Mereveld (Museen der Stadt Bamberg, Inv. No. 1237).

10. The Arrival at the Sabbat, by David Teniers, 1632, showing witches engaged in digging up a corpse from under a splintered gallows, gathering herbs and employing image magic to seal their charm. A host of demons, *striges* and familiar spirits look on. Though Teniers was a Dutch artist, and his painting was bought for the 'Cabinet of Curiosities' of an aristocratic Parisian, this image was engraved and sold for a German audience, giving form to the fears of Bamberg's elite (Author's Collection).

11. 'Love Magic' by the Master of the Lower Rhine, *c.*1498 (Private Collection).

12. Apuleius of Madura, as envisaged for a 1624 edition of his works, published in Amsterdam. Laurels crown his portrait, taken from a surviving cameo from late pagan antiquity, and the goddesses Isis and Panacea frame the scene, but the Platonic philosopher (depicted in the bottom panel) is oblivious to both the braying of Lucius – transformed into the Ass – and the obscene gestures of a demon (Author's Collection).

13. Fotis the slave girl and Lucius, the aristocrat, transformed through a witch's magic into a humble ass. Webster Murray, the artist who produced this delightful study in 1946, realises the story's full bawdy, comic potential. Yet, the bashful ass is already wreathed in the rose garlands that will break his enchantment (Private Collection).

Ah! lampe audacieuse et téméraire tu brules
l'auteur de tous les feux du monde

14. Cupid & Psyche, engraved for an edition of Apuleius' works, published in Amsterdam in 1788. Classical paganism had no problem in juxtaposing the sacred with the profane, and with encompassing humour and sexuality alongside all that was mystical and most profound, within its religious schema (Author's Collection).

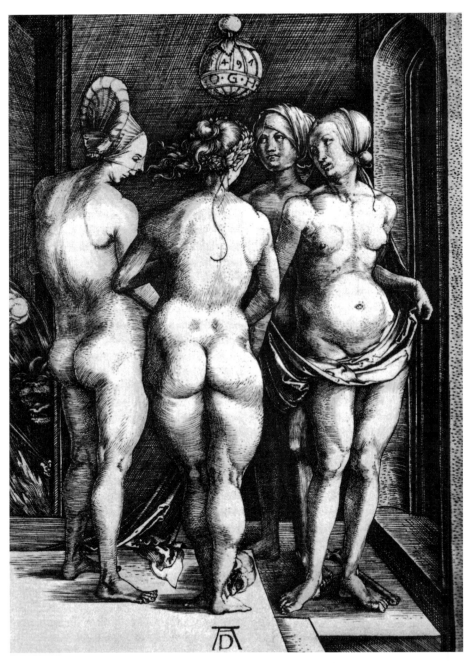

15. The Four Witches, by Albrecht Dürer, 1497 (Private Collection).

16. **Witch Riding Backwards on a Goat**, by Albrecht Dürer, c.1500–7 (Private Collection).

17. **Salvator Rosa (1615–73): The Painter of Witches** (Author's Collection).

18. The Temptation of St Anthony, by Salvator Rosa, *c.*1646. In this later, French engraving, the demon has been somewhat sanitised, with the flapping folds of genital skin that appear in Rosa's original painting smoothed away from an eighteenth-century vision of hell (Author's Collection).

19. The Witch, by Salvator Rosa, *c*.1646–9. Rosa contrasts the lowly status of a degraded and dishevelled witch with her intent to practise High Magic. Thus, she pores over a grimoire that she is, probably, incapable of reading (Private Collection).

20. King Saul and the Witch of Endor, by Salvator Rosa, 1668 (Author's Collection).

21. Witches' Sabbath, woodcut by Hans Baldung Grien, 1510 (Private Collection).

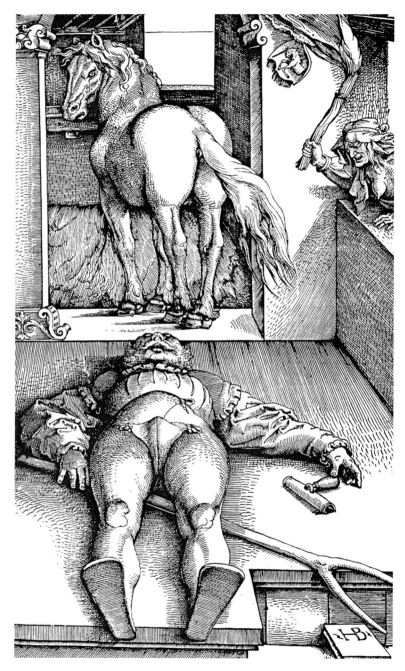

22. The Bewitched Groom, by Hans Baldung Grien, 1544 (Private Collection).

23. The Worm in the Bud. The strength of the witch-hunter lay in his plausibility, rectitude and charisma. The late Michael Gothard's portrayal of Father Barré in *The Devils* as a 'rock star' figure, with love beads and John Lennon shades, perfectly captured this dangerous essence. Sister Jeanne (played by Vanessa Redgrave) hangs – and is prepared to hang others – upon his every word (Private Collection).

24. Urbain Grandier Confronts the Hooded Tribunal, Oliver Reed's finest moment as an actor and the climax of *The Devils*, as the doomed Grandier tears apart the terror and the lies of the witch-hunters at Loudun. Detail from an American film poster, 1971 (Private Collection).

25. The Witches' Sabbath, an engraving by Michael Herr, 1620. The hollow hills, riotous dancing and feasting shown here, when taken out of context, could distort Isobel Gowdie's tales of night flight, 'elf bulls' and meetings with the 'king and queen' of the faerie, into something altogether darker and more threatening to the Kirk and the State (Author's Collection).

26. 'Credulity, Superstition & Fanaticism', by William Hogarth, 1762. The Anglican clergyman attempts to strike fear into his congregation by brandishing images of the broomstick-riding witch and the trident-carrying devil. However, his wig flies off to reveal the tonsure of a Catholic monk, while Mary Tofts – who was believed to have given birth to a litter of rabbits – and a 'Demoniak', who vomits forth pins and nails to order, are satirised. A bewildered Turk (no doubt a relation of Montesquieu's *Usbek* and *Rica*) peers in at the window (Author's Collection).

27. Tam O' Shanter and the Witches, as drawn by John Faed. Robert Burns' poem, written in 1790, is an Enlightenment satire against superstition and drunkenness. The account of the coven meeting in the ruined Kirk would seem to be based on the account of the trials of the witches of North Berwick. Yet, fear has turned to laughter, the devil has become a figure of fun – corpulently blowing upon the bagpipes – and the 'maiden' of the Coven is now both young and inviting (Author's Collection).

28. Hansel and Gretel, by Hermann Kaulbach, 1872. This illustration to the Grimms' *Nursery and Household Tales* emphasises the bestial nature and murderous cannibalism associated with the witch figure. If her femininity is negated and perverted, then Gretel's mixture of kindness and cunning, as pictured here, fulfils a feminine archetype (Author's Collection).

29. **'The Singing Ringing Tree'.** Despite the petulant commands of Princess 'Thousandbeauty', the little tree will neither sing nor ring, until her heart is true. Christel Bodenstein stars in the definitive DEFA fairy tale, released in East Germany in 1957 and brought to the BBC in 1964 (Author's Collection).

30. **Jules Michelet (1798–1874).** A photograph taken in a Montmartre studio towards the end of his life (Author's Collection).

31. The Witch, by Luke Fieldes, an engraving reproduced in a popular magazine at the end of the nineteenth century reflecting Michelet's archetype (Author's Collection).

32. Michelet's Witches? Two young women pose for a photograph in their carnival costumes, in 1901 (Author's Collection).

33. The Reality of Witchcraft? At the turn of the twentieth century, the *Journal des Voyages* published this photograph of the 'Witch of Rochefort' in Brittany. Prematurely aged and frail, she is a world away from Michelet's emancipatory vision (Author's Collection).

34. The Witch's Sleep, an engraving after a painting by Albert von Keller, 1888. The witch now appears as the epitome of German womanhood, as she goes to the flames, to the fury of the monk and the sorrow of her family and friends (Author's Collection).

35. Února: The Witch of Prague, an illustration to F. Marion Crawford's novel, 1892. The witch is now sophisticated, urban and – most worrying of all to the Victorian psyche – independent of male control (Author's Collection).

36. The Witch on the Barbican, Lenkiewicz's great mural depicting the Elizabethan occult, Plymouth, 1971–2 (Author's Collection).

37. 'Beware: I'm a Woman – the Source of All Evil': The Witch as Situationalist, a protestor at a Women's Liberation demonstration held at Trafalgar Square, in 1973. Identifying with the traditional imagery surrounding the witch, she carries a broom and has pinned a pointed hat to her placard (Author's Collection).

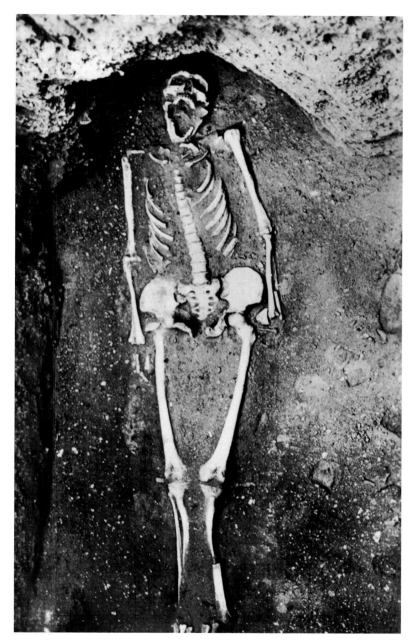

38. The Skeleton of Ursula Kemp, photographed *c.*1921 for a tourist postcard at St Osyth. The nails that were thought to have shackled her into her grave can clearly be seen, beside her knees and the remains of her left wrist (from the Collection of Suzanne Vincent).

39. The Ravages of Time. Lenkiewicz's portrait of Frances Howard stares out from the faded ruins of his mural. The Plymouth Barbican, July 2008 (Author's Photograph).

40. The Witch as Enchantress. Robin Hood – played by Michael Praed – is bewitched by one of Simon de Bellême's acolytes, played by Gemma Craven, in a production still from *Robin of Sherwood* (Private Collection).

41. Herne the Hunter, pencil study by Mary Fairclough, 1947 (Author's Collection).

42. Herne the Hunter, print by Chesca Potter, *c*. mid-1980s. Although owing much to John Albineri's TV portrayal and Kip Carpenter's vision of the shamanic forest god, Potter's 'Herne' has lost his human aspect and stands at the gateways of life and death (whereabouts of the original unknown).

43. Drawing Down the Moon – or Raising Hell? Morgwyn of Ravenscar, the high priestess of the Coven – played by Rula Lenska – performs her art, in a still from *Robin of Sherwood* (Private Collection).

However, in his treatment of the script, which he produced in just under three weeks, he did far more than just adapt the work of Huxley and Whiting. He wove together influences from Dumas and from Michelet, effectively dramatising their accounts of Grandier's triumphant entry into the city and his humiliation of Father Mignon during a church parade.[56] In the film, the self-confident and virile Grandier (played with gusto by Oliver Reed) contemptuously brushes aside the slight and prissy figure of Father Mignon (Murray Melvin) at the head of the procession. He gives a boyish wink to the altar boys, who immediately drop Mignon's train to pick up his own. Grandier forgets his bravado in a minute, but Mignon – having been made to look foolish and unimportant at the hands of a man who is bigger, both physically and intellectually – neither forgets nor forgives the slight, determining to drag down the man he could never hope to be.

Russell understands the nature of politics: petty jealousies and stupidities that can be cloaked in policies and dressed up in high-sounding rhetoric. They will ruin lives in order for a moment's satisfaction. His Grandier – unlike Whiting's – is politician as well as priest. He is the de facto governor of the city, who uses his power to remind his fellow citizens of their unique possibilities, and to urge religious toleration between Catholic and Protestant. 'The religious wars are over,' he tells them, 'Catholic no longer fights with Protestant' and the people must now 'build a temple in their hearts'. This does little to endear him to his own side, but the handful of sober-suited Calvinists in the square push forward to hear his words and congratulate him. However, in pushing out the quack doctors from a woman's deathbed, he saves her from suffering her final agonies at their hands but gains the enmity of a rich cabal of businessmen and medical entrepreneurs who hold influence within the city government. He then compounds his talent for making enemies by cynically rejecting his lover, Philippe Trincant, as soon as she announces her pregnancy – effortlessly shifting his role from that of attentive suitor to admonishing cleric. Taken apart, none of these squabbles and unkindnesses are insurmountable for – or threatening to – the clever and worldly priest. But, when taken together they can be seen to have already alienated him from Loudun's elite, long before talk of possessions and witchcraft have taken hold of the neighbouring convent. This is, after all, as Russell suggested, the story of the 'self-destruction of a citadel from within'.[57]

For Russell, the persecutions are triggered from above. Sister Jeanne is simply a pawn, who provides the pretext by which a grander political design – encompassing the extirpation of the French Protestants and the centralisation of royal power – might be achieved. Moving as though on casters, Richelieu masterminds and controls events from afar, while a decadent playboy king provides an allegory for absolutist monarchy: shooting fleeing Huguenots, dressed up as fowl, to the gramophone soundtrack of 'Bye Bye Blackbird.' In another example of the mix between know-ing anachronism and scrupulous attention to historical detail, Russell divided responsibility for the film-score between the brilliant young specialist in Early Music, David Munrow – who used the seventeenth-century compositions of Michael Praetorius for the court masque – and the contemporary classical composer, Peter Maxwell Davies, who in the late 1960s and early 1970s was at the cutting edge of the avant garde. This was not the product of a simple division of labour, or a lack of care. Rather, it was born out of a powerful appreciation of historical processes and the ways in which past societies have chosen to view and to define themselves. 'I wanted,' Ken Russell later explained,

> to get a feeling of this happening to a set of people who considered themselves modern. I'm sure to every person at every stage in history their town has not been an old-fashioned town, their town has been a modern town and they are modern people.[58]

As a result, his Loudun would not be a picturesque vision of half-timber and over-grown walls; it would be sleek, and modernist and would gleam in the sun.

He was fortunate, indeed, to have discovered Derek Jarman at the outset of his career, a youthful designer who could fully realise and expand upon his ideal, con-structing a monumental cityscape on the back lot of Pinewood Studios. Clinical and impersonal, it dwarfs the actors and suggests in the sterility and starkness of the white-tiled convent – where scale collapsed in upon itself – a nod to Eisenstein's *Ivan the Terrible*. Sister Jeanne is suddenly forced to stoop through narrowing pas-sages and to squeeze herself into improbable contortions so that she might gaze at Grandier's passing feet, through the grill of her subterranean cell. Suggestive of the shower blocks of the Nazi death camps, and of Huxley's evocation of the stricken convent resembling 'a public toilet'; the building is clad in wipe-down tiles, with perfectly polished floors, acrylic doors and stainless steel surfaces. Jarman's taste for the opulent and the Baroque was realised in Grandier's tower-room study, hung with an equally anachronistic copy of Poussin's *Triumph of Pan* and deco-rated with plaster casts from the tomb of King Mausolus.[59] His relationship with Russell, during the making of the film, appears to have been symbiotic. Jarman had originally suggested the scene in which Louis XIII leads his hunting party against the caged Protestants, stripped of all humanity in their new costumes as blackbirds; and had story-boarded a dream sequence – which in the event was not shot – in which Sister Jeanne was laden down with thousands of crucifixes and con-demned to crawl through a desert landscape, where martyrs hung from stunted and withered trees.[60]

The Devils, filmed over the course of 1970 and released a year later, was steeped in the counterculture of the late 1960s. Here, Russell revealed the measure of the acuteness of his genius and perception. The composite figure of the exorcist, Father Barré (played by the late Michael Gothard) could have been used as a vehicle to tilt at the mores of 'straight' society. Instead, Russell used Barré to shine a harsh, ironic, light upon the hippy ethos. In this way, Barré is dangerous because he is just as charismatic as Grandier. He is attractive and plausible and – with his long hair and rosaries that drape like love beads – he is part of the zeitgeist, as at home in the front row of the audience watching The Rolling Stones play Hyde Park as he was presiding over a gruesomely invasive exorcism.[61]

Russell appreciated that witch-belief in the sixteenth and seventeenth centuries stemmed not from stupidity or a lack of learning, but from a desire to reform behaviour and morality in both public and private spheres. Thus, Barré – who scripts the confessions – can declare that 'sin can be caught as easily as the plague', conflating the recent epidemic in Loudun with what he feels to be the city's spiritual sickness. As we have seen, witchcraft was systematised by an intellectual movement, rooted in the universities that attempted to construct a coherent 'science' of demonology from theological, literary and philosophical sources that went back beyond St Augustine and the New Testament to Plato and the Academy at Athens. Therefore, Barré is no fool or simple charlatan. He mirrors Grandier in exerting a sexual and intellectual power on his audience. It is for us to make up our own minds which one truly smells of sulphur.

Were Grandier not flawed, and compromised by the transgressions of his sex life, then he would not have been fair game for the Inquisition. He falls because he is guilty, though not of those things with which he was charged. In shifting the stronger and more reflective dialogue from the mouth of the Prince de Condé to Grandier himself, Russell stripped away the fatalism from Whiting's rendering of the character, ennobling the central figure of the priest and accentuating the tragedy of his destruction. This is possible, to a large extent, as the result of the brooding intensity and dynamic energy invested in Grandier by Oliver Reed, in what quite simply was his greatest film performance. His well-founded reputation for hell-raising and drunken boorishness should not be permitted, here, to obscure his brilliance as an actor, who combined sensuality with sensitivity and whose rich inflections could turn dialogue into poetry just as easily as they could summon the intensity of anger and pain. His Grandier is not a self-pitying and self-destructive ascetic, but a man who, while he might have 'loved women and power', regains his sense of purpose through his union with Madeleine de Brou and discovers a new sense of spirituality. While the cathedral is profaned by Barré's exorcisms, which reduce religion to 'a circus and its servants into clowns', seducing the people only 'in order to destroy them', Grandier finds his religion in nature, celebrating mass in the open, beside mountain streams, while Madeleine walks back to the city through a forest of flowers. In many respects this epiphany, on the part of Grandier, represents the climax of the film.

Contrary to opprobrium heaped upon Ken Russell and the wilful misreadings projected onto *The Devils*, he establishes a sense of spirituality and true religious revelation at the heart of the film. Rather than simply revelling in the shock value occasioned by obscenity and profanity, *The Devils* attempts to present an account of the persecutory impulse, expressed in the clash between the human spirit and the authority of an absolutist state and a totalitarian church. Grandier is re-formed through his selfless love for Madeleine and this, in turn, has a profound impact upon his personal theology. Their communion is now one of equals. The female is no longer subject to, and subjectivised by, a male God and a patriarchal Church. Grandier is no longer a cynic, and the self-destructive melancholic of Whiting's play; but an idealist and a forceful political actor in his own right and as a consequence of the force of his own, highly original, inspiration. 'Each morning', Grandier/Reed informs the audience,

> I wake up with a feeling of optimism so strong as to be almost absurd ... Strange thoughts come to me. I am like a man who has been lost, who has always been lost. Now, for all kinds of reasons, I have a vague sense of meaning and can think of myself as a small part of God's abundance which includes everything, and I know I want to serve it. I want to serve the people of Loudun.

He would show the king 'that the city is the strength that lives in the hearts of men. That greed and dissension will never destroy her, and with God's help, we will change her walls to terraces that have the colour of stars.'[62]

Unfortunately, what he finds upon his return to the city is Barré's own carnival of reaction. By confronting the exorcists while they are at work in the cathedral, this Grandier re-enacts Jesus' own rout of the moneylenders from the Temple in Jerusalem. In his first hearing before the court, he dominates the proceedings, facing-down the hooded tribunal and the masked spectators. He urges them to go ahead and:

> Accuse me of exposing political chicanery and the evils of the state, and I will plead guilty. But what man can face arraignment on the idiocy of youth, old love letters and other pathetic objects stuffed in drawers or at the bottom of cupboards? Things kept for a day when he would need to be reminded that he was once loved.

What is at stake is neither his own life nor the presence of demons at Loudun, but the fate of the city's independence, integrity and financial prosperity. The demons are simply a sideshow and 'this new doctrine' of witch-hunting and demonology is

> especially invented for this occasion ... the work of men who are not concerned with fact, or with law, or with theology, but with a political experiment to show how the will of one man can be pushed into destroying not only one man or one city,

but an entire nation.

Grandier leaves the courtroom in triumph, swathed in his ecclesiastical finery. However, what follows is an insightful portrayal of the apparatus of witch trials, and the judicial use of terror and humiliation, which enabled their success. Grandier's apartments have been stripped, his paintings slashed and his classical statues overturned and gelded by musket butts. Now, it is his own turn to be humiliated. Laubardemont – who has increasingly taken on the form of Gletkin, Arthur Koestler's Stalinist interrogator in *Darkness at Noon* – complete with his own brand of 'double-think', implores him to consider that he is no longer important. He is already dead. Through his confession, however, he might render 'one last and supreme gesture for the Roman Catholic Church'.

With his head shaved and every hair plucked from his body by order of the tribunal, Grandier's reappearance in court is greeted by howls of laughter and derision. The sack-cloth of his penitent's garb serves to neuter his gender and to emphasise in his, now halting, gait an almost matronly form. Reed, a humiliated Sampson, encapsulates Whiting's earlier description of Grandier, 'completely shaven', reduced before the court to the status and form of 'a bald fool'.[63] Women who once lusted after him, now laugh in his face. Depersonalised – without his magnificent curls, waxed moustaches and even his eyebrows – his is one step nearer the final stage of his dehumanisation, as the bonfire strips away the flesh from his bones. The shaving of the accused was a process common to all formal witch trials, and codified as a means of flushing out the devils and familiars who might seek to hide away from witchfinders and exorcists in strands of hair, or secrete their devil's mark, or supernumerary teat, in the follicles that protect shins, armpits and the pubic glands. Thus, in 1590, Henri Boguet, had recorded the details of a case of witchcraft in Burgundy, whereby:

> Francoise Secretain refused to confess anything, saying that she was innocent of the crime ... Accordingly, it was decided to shave off her hair and change her garments, and to search her to see if she were marked in any way. She was therefore stripped, but no mark was found; and when they came to cut the hair off her head she submitted with utmost confidence. But no sooner was her hair cut than she grew

perturbed and trembled all over her body, and at once confessed, adding to her first confessions from day to day.[64]

For Boguet, the witch-hunter, this demonstrated the veracity of demonological theory. The demons had flown, as soon as her locks had dropped to the floor. Today, we might perceive a different explanation, lying in the forcible erasing of self, and self-image and the assault upon established notions of gender-specific beauty. Thus, Francois Secretain was literally shorn of her femininity, just as surely as Grandier was emasculated by the redeployment of the surgeon's blades.

The blurring of gender lines and the refashioning, and reappropriation, of sexual identities are reoccurring themes at the heart of *The Devils*. In the opening scene, the effeminate Louis XIII appears from out of an oyster shell, to dance in a masque in parody of both his office and Botticelli's vision of *The Birth of Venus*. During the performance, only his crown and strategically placed shells preserve his modesty, but upon the completion of his dance, the spreading concertina of his cloak fans out to transform him into a parody of the statues of the Madonna, seen on the altars and side-chapels of the Counter-Reformation. While the king cuddles his minions, a withered – and withering – Richelieu sits impassively in his wheelchair, as crow-like nuns peck at his icy cheek. Similarly, if one looks closely enough – over Father Barré's shoulder, during the exorcism scene – then both Twiggy and Justin de Villeneuve can be spied, in drag, among the throng of courtiers and fellating nuns, in the cathedral. The ambiguity of their dress – as of many others during the scene – leaves the audience in doubt as to just what they are witnessing. Are they girl and boyfriend, or young boy and older man? And, are they engaged in a platonic, hetero- or homosexual relationship? What is clear is that London's 'top Mods' of the mid- to late 1960s have forsaken the sharp suits and short crops that had made them famous – abandoning the fashions of one elite for that of another – and adopted the silks, satins and long, crimped wigs that characterised both seventeenth-century Loudun and the contemporary counterculture. In fact, the couple pre-empt the Bohemian images that they, themselves, would adopt in real life by the mid-1970s. Within the film, transgression and inversion have become the order of the day and, at Loudun, even Twiggy's familiar androgyny has been distorted and channelled in order to fit a new paradigm of beauty. The girl who looked like a boy, is now the boy who aspires to be a girl.

Grandier's de-gendering is the most graphic and extreme example of this process, and the one that produces the most fearsome results. However, as in life, Grandier's incredible resolve and bravery in the face of brutal torture and a horrendous death ensured a posthumous triumph that stunted the witch-hunt at Loudun and saw the trial deviate from the standard pattern. Despite the shattering of his legs, and the physical and intellectual force of Laubardemont's cross-questioning, he steadfastly refused to implicate others. As a result, the widening cycle of persecution upon which the 'classic' witch persecution relied, was absent. There were no more suspects, and so the accusations of *maleficia* and devilment had nothing fresh to feed upon. It was the absence of a fresh focus that permitted Madeleine de Brou to slip back into obscurity and Sister Jeanne of the Angels to acquire an aura of sanctity capable of transferring from the cloister to the royal court.

The Devils is able to convey something of this sense in its final scenes. Laubardemont visits Sister Jeanne in her cell, to find her compulsively purging her womb, self-administering the clysters that have ruined her body and her mind. The witch mania has passed the city by; shaken and shamed by Grandier's death, Father Mignon has lost his sanity and has taken to repeating the mantra that they have burned an innocent man, while the ever-enterprising Father Barré has left on another mission, this time to exorcise a nun possessed by a devil in the form 'of a three-legged dog'. Patiently, Laubardemont explains to Jeanne that there will be a few tourists who will come to see her, 'to brighten things up' from time to time, but that these visits would soon dry up as the city – stripped of its military defences and political defender – would soon dwindle away to the status of a rural backwater. Her fame, and her purpose, would disappear along with it. Now she really would be 'stuck in this convent for life'.[65]

Amid the fallen masonry, the smoking tinders and the ashes of her dead husband, Madeleine de Brou is permitted to walk free from the ruined city, and across an apocalyptic landscape. Despite everything, *The Devils* still presents a more optimistic message than either *Mother Joan of the Angels* or Whiting's stage play. Though they have lost, both Grandier and Madeleine knew precisely what it was they fought against, and why. They attained a shared religious revelation and attempted to re-mould their city as a heaven upon earth, a new 'city upon a hill'. Madeleine, at least, had lived to tell the tale and tomorrow would be her own.

CHAPTER SEVEN

I Shall Go Unto a Hare

I shall goe until a hare,
Wi sorrow and sick mickle care,
I shall goe in the devil's name,
An while I come home again.

I am ruled by the moon,
I move under her mantle,
I am the symbol of her moods,
Of rebirths' cycle.

I am companion to the gods,
I can conceive while I am pregnant,
I call the dawn and spring in,
I am the advent.

… I've been cursed, I've been despised,
As a Witch with darkest powers,
I shall goe until a hare,
I've been hunted, trapped and punished,
In these my darkest hours,
Wi sorrow and such mickle care.

(Maddy Prior, 'The Fabled Hare', 1993, Park Records)

I

A moment or two is often enough to define a life. Isobel Gowdie was born, lived, kept house and worked the fields at Auldearn for the great majority of her life without ever exciting comment, or causing so much as a ripple to trouble the keepers of official records. She would, doubtless, have gone to her grave under the sodden Highland turf and troubled no one had she not walked into a courtroom, seemingly of her own volition, in the spring of 1662, in order to confess her crime of witchcraft. Struggling with overwhelming feelings of guilt and fearful that she had harmed a close neighbour through her practice of malefic magic, she confessed that she had been 'over long' in the service of witchcraft. Between 13 and 17 May, she went on to give four separate confessions to the local magistrates and it is from these very different and, at times, difficult and conflicting testimonies that we owe our only glimpses into her life, her activities, and the wellspring of fear that came to consume her.[1] Either side of those dates we know nothing of her movements or biography, everything else is pure conjecture.

We do know from the court records that she was married to John Gilbert, a cottar; that she was approaching middle age but still sexually active at the time of her trial; and that she lived in a farmstead at Loch Loy, on the outskirts of Auldearn, with her husband. All else that might be considered to be the stuff of a conventional biographical narrative is entirely absent from her statements before her judges. We do not know if she had children, if the oppressive nature of the Kirk's dominance in Scotland stunted her horizons and limited her powers of self-expression, or whether she had witnessed, as a young girl, the bloody fight among the village enclosures, on 9 May 1645, when the Marquis of Montrose's Royalist host routed the army of the Covenant and left Auldearn a smouldered parchmark among the ripening corn.[2]

What we can be sure of is that, in presenting herself before the authorities, Gowdie hoped to unburden herself of her worries and to give a good account of those of her activities that, she felt, had grievously harmed her chances of salvation and a life hereafter. It was her particular tragedy that the authorities had their own, very clear, preconceptions about exactly what did – and did not – equate to the practice of witchcraft and were not prepared to allow her the freedom to present her evidence in the manner that she had carefully planned. Indeed, over the course of the four separate interrogations, her judges made sure that the list of her crimes and the names of her accomplices were constantly reworked, refined and clarified, in order to fit with a more conventional stereotype that was familiar to them through the standard witchcraft texts. As a result, her initial desire to tell her examiners of her adventures in faerie land was subsumed in a darker narrative of demonic pacts and murderous vengeance against all those who had wronged her.

Thus, she described how, in 1647, she had met the Devil while out walking and had entered into a covenant with him, in parody of both the Old Testament accords of the Jewish people with Jarweh and also the founding document of modern Scottish political life, signed in Greyfriars Kirkyard in February 1638. That same night, she claimed that she had gone to the Kirk at Auldearn, where she denied her Christian baptism before the Devil and received his mark upon her shoulder. While she was held fast by her neighbour, Margaret Brodie, the Devil had supposedly sucked the blood from out of her mark and sprinkled it upon her head, declaring that: 'I baptise thee, Janet, in my own name!'³ Having given herself in spirit to the Devil, Gowdie proceeded to give him exhaustive use of her body. In her third confession, she provided lurid details of their sexual relationship, explaining to the court how she had deluded her husband, creeping out of bed at night to meet with the Devil and leaving a broom behind her, which doubled for her image in her husband's mind until the breaking of the dawn. She revelled in tales of the Devil's sexual prowess, of the enormous size and blackness of his penis, and how his semen dripped cold into her, searing and thrilling her to the core of her being, while he rode her 'like a stallion among mares'.⁴

Equipped with her new name and backed by a strong network of covens, Gowdie then, supposedly, began to wreak havoc upon her local community, with the aid of her familiar spirit, known as the 'Read Reiver'. She claimed to have ruined crops and to have soured milk, to have transformed herself – at will – into jackdaws, hares and crows, and to have stolen into the houses of the local gentry in order to 'eat and drink of the best'.⁵ Indeed, the procuring and consumption of rich foods is a constant theme in all of her confessions and seems to have been one of the greatest benefits that she felt she had received during her service to her dark master. However, it is patently obvious that Isobel, in 'professing [her] repentance' and her 'great grief and shame' was only too keen to please her interrogators and that her spoken testimony was heavily edited and led by them. Thus, her initial enthusiasm to tell of her meetings with the King and Queen of the Faerie, up in the 'Deunie-Hills', and to describe their appearances, together with the fearsome activities of the herds of 'elf bulls' that milled about them, was brusquely cut short and went largely unrecorded in the official case notes.⁶ A clearly bored official simply noted 'etc. etc.' in the middle of her testimony as she struggled to explain her encounter with the faerie realm and stopped writing altogether. We will never now know just what she felt impelled, at the risk of her life, to tell her judges.

It was demonology, and not folklore, that concerned and motivated the authorities. Thus, the tales of 'elf bulls' and of feasting, on equal terms with the King and Queen, were ignored or struck from the record. The cataloguing of her murderous crimes as a witch was what was demanded of her, and it was precisely this which was duly revealed in her subsequent depositions. Consequently, Isobel informed her interrogators that she had raised an unchristened child from its grave at Nairn; caused the heirs of John Hay, the Laird of Park, to sicken, wither and to die; and had killed many men by flying through the air above them upon straws and shooing them down with special 'elf arrows' – most likely Neolithic flint-knappings – that came to her straight from the hands of the Devil, himself.⁷ Minister Forbes seems to have been singled out by the coven for particular attention and an underlying antagonism between him and Gowdie appears to have existed, which drove forward both the witches' supposed reign of terror and the legal prosecution that followed in its wake. Gowdie claimed, in court, that she had begged the Devil to be allowed to shoot at him again, after another witch's arrow fell short of its intended target. Moreover, she maintained that, in the winter of 1660, the coven had sought to make fatal an illness that he was suffering by uttering incantations over a bag containing the 'galls, flesh and guts of toads', together with barley grains and nail and hair clippings, before hacking it to pieces and throwing the remains into water.[8] However, in repeatedly expressing her profound sorrow for the killing of her neighbour, William Brower of Milltown Moynes, Gowdie appears to have seen herself as having acted against her own will, and to have genuinely believed that she had been directly responsible for his death through her use of demonic magic. It is conceivable that this powerful sense of guilt was a major factor in prompting Gowdie to make her confessions and to demand that an exemplary sentence should be passed upon her, desiring that she should be riven upon iron harrows or 'worse, if it could be devised.'[9]

Though Pitcairn believed that Gowdie was probably convicted of witchcraft and subsequently burned at the stake – together with her accomplice, Janet Breadheid – there is no record of her eventual fate.[10] Her papers were forwarded to the Scottish Privy Council, in the summer of 1662, and Sir Hew Campbell of Calder, together with eight others, was empowered to try the case, on 10 July 1662. However, it was recommended that the death sentence were only to be passed if a whole list of conditions, regarding the prisoner's physical well-being and the state of her mental health, were met in full. Not only was it important to prove beyond all doubt that Gowdie had confessed voluntarily and 'without any sort of torture', but, significantly, solid evidence was also required that 'at the tyme of their confessions ... [Gowdie and Breadheid] were of sound judgment, nowayes distracted or under any earnest desyre to die.'[11] Only if Gowdie insisted upon reiterating and renewing her former confessions, before the judiciary, 'then and in that case and no otherwayes' should the death sentence be invoked.[12] Whatever the societal tensions in Auldearn, central government in Edinburgh was clearly sceptical about witchcraft as a crime and the need to hand down capital sentences to deal with transgressions that appeared so outlandish and outdated to an increasingly confident urban elite. Sir Hew Campbell was, thus, able to arrive at a formula that appeared to satisfy all parties and quickly, quietly and probably bloodlessly put the matter to rest. The Privy Council had praised the local authorities for detecting and successfully prosecuting the crime but also offered so many provisions for allowing an acquittal that its own preferences in the matter were made crystal clear. Local government had been allowed its honour, but would have to risk confrontation with the centre if it wished to proceed further in seeking the deaths of Isobel Gowdie and Janet Breadheid. While in the cases of the witches of

Bamberg and Loudon, the nation's political elites had been actively engaged in seeking convictions, in the case of the witches of Auldearn, they were playing the opposite role and were seeking – in the wake of a quarter century of war and revolution – to downplay localised disputes and social tensions. The *realpolitik*, an emergent sense of rationalism and an enlightened, more humane, attitude to the law, now coincided and seem to have provided for acquittals, even at the point when the Scots judiciary was prepared to unleash the greatest witch-hunt ever known in the land upon its peoples.[13]

The evidence for Isobel Gowdie's fate is, therefore, in essence negative. There is no record of a subsequent trial under the direction of Sir Hew Campbell, no accompanying popular ballad or pamphlet literature to celebrate the conviction of two such notorious and garrulous witches, and no account of a dramatic public execution through their burning at the stake. Given the volume of salacious material provided by Gowdie's evidence to the court at Auldearn and her talk of devils, murderous plots and faerie kingdoms lying under the hills, it seems unlikely that an enterprising publisher – in either Edinburgh or London – would have chosen to pass over the chance of producing a sure-fire bestseller. It would appear likely, though by no means certain, that Isobel Gowdie was eventually discharged – at some point in the later summer of 1662 – and allowed to slip back into the quiet obscurity from whence she came.

II

With no accompanying pamphlet literature to accompany it, the case was quickly forgotten, until – that is – Robert Pitcairn rediscovered it in the archives of the Edinburgh High Court and transcribed a version of Isobel's testimony which appeared in the published version of his *Ancient Criminal Trials in Scotland*, in 1833. Pitcairn had been greatly influenced and inspired by the work of Sir Walter Scott and sent copies of the more dramatic cases to the author, for use as possible source material in his historical novels, almost as soon as he found them. In this manner, the disciplines of the dryly empirical archivist and the myth-making Romantic novelist cross-fertilised, as both men clearly recognised in their correspondence. Scott had long harboured the idea of writing about witchcraft, possessed a large occult library at his stately home at Abbotsford, and had made three earlier, ill-fated, attempts to publish upon the subject. In 1809, he had suggested collaborating on a treatise on demonology with the north-eastern antiquarian, Robert Surtees; in 1812, he considered writing a selection of light-hearted supernatural tales with Charles Kirkpatrick; and in 1823, he had begun a dialogue on superstitious practices and popular magic which, like his other ventures, ground to a standstill as the result of a lack of interest and financial support from his publishers. However, Pitcairn's private generosity with his research notes, and the public interest they generated through their serialised publication in popular literary magazines, transformed the situation and ensured that there would be a ready market for a book upon witchcraft by Scotland's foremost historical novelist. The idea seems to have originated with Scott's son-in-law, John Lockhart, who had increasingly come to act as his literary agent as the author's health began to fail and who drove the project along to its successful completion.

The resulting book, *Letters on Demonology and Witchcraft*, was written very quickly during the summer months of 1830 and, published together with a series of illustrative plates by George Cruikshank in time for Christmas, became a bestseller, helping to stabilise Scott's flagging fortunes. It took the form of ten 'letters' sent by Scott to his son-in-law, in response to questions from the readers of *Murray's Family Library* – the publisher of popular serialised works – about 'the history of a dark chapter in human nature'.[14] Scott had been quick to realise the importance of Gowdie's confessions as an important and sensational new source for Scottish witchcraft, bringing the term 'coven' – to denote a group of witches – into popular usage and attesting to a wealth of fairy lore in the Highlands of Scotland, that was far removed from the learned traditions of elite demonologists.[15] However, he went further in attempting to codify the practice of witchcraft from the atypical confessions of a single individual and to make the experience of Isabel Gowdie appear general. Thus, he stretched the original evidence to form the following picture of the

> witches of Auldearne ... [who] were so numerous that they were told off into squads, or *covines* [sic], as they were termed, to each of which were appointed two officers. One of these was called the Maiden of the Covine, and was usually, like Tam O' Shanter's Nannie, a girl of great personal attractions, whom Satan placed beside himself, and treated with particular attention, which greatly provoked the spite of the old hags, who felt themselves insulted by the preference. When assembled, they dug up graves, and possessed themselves of the carcasses (of unchristened infants in particular), whose joints and members they used in magic unguents and salves ... praying the devil to transfer to them the fruit of the ground ... and leave the proprietors nothing but thistles and briars ... They entered the house of the Earl of Murray, himself, and such other mansions as were not fenced against them by vigil and prayer, and feasted on the provisions they found there.[16]

Scott thought that the witches of Auldearn 'were the countrywomen of the weird sisters in *Macbeth*' and provided his readers with some of the 'spells' that they had employed in their working of harmful magic.

Metamorphoses were, according to Isobel, very common among them, and the forms of crows, cats, hares and other animals were on such occasions assumed. In the shape of a hare, Isobel herself had a bad adventure. She had been sent by the Devil to Auldearne in that favourite disguise, with some message to her neighbours, but had the misfortune to meet Peter Papley of Kilhill's servants going to labour, having his hounds with them. The hounds sprang on the disguised witch, 'and I', says Isobel, 'ran a very long time, but being hard pressed, was forced to take to my own house, the door being open, and there took refuge behind a chest'. But the hounds came in and took the other side of the chest, so that Isobel only escaped by getting into another house, and gaining time to say the disenchanting rhyme:

'Hare, hare, God send thee care!
I am in hare's likeness now;
But I shall be a woman even now –
Hare, hare, God send thee care!'[17]

So influential was Scott, as both a Romantic novelist and interpreter of Scotland's core national myths, that the idea of the 'coven' – which had no basis in English trials – with 12 members and a 'maiden', now became rooted in the popular consciousness, while Isobel Gowdie was recast as a beauty, particularly favoured by her lord, the Devil.

Both visions would appeal to another – though less well-known – novelist, John William Brodie-Innes, an Edinburgh barrister, friend to Bram Stoker and leading figure in one of the many offshoots of the Temple of the Golden Dawn. Published in 1915, his gothic novel *The Devil's Mistress*, combined appeals to archival sources with outright invention. 'Mistress Isabel' is recast as a young girl, from a monied family, the

daughter of a country lawyer, [who] was exceptionally well educated for her time and class ... [who] read much, played fairly well on the spinet, and could dance a minuet as well as any lady in the land ... In person she was strangely unlike the women of the farmer class in the province of Moray, being tall and slight, with a mass of flaming red hair, deep brown eyes that seemed as though brooding over hidden fires, dark eyebrows almost straight in a face that seemed unnaturally pale ... and full red lips.[18]

It was her misfortune to be a secret Roman Catholic, in a land dominated by a dour and repressive Kirk, and to be married for money to John Gilbert a 'grim, heavy, untidy farmer, with his ragged hair and unshaven chin, his clothes rarely changed save when he donned his rusty black on the Sabbath day ... to ... listen to the edifying discourses of Master Harry Forbes, the minister'.[19] Spurned by her husband, lusted after by the local laird and preached hell fire by the minister, she seeks solace in the visitations of the Catholic missionary priests and 'gossip' afforded by her one friend, Janet Broadhead, 'a great teller of stories ... [whose] tales of wild adventure ... afterwards made her own life look so grey and colourless' by comparison. Yet, all of this changes through a chance encounter with a stranger upon the road. Thoughts of this stranger, with the 'face of a student, grave and somewhat sad', a natural dignity, lilting voice and 'eyes [that] were piercingly bright with a strange magnetic attraction', soon come to possess her every waking moment, as she yearns and lusts for his danger and charm.[20] At the price of her soul, she finds self-expression and sexual fulfilment in the arms of her 'Dark Master' who – of course – soon transpires to be none other than the Devil, himself.

This association between witchcraft, free love and the sensuous is embodied in a passage in which Isobel performs a magical rite, naked, at full moon in Auldearn kirkyard.

> On this night the moon at her full would rise exactly in mid-heaven at midnight, and now she hung clear and dazzling brilliant, almost in the centre of her arc ... The stillness was intense ... the usual night sounds were hushed, all nature seemed pausing ... to observe her. The very stars seemed to be a thousand eyes, watching with shameless curiosity. Then the fascination of the daring took her. She drew a long breath, stood erect for a moment, and then loosening the clasp of her robe at the neck she dropped her arms and let the dark robe and the white smock together slip rustling to her knees. One second she held her arms aloft, then she loosed the silver snood and shook out the mass of her tresses, stepped from the confining entanglement of clothes about her feet, and stood forth, a beautiful white, naked figure in the strong moonlight

attempting to draw down the moon in the name of the goddess, Hecate.[21]

The novelist leaves the reader in no doubt of the physical reality of the Devil, the malignity of witchcraft and the existence of an underground pagan cult which worshipped the goddess; Isobel is neither deluded, nor half-crazed, but clear-sighted in her resolve to achieve her desires through the dark art. Yet, in the end, the denouement of the tales hangs upon Isobel's desire for Christian redemption and, in particular, her whole-hearted re-engagement with the Roman Catholicism of her youth. The element of mild sexual titillation is balanced, in the last few chapters, by an improving religious homily, which attempts to excuse much of the narrative that went before it. Exorcised of the devil by Father Blackhall – another of the missionary priests – she, at last, witnesses Satan's true form 'cringing and cowering, but insolent to the last'.[22] Retiring to a remote convent in the calm, regular life of devotion, all the restlessness and heart-hunger passed away from her, and ... the second sight which she had by nature, aided by prayer and the rigid austere rule of the community developed into visions as were accorded ... to the saints.

In the course of a 'truly' religious, as opposed to sexual, ecstasy, Jesus appears to her in her cell and leads her, on her path of atonement, to the courtroom and, finally, to the executioner's stake.[23] Brodie-Innes, therefore, sought to establish for his readership, the demonic malignity of witchcraft, the physical reality of Satan, and the ability of witches – in line with the occult philosophy of the Golden Dawn – to be able to visit, and flourish, upon the astral plane. Unwittingly, he also gave credence to a vision of female magic and power – worked naked, under the moon and by a beauty as opposed to a hag – which would find strong resonance within the modern Pagan religion.

This vision of witchcraft appeared to receive intellectual credence through the success of Margaret Murray's popular studies of witchcraft – *The Witch-Cult in Western Europe* and *The God of the Witches* – published respectively in 1921 and 1933. Having trained as an Egyptologist, participated in the direct actions of the suffragette movement and joined Sir Flinders Petrie's excavations in the Nile delta, Murray found that amid the destruction of World War I, 'I had practically no students, the learned societies were neither meeting nor publishing, and Egyptology seemed, for the moment, to be flat and unprofitable'. Instead, she turned her attention to witchcraft and spent the rest of the war years compiling the notes that would form the basis of *The Witch-Cult in Western Europe*. 'I had started', she later recalled,

> with the usual idea that the witches were all old women suffering from illusions about the Devil ... I worked only from contemporary records, and when I suddenly realised that the so-called Devil was simply a disguised man I was startled, almost alarmed, by the way the recorded facts fell into place, and showed that the witches were members of an old and primitive form of religion, and the records had been made by members of a new persecuting form.[24]

Isobel Gowdie's confessions seemed to stand out among all of 'contemporary records' consulted by Murray as proof-positive of a powerful and enduring, underground, pagan tradition at work within the British Isles. Indeed, Gowdie's testimonies – harvested from Pitcairn's volumes and owing a debt to Scott's expert retelling – formed the single most potent, and directly quoted, source to support Murray's vision of the witch. At a single stroke, her evidence seemed to provide a highly detailed insider's account of the operation of a coven and the practical workings of magic.

She gives details of enchantments, 'pagan' religious rites, familiars, of the Devil acting more like a brutish man – giving her frequent beatings – than a fallen angel, and of the organisation of the underground religion, including the initiation by 'blood-rite'.[25]

The vision of their meetings as 'joyous assemblies', forming part of a pagan ritual calendar, seemed to be substantiated by Gowdie's first confession at Auldearn, when she told the magistrates that:

> The last tyme that owr Coven met, we, and an vther Coven, wer dauncing at the Hill of Earlseat; and befor that betwixt Moynes and Bowgholl; and befor that we ves beyond the Meikleburne; and the vther Coven being at the Downie-hillis we went from beyond the Meikle-burne, and went besyd them, to the howssis at the Wood-end of Inshoch ... Befor Candlemas, we wentbe-east Kinlosse.[26]

The trouble was that only one of these gatherings is dated and, even then, she does not say that the witches met *on* Candlemass but at some unspecified time *before* it. Moreover, for Minister Forbes, the members of the Dunbar family and William Dallas, Sheriff of Nairne, who sat in judgement upon her, the reference would have inspired thoughts of the Christian Gaelic, as opposed to the pagan universal, ritual year. Indeed, the whole concept rests not upon Isobel Gowdie or her coven, but upon the confession of one solitary witch, Isobel Smith, recorded at Forfar in 1661.[27] What is omitted from the passage is, perhaps, just as significant as when Murray left out the wilder parts of Isobel's testimony, which sat askance with the veracity of her evidence regarding the operation of the covens. If we extend the quotations beyond her account of the meeting at Kinloss, we discover through Pitcairn's trial records that they yoked frogs to a plough, which the Devil and John Young, the 'Officer' of the Coven, supposedly drove through the turf while the witches went up and down with the plough, praying to the Devil 'for the fruit of that land', that thistles and briars might grow there.[28] Now, we are faced with the decision, whether or not to accept Gowdie's confessions in their entirety as truth or to dismiss them as the products of coercion or mild mental illness. What we cannot do, with clear conscience, is to cherry-pick selected quotations from four wild and wildly conflicting confessions in order to try and justify a picture of a secretive, but highly organised, underground religion.

Unfortunately, the desire to make this one, particularly detailed, account general and to apply it, uncritically, to the *modus operandi* of English witches is precisely what Margaret Murray did through much of her work. In scholarly circles, attempts to prove that Gowdie represented a powerful and enduring, underground, pagan tradition at work within the British Isles, through the use of these selective quotations, have been increasingly viewed as being both misleading and unhelpful. From the 1960s onwards – beginning with Elliot Rose's critique, *A Razor for a Goat*, and continuing through Hugh Trevor-Roper and Keith Thomas to Norman Cohn – academic writers, from across many different disciplines, began to pick-apart the Murray thesis by recourse to the original sources and to a growing number of local case studies. Thus, as Norman Cohn points out, Murray systematically plays 'down the manifestly impossible features in the accounts of the sabbat'.[29] In particular, Murray's contention that the Dianic cult survived through an aboriginal race – pushed further and further north and, ultimately, driven underground – finds no trace in the archaeological record, and appears at best fantastic and at worst laughable. The collapse of the Murray thesis, hastened by the increasing academic engagement with the subject, seemed total when her former stronghold, the Folk-Lore Society, took a more measured and nuanced view of her work and Carlo Ginzburg, a leading authority who had once taken inspiration from her work, could declare her concept of the Gowdie trial 'absurd' and that by 1989, 'almost all historians of witchcraft concur in considering Murray's book (as had its first critics) amateurish, absurd, bereft of any scientific merit'.[30]

Though this might have been the case among academics, in the meantime, Murray's views profoundly shaped the nascent Pagan movement, in general, and to popularise Gowdie's account, in particular. Her concept of the coven, 'the cult group of thirteen ... generally, though not invariably adhered to', became formalised as the basis of a new, world religion, while Isobel's testimony – with a 'wild air of poetry about it' – became an important source for spells and ritual language when Doreen Valiente attempted to codify the practice of modern witchcraft, for a new generation, in 1973.[31] Valiente accepted Murray's idea that Gowdie had presented herself to the authorities in order to escape a 'cruel and sadistic man' who had acted the part of the Devil in the coven's rituals, but added an interpretative twist of her own that seemed to reinforce Murray's linkage of paganism with divine sacrifice. The desire to die, to offer herself up to the executioner, and to confess her crimes before the court, suddenly became explicable to Valiente if Isobel Gowdie was viewed as 'a voluntary human sacrifice'. The Maiden of the Coven willingly enacted a religious, and triumphant, act: defying and double-crossing the dominant Christian order in the Highlands and, at the same time, feminising the image of the sacrificial pagan 'Corn King' who died in order to save his people and secure the harvest. In this version, Gowdie emerges as a brave, powerful and empowered woman who acted out of clear conviction, as opposed to a frightened cottar's wife, consumed by her doubts and running heedless towards her own destruction.[32] She was now defined and repeatedly described as a 'young Scottish witch' and as a 'beautiful, red-haired girl', turning the conventional stereotype of the solitary, poor old crone upon its head.[33] Such singular empowerment was core to Valiente's own conception of witchcraft: she had been initiated by Gerald Gardner into his own coven and had served as his High Priestess, bringing a strong sense of the power and rhythms of language to Pagan ceremony, and investing – in her adaption of Gardner's *Book of Shadows* – a sense of poetics and the feminine into its dominant liturgical expression, which had hitherto been largely masculine. Isobel Gowdie's ability to shape rhyme in order to effect and define her dark art had an instant and understandable appeal to Valiente. They gave modern witchcraft a vocabulary and solid evidence for the working of sympathetic magic in the past; which could barb 'Elf arrows', visit sickness, strike down new-born lambs or enable night flight.[34] Furthermore, Isobel's ability to recall, recite and improve upon magical verses – while under the scrutiny of the courtroom – marked out her own testimony from that of her co-accused, Janet Breadheid (or Broadhead), and gave her a distinctive and creative voice that drew successive generations of writers and musicians to her tale.

In choosing to depict Gowdie as a beautiful, young redhead, Valiente was not following the court records, but a literary convention established by Brodie-Innes and popularised by Dennis Wheatley, who wrote of Isobel's 'exceptional beauty of face and body crowned by a mass of flaming red hair', as though he was expressing an opinion formed after consulting original sources rather than providing a simple précis of the novel's plot.[35] More remarkable still, was his readiness to accept Isobel's demonic liaison at face value. 'One day in the forest', he tells his readers, Isobel Gowdie

> meets a most attractive man. She instantly falls in love with him, and he with her. He is Satan, yet not represented in accordance with Christian teaching – a hideous monster – but as Lucifer, the Lord of this World and Son of the Morning. Isabel readily gives herself to him, joins his coven and becomes its queen.[36]

The testimony before the court is passed off as veracity, while Brodie-Innes' redemptive homily full of visions, temptations of the flesh and religious ecstasies, is sensationalised and sexualised, with an added emphasis placed upon Gowdie's Satanic encounter. This notion of Gowdie as a predatory succubus was later to find its niche in the horror fiction of Graham Masterton. In his 1991 novel, *Night Plague*, Isobel Gowdie's role as witch is entirely subsumed by her sexual deviancy, played out in dreamtime, and by her status as the Devil's 'mistress', the queen of pain and punishment. Her own history is thoroughly conflated with that of Ursula Kemp as we encounter her, bound fast to a limestone outcrop, 'her forehead still crowned with corroded screws [from her coffin] ... once imposed on her, in the hope that she would never be able to think Satanic thoughts again'.[37]

In the popular imagination, Gowdie had made the journey from victim to liberated woman, to oppressor. However, the tale came full circle with the publication in 2005 of *The Drowning Pond*, a novel aimed at a teenage readership, which reimagined Isobel crying out to her accusers on her way to the scaffold that she was

> too blind and lame to work the land … All you've ever done is ease bokes, calm skins and break fevers with your oils and veneficiums. But who'll stand up for an aul crone who walked the woods at night talking to herself for company, gathering roots and herbs? Who's going to admit Mother Gowdie wasn't exhuming the corpses of unbaptised bairns for sorcery when they saw her digging earth in the churchyard, but tending her mother's grave. You saw me, Meg Pirrie, Janet McLean. You know I was praying in Latin, not summoning Satan with my incantations … You were only gossiping because you didn't like the look of me.[38]

The point of departure for adolescents coming to terms with feelings of anxiety about themselves and hostility towards others, perceived as being wanting or simply different, was the music of James MacMillan and it was his symphony, premiered at the Proms season in 1990, that introduced modern elites to Gowdie's story.[39] However, as an inspiration for popular music, Gowdie had a far longer pedigree.

The Sensational Alex Harvey Band paid homage to Isobel – renamed as Isobel Goudie – in December 1972, on their debut album, *Framed*. The song, a three-part opus respectively titled 'My Lady of the Night', 'Coitus Interruptus' and the 'Virgin and the Hunter', rather than reflecting a 'bawdy tale of prostitute, Isobel Goudie' – as the sleeve notes on a recent re-issue would have it – actually retold the encounter between Isobel and the Devil on the high road, their liaison and the cuckholding of John Gilbert.[40] Alex Harvey, a hard-drinking, straight-talking, hard-partying son of the Gorbals, was also a born entertainer. Charismatic, well read, with a love of science fiction and historical tales, he had come across Gowdie via Walter Scott and Pitcairn and began working and reworking the song as part of his band's repertoire several years before it was committed to vinyl.[41] Yet, the performance was key: stage shows brimming with theatrics and bravura; a guitarist, leering over the footlights, clad in tight particoloured breeches and skull-white clown make-up; Harvey, in faded tailcoat, spitting out the lyrics, serenading the dressmaker's mannequin that he was dragging along behind him. Gowdie the witch, who 'does not do the things she should', fitted easily into the purposefully unsettling, macabre scene. If Harvey's genius illuminated the charts all too briefly, and cascaded to earth before dull corporate conformity wrapped them in a cola-pop, dollar-strewn grasp, then his contemporaries on the scene, the folk-rock band Steeleye Span, enjoyed considerable artistic and commercial success with a number of songs and border ballads featuring witchcraft as an explicit theme. Bob Johnson, their guitarist, revelled in stories of murder, faerie law and dark magic and if the creative drive and excitement that powered 'Alison Gross' – 'the ugliest witch in the north country' – 'Two Magicians' or 'Thomas the Rhymer' had dwindled away by the time of their twenty-fifth anniversary – when a song about the witch-hunts, 'You Shall Burn,' sounded like an Angela Dworkin tract stitched onto a plodding and tinny backing-tape – then, at least, their erstwhile lead singer had left for fresher fields. Maddy Prior, one of the most gifted and original talents of the British folk revival, wove traditional motifs – many drawn from Scotland and the borders – with modern themes and, in 'The Fabled Hare,' which is quoted at the head of this chapter, tied Isobel Gowdie's account of shape-shifting to the turning of the seasons and wider, ecological, issues to great lyrical and musical effect.[42] This theme of Gowdie's magical transformation would appear again, in 'Woman to Hare,' a rock song by Inkubus Sukkubus, a band who trod their own distinctive line between Goth style and folk themes, overtly celebrating the Pagan revival and modern witchcraft in all their albums. 'Woman to Hare' envisages:

> Woman to hare and back …
> I have watched many men in their beds as they lie …
> They may think they are strong and are brave and rule this world,
> But with quiet and with magick and with hare,
> They do not compare.[43]

Fresh, emancipatory and defiant of social and religious convention, popular music's Isobel Gowdie – free, magical and avowedly pagan – sits askance with MacMillan's symphony, which casts her as Christian, devout and utterly repressed. In this revisionist take on the story, MacMillan – himself, a strong Roman Catholic – identifies the Reformation as the prime impulse behind the witch-hunt in Scotland. Gowdie – echoing whether consciously or unconsciously, Brodie-Innes' novel – is a secret Catholic destroyed by the paranoia of a Calvinism 'suspicious of anything that suggested Satanism, from the "papist" practice of praying to saints to the old custom of leaving out milk for the faeries'.[44] Indeed, Catholic liturgy and church music are referenced throughout the work, with the plainsong requiem 'Lux Aeterna' used to mourn Gowdie's plight. Indeed, the composer wrote that the piece was designed: 'On behalf of the Scottish people, the work craves absolution and offers Isobel Gowdie the mercy and humanity that was denied her in the last days of her life … This work is the Requiem that Isobel Gowdie never had.' One history of Scotland, of Kirk and Covenant, of Greyfriars Churchyard and heroic martyrdoms, collapses amid allegations of overturning the orderly Catholic consensus with fire and sword. Gowdie is a victim on account of her faith, and her status as a victim demands that she should suffer torture and death in order that we can repudiate one past, and substitute another. In this manner, Knox and Henderson, the hodden grey Covenanters and field preachers might be seen to retreat before the shades of Mary Queen of Scots, Cardinal Beaton and the Highland Host. However, in this case the confessional and societal paradigm does not fit. The problem is, of course, that Gowdie was neither a Roman Catholic, nor – as far as we can tell – either tortured or put to death. This Scottish Golgotha, is simply a misshapen hill if, after all, it lacks a cross.

Academic research, and the belief that somewhere amid the local records offices and boxes of neglected, crumbling legal documents there has to be the resolution to our questions, can often transform the frontiers of our knowledge and alter the parameters of debate. Certainly, Emma Wilby's monumental study of *The Visions of Isobel Gowdie*, published in 2010, seemingly left no stone unturned in attempting to reconstruct Gowdie's life and to forge a conventional biography for her, from out of a few pages of court records and a mass of supportive cultural and theological detail.[45] Particularly exciting was the claim to have rediscovered manuscript trial records of Gowdie's committal that supplemented Pitcairn's transcripts. The book certainly represents a labour of love and builds, for the most part successfully, on the hypothesis advanced in Wilby's earlier study of familiar spirits, which rejected the charge that Gowdie had been mentally ill and, instead, celebrated her 'visionary experience'.[46] The mutation of the counterculture, from the late 1980s and not least through the impact of dance or rave culture, had given rise to neo- or urban shamanism, with examples and practices drawn overwhelmingly from Native American, as opposed to Siberian, experience. Engagement with spirit flights, animist religion, altered states of consciousness and another world free of demonic influences, enabled Isobel Gowdie to no longer be seen as a witch or simple maniac, but as an experienced shamanic practitioner whose only misfortune was to have run foul of the authorities. The thesis dispensed with the untenable aspects of Margaret Murray's work but neatly found an explanation for Gowdie's accounts of night flight and shape-shifting, which gave them purpose and an element of rationality. Yet, there would seem to be an immediate problem in attempting to establish the existence of an *a priori* culture based upon shamanistic visions that was once general across the northern hemisphere, both East and West, before being driven underground at the advent of Christianity. First, it sounds too close for comfort to the discredited Murray thesis – substituting the figure of the shaman for that of the witch – and second, there would seem to be a danger in trying to establish a 'core' set of shamanic practices, supposedly common to all indigenous peoples, that went entirely unnoticed by Europe's elites – outside a Siberian or Lappish context – for almost a thousand years.[47] Moreover, while Isobel Gowdie's evidence is suggestive of spirit flights, her testimony is entirely devoid of any sense of contact with dead ancestors who advised or empowered her, as one might expect from recourse to anthropological studies of shamanism. Perhaps more surprising, given the strong biographical focus, is the comparatively modest attention paid to Gowdie's fate. She is assumed to have perished, as a convicted witch, amid the flames but, after more than 500 pages of closely argued detail, there is no significant discussion of her actual conviction or of the deliberations of the Privy Council.

The cautionary point of Isobel Gowdie's tale is that we can only go so far in reconstructing cases of, and motives for, witchcraft, as the sources available to us will allow. Courts, victims and witnesses can only tell us as much as they wished to, on subjects that, at the time, were considered germane. Our understandable urge to recover the totality of the picture and to attain a historical truth is negated, for the most part, by the fragmental nature of the documentary sources. It is also limited by the fact that our modern concerns and questions are not necessarily those of the Early Modern period. It is a frustrating state of affairs but one which leads the artist and the historian into very different territories, in their quest for 'real' or purely imagined pasts. It is possible for MacMillan to have Isobel Gowdie executed at the stake, for what is a tragedy without an injustice or a sacrifice? Brodie-Innes' Gothic romance would fail to captivate if its heroine were unremarkable, plain or unsympathetic. However, the nature of history is the art of forensics, as opposed to the business of speculation; and the only honest response to limited, incomplete or partial testimonies is to admit that there are some things that we do not, or cannot, now know.

With this in mind, it is probably safer to conclude that the Gowdie case was the product of conflicting cosmologies, on the fault-line between a Gaelic-speaking Highland culture, on the one hand, and an English-speaking Lowland culture, harnessing the power of a centralising Scottish state, on the other.[48] Without the evidence of an execution, Isobel Gowdie would seem to have left the courtroom for one last time and returned to the obscurity she had previously known. In this light, rather than speaking for a prior folk culture – defined by witchcraft or shamanism – Gowdie's wild imaginings can be more accurately viewed as articulating the concerns and frustrated desires of a poor, and frequently hungry woman, who wished for plentiful meat to feast upon, and a level of social and sexual freedom that was all too lacking in the hierarchical, and Kirk-dominated, Scotland of the mid-seventeenth century. The power of her testimony, her imagination and her ability to give form and rhyme to folk charms elevated her, however briefly, from the anonymous mass and permitted her a limited degree of expression, which bears constant reinterpretation and the ability to truly entrance, not through some arcane magic, but through the beauty of language and the power of the written word.

CHAPTER EIGHT

The Flight of the Witch
From Reason to Romance

I

'Before printing', thought John Aubrey,

> Old-Wives Tales were ingeniose: and since Printing came in fashion, till a little
> before the Civil-warres, the ordinary sort of People not taught to reade; now-a-dayes
> Bookes are common, and most poor people understand letters; and the many good
> Bookes and variety of Turnes of Affaires, have putt all the old Fables out of doors;
> and the divine art of Printing and Gunpowder have frighted away Robin-good-fellow
> and the Fayries.[1]

Writing during the reign of King James II, Aubrey had clearly come to view the
violence, the coarsening of social attitudes and profound social changes that were
injected into English rural life by the Civil Wars as marking a profound cultural
watershed in the development of the nation. Yet, these folkloric visions seemed to
retreat further into the background – like so many fleeting Will O' the Wisps – every
time an attempt is made to capture, codify and define them.

As Aubrey amassed his notes on customs, folklore, faerie belief and the detection
of witchcraft, he returned to the sense of loss of an idealised and socially harmonious vision. In seeking to record the words and rhythms of charms spoken for the
preservation of cattle; examples of counter-magic to release horses or human households from the bewitchments they laboured under; or accounts of the efficacy of the
'evil eye', the 'evil Tongue' and even a spell to draw down the moon, Aubrey has the
sense of a world which is gathering pace and reordering its priorities.[2] Tradition is
inexorably giving way in the face of fashion, technical innovation and novelty; yielding
to an uncertain brand of modernity, characterised by faction, new forms of learning
and the acrid burn of gunpowder.[3]

Aubrey straddled two very different belief systems. On the one hand, as a member of the new Royal Society – and a representative and creation of a social and
intellectual elite – he typified the sense of enquiry and creative use of reason that

enabled him to virtually found the science of archaeology in these isles, through the evaluation and recording of prehistoric sites for his projected *Monumenta Britannica*. On the other, as antiquarian and folklorist, he anxiously sought to preserve the tales and superstitions of the 'Common' or 'Countrey' people, without criticism or editorial comment. Thus, he noted the 'swimming' of witches at Leominster, the Midsummer revels of German witches upon the Blocksberg mountain, and 'a world of things from these Portents and Prodigies' of demonic possession and love magic.[4] A close friend of that arch-materialist and pragmatist, Thomas Hobbes, he was also deeply influenced by the Rev. Richard Baxter's *Certainty of the World of Spirits* and thought it entirely appropriate to include magical and preternatural occurrences in his study of the *Naturall Historie of Wiltshire*, alongside considerations of human geography and natural geology.[5]

Aubrey seemed to typify the ambiguous position of many intellectuals – such as Isaac Newton, John Wesley and Ezekiel Chambers – who attempted to square biblical and deeply rooted cultural beliefs in witchcraft, with a society that was becoming more sceptical, more atomised and far more favourable towards, and tolerant of, individual modes of expression and thought. At the elite level, the second-half of the seventeenth century saw the steady growth in Western European confidence in the ability to fashion, and refashion, the world according to its own image and priorities. Limited enclosure, fen and sea drainage, the discovery of potential new colonies abroad and increased urbanisation at home helped to show that humanity was more than capable of controlling its own physical and social environment and was not just the helpless plaything of beings – both demonic and angelic – more powerful than itself. Moreover, the gradual acceptance of Cartesian philosophy, which effectively demystified nature and replaced Aristoteleanism and Hermetic thought, created an intellectual climate whereby science could act as an integrated, observable and mechanical whole. Its operation was to be found equally in the movement of the heavens as in the lifecycles of plants and the now observable microscopic organisms, reducing or even eliminating the need for the agency of demons, and marking – as Hugh Trevor-Roper memorably remarked – the 'liberation of Nature from Biblical fundamentalism'.[6] Increasingly, God, himself, was seen to act through natural forces, as opposed to portents or miracles. He was now the 'divine Clockmaker', the driving force of Cartesianism, operating via the natural laws that he had imposed upon the mechanism that he had set in motion.[7]

At the same time, at the popular level, 'traditional' beliefs and cultures were proving themselves to be far from static. In order to survive, they needed to adapt and to change.[8] Witch-belief – that had once been general – was squeezed at both ends of society, and became increasingly class and even age, specific. The witch was increasingly relegated to the societal margins, and – for the educated elites, at least – she was fast becoming an object of derision, or pity, rather than of tangible fear. Consequently, by the early years of the eighteenth century it was possible to hold that, in every English village:

> When an old Woman begins to doat, and grow chargeable to the Parish, she is generally turned into a Witch, and fills the whole Country with extravagant Fancies, imaginary Distempers, and terrifying Dreams … the poor Wretch that is the innocent Occasion of so many Evils begins to be frighted at herself, and sometimes confesses secret Commerce and Familiarities that her Imagination forms in a delirious old Age. This frequently cuts off Charity from the greatest Objects of Compassion, and inspires People with a Malevolence towards those poor decrepit Parts of our Species.[9]

It is likely that popular beliefs in magic and witchcraft finally began to break down with the introduction of the New Poor Law in the nineteenth century, and with the provision of the Old Age Pension at the beginning of the twentieth. Once the localised production of foodstuffs declined, the agrarian rhythms of buying, begging and borrowing, that had defined witchcraft as an economic crime, started to vanish from village life. The disappearance of the social inequalities which had, in part at least, given rise to the stereotype of the witch figure, served to remove the witch, herself, from the local community. Thus, when in the 1880s the child, Laura, in Flora Thompson's *Lark Rise to Candleford*, asked her mother whether there really were witches, she was told that: 'They seem to have all died out. There haven't been any in my time: but when I was your age there were plenty of old people alive who had known or even been ill-wished by one.'[10]

Such a view of the incremental workings of the changes detected by John Aubrey, a full 200 years earlier, would seem to be reflected in the statistics for official witch persecution, from the mid-seventeenth century onwards. Though Anna Goldi, the last European victim of a witch trial, would perish as late as 1782, in the Swiss canton of Glarns, and – as Owen Davies has charted – rough justice remained an unpleasant, and sometimes fatal, aspect of rural life in England until the mid-eighteenth century, legislatures and judiciaries across Europe began to feel increasing discomfort at the thought of handling witchcraft cases.[11] As Jim Sharpe, Ronald Hutton and Owen Davies have emphasised, the repeal of the English witchcraft statutes, in 1736, provided an ingenious display of Enlightenment idealism, and Whiggish pragmatism, working hand in glove.[12] Accordingly, while the Act did not provide an explicit challenge to the biblical framework of witch-belief, it removed the entire legal basis for: 'Prosecution, Suit or Proceeding … against any Person or Persons for Witchcraft, Sorcery, Inchantment, or Conjuration ... in any Court whatsoever in Great Britain'. At the same time, it struck at the popular basis for witch persecution through criminalising the fraudulent, or pretended, use of magic. Thus, in one neat, legalistic package; the beliefs of Anglican and Nonconformist clergymen were respected, while the official sanction for the persecution of witches was removed, and the criminal definition of witchcraft moved from the realm of the demonic and the murderous, to that of the simple-minded and the village confidence trickster.[13]

In this sense, William Lecky was probably nearer the mark than many of his recent detractors would care to admit, when he suggested that the decline in prosecutions was not the result 'of any series of definitive arguments, or of new discoveries, but of a gradual, insensible, yet profound modification of the habits of thought prevailing in Europe'.[14] As Norman Hampson has argued, the European Enlightenment was a state of mind, and a way of life, just as much as it was a series of clearly defined philosophical propositions, the embodiment of new scientific theories and the creation of a major social movement.[15] Furthermore, despite the revisionist turn in academic thought, which seems to limit or even deny the impact of the Enlightenment – emphasising the survivals, rather than the rapid disjunctures in witch-belief – it seems fair to concur with Christopher Hill's assertion of the simple, but revolutionary, fact that: 'In 1600 most respectable people believed in witches ... by 1700 this was no longer true'.[16] Though judicial responses varied, with persecution slackening at different rates – England saw its last trial in 1717, the Dutch Republic in 1659, France in 1693, Westphalia in 1732, Bavaria in 1792 and Spain in 1820 – the elite notion of the witch was increasingly taken up with debates centring around clericalism, rather than with the imminence or transcendence of God. In similar fashion, the conception of the Devil was shifting from the realm of the corporeal to the metaphysical, and even on occasion to the purely metaphorical. Once the witch was stripped of her demonic powers, to hurt and damn, she could appear as she really was: often no more than frightened, poor, old and unfortunate. She was a figure of pity, not of fear. Within this schema, the nature of the crime was inverted. The witch was now the innocent, the Christian Church now the bloody persecutor.

For the leading figures of the European Enlightenment, the 'philosophes' and for Voltaire, in particular, witchcraft was the theme that best summed up all the hatred, irrationality, superstition and credulity enshrined by the *ancien regime*. Magic, in Voltaire's eyes, was 'an impossible thing' and superstition 'immediately after the plague, [was] the most horrible flail which can inflict mankind'. With judicial murders sparked by 'tyranny and fanaticism', it had become 'sacred to put girls to the torture in order to make them confess that they had lain with Satan, and that they had fallen in love with him in the form of a goat'. Convicted by magistrates, who as educated men should really have known better, 'They were burned at last, whether they confessed or denied; and France was one vast theatre of judicial carnage'.[17] This radical recasting of witchcraft, combining political polemic, free thought and concern at human suffering, was expounded at length in the pages of the *Encyclopedie* and proved enormously influential in shifting the mindset of Europe's ruling and emerging commercial classes. It made witch-belief seem brutal, stupid and, perhaps most significant of all, outdated and increasingly unfathomable. Condescension is, often, the most deadly weapon of all in any intellectual argument, and armoury, and from the late eighteenth century to the immediate postwar period European witchcraft was seldom accounted as a serious, or fitting, subject for academic enquiry. This position did not necessarily reflect the hubris of Enlightenment scholars, or the sense that belief in witchcraft had been extirpated at a village level; rather, it was testament to the understanding of the educated elites that toleration, plurality of belief and the exercise of civil and economic liberties were hard won. Scratch the surface of society at any point and it is possible to witness the same persecutory impulses, expressed in different forms, in the clerical and political reaction that gripped Spain after the expulsion of Napoleon's armies in 1814; the rise of the Third Reich in Germany in the 1930s; or in the re-emergence of murderously competing nationalisms that collapsed the Federal Yugoslav state in the 1990s. As Goya knew all too well, it was the sleep of reason, rather than its triumphs, which produced monsters.

The argument for reason had to be made again for each successive generation, lest the gains brought about by the Enlightenment were lost. If today it is often the irrational impulse which is celebrated and studied by academia, then it is worth recalling that it was the much-maligned 'Age of Reason' that afforded that spirit of enquiry, within Europe, in the first place. This concern explains, in part at least, the critical distance placed between mainstream academic writing and the examination of witch-belief for the best part of 200 years.

While philosophers and historians were pushing the witch to one side, linguists and folklorists were concerned to recapture the essence of an *a priori* culture, that John Aubrey had already seen fading before his eyes in the 1660s. The witch now shrank to the realm of the storyteller and the nursemaid. Once confined, adults no longer questioned – or had cause to fear – her image and, in Tolkien's words, her stories were relegated like 'shabby or old fashioned furniture ... to the play-room'.[18] However she was shackled and silenced, the uncomfortable sense remained that she was still waiting in her dusty attic for the right moment when the spindle could be turned, and the finger pricked.

II

In popular culture, this palpable tension between reason and romance is, perhaps, nowhere better explored than through the films of Terry Gilliam. Gilliam's fantastical reimagining of *The Brothers Grimm*, which sets them within the conjoined narratives of their own fairy tales, challenges liberal, modernist sensibilities by turning our historical perspective, and sympathies, upon their head. Thus the opening scene of the film, which was released in 2005, boldly informs us that we have been transported back to 'French Occupied Germany', during the Napoleonic Wars, when the traditions and liberties of the indigenous population are being crushed under the heel of the new regime.

At the outset, the brothers are little more than confidence tricksters, phoney witch-hunters on 'the make', preying on the fears of the vulnerable and superstitious. As Jacob confides to Wilhelm, 'there is definitely money in witches'. Yet, once they are called out of town and journey deeper into the forest at Marbaden the motifs of their imaginary tales begin to take on a life, and an uncanny physical reality, of their own which pits the materialistic Wilhelm (played by the late Heath Ledger) against the idealistic Jacob (Matt Damon). Thus, while Wilhelm has an eye for the girls and the gold, embracing adulthood, Jacob still 'wishes his whole life was something out of a [child's story] book' and wants every tale to have a happy ending.

Though influenced, to an extent, by Hayden Middleton's novel, *Grimm's Last Fairytale*, Gilliam's film holds in dramatic tension the demands of adulthood and the appeals of reason with the creativity and unfettered imagination of the child.[19] Progress, in Gilliam's view is brutal, unfeeling and inexorable: it is encapsulated by the refined string quartet that provides the musical accompaniment to the sadistic torture meted out by the French to their prisoners. The antithesis of order is found in the forest of Marbaden, where the forest paths move, shifting at will, the lycanthrope bays at the moon, and at the heart of it all, a witch-queen lies entombed in her overgrown tower.

The trees have grown up to fill a vacuum created by human agency. We are told, in a series of flashbacks, that a proud Christian king had destroyed the pagan forest people and founded his city upon their bleached bones. Yet, blinded by desire and beauty, he took a witch for his wife. On their wedding day, the plague came to Marbaden and the king fell, as its first victim. The new witch-queen proved vain and cruel, abandoning her subjects in the dying city and retreating into a specially built tower, without an entrance. However, this plague was borne by the wind, and when she caught it and her beauty turned to corruption before her own eyes, 'you could hear her screams across the oceans'. On the ruins of the abandoned Christian city, a pagan forest again takes root, obliterating all save the spire of the witch's tower until the arrival of the Brothers Grimm. The forest, we are told, 'makes traps' but had never turned against the people of Westphalia until the French invasion. In keeping with Gilliam's celebration of the anarchic and irrational – it is the trees, themselves, that eventually destroy the occupying Napoleonic army.

The fairy tale and the figure of the witch appear particularly well suited in order to underscore Western society's post-industrial disengagement from, and disenchantment with, a rationalist project centred upon the values of the European Enlightenment. Yet, Gilliam's work goes much further than this. It manages to combine studio demands for fast-paced popular, and populist, entertainment – turning upon sibling rivalry, the age-old conflict between good and evil, and a conventional love story – with high-end production values, stunning art direction and a true appreciation of the essence of the folk tale. Furthermore, it enacts Schiller's contention that: 'Deeper meaning resides in the fairy tales told to me in my childhood than in the truth that is taught by life.'[20] The constant referencing of themes extrapolated, or reworked, from the Grimms' own tales – not least of these Rapunzel, Sleeping Beauty, Snow White and Hansel and Gretel – reconnects the adult audience with their own childhood remembrances. However, it is their mature insights which inform the context of the film and make sense of its layered, and surprisingly nuanced meanings. Thus, in the closing scenes, the liberated villagers and their daughters dance to Jewish folk music in a final tilt at ingrained prejudices and preconceptions. It is possible that these sturdy Teutonic villagers, formed from the very soil of Marbaden, are also German Jews. The plurality of cultures and mythologies, and the readiness with which the Grimms join in the festivities, removes any lingering sense of the Nazi appropriation of folk culture and tales. Gilliam shows us the Germany of Goethe, Schiller and Beethoven, not that of Wagner, Goebbels and Riefensthal. Moreover, the Grimms themselves, in both celluloid fantasy and historical fact, were firm and principled liberals, who sacrificed their own careers in protest at an attempt to turn the clock back to an absolutist monarchy in Hanover.[21]

It is not surprising that Gilliam felt compelled to end his film on this note, as the Grimms' tales have been periodically bowdlerised and, in the immediate aftermath of World War II, banned in the liberated sectors controlled by the British and Americans as being representative of the literature of fascism.[22] The brutal irrationality of Nazism appeared to the Allies as having been prefigured in the random violence of folktales, and the two were linked to try to account for the spiral of a supposedly civilised nation into barbarity. The general trend, at present, towards the 'Disneyfication' of children's film and cartoon – which stresses all that is 'cute', up-tempo and unambiguously saccharine – does not sit well with either the content or purpose of the folk tale.[23] However, on another level, while heterogeneous or discordant projections of evil have been decried, or removed from the canon, the witch figure has continued to thrive, largely on account of her contemporary de-sexualisation.[24]

Such attempts to sanitise the fairy tale are in no way new, or particular to our own generation. In fact, the Grimms themselves, were acutely aware of them. In reviewing the publication of the first edition of their *Nursery and Household Tales* in 1815, Friedrich Ruhs proclaimed that whatever its merits for an adult readership, it was certainly not a book that should be put into the hands of children as it evoked 'uncomfortable' and unrestrained feelings.[25] Yet, if the Grimms' stories were harsh, or even on occasion cruel, then this was to large extent merely a reflection of the terms of existence for the vast majority of the labouring poor, and many of the artisanate, in the early nineteenth century.[26] This was not lost upon the Grimms. They had spent much of their early lives in the countryside, becoming attuned to agrarian cultures and customs, before tasting want and a bitter fall in social status, after the death of their civil servant father forced them into an urban existence and the acceptance of a genteel form of poverty. Their youth was, indeed, as Terry Gilliam suggests, shaped by the wars of the French Republic and Empire, the threat of the draft, grapeshot, and the spread of epidemic brought by the savage tramp of rival armies across Westphalia.[27]

Now, while it may be a step too far in causality to see the tales, as Taylor and Rebel have done, as a projection about fears of conscription in Hesse, the abandonment of children and the wider militarisation of society, it is perhaps not altogether surprising to discover that the tales that the Grimms recorded contained numerous examples of poor soldiers, discharged from the wars, alongside foundlings, honest but poverty-stricken tailors – squeezed by the trade depression – and all manner of changelings.[28] Indeed, the majority of the Grimms' heroic protagonists are, at the start of their tales, young, wronged – in some way or another – poor, yet clever and highly socially mobile. Therein lay a highly progressive trait, inasmuch as society and hierarchical order were not immutable. As Ernest Bloch noted,

> courage and cunning in fairy tales succeed in an entirely different way than in life … While the peasantry was still bound by serfdom, the poor young protagonist of the fairy tale won the daughter of the king. While educated Christians trembled in fear of witches and devils, the soldier of the fairy tale deceived witches and devils from beginning to end – it is only the fairy tale which highlights the 'dumb devil'.[29]

III

The Grimms' fairy tales acted as a palliative against hunger, a check upon fear and a hope for justice in an unfair and often, unfathomable world. Similarly, for a brief, enlightened and enlightening period, the national broadcaster in Britain threw open a window upon the imagination and encouraged a process by which the individual child might have a means to realise her, or his, full potential. During the 1960s–70s, the television 'children's hour' existed in tension with socially defined, and often more conservative and manipulative, formal education, and was shaped most surely and skilfully by a producer of enormous energy and creative talent. Peggy Miller (1919–93) was an accomplished linguist, who had gained a doctorate from the University of London, and penned two elegant and well-researched studies of the Jacobite cause.[30] At a time when the strength of the dollar and the balance of payments deficit effectively precluded the import of films and series' from Disney and the other Hollywood studios, Miller seems to have been committed to encouraging the development of a pan-European culture that bridged Cold War divisions and stood in conscious opposition to the consumerist ideals and rampant individualism that defined the dominant cultural values and cinematic output of North America. Fluent in French, Italian, German, Polish and Czech, and possessing the skills of scriptwriter and adaptor, she was uniquely placed to make good use of the plentiful, high quality and comparatively cheap films and drama series being produced across mainland Europe, in the postwar era. There was hardly a major children's series aired on the BBC, from the late 1950s to the early 1970s, that did not bear her direct imprint.[31]

In particular, she excelled in the adaption of Eastern European fairy tales and it is for these that she is, probably, best remembered. Between October and December 1964, BBC1 broadcast four individual folk tales – under the collective title of *Tales from Europe* – that were dubbed and rescripted under her direction. The series was prominently scheduled, filling a teatime slot each Thursday between *Blue Peter* and the *Six O'Clock News*, and quickly gained a large audience. Frequent repeats – and the addition of two more films to the series in December 1966 – helped to keep *Tales from Europe* in the consciousness of a generation of children and parents, with its rotation ensuring that younger sisters and brothers were introduced to the stories. From the point of view of the Corporation, it was an extremely cost effective way of programming, which continued on into the late 1970s, with *Three Wishes for Cinderella/Drei Haselnüsse für Aschenbrödel*, released in 1974 and periodically repeated for almost a decade, providing a last flourish and a fitting coda to the project. On a wider level, the series succeeded in embedding a particular vision of the

European folk tale within British cultural life that, for almost two decades, had the power to challenge and supersede the cloying Disneyfication of the genre.[32]

Of the six tales broadcast between 1964 and 1966, one – *The Boy and the Pelican* – was made in the USSR; one – *The Proud Princess* – hailed from Czechoslovakia; and the other four – *Snow White, Rumpelstiltskin, The Tinder Box* and *The Singing Ringing Tree* – were all filmed in the German Democratic Republic (DDR). The dominance of East German film is not difficult to explain, as Berlin's DEFA studios had built upon, and swiftly eclipsed, the early Soviet engagement with the fairy tale, which had demanded high production standards, a healthy respect for the source materials, and the allocation of substantial budgets for children's cinema.[33] For Peggy Miller, there was a sense that British children – raised in an atmosphere of grey, postwar austerity – would never have experienced anything quite like these films: they were opulent, strange and challenging, and just a little bit dangerous.[34]

Some worked better than others. DEFA's version of *Snow White* was a rather slight, and unmemorable, pastiche of the Disney studios' greatest work. By way of contrast, *Rumpelstiltskin* provides a successful and thoroughly subversive retelling of the Grimms' tale. The dwarf is no longer the villain of the piece, but a child-like hero; who kidnaps the baby prince in order to protect him from becoming corrupted by materialism and the lure of gold. It is certainly the most polemical and the most freely rendered of DEFA's reimaginings of the Grimms' tales, and gives lie to the accusation that the studio was unsympathetic in its stereotyping of those with restricted height or disabilities.[35]

The Tinderbox follows Hans Christian Andersen's text far more closely, but is distinguished by superior art direction, strong scripting and a superb performance by Rolf Lugwig as 'the soldier', and combines warm-hearted innocence, with courage and a judicious sprinkling of cunning.[36] An establishing shot sees the soldier, newly dismissed from the Prussian army, humming a jaunty tune as he reflects that his king and country owe him much, but have paid him little. The music changes its register – from cheerful to sinister – then cuts; as the wind rises and leaves swirl, the soldier finds himself in an unfamiliar part of the forest and is assailed by a stooped and brutally disfigured witch. The soldier's bravery gains what she cannot; the magical tinderbox from inside a lightening-blasted tree, but the soldier – despite his own lack of guile – is shrewd enough to see through the witch's evil designs. With the witch slain and his knapsack filled with gold coins, the soldier spends freely upon others. He uses his money to rescue struggling craftsmen, to endow a street urchin with an apprenticeship as a bootmaker; to buy food for the hungry; and to buy toys for poor, but deserving, children so that they, too, can enjoy a happy childhood. Tried and convicted on account of his love for the princess, he escapes from the gallows at the last minute, through the magical agency of the tinderbox. The film ends with the flight of the king and his courtiers, and the joy of the townsfolk and their children at the soldier's rescue and triumph against all the odds. Having recognised his true friends and rejected those who had proven false, we are left assured that he will now rule alongside the princess, for the greater good of the people.

The Tinderbox brings out a number of features inherent in Hans Christian Andersen's original story, not least a profound sympathy for the plight of the poor and a sense of sorrow at the soldier's unjust treatment and death sentence. Significantly, for Andersen writing in Odense in the mid-nineteenth century, magic and witchcraft possessed rather different qualities to those that they had been thought to possess some 200 years earlier. Magic appears to be 'value free', neither demonic nor angelic in origin and inspiration. It simply exists, to be harnessed – for either good or ill – depending upon individual will, and predisposition. In similar fashion, Andersen's witches are rarely described in any detail; they act as cyphers – the embodiments of pure evil that drive forward the plot line of his tales – and, at times, appear almost as a separate species, or entity, rather than as a maleficent human being. Unlike the Grimms, Andersen was creating his stories to fulfil a burgeoning new market for children's literature. He was not attempting to recover voices from the past or connect with a greater truth born from the timeless labours of the peasantry. Consequently, we should not be surprised that Enlightenment attitudes work their way, as if by osmosis, deep into the pages of his romances. The Danish shoemaker *knows* that the witch does not exist among us and that she is only the childhood summation of our fears. He speaks to children, about children, and all that concerns them – in itself, a revolutionary development in the history of literature and pedagogy.[37] However, the witch has been diminished and, accordingly, we should not be surprised that in the filming of *The Tinderbox*, for all its other strengths, she plays no more than a walk-on, one-dimensional part.

Some forms of enchantment are more enduring. The greatest, and one of the earliest, of DEFA's fairy tales, *The Singing Ringing Tree*, was shot entirely on an East Berlin soundstage, in 1957. Though it claimed, in its title sequence, to be based upon a 'traditional' tale of the Brothers Grimm; the screenplay was an entirely modern creation rooted in the fertile, and sensitive, imaginations of the screen-writer and director, Francesco Stefani, and the original author, Anne Geelhaar.[38] In this case, the Iron Curtain appears to have been extremely permeable, as both Stefani and Richard Kruger – who played the 'evil dwarf' – normally lived and worked in West Germany. Stefani (1923–89) had just launched a film version of the popular, if savagely humorous, children's story *Max und Moritz*, which combined stylised sets with modern dance and proved a big box office success. However, while this brought him justified recognition and critical acclaim, it was probably his earlier work on *The Dwarf's Nose*, in 1952–3, that attracted the attention of the East German studio to his work. In some ways, this short film prefigures some of the themes – not least those of transgression, transformation and the figure of a reviled dwarf – that run through *The Singing, Ringing Tree*. Jacob is a little boy who helps his mother sell fruit and vegetables from her market stall. One day, he is told to help an old lady carry home her shopping basket. He cruelly taunts her on account of her long nose, without realising that she is actually a witch. Childish name-calling fades into silence and tears as the witch curses him, changing him into a misshapen dwarf with a long nose that matches her own. Now, he can see how he likes it! Reflection, empathy and restitution eventually lead to the breaking of the enchantment but the idea that juvenile behaviour – in particular, mockery of those older, less fortunate or simply different to themselves – could be ameliorated and dispelled, through improving stories that championed reason, would become a central motif guiding DEFA's fairy tales, from *The Story of Little Mook*, released in 1953, onwards.[39] Fairy tales were, after all, intended to be a treat and the studio – and, for that matter, the authorities – were quick to emphasise, 'Children that are good go to the *Märchen/Fairy Tale film*'.[40]

As already noted, it was Anne Geelhaar (1914–98) – rather than the Brothers Grimm – who seems to have been responsible for the scenario, that Stefani filmed. Born in an area of East Prussia that, after 1945, was returned to Poland, she enjoyed a long career as a children's author in the DDR, specialising in stories that took their inspiration from traditional folk tales, or tried to make sense out of Germany's all too recent past for youngsters traumatised by the legacy of the Nuremberg rallies and Auschwitz.[41] Her personal warmth, love of animals and commitment to a humanistic brand of Socialism, hallmark all of her books and film scripts. Just like Peggy Miller, she was immersed in a world of fairy stories that she both adored and absorbed, before seeking their glorious recapture in her own, highly original works. Indeed, her respect of her source material and concern for authenticity added a sense of timelessness to *The Singing, Ringing Tree* that fostered the sense that – contrary to all the evidence – it was a product of the 1450s, as opposed to the 1950s; and of a collective, as opposed to a singular, imagination.[42]

The film centres around traditional archetypes: the prince is 'handsome', the princess is known as 'Thousandbeauty', and the dwarf is irredeemably 'evil'. Yet the creation of vast papier-mâché sets, the use of brilliant colour and the innovative use of an early synthesiser to create brooding, or discordant, electronic walls of sound, was entirely new. It is also, perhaps surprisingly, far less a product of patriarchy, than many fairy tales. The story is largely seen from the perspective of the princess (played by an 18-year-old Christel Bodenstein) and it is her journey from a selfish childhood, to an altruistic maturity, that is key to the tale's sense of drama and charm. Even the source of witchcraft is re-gendered, with the dwarf taking the place more usually occupied in traditional tales by the 'bad queen' or the 'wicked fairy'. His inability to love both fuels his malice and seals his doom. In this way, Anna Geelhaar's script is also concerned with self-realisation; and an adult acceptance of one's own sexuality, and sexual power over others. At the beginning of the film, it is – on this level – perfectly rational for 'Thousandbeauty' to reject the prince as a suitor. Subconsciously, she may be aware that she is not yet mature enough for any kind of a sexual relationship and sending the would-be lover away on a quest might act as a sensible delaying tactic, postponing the moment of decision and sexual awakening until a time of her choosing.[43] Both her father and the prince should have been aware of this, and the appropriateness of their own designs. That they were not, occasioned the initial chain of disasters that engulfed all concerned. We might, therefore, choose to read Anna Geelhaar's fairy tale as an allegory about the shedding of childish and irrational impulses, and the realisation that sexual fulfilment stems as much from playing a full role within society and finding a common cause with a partner, as it does from a sudden and purely superficial sense of attraction. The sexuality of 'Thousandbeauty' is far from passive. She triumphs, despite lacking magical powers or other extraordinary properties, through her gradual adoption of moral principles – not least of which are a belief in co-operation over greed, and a kindness to animals – and the rejection of the self, in favour of the liberating practice of reason. In stepping through the dwarf's fires to claim the tree, she symbolically conquers her fears and arrives at an adult conception of her own sexuality, which makes possible the traditional happy ending of her union with the prince.

Some of the force of the original film was undoubtedly lost when it was screened by the BBC, as it was stripped of its magnificent colours, shown only in black and white, and cut into three separate episodes. Yet, at the same time, it benefited from Peggy Miller's sympathetic script editing – which tended to speed up the action and iron out any apparent ambiguities, while even the monochrome led, curiously enough, to a heightened sense of atmosphere, with the exaggerated play of light and shade inducing a heightened sense of fear and foreboding.[44] The dwarf's ice storms that, in the original coloured version are shown to be quickly dispelled, appear – in black and white – to hold the valley in their grip until the final scenes and the breaking of his bewitchment by the princess. Only then could the flowers bloom again and the waterfall run free.

IV

If the folk tale is 'the result of a story being shaped and reshaped' by constant retelling; then the partnership wrought by Anna Geelhaar's words, Francesco Stefani's images and Peggy Miller's potent advocacy and deft reimagining, confirmed both Bruno Bettelheim's definition of a 'true' fairy story as 'a unique work of art', and Tolkien's criteria which synthesises 'Fantasy, Recovery, Escape, [and] Consolation.'[45] Its innovations within the genre – and extremely stylised, storybook format – seem, paradoxically, to place it outside a strict periodisation and to imbue it with a tremendous feeling of weight and authenticity. It is true to the Grimms' vision, not least because – like their work – it is a highly creative mediation of popular themes, fears and thoughts, via the imagination of an educated and highly literate elite. 'Looser, less fettered than legend', argued Jacob Grimm,

> the Fairy-tale lacks that local habitation, which hampers legend, but makes it the more home-like. The Fairy-tale flies, the legend walks, knocks at your door; the one can draw freely out of the fullness of poetry, the other has almost the authority of history.[46]

Contrary to popular belief, the Brothers Grimm were not in the habit of journeying through vast tracts of forest and remote stretches of the German countryside, in order to glean 'original' tales from the peasants and to transcribe all that they heard. In fact, most of their stories came from a circle of young, educated and relatively well-connected, female storytellers in the circle of the Wild and Hassenpflug families, in Hesse-Kassel. These were tales told in the drawing room, rather than around the open hearth; in the context of the town house or country estate, rather than the isolated cottage or decaying, rural inn. Thus, the ladies would regularly invite the Grimms to visit their homes and, in the course of a wider social occasion, would attempt to recall and re-tell the stories that they had heard from their nursemaids or servants. On occasion, they would even recycle tales from the chapbooks and pamphlets that they had read, conflating literary and purely oral sources.[47] This is not to suggest that the Grimms were isolated from the popular voice, or that their stories were polite inventions. Rather, they were the products of a myriad of retellings, by generations of storytellers, and the free movement of ideas across artificially created frontiers. Many of the Grimms' other tales originated in France, as opposed to Germany – and often, as in the case of *Bluebeard* and *Puss in Boots*, with Perrault's earlier printed editions – as the Hassenpflug family had been Huguenots, before being driven into exile. Thus, rather than being the 'authentic' articulation of the wisdom of the *Volk*, the fairy tale was truly international, and internationalist.[48]

The success of the *Nursery and Household Tales* brought the Grimms popular fame, academic recognition and – more importantly – the financial freedom to pursue their scholarly and artistic interests. Moving from Hesse-Kassel to Hanover to accept a tenured position as a professor at the university of Gottingen, Jacob Grimm published his sourcebook of *Teutonic Mythology*. Careful, systematic and groundbreaking, these volumes provided a vocabulary and a methodology for the academic study of the interplay between mythologies, linguistics and folk-beliefs. For our purposes, they did two very important things: first, they suggested that pagan religion and custom had been overlaid by Christian beliefs, but had not been irretrievably lost; and second, they provided a scholarly overview of witch-belief that proved highly influential for writers and artists operating within the Romantic movement.

Grimm provides an account of 'the German witch-world' that is rooted in the moral and intellectual values of the Enlightenment, as he declares that, while 'Fancy, tradition, knowledge of drugs, poverty and idleness turned women into witches', the 'whole wretched business rested on the imagination and compulsory confessions of the poor creatures'.[49] The simple application of reason led – as it had for the critics of witch theory in the late sixteenth and seventeenth centuries – to the conclusion that the pursuit of witchcraft was illogical, dangerously precarious and deeply unprofitable. 'Witches,' wrote Jacob Grimm,

> with all their cunning and the devil's power to boot, remain sunk in misery and deep poverty: there is no instance to be found of one growing rich by sorcery, and making up for the loss of heavenly bliss by at least securing worldly pleasure ... These hook-nosed, sharp-chinned, hang-lipped, wry-toothed, chap-fingered bedlams practise villainy that never profits them, at most they may gratify a love of mischief. Their dalliance with the devil, their sharing in his feasts, never procures them more than a half-enjoyment.[50]

So far, so good, but in terms of its detailed substance, the *Teutonic Mythology* presents an altogether more imaginative, romantic and Gothic picture of the witch and her crimes. These are 'women of ill repute who clung to heathenism, fantastic old wives ... to whom the forest becomes mother.'[51] 'Our Hexe,' confides Grimm with a tangible sense of pride, 'is a deep, sly woman.'[52] Wherever three lights burn in a room, she is thought to have power. She can draw milk and honey from a neighbour's house to her own, her compliments upon entering a house will turn the drink sour, and her mere look, 'let alone breath and greeting, can injure in a moment, dry up the mother's milk, make the babe consumptive, spoil a dress [or] rot an apple.'[53] Witches 'make blue lights trickle into the water, throw flintstones into the air, or trundle barrels whose bursting begets tempest'. They bathe naked in the sand or corn, and 'stroke or strip the dew off the grass' to harm cattle or to 'make the grass grow ranker'.

> They gather oak-leaves in a man's shirt, and when it is full, hang it on a tree: a wind springs up directly, that drives all the rain away, and keeps the fine weather. Out of a small piece of cloud a witch made a deal of bad weather.

If a witch should be invited to a wedding, 'just as the blessing is pronouncing, she snaps a padlock to, and drops it in the water: this is called *tying up the laces*; until the padlock can be fished up and unlocked, the marriage proves unfruitful'.[54] Jacob Grimm's witches are dark, decadent and dangerous beings: 'Lashing the brooks with their brooms, squirting water up in the air, shooting gravel, scattering sand toward sunset ... [to] bring on storm and hail' but they are still crones and child killers. 'Our present fairy-tales,' says Grimm,

> represent the witch as a wood-wife, who feeds and fattens children for her own consumption; if they escape she goes after them in league boots. Grimly the witch in the tale of *Frau Trude* throws a girl into the fire as a log of wood, and snugly warms herself thereby.

The witch is transgressive – 'young wanton makes old witch,' observes the professor – but she is not yet alluring, beautiful or rebellious.[55] That transition was, however, already underway in the fertile historical imagination of a youthful French Republican, who grew up knowing poverty amid the ruins of a deconsecrated church and became the tutor not to fairy tale, but to real live princesses.

V

Jules Michelet transformed the writing of history. Like the Grimms, he consciously produced national epics – grand sweeps of emotive, popular, narrative history – and, just as surely, transformed our conception of the witch. But, he went even further than they in conjoining the figure of the witch with that of the entire female sex, of celebrating her glamours and of making her emblematic of the power latent within every woman. A feminist, of sorts, he was also very much a revolutionary. 'Man hunts and fights,' Michelet contended:

> Woman contrives and dreams; she is the mother of fancy, of the gods. She possesses glimpses of the second sight, and has wings to soar into the infinitude of longing and imagination. The better to count the seasons, she scans the sky,

for 'she is a Witch, and casts spells, at least and lowest lulls pain to sleep and softens the blow of calamity'.[56]

For Michelet, the process of writing history was a 'violent mental chemistry, where my individual passions evolve into generalities, [and] where my generalities become passions' and every book should be shot through with 'energy, continuity [and] progress.'[57] In this sense, Victor Hugo caught his essence when he told Michelet: 'All your books are acts. As a historian, as a philosopher, as a poet, you win battles. Progress and Thought will count you among their heroes.'[58] He championed a strident teleology, in which the destiny of a France shaped by Enlightenment values, and the triumph of Liberty born amid the ruins of the Bastille, would lead in measured, progressive steps to the ultimate liberation of the individual and the nation state. His use of elliptical language, imaginative gifts and willingness to intertwine fact and fantasy ensured that he could be posthumously celebrated by both modernist authors, who approved of his optimism and faith in human capacities, and post-modernists, who valued his ambiguity and use of the linguistic turn.[59]

Michelet sought to open a dialogue with the past, with the aim of resurrecting past – and forgotten lives – in order that the dead might speak to his own age. 'They appeal to me,' he confided to his journal in June 1841,

> so that I will make them live ... that they and I were but one, that our hearts suffered in the same way, that their life lived in my life, that these pale phantoms were my phantom, or rather that I myself was the living, fleeting phantom of peoples fixed in real existence and changelessness.[60]

His study of the Witch, *La Sorcière*, was conceived in the same manner and was intended as both a lyrical appeal and a strident polemic, that was intended to rehabilitate and celebrate the figure of the witch. It was written at a time of professional eclipse and personal tragedy, when the author had been forced out of his university post by Napoleon III and desperately needed a popular success in order to underpin his personal fortune and to act as a form of compensation for the loss of his livelihood. However, the idea of the Witch as a positive, feminine archetype was no sudden development, or opportunist ploy, on Michelet's part. It had been signalled by his earlier studies celebrating the 'profundity' of women, namely *L'Amour*, published in 1858 and *La Femme*, published in 1859.[61] Here,

> woman has a language of her own ... woman, above man's word and the song of the bird, has an entirely magical language with which she interrupts that word or that sigh, her impassioned breath. Incalculable power. No sooner is it felt than our heart is stirred. Her breast rises, sinks, rises again: she cannot speak, and we are convinced in

advance, won over to all she wishes. What argument of a man's will act so powerfully as a woman's silence?

'She is the Melusine of the fairy tale: a lovely fairy who was often, below the waist, a pretty snake, hiding herself away in order to molt. Happy the man who can reassure Melusine.'[62]

Michelet both idealised and objectified the women in his life. Thus, he wrote just hours after the death of Pauline, his first wife, that she retained 'the vivacity of ancient France which would have raised her, as ignorant and unformed as she was, to the highest level of society'.[63] His 'White Angel', Madame Dumesnil, combined beauty with a cultured intelligence, and – in her escape from an unhappy marriage – defined herself through her devotion to her son. Her debilitating illness and early death from cervical cancer had, for Michelet, effectively sealed her image in aspic. She was truly without peer or reproach, womanly yet chaste, profound yet unknowable. Athenais, his second wife, was almost 30 years his junior, an orphan and ingénue, who had sought solace in his writings in order to escape the grasp of the Church, and acted as his muse until his death in 1874.[64] It is, perhaps, not too causal an argument to suggest that Michelet's projections upon his partners, and the composite image he formed from them, contributed to the development of an archetype that developed gradually in his writings, from the 1840s onwards, and reached its fullest expression in the pages of *La Sorcière/The Witch*. His anti-clericalism increasingly out-stripped the traditional bounds of Christianity, as he began to formulate 'the idea of a God-mother and of death as a childbirth' and 'a religion of nature, of sensual nature, epitomized by woman'.[65]

Michelet had already encountered, and explored, the theme witchcraft in the course of writing his *Histoire de France*. His heroine, Jeanne d'Arc, had been convicted of the crime by a scholarly jury, drawn from the University of Paris, and burned as a witch by the English, in the market place at Rouen, in 1431. His researches on Cardinal Richelieu – whom he despised with a passion, as representing all that was most cankerous and rotten at the heart of the Catholic Church – brought him into contact with the career, and destruction, of Urbain Grandier; while the latest volume of his work, completed in December 1861, had chronicled the reign of Louis XIV and the 'Affair of the Poisons', in 1679–80, which had turned a number of Parisian fortune tellers into a cabal of poisoners, child-murderers and devil worshippers, intent on bringing down the monarchy of the 'Sun King'.[66] As a consequence, Michelet had the accounts of the murders, sacrileges and black masses allegedly practised by Madame la Voisin and her clients, very much in mind when he wintered at a rural retreat, outside Toulon, in 1861–2.[67] His was a mind that never stayed still; within eight days of completing the fourteenth volume of his *Histoire de France* and despatching the manuscript to his publisher, on 22 December 1861, Michelet suddenly hit upon the idea of a new work that would grip the reader's imagination with pity and tenderness, before achieving 'finally a rehabilitation of the witch'. This, he noted in his journal, would be a 'very pleasant' project and one that was 'close to my heart'.[68]

Yet, after his revelation, he immediately hit a major interpretative problem. His commitment to the Enlightenment, and his own matrix that demanded a progressive and positivist writing of history, caused him difficulties. He intended to contrast the murderous irrationality and superstition of the Mediaeval clerics that triggered the witch-hunts with the growing sense of rationalism, stemming from the Renaissance – a term he created – and culminating, with the Enlightenment, in a modern age of secularism and greater religious, political and sexual freedoms. The trouble was that the available source materials did not, necessarily, reflect this trajectory and that a gap of more than 150 years separated the isolated, politically driven and atypical trial of Jeanne d'Arc from the multiplicity of hunts and convictions that scarred the late sixteenth and seventeenth centuries. He seems to have begun with the last chapters of the book, charting the Jesuit-led persecution and trial of Charlotte Cadière, 'a delicate, invalidish young girl of seventeen, entirely devoted to piety and works of charity', in 1730–1.[69] However, even though 'this melancholy blossom was a pure product of Toulon', Michelet could find little in the way of satisfactory material in the local archives. His work progressed in fits and starts. It was an infuriating situation for a compulsive writer, who rose at 5 a.m. every morning in order to practise his art, increase his word tally for the day, and drive forward the project at hand by dint of his ambition and capacity for sheer hard work. He broke off the writing of the book in order to consult the notes taken years before by Alfred Dumesnil, the son of his lost love, on 'the legends and myths of the Middle Ages'.[70] These, together with a collection of trial extracts, the pamphlet literature for the outbreak of witchcraft at Loudun, and the writings of the demonologists – Kramer and Sprenger, Bodin, Boguet, Del Rio and de Lancre – fired his imagination and provided the bedrock of his research. Though the speed with which he wrote *La Sorcière* – often completing a chapter a day between 2 February and 28 March 1862 – cannot be doubted, his industry has perhaps been too easily equated with hack work and dismissed as being suggestive of slapdash methods.[71] Michelet approached the subject of the witch with as much verve and dedication as he did when approaching any other of his works, and in some respects to a far more subtle, and greater, cultural effect. However, the creation of *La Sorcière* was neither a happy, nor a straightforward process. At the beginning of April 1862, as he was consolidating and re-writing the text, fashioning an epilogue, he was called away to the bedside of his son, Charles, who worked for a railway company in Alsace. He arrived just in time, for the young man died on 16 April and, heartbroken, Michelet abandoned both his lodgings in Toulon and the writing of his book, to return to Paris. It was August before he looked at it again.

Unfortunately, but not surprisingly – considering its subject and content – the Parisian printers who had pushed Michelet on towards completion, in expectation of fat profits, began to get cold feet when the final text was delivered, in November 1862. Louis Hachette, his old friend and publisher, fearful of the reaction of the authorities and the attention of Napoleon III's secret police, panicked and sought to stall the project and distance himself from such a controversial title. Even the offer of expedients – holding over the strident and inflammatory epilogue until a second edition, and retailing the book through a third party – caused one possible editor to declare that Michelet was willing a heart attack upon him. Hachette's fears were well grounded.[72] The authorities did haul in two of the printers, Templier and Hetzel, for questioning, and succeeded in frightening the latter into giving a long, and potentially damaging statement. However, the police held back from Michelet, himself. In the bourgeois empire of Napoleon III – all tinsel and swagger – status and connections mattered; and it could not be doubted that Michelet possessed these qualities in abundance, together with a heady dose of fame. Perhaps, if the book had failed, he might have been fair game for the prosecutors but it was a runaway success, selling out a first edition in days and repeating the success, and evading the censors, through the publishing of a second edition in Brussels. Lacroix, who had just completed the publication of Victor Hugo's *Les Miserables*, took the risks and reaped the rewards. In February 1863, within a month of the book appearing on the streets of Brussels, the print-run had been carted across the border and again been sold out in Paris. *La Sorcière* has never been out of print since that time in France, and carved itself an influential niche through inexpensive English language versions that, significantly, sensationalised its title – and the presentation of its contents – transforming Michelet's 'Witch' into either *Satanism and Witchcraft* or *Witchcraft, Sorcery and Superstition*.[73] In a sense, this reframing of Michelet's work was precisely what some of his own friends had feared, and warned against, over the winter of 1862–3. The publication of *La Sorcière* divided, even, his own circle. Eugene Noel, a supporter and confidant, denounced both the effort expended and the unworthy choice of subject that had produced 'a whining novel, without invention, without truth, without interest'.[74] While it is tempting to observe that with friends like these, the author did not really need enemies, it is more important to note that Michelet's work was a consciously inflammatory challenge to the power and authority of clerical France and was, rightly, judged by his contemporaries alongside Hugo's *Les Miserables*, and Baudelaire's *Les Fleurs du Mal*, as representing a new wave of highly subversive, charged and challenging literature. Moreover, as Noel appreciated in his critique, audiences – both at the time and since – were divided in viewing *La Sorcière* as being a straightforward historical account, a fictionalised romance or an uncomfortable composition of the two.

In part, this is a result of the limitations of Michelet's source materials. As we have already seen, he sought to locate the horror of witch persecution within the narrowing world view of Mediaeval Catholicism and its crushing of the human spirit. 'The Church,' he wrote,

> has cast away and condemned – Logic, the free exercise of Reason ... The Church has built of solid stone and tempered mortar a narrow in pace, vaulted, low-browed and confined, lighted by the merest glimmer of day through a tiny slit. This they called the schools. A few shavelings were let loose in it, and told 'to be free', they one and all grew halting cripples.[75]

However, the lack of any but the most salacious and credulous accounts of Mediaeval heresy and witchcraft trials – those of the Knights Templar and Jeanne d'Arc's erstwhile confidant, Gilles de Rais spring to mind – led Michelet to divide his study in half. In the first, he used largely imaginative reconstructions of Mediaeval village life, the impact of Feudalism, the revolts of the peasantry and the 'Black Mass' to create a vision of, and a feel for, the *mentalité* of the witch. In the second, he skilfully deployed a number of well-reported witch trials – those of the Basque Witches hunted by de Lancre; that of Urbain Grandier, and the possessed nuns, Madeleine Bavent and Charlotte Cadière – from the seventeenth and early eighteenth centuries, to act as case studies and to attest to the blind cruelty of the religious orders and the guiltlessness and purity of those women accused of witchcraft. This produces a rather odd tension within the text; on the one hand Michelet's scholarship in the second-half of the book can be seen to legitimate his speculative arguments in the first; while his acceptance of the physical reality of both magic and the Devil, in the first, sits somewhat at odds with his attempts to exonerate those convicted of malefic witchcraft, in the second. In effect, he advances two separate ideological positions in the course of the book: 'Part One' is a polemic and lyrical novella, breathing the air of rebellion fashioned by the Romantic movement; while 'Part Two', despite its flourishes, is grounded in the Enlightenment view of human rights, secular government and universal freedoms.

Despite these incongruities and contradictions or perhaps, even because of them, *La Sorcière* exerted an enormous power over the imagination of its readership and threw out a large number of incendiary, creative, and potentially liberating ideas about witchcraft that would be developed and honed by writers as different as Francis Marion Crawford, Aleister Crowley, Margaret Murray and Gerald Gardner, over the space of the next century.

Michelet's witch is an eternal, female archetype. Nature forms her, with a 'genius peculiar to woman and her temperament ... She is born a creature of Enchantment. In virtue of regularly occurring periods of exaltation, she is a Sibyl; in virtue of love, a Magician ... often fantastic, often beneficent.'[76] We find her at the cottage door, or treading upon the woodland path, 'this little peasant wife' who 'keeps the house ... spins as she watches her sheep ... trips to the forest and gathers her little bundle of firewood'. This witch is 'not the repulsive-looking countrywoman of a later time, disfigured by unremitting labour' but she does carry with her a potentially deadly secret:

> a secret she never, never confesses at church. She carries shut within her breast a fond remembrance of the poor ancient gods, now fallen to the estate of spirits, and a feeling of compassion for them. For do not for an instant suppose, because they are gods, they are exempt from pain and suffering. Lodged in rocks, in the trunks of oaks, they are very unhappy in winter ... Having no more incense, no more victims, poor things, they sometimes take some of the housewife's milk. She, good managing soul, does not stint her husband, but diminishes her own portion, and when evening comes, leaves a little cream behind in the bowl.[77]

But, 'Great heavens!' Michelet reminds us, think of the consequences if she were to be discovered; her God-fearing husband would beat her; and the Church would torture her and burn her at the stake. Over the course of a few, short paragraphs, Michelet thus sketches out the framework for a future Pagan revival, emphasising

> the host of indigenous gods, the crowd of deities still holding possession of boundless plains, of woods and hills and springs, inextricably blended with the life of the countryside. These divinities, enshrined in the heart of oaks, lurking in rushing streams and deep pools, could not be driven out

despite the fact that the

> priest makes fierce war on the poor spirits and hunts them out of every corner. Yet surely they might be let live in peace in the old oaks. What harm do they do in the forest? But no! Council after Council launches its anathemas against them. On certain days the priest even goes to the oak, and mumbles prayers and sprinkles holy water to drive away the evil spirits.[78]

In a later age, the seventeenth century, when every hand has turned against her, the witch has also become

> another type altogether – a delicate Devil's plaything, the little Witch-wife, child of the Black Mass ... blossoming into being, with all the wily ways and sportive grace of a kitten ... she is soft and silky, stealthy of approach and treading so softly, softly, and loving, above all things, to be caressed ... As a child, she loved dirt. Grown a big girl and a pretty ... her Sorcery will become the strange laboratory of a ... mysterious alchemy. From a very early period she handles, by predilection, repulsive matters, drugs and medicaments to-day, to-morrow nauseous intrigues. This is her element, love and disease; she will turn out an apt go-between, a clever, bold experimenter. She will be prosecuted for alleged murders, for the concoction of poisonous brews; but unjustly. Her instinct by no means lies in that direction; she has no hankering after death ... she ... loves life, prefers to heal the sick, and prolong existence.

Yet, she is dangerous to men in two ways:

> She will sell recipes to produce sterility, perhaps abortion. On the other hand, with her wild, reckless wantoness of fancy, she will be only too ready to help women to their ruin by her accursed potions, and find cruel joy in crimes of the sort.[79]

This, then, is the germ of the modern witch, popularised by Wicca and owned as a symbol and source of empowerment, in the 1990s, by many young women who came to her through such mainstream, network TV series as *Charmed* and such major Hollywood movies as *The Craft*.[80] Yet, true to Michelet's overarching vision, she was also a symbol of social and political change, of optimism and faith in a brighter future. Patriarchy and Capitalism were the problems, and a re-gendered, feminine-inspired and nurtured, form of egalitarianism – based around the values of 1789 as opposed to 1793 or 1871 – offered a means of solution and, ultimate, salvation. In this manner, 'Reason, Right, and Nature' might act in concert to fashion such a 'triumphantly victorious ... new spirit' capable of forgetting its previous sufferings and even being unmindful of its own triumphs but, yet, recalling its roots

> in the days of persecution, when a woman, the unhappy Sorceress, gave the first impetus to its scientific and popular vogue. Bolder far than the heretic, the doubting half-Christian, the man of knowledge who still kept one foot within the sacred circle, she eagerly fled from such constraints, and free on the free soil, strove to build herself an altar of the rude wild boulders of untrammelled nature ... Woman, bruised during the later centuries with men's affairs, has in requital lost her own true role – that of

healing, and consoling, that of the fairy that restores to health and happiness. This is her true priesthood – hers by right divine, no matter what the Church may have said to the contrary. With her delicate organs, her love of the finest detail, her tender appreciation of life, she is called to be its quick-eyed confidante in every science of observation. With her gentle heart and sweet pity, her instinctive kindness, she is a heaven-sent healer ... She will pursue the sciences, and bring into their domain gentleness and humanity, like a smile on Nature's face. Anti-Nature pales in death: and the day is not far off when her final setting will mark a dawn of blessed augury to mankind.[81]

VI

Ironically, Michelet's witch did not settle naturally, in the way that he had intended, upon the soil of France; but rather took flight to other shores, embedding herself in the Anglo-Saxon psyche of England and North America. In the *fin de siècle*, she became a cultural hybrid, standing at the intersection of empires and religious movements. She returned to prominence through the pen of a North American ex-pat, devoted to ultra-montagne Catholicism. Francis Marion Crawford (1854–909) the son of a renowned sculptor and a New England heiress, spent a few terms riotously spendthrift but academically unsuccessful at Cambridge University before completing his education at a technical school in Karlsruhe and the University of Heidelberg.[82] Unable to find employment in North America, he sailed for Bombay in 1879, and took a post as editor of the *Indian Herald* newspaper and began writing both articles and short stories. As a linguist and Orientalist, he knew Sanskrit and Urdu as well as Italian, German and Czech; as a traveller he was fascinated by all that was most opulent and religiously ceremonial. Significantly for his writing career, he was also fascinated by the occult.[83] His first adventure novel, *Mr. Isaacs: A Tale of Modern India*, was an immediate success, establishing Crawford as a professional novelist in Britain and the USA, just short of his thirtieth birthday; but for our purposes it also served to establish certain plot devices – foreign travel, exotic locations, forbidden desire – and philosophical principles – a feel for esoteric mysticism, religious asceticism and the transcendence of love – that would later hallmark his work on witchcraft. Thereafter, signed on a profitable contract to the prestigious Macmillan Publishers, his novels appeared almost annually, on both sides of the Atlantic, for the next quarter of a century.[84]

Unusually popular in its own time, though today largely forgotten despite being celebrated as part of post-Communist 'magical Prague', *The Witch of Prague* was reprinted no less than four times in Great Britain and North America, in 1891–2,

and was made available in Germany and Austro-Hungary through a cheap paper-
back edition published by Tauchnitz.[85] Crawford had spent some time in Prague; he
had walked its streets and knew its cadences. He had a good ear for the Czech language, a feel for the Czech soul and the significance of Czech history. He was intent
upon celebrating the *Malá Strana* and the *Staré Město*, and upon exploring the Jewish
ghetto of Prague, even as the developers began clearing away the slums and effacing
the Mediaeval tenements of Josefov.[86] He would have known the Hunger Wall and
the Petrin Hill, where today the hares still race through the snows and where an art
gallery, lodged in an old villa, offers mulled wine and a chance to view paintings of
witches, demons and other occultist scenes. He would have also known the *Havelska*
market, where fruit and vegetables have given way to postcards and wonderful
wooden toys; but he might have been saddened to know that the witches that hang
upon their broomsticks, suspended from the corners of the stalls, cackle with a
venom and discordancy that would never have come from the full, and eloquent, lips
of his own creation. His witch has long since flown from Prague. And this knowledge provides a melancholic coda to any contemporary approach to his novel, for
its strengths lie in the envisaging of a witch born out of our own modernity and in
the atmospheric passages that reveal a city of beauty and decay, of love and of terror.
Indeed, in one sense the entire narrative acts, as Ripellino has suggested, as a simple pretext for the main character, the 'Wanderer' (we never learn his name) to lead
us on a journey through the labyrinthine heart of the old city and 'to roam through
misty, dark, mournful Prague'.[87] Crawford's city is the Baroque Prague, fashioned by
the Counter-Reformation, dominated

> by huge figures of saints, standing forth in strangely contorted attitudes, black
> with the dust of ages, black as all old Prague is black, with the smoke of the brown
> Bohemian coal, with the dark and unctuous mists of many autumns, with the cruel,
> petrifying frosts of ten score winters.[88]

The story begins with a service, in the gloom of the historic Týn Church, and with
a chase through a maze of alleyways in pursuit of the hero's lost love. Through the
darkening day, 'the Wanderer' pursues the 'shade' of his Beatrice 'speeding onward,
light as mist, noiseless as thought, but yet clearly to be seen and followed'. At each
turn and crossroads, he catches a fleeting glance of her 'black garment', and the swirl
of her skirts, 'just disappearing', tantalising, out of reach of both touch and call. Yet,
at last, through misdirection or the workings of an old magic, he comes to the witch's
door, 'studded with iron nails' and 'invariably shut'. However, this is not the entrance to
a tumble-down forest cottage, that reeks of poverty and want, but the gateway to an

elegant, if secluded, town house, that Crawford locates, precisely, within the city's contemporary street planning: flanking the wall of the Jewish ghetto and the commercial
thoroughfare of the Karlsgasse.[89] What he finds, inside, is not the witch as primitive,
country crone but the witch as an urban sophisticate and beauty. He is introduced to
her within a palm court, where – in contrast to the penetrating cold of the city – the
'air was very soft and warm, moist and full of heavy odours as the still atmosphere of
an island in southern seas, and [where] the silence was broken only by the light splash
of softly-falling water' from an unseen fountain.

Února, the witch of Prague, is a woman

> who dwelt among the flowers ... sitting before him, motionless and upright in a high,
> carved chair ... so placed that the pointed leaves of the palm which rose above her cast
> sharp, star-shaped shadows over the broad folds of her white dress.

Alabaster hands, as white and as cold as if they had been sculpted by 'a Praxiteles or a
Phidias' cradle a 'great' grimoire; but it is the gaze of the witch that captures, holds and
'fascinates', the 'Wanderer's' attention. For, he

> did not remember that he had ever seen a pair of eyes of distinctly different colours,
> the one of a clear, cold gray, the other of a deep, warm brown, so dark as to seem
> almost black, and ... would not have believed that nature could so far transgress the
> canons of her own art and yet preserve the appearance of beauty.[90]

Later, we learn that Února – whose name means 'belonging to February' in Czech –
was a foundling, who 'from childhood' possessed 'the power to charm with eye and
hand all living things, [with] the fascination which takes hold of the consciousness
through sight and touch and word, and lulls it to sleep. It was,' Crawford tells us, pure

> witchery, and she was called a witch. In earlier centuries her hideous fate would have
> been sealed from the first day when, under her childish gaze, a wolf that had been
> taken alive in the Bohemian forest crawled fawning to her feet, at the full length of its
> chain, and laid its savage head under her hand, and closed its bloodshot eyes and slept
> before her.

However, those who had seen her charm the wolf 'had taken her and taught her how
to use what she possessed, according to their own shadowy beliefs and dim traditions
of the half-forgotten magic in a distant land', and had, 'filled her heart with long-
ings and her brain with dreams, and she had grown up to believe that one day love
would come suddenly upon her and bear her away through the enchanted gates of the
earthly paradise.'[91] It is this belief, and her unrequited love for the 'Wanderer' – who

refuses to abandon his quest for his own beloved, Beatrice – which proves her undo-
ing and provides for the central tragedy of the novel.

Uneven, overwrought and weighed down by too many unnecessary sub-plots, *The
Witch of Prague* harvests themes drawn from Goethe's *Faust* – through the conclusion
of Února's demonic pact – Mary Shelley's *Frankenstein* – with Února and Keyork
Arabian's quasi-scientific search to find the key to prolonging human life – and from
Czech and Jewish folklore, in the shape of the tales of the necromancy of John Dee
and Edward Kelley, and those of protection of the ghetto by the magical Golem and
the wise Rabbi Loew.[92] Herein lies the tension and the major trouble within the novel,
as Crawford's desire for grisly occultist stories and arcane law vies with his personal
religiosity, and love for the Mediaeval Roman Catholic Church. Thus, he is prepared
to take the worst of the 'blood libels', and stories of host desecration levelled against
the Jewish people by the Christian Church, entirely at face value. It does not seem
to trouble Crawford that these fabrications, which turned each and every Jew into a
proto-typical witch figure or would-be 'Christ killer', were responsible for the worst
massacres of Western Jewry across the Middle Ages and Early Modern period, or
that they formed the basis for the *Protocols of the Elders of Zion*, which was fuelling
anti-Semitism in Crawford's own day, and was a text with which he appears to have
been familiar. As a consequence, at one level, *The Witch of Prague* is a deeply unpleasant example of just how far a virulent form of anti-Semitism could be held to be
respectable and seeped into Victorian drawing rooms under the guise of acceptable
and truly popular, romantic literature.

In one of the many sub-plots, as a particularly brutal form of revenge, Února
regresses a Czech Jew – the splendidly named Israel Kafka – to a former life, in
which he assumes the guise of Simon Abeles; a young Jewish boy, who had allegedly
converted to Christianity, in 1694, and was supposedly abducted and ritually murdered by members of Prague's Jewish community.[93] Here, Prague's Jews appear as
gross caricatures

> crooked, bearded, filthy, vulture-eyed … chattering, hook-nosed and loose-lipped,
> grasping fat purses, in lean fingers, shaking greasy curls that straggled out under caps
> of greasy fur, glancing to right and left with quick, gleaming looks that pierced …
> like fitful flashes of lightening, plucking at each other by the sleeve and pointing long
> fingers and crooked nails … intoxicated by the smell of gold, mad for its possession,
> half hysteric with the fear of losing it.[94]

Abeles is baptised in the Týn Church – around which much of the action of the
book is played out – and is transfigured by the power of Christ's teachings. Seized
by former friends and his family, he is tried by a panel of Rabbis and, after refusing

to recant, he is crucified in a savage mockery of Christ's own Passion. That Crawford chooses to set the scene for the bewitchment and degradation of Kafka within the Old Jewish cemetery, in Josefov, a few yards away from the spot where Simon Abeles' hurried burial had allegedly been uncovered by the Jesuits; or that he seeks to ground his tale in historical events, through recourse to a spurious trial account that he had consulted 'in the state Museum in Prague', adds an undercurrent of perverse and deadly hatred to his prose.[95] Moreover, at the climax of the novel, Února attempts to destroy Beatrice – a model of piety, and of chaste religious devotion – through the ultimate 'crime against Heaven': the desecration of the Host.[96] Look around, he suggests, the war between heaven and hell has not ceased. These are not simply fables drawn from the past, these are demonic enchantments that threaten to ensure our own present: the faces of your friends or neighbours may be those of would-be Christ-killers, anxious to draw the blood of the saviour and re-enact the pain of his sacrifice each and every day. In this, for Crawford – as for many Mediaeval demonologists – the figures of the Jew and the witch have become as one.

The power and virulence of Crawford's position is derived from his choice of setting. This is not a simple historical romance, but a devotional tale. Crawford's particular gift, for better or worse, was for giving these stories a decidedly modern grounding. He reimagined nightmare figures drawn from folklore within the context of the decaying and beleaguered Jewish quarter; and populated the palaces and salons of a doomed Empire with larger than life heroes and heroines, at precisely the point when Czech nationhood was again beginning to be expressed through the pens of his contemporaries, Masaryk and Neruda. *The Witch of Prague* makes for often unpleasant reading, but it is the racism and intolerance of an outwardly rationalistic and industrial society that gives it its virulence and empowers its hatred. It is, therefore, a work of modernity. Within this context, Keyork Arabian – Února's *Mephistopholis* and a character who, once again, reflected and explored Crawford's equation of orientalism with occultism – conducts his research in a laboratory, crammed with Darwinian texts and specimens.[97] Part scientist, part necromancer, part alchemist, Keyork Arabian seeks to intrude upon God and to unlock the secret of eternal life. 'Strange and wild,' says Crawford, 'were the trials he had made; many and great the sacrifices and blood offerings lavished on his dead in the hope of seeing that one spasm which would show that death might be conquered.' Yet, the

hidden essence was still undiscovered, the meaning of vitality eluded his profoundest study, his keenest pursuit. The body died, and yet the nerves could still be made to act as though alive for the space of a few hours – in rare cases for a day. With his eyes he had seen a dead man spring half across a room from the effects of a few drops of musk – on the first day; with his eyes he had seen the dead twist themselves, and move and grin under the electric current – provided it had not been too late.[98]

It is through the mysterious figure of Keyork Arabian that Crawford also reintroduced the concept of the demonic pact. Února's white magic is subordinated to his black, as her love for the 'Wanderer' leads her to guilelessly promise Keyork anything – including her immortal soul – if he can ensure that her passion is fully requited. She makes her pledge three times, within earshot of Keyork Arabian, who suddenly appears at her elbow, with 'an odd smile on his usually unexpressive face' to accept, quite conversationally and seemingly half in jest, that 'that soul of yours' is now his.[99] Before Února realises it, the damage has been done, the pact concluded and her fate sealed. Only her last minute contrition, can banish the demonic Arabian back to hell, reunite the lovers at long last, and attest to the triumph of Christianity over dis-belief, worldly cynicism and the Devil.

However, if Února's selfless death is demanded as the price of her salvation, and fashioned as the hackneyed plot device by which the novel can end happily and neatly, to the benefit of the hero and heroine, and the comfort of the faithful; then Crawford does, in the meantime, manage to create an original character for his witch, who man-ages to speak to – or at least channel – some of the themes confronting the feminine ownership, and expression of, spirituality at the close of the nineteenth century. For, while Beatrice (the nominal heroine) is largely silent and compliant, led equally by the nuns in the cloister and by the witch upon the hillside, Února possesses her own voice and is unafraid to seek out and articulate her own desires.

Crawford is at great pains to encompass his witch within the bounds of science and reason, devoting several long passages to an explanation of her powers, which defines her as both mesmerist and medium.[100] Února, he tells us, 'possessed the power of imposing ... hypnotic sleep' and suggestion through the 'fascination of her glance'. She was

> superstitious ... She did not thoroughly understand herself and she had very little real comprehension of the method by which she produced such remarkable results. She was gifted with a sensitive and active imagination, which supplied her with semi-mystic formulae of thought and speech in place of reasoned explanations, and she undoubtedly attributed much of her own power to supernatural influences. In this respect, at least, she was no farther advanced than the witches of older days, and if her inmost convictions took a shape which would have seemed incomprehensible to those predecessors of hers, this was to be attributed in part to the innate superiority of her nature, and partly, also, to the high degree of cultivation in which her mental faculties had reached development.

And while her influence was held to be

> purely a moral one, exerted by means of language and supported by her extraordinary concentrated will … She fell back upon a sort of grossly unreasonable mysticism, combined with a blind belief in those hidden natural forces and secret virtues of privileged objects.[101]

Modern, educated, privately wealthy and self-assured, Února is also an elemental child, ruled by nature and her passions. This is precisely what makes her dangerous. Unlike the submissive Beatrice, she has grown up without any sort of male influence, untouched by, and unbeholden to, patriarchal authority. Raised by the peasants in the forests of Bohemia, and briefly – but unsuccessfully – schooled by Sister Paul in a convent inside the city walls, she is the social superior to the unfortunate Israel Kafka and the equal to both the 'Wanderer' and Keyork Arabian. We are told that 'her wild bringing-up, and the singular natural gifts she possessed, and which she could not resist the impulse to exercise' would have 'rendered a marriage with a man of that [aristocratic class] all but impossible', while her own proclivities 'would have entirely excluded her from the only other position considered dignified for a well-born woman of fortune, unmarried and wholly without living relations or connections – that of a lady-canoness on the Crown foundation'.[102] She shuns would-be suitors, 'who for her beauty's sake, or out of curiosity, would have gladly made her acquaintance' and raises 'an impassable barrier of pride and reserve' that ensures, 'in a strange fashion', that she 'kept her name free from stain.' 'If people spoke of her as the Witch,' Crawford tells us, 'it was more from habit and half jest than in earnest.' For, in 'strong contradiction to the cruelty which she could exercise ruthlessly when roused to anger, was her well-known kindness to the poor, and her charities to institutions founded for their benefit were in reality considerable, and were said to be boundless'.[103]

Only when she seeks to free herself from her 'extreme seclusion' in pursuit of love and sex with a man of her own class does she seem to fatally transgress, stepping outside the permitted bonds set upon her gender and status, and setting in train the forces that will conspire to destroy her. Intensely self-aware and reflexive – in a way that the 'Wanderer', a silently brooding, humourless 'alpha male', is certainly not – she gladly owns and celebrates her identity as 'the Witch'. Significantly, she also articulates a belief, enshrined within revived Paganism, that the witch is healer and comforted, as much as tormentor and destroyer. They call me a witch, she tells Sister Paul, 'because I can make people sleep – people who are suffering or mad or in great sorrow, and then they rest. That is all my magic.'[104]

Února, therefore, is a reflection of those women – bright, and increasingly both economically and societally independent of men, and male control – who took the lead in the Spiritualist movement of the late nineteenth century. Denied a meaningful role with organised religion, that, itself, was shuddering under the shock-waves produced by Darwin, Marx and Freud, it was natural that they should seek to find a meaningful expression for their religiosity that was neither hidebound nor entirely mediated through patriarchal norms. She also represents a new archetype (as opposed to the clichés that litter much of Crawford's work) and one that the 'Wanderer', as the conscious embodiment of bourgeois authority and machismo, really should have had cause to fear.[105] The witch had come full circle, with Února as Circe, reborn. No longer mocked and reviled, for her poverty and stupidity, this new witch had thrown off the rags which had accrued to her over more than 300 years and was preparing to renegotiate the terms upon which her power was based. Confident, sexual – rather than sexualised – and erudite, she had taken form as the result of the liberties bestowed upon individuals by the European Enlightenment and the imaginative powers unleashed by the Romantic Revival. Her substance would be defined in the twentieth century, by writers who had somehow to make sense of the poisons that had stemmed from those new freedoms – the anti-Semitism that had lodged, like the worm in the bud, in the pages of pseudo-science and popular literature – and which had led to the wreck of modernity amid the smoking chimneys of Auschwitz.

CHAPTER NINE

The Witch on the Barbican

I

The greying heads, sober suits, twin sets and sensible shoes, that filled a Plymouth hall one summer's evening in 1973, had come to be challenged. They sat fixed on the edge of their stacking seats, to hear tales of witchcraft, magic and the occult. As the lights dimmed, Robert Lenkiewicz strode majestically across the floor, dressed in a flowing cloak, bucket-top boots and the doublet of an Elizabethan *magus*, carrying a human skull and surrounded by his acolytes. The tramp, Diogenes – otherwise known as Edwin McKenzie – followed in his wake, dressed up as a court jester, Lenkiewicz's 'pretty shawl-clad girlfriend', Belle, brought up the rear. Amid gasps, and the odd grumble, the young artist uncoiled a length of rope, scribed 'a magic circle' complete with pentagram and, in deep sonorous tones, invoked the presence of 'a demon' to walk among his audience. After talking 'authoritatively for an hour about witchcraft, alchemy and magic', the performance came to an end and he and his retinue were gone as quickly as they came, off into the night.[1]

Timing can be everything. And Robert Lenkiewicz – 'The Portrait Painter', as his shop-sign on the Barbican, styled himself – was never one to forget the maxim. He knew how to make an entrance; he knew how to create a mystique about himself, how to captivate an audience, and how to enchant a lover. Sometimes it could be accomplished with a word, an expression of interest in a woman's fleeting thoughts, or with a sudden burst of creativity, breathing life and genius on to a blank canvas or a drab expanse of wall. On occasion, it simply required showmanship and a feel for all that was dangerous, exotic and intoxicating, especially if glimpsed from the outside and from a safe distance.

Lenkiewicz, we are told, was

> a first-rate mimic [who] likes to declaim. His urge is to dramatise situations, and that means an instinct to recreate them, pump fresh life into them. People are curious, leaving aside [his] metaphysical speculations, his sense of history, erudition, his preoccupation with *Death and the Fool*, this statement would perhaps be a fair summing-up of his attitude to the misfits of all kinds who pass through his studio, and in and out of his life. As far as I can understand, this flow of people is not

something that just happens to him, it is something that he invites, that he wants to happen. This is his element, if you like. These are his characters, his performers, they climb on to his stage, they are his passing show.[2]

For the time being, at least, this show had alighted on the theme of witchcraft.

In 1970, the artist had begun to work upon a series of occult paintings on cardboard, sailcloth and parachute silk. Several of these survive, preserved at the *Museum of Witchcraft* in Boscastle, and reveal the influence of the works of both Margaret Murray and Denis Wheatley – not to mention the Hammer Horror films – upon Lenkiewicz. One shows an initiation ceremony into a demonic cult, set in a darkened library, with the coven staring at a door thrown open to reveal a shard of light and a cloaked, goat-headed figure. A second canvas, depicting a *Witch with Foetus*, shows a naked woman staring at the unborn infant, enclosed within a glass jar, while prodding at her vagina with a thyrsus staff – echoing Dürer's aged crone – her reflection caught in a mirrored pentagram. The third painting in the series, *Witch with Demon*, reveals a newly summoned incubus materialising beside a prone witch. As she writhes across the floor in ecstasy towards her new master, the instruments of her art – a broomstick and cauldron – lie beside her.[3] In comparison to Lenkiewicz's later work, all three, though very much of apiece, are rather naïve and stilted, both in terms of their rendering and subject matter. They appear to have been quickly conceived and executed, probably for the same client, and with a view to gaining swift renumeration. Though not ranking among the artist's major works they do, however, indicate the first expression of his interest in the subject and led him, within a matter of months, to a far deeper study of the available sources for witchcraft. This resulted in him – quite literally – raiding the local library for books and starting work on the greatest of all his public murals: a celebration of occult influences on Elizabethan and Jacobean England.

For once, Lenkiewicz, the perennial scourge of Plymouth councillors and civic planners, played his hand very astutely when it came to gaining official approval for the project and was wise enough to disguise the mural's true subject matter until it was too late for the authorities to change course. Indeed, when he presented his outline sketches to the city's planning committee, his stated theme – 'Elizabeth and Her Heroes' – seemed particularly well chosen. Britons were still being encouraged to think of themselves as 'New Elizabethans', so a panoply of figures including the Virgin Queen, Drake, Raleigh, Frobisher and Sidney, and supplemented by Shakespeare, Marlowe, Jonson and their companies of actors, was calculated to appeal to local pride in the Armada fight and, more generally, to a vision of the cultural and intellectual richness of the Elizabethan world, which came straight out of the school textbooks.

From the winter of 1969 to the spring of 1971, Lenkiewicz worked on more than a hundred preparatory studies, in pencil, pen and Indian ink of costume, weaponry and heraldic devices, which revealed his consummate gifts as an illustrator together with a real talent for historical research. Knights of the Garter competed for space in his notebooks, with Yeomen of the Guard, Quarterstaff-Men, heralds and courtiers, while the faces of Philip Sidney, Walter Raleigh, Francis Bacon and Inigo Jones – surrounded by comprehensive, descriptive notes and *aide memoire* – were meticulously copied from original portraits in The National Portrait Gallery, Victoria and Albert Museum and the Ashmolean. It seemed that the finished mural would be an historical epic, rooted in Plymouth's seafaring past, and echoing the artist's other large mural painted in *The Mayflower* cinema, the year before, which depicted the landing of the Pilgrim Fathers in The New World. The original Mayflower had, of course, set sail from the Barbican and Lenkiewicz, in the eyes of the planning department, was therefore making an understandable pitch to record the next chapter of a proud civic, mercantile and religious history.

Fortunately, while the artist would never tire of criticising other politicians and other local government officers, he was surprised to find that his encounters with Mr C.C. Gimingham, the City Planning Officer and Councillor Harry Cooper were both productive and amicable. Far from being dull time-servers who could be expected to dismiss anything that smacked of bohemianism out of hand, Lenkiewicz found them to be intelligent, enlightened and highly supportive of his own creative endeavours. To his credit, the artist was unstinting in his subsequent praise of their generosity, 'common sense' and progressive vision. They certainly agreed with him that the chosen site for the mural – 3,000 square feet of wall on the side of a derelict Victorian warehouse – could hardly be anything but an improvement on the existing graffiti and crumbling stonework that confronted visitors to the corner of the Barbican. Lenkiewicz had recently opened his own studio next door, in premises formerly occupied by a family of greengrocers, and the great expanse of brick fronting onto a surprisingly secluded square, faced on three-sides by 'plain, modern, angular' flats, proved enormously tempting to both the artist's creative eye and his inquisitive if not positively acquisitive, magpie nature.

With planning permission granted, work began on the mural towards the end of July 1971. The paints were supplied for free by a local building firm, while the owners of the warehouse space – then used as a furniture store but later incorporated as part of Lenkiewicz's expanded studio – contributed to the resurfacing and plastering of the wall. Initially, the artist thought that the whole project would take five weeks, but the work soon overran and would, in the end, take almost a year to reach completion. This was due in part to the inexperience of Lenkiewicz's youthful band of helpers, as well as to the artist's own spiralling ambitions and expectations. With time, the emphasis of the Barbican project shifted dramatically and the initial vision of an Elizabethan 'golden age', of national triumph and social order, grew altogether darker and more anarchic with every brushstroke.

Though their imagination had been grabbed by Lenkiewicz's early sketches, the local councillors had perhaps not listened with sufficient attention to his words. 'It is intended,' he wrote, 'that the Barbican mural should convey some feeling of the demonic brilliance of the Elizabethan age, a time of tremendous skills, flights of imaginations, and great brutalities, a time – very much like our own'.[4] His days were filled with trips up to London – to the British Museum and Library – in order to sketch John Dee's seal and scrying stone, and to take notes from the works of his favourite occultists, Cornelius Agrippa, Artephius and Robert Fludd. His sketchbooks were filled with copies of alchemical symbols, images of Rabbis, would-be magicians and 'Yorkshire witches and imps', culled from Aristotle, Ramon Lull and from Edward Fairfax's *Treatise on Witchcraft*. Soon he was telling his friends and the local media, that the finished mural would 'represent a limited period of Elizabethan [and actually Jacobean] culture from 1580 to 1620, the philosophy, the poetry, the music and, above all, the magic, the witchcraft and the alchemy of the time'.[5] 'It is to be imagined', he wrote,

> that a large group of Elizabethan contemporaries numbering a little more than one hundred individuals are walking through an alley flanked by buildings; the whole group is moving rapidly towards the spectator in a dynamic left hand motion … The whole composition is based on the shape of the Hebrew letter 'aleph', which according to the Cabala, may imply unity as well as man in relation to the cosmos. The areas coloured green, number only five, and when a line is inscribed, forms the shape of the pentagon, [the] common geometrical image, and symbol of the 'Golden Section', an allegedly divine proportion that was still being used in architecture and poetry.[6]

Now, a depiction of witchcraft and the influence of the Cabala upon the alchemists was more than a subtle variation on the theme of the Spanish Armada. While he may have pleased the councillors by painting the frontage of the well-known Elizabethan House in New Street into the composition, Lenkiewicz also scoured the backstreets and alleyways of Plymouth in search of contemporary models for his mural, permitting the faces of local vagrants, hippy squatters, buskers, alcoholics and drifters to crowd out the historical portraits, with many of the original figures, not least Drake and Raleigh, themselves, being reimagined within a decidedly modern and counter-cultural context.

The central figure of Lady Frances Howard, boldly returning our gaze across the Barbican, has abandoned her ruffs and shaken out her hair, appearing as very much the liberated young woman of the 1970s as opposed to the aristocrat, adulterer, suspected poisoner and alleged witch of the 1610s. Her partner in crime, the astrologer and alchemist, Simon Forman – whom she paid to provide her love potions – is shown beating a hasty retreat from the scene, clutching his illegible notes and practically tumbling over the fallen figure of Robert Fludd. It is Frances Howard – and not the Virgin Queen – who commands our attention. For many of her contemporaries, she represented all that was worst in the vice-ridden Jacobean court. Her infidelities and her ambition appeared boundless, she humiliated her stolid and brave soldier husband, the 3rd Earl of Essex, and was tried for the murder of Sir Thomas Overbury, a servant of the Crown, who stood between her and the man she desired. The Earl of Cumberland's broken lance, which transects the scene, could as easily refer to Essex's impotence – allegedly visited upon him through his wife's witchcraft – as to the degradation of chivalry with the coming of firearms and mercantile power. It is Frances Howard's beauty, self-awareness and predatory sexuality that Lenkiewicz chooses to celebrate and the casual observer would not automatically associate her figure with that of an accused witch. Her pride, wealth and exalted social status protect her – then as now – from such associations and her escape from the gallows owed far more to her family connections than her innocence or a spirited defence.[7]

For those without such privileges, the reality of witchcraft allegations was a far briefer and more brutal affair. Lenkiewicz, from his intensive reading of witchcraft sources, which bordered upon the compulsive, was well aware of this and sought to contrast the elite with the popular experience of magic and persecution. Thus a gibbet, hung with the corpses of dogs – strung up as suspected familiars – dominates the top of the wall. A cowled monk carrying a crucifix, followed by a devil – both copied from an early sixteenth-century engraving by Urs Graf – push their way through the crowds, leading a half-naked man, writhing with his arms pinioned behind his back; and a plump doe-eyed blonde, still incredulous, on her way to execution. Below them, an older witch seeks comfort in the arms of a pert little demon, who seems dismissive of her but intent on the motions and mischievous form of Alexander Seton, another of the alchemists. He clearly values the acquisition of some souls over others. Lenkiewicz provided his own explanation of the scene and the last minutes of

a victim of the extraordinary witch mania that was beginning to develop at this time. It was not to be long before witch hunting became a popular pastime and financially lucrative ... The silhouetted figure of the animal on the gibbet would have been a common sight, as well as the hangings and tortures of many thousands of people who were in all probability innocent, but trapped by their inability to be articulate, as well as by popular hysteria and exploitation.[8]

Witchcraft belief, in his eyes, was a form of obsessive behaviour and the result of individuals conceding 'their lives for an idea'. What particularly enthralled him was 'the root cause of fanatical behaviour, whatever form it takes. It could be alcoholism, heroin addiction ideological or political systems or "falling in love"'. Witchcraft was a clear example of such fanaticism and the artist's sympathy with the disadvantaged and the underdog – alcoholics, obsessives, the homeless and drug addicts – led him naturally to an appreciation of the witch and

vibrant ... violent [images that] dealt with male domination and ... smacked of the same kind of fanaticism that one sensed in the *Malleus Maleficarum* and the witchcraft phenomenon, which can be seen nowadays as the history of male violence against women.[9]

In this way, he thought that his mural, and the arts in general, could 'offer one of the only means of developing skills to help us live in the shadow of infinite black space' formed from ignorance, intolerance and fanaticism.

The figure of the Rabbi presides over all, hovering above the other figures; physically detached of necessity, as save for a handful of Portuguese merchants, there were no Jews in England between Edward I's edict of expulsion, in 1290 and Cromwell's readmission of the community in 1656. However, it is the intellectual impact, not the physical presence, which interests the artist. His rabbi wears an enormous white scarf, that unravels out like the scrolls of the Torah, flapping in the wind while he 'screams down at the crowd, much as any member of a persecuted minority might. He represents the man who to some extent can see the problem but is inextricably part of it'.[10] The mural also owes a profound debt to Lenkiewicz's own Jewish heritage and makes the argument that cabbalistic thought was integral to the development of alchemical thought in the West. Elizabeth's England is no longer an isolated 'sceptre'd Isle' but an integral part of Europe and the wider world, the home to immigrants, open to the transference and transmutation of cultural values and deeply indebted to the Jewish people for the inspiration that fired Shakespeare, Marlowe, Donne and Spenser.

The only other figures to fly are the alchemists. One circles the rabbi, holding a kingly homunculus captive in the bottle at his side. Thomas Charnock looms out of the mural towards the viewer, proffering a phial containing three dead birds – one black, one white and one red, representing the body, soul and spirit according to alchemical symbolism. They also depict the colour change from black to red, being death to knowledge – the symbol of the 'black crow' – putrefaction – one of the few images common to most alchemical treatises.

A similar colour change is seen in the clothing of the figure of Alexander Seton, who floats impishly above the head of Sir Philip Sidney.[11] At the left of the mural, John Dee and Edward Kelley are depicted, flanking Simon Forman. Dee is plump, inscrutable and aged, clutching his manuscripts written in his 'Enochian' script. In Lenkiewicz's opinion':

> It would be fairly safe to say that John Dee has been one of the most underestimated individuals of the Elizabethan scene ... And he can certainly be viewed as the hub of the intellectual, metaphysical and possibly economic-political wheel of the Elizabethan age.[12]

Kelley is similarly shown as an old man, his sparse locks brushed forward to cover his mutilated ears, holding an inscribed wax disc that formed part of one of the tables created by him, and Dee, to assist in their conversations with the angels.

The majority of the alchemists pictured were modelled upon Lenkiewicz's homeless friends and acquaintances. So, for all his pretentions to nobility, Edward Kelley looks out at us with the features of Edward McKenzie, a local down-and-out, beloved by Lenkiewicz who had styled him as 'Diogenes', on account of his makeshift home in a barrel. At the foot of the mural, holding a phallic fool's staff, is another one of Plymouth's vagrants, Albert Fisher, whom Lenkiewicz styled as 'the bishop' – 'an extraordinary man with large hands and a great red beard' – who slept rough in the city's graveyards and believed that he experienced mystical visions of the hereafter. In his left hand he holds a pamphlet on the problems of London crime, written by the Elizabethan pamphleteer Robert Greene. Lenkiewicz thought that Fisher's sleeping figure alluded 'to the whole cult of melancholy that permeates the Elizabethan arts', and it certainly echoed the complexity inherent in the elderly vagrant's character, his learning, sudden abandon, affected 'posh' accent and utter inability to live within the bounds of mainstream society. Many of these figures would be painted for his *Vagrancy Project*, which overlapped with the work on the mural, and would later feature in his *Burial of John Kynance*.[13]

Alongside the melancholy, the mural espouses a sense of fun and iconoclasm. A rough hand moved to snatch the hat – distinguished with Queen Elizabeth's favour – from the Earl of Cumberland's head. The broken carving of the figure on Fisher's staff is baring its arse; underneath the jesters, one of Lenkiewicz's cronies pokes out his tongue; the distinguished Dr Fludd is pushed to the ground; and the artist, himself, is portrayed crawling up out of a subterranean cellar, shaking a begging bowl at the passers-by, his eyes appealing for their favour. On a more subtle and gentler level, the kindnesses Lenkiewicz received from the occupants of the council flats, opposite his studio, was returned through a carefully observed and touchingly executed study of the estate children that fills the whole bottom right corner of the old warehouse wall.

Yet, while their parents were delighted with the mural, not everyone was so impressed by it. The local council had not got quite what they had bargained for, while the Reverend of the nearby St Judes' Church in Plymouth commented that:

> I was rather appalled when I saw it. It seems to be negative, macabre and horrific, not the sort of thing one really wants the public to feast its eyes on. The Barbican is a big tourist area and lots of children visit it. I think they might find this kind of thing rather repulsive. There is no Christian message of death in it. There is nothing of heaven, light and purity. It is all destruction and hellish.[14]

Curiously, for what might still be considered to be Lenkiewicz's major public work, the artist – within a matter of weeks of its completion – expressed somewhat ambivalent feelings about his mural. He had himself photographed beneath it, sitting in a rubbish bin with his seventeenth-century-style, seven league boots poking out and barely alluded to it in his later collections of catalogues and interviews, seeming to dismiss it as being 'fairly skilled but illustrational'.[15]

A plan to expand on the themes of witchcraft and alchemy, making use of his own rapidly expanding collection of occult books, by writing *Notes on the Elizabethan Esoteric Tradition*, was scheduled for publication in 1973. Though it aimed to discuss 'in an academic way, with the magical and symbolic thought of the period 1580–1620', the promised work never appeared.[16] Instead, he pursued a project on *Death and the Maiden*, linking sex with death and the Mediaeval *danse macabre*. However, while his artistic output diversified, taking the form of discourses upon mental and physical handicap, addictions, homelessness, local education and old age, his intellectual preoccupation with the subject of witchcraft only intensified with the passing years. His restless desire to acquire ever greater numbers of occult books, manuscripts and artefacts came to dominate his every waking moment and led him to create the largest private library of witchcraft texts in the country.

II

With Lenkiewicz, everything – the number of his lovers, the scale and scope of his paintings, the total of completed canvasses and the number of books owned – had to be bigger and better than that which went before.[17] 'It doesn't matter how much of the Renaissance I've got on my shelves,' Lenkiewicz told one interviewer,

> I've *got* to have that Ficino or that Pico della Mirandola for the library! ... What appealed was that I didn't just have Renaissance literature on the shelf in the form of paperbacks, but that I had the actual artefact, the first edition as it would have looked hot off the press. So my Antoninus for instance, published in 1511 in Florence, may have been read in a room next to Leonardo da Vinci's.[18]

Warming to his subject, he went on to explain that the

> impulse stems from my feeling that some of the craziest notions in Western culture – witchcraft, ceremonial magic or alchemy for instance – in all their extraordinary variations are represented not just by the contents of the book but by the real thing. Quite often, part of the fanaticism shows up in its binding, its dimensions or its longevity; the mere fact that it has survived for so long. There are often frequent annotations in the margins or inscriptions made a century or more after publication which are just as crazed as the original text. These provenance details give the artefact extra pathos. I often think of parts of the library as a time machine. My interest in alchemy or witchcraft is not that dissimilar to my interest in philosophy; these are all aesthetic packages with time-trapped capacities for survival.[19]

Plymouth offered Lenkiewicz comparatively inexpensive premises and warehouse space into which he could expand as his library grew exponentially. If he was to be believed, he owned anywhere between 250,000 and 700,000 books, stored in various buildings all around Plymouth. Though according to his estate, the figure was closer to the 25,000 books, estimated to be worth around £3 million, which were located and catalogued at the time of his death. He had book collections corresponding, roughly, to the themes of his projects, 'on theology; philosophy; art biography; art history; there's a room on death, euthanasia and suicide; on fascism, anti-Semitism and slavery; erotica and sexuality; a room on poetry and literature.'[20]

Most important of these, and the dearest to Lenkiewicz's heart, was the witchcraft collection located in his Barbican studio, in what the artist always referred to as his 'Metaphysics Room'. This contained the bulk of his antiquarian volumes, split into three sections – Neo-Platonic thought; demonology, alchemy and the Cabala – amounting in all to probably about 3,000 volumes, supplemented by a range of magical artefacts. He owned no less than ten different editions of the *Malleus Maleficarum*, including one published in 1487, in Speier, by Peter Drach; a second edition of Johannes Nider's *Formicarius*, published in 1484; Joseph Glanvill's *Saducismus Triumphatus*; a stunning edition of Ulric Molitor's *De Lamiis et Phitonicis*

Mulieribus, published in Cologne *c.*1500, and early editions of practically all of Robert Fludd's extant writings. There were two manuscripts 'possibly in the hand of Sir Edward Fairfax', dated 1623, describing the demonic possession of his two daughters, and numerous grimoires.[21] One of these, written between 1590 and 1620, contained 30 pages of Latin invocations, instructions on how to draw a 'magical eye' in order to identify and punish thieves, spells for calling upon the support of angelic hosts, and how to attract and bind a lover. According to the latter charm, a male suitor should 'take a frog and put him in a pot and stop it fast' before burying it, for nine days and nights, in the midst of an ant hill at a crossroads. When the time was up, the frog's bones should be dug up and cast into a stream or running water. 'One of the bones will', the grimoire claimed, 'float against the stream' and this was the one required for the spell to work. 'Make thee a ring', continued the spell, 'and take the part swum against the stream and set it in the ring, and when you will have any woman put it on her right hand ... she shall never rest till she hath been with thee'. When the book was opened by an auctioneer, in 2007, 'something black and scaly fell out into her hands ... the body of a frog, wizened by time and pressed flat between the pages'.[22] It was either the remains of an Early Modern spell or, perhaps far more likely, another of Robert's dark practical jokes.

Lenkiewicz's own view on the collection, that: 'My own outlook is not to take sides on anything; I like simply to look down the historical highway', actually served to ensure that he bought everything on witchcraft that he could lay his hands on, without a specific research project in mind or an academic's narrow filter. Consequently, the collection proved both a representative selection of original demonological texts – both published and unpublished – from the Early Modern period, and a similarly thorough overview of recent scholarly research on witchcraft, running from the 1960s right up until his death. Thus, copies of Keith Thomas' *Religion and the Decline of Magic* and Alan Macfarlane's *Witchcraft in Tudor and Stuart England* sat alongside Frances Yates' *The Occult Philosophy in the Elizabethan Age* – which in some ways echoed the conceptual themes of Lenkiewicz's mural and own published writings – the works of Margaret Murray and shelf-after-shelf of monographs, both scholarly and self-published, on John Dee.

We do, however, have to face the fact that these books might have been acquired for no other reason than show.[23] It is clear that he never found the time to read, or even open, some of his newly acquired volumes.[24] The great majority of the rare, Early Modern, texts were written in either Latin or High German, neither of which languages he knew. Indeed, it might have simply been the case that 'some of his collection were just a revered presence, not something he could truly use'.[25] On the other side of the equation, a young doctoral student who made use of his witchcraft library for their thesis recalled that they were 'left undisturbed, but for occasional visits from Lenkiewicz himself, who would often, rather apologetically, ask me if I wouldn't mind translating a bit of Latin for him', while one of his friends reflected that he

> bought books in Latin and on the occult – books he couldn't read himself. He bought them because the reputation of the book appealed to him. The classic example of that was a manual of the Roman Catholic Church [presumably the *Malleus Maleficarum*] on how to find witches … He had eight copies of it and they are worth 10 or 20 thousand each. He couldn't read them himself, so I translated passages for him.

Yet these books did not go unheeded or uncared for, once purchased, and Lenkiewicz, according to another of his friends, 'would go diving off into his bookshelves to pull out some arcane pamphlet to make his point. He knew where everything was.'[26] It seems that, like many authors and artists, Lenkiewicz stored materials away in the hope that, one day, he might have the time and the leisure to embark on an all-embracing project that would guarantee his reputation and genius for all time. The irony was that amid the spiralling debts and piles of books, Lenkiewicz had already achieved his monument in the witch who stared down from the wall of the Barbican.

III

Death had often been at Lenkiewicz's shoulder. He bought a secluded cottage, known variously as 'the Witch's House' or 'Death's House', with a skull and inscription on the lintel – echoing Dürer's charcoal of a skeletal, plague-ridden horseman – proclaiming 'Death succeeds, Death is King.'[27] At the bottom of the Barbican mural, the portrait of the artist – begging bowl in left hand, beard just beginning to sprout – has his right hand curled over a skull as a grim *memento mori* to the holidaymaker and the unwitting passer-by. When his friend 'Diogenes' – 'a picture-postcard kind of tramp. Barely … five foot two … [be-whiskered and] petite in every sense' – fell terminally ill in 1984, and Lenkiewicz suggested that he might permit the artist to embalm his remains and display them as a permanent installation in his studio, the old man 'was delighted with the idea'. The authorities, however, were not quite so enamoured with the prospect of a cadaver being on public view and the police were informed of 'body snatching.'[28] The story made the BBC's 6 o'clock news and further added to Lenkiewicz's *Rabelasian* lustre, with the artist triumphing once it had emerged that he had had all the proper permissions signed and approved before his friend died. He observed to the media that the authorities appeared to have been far more interested in the fate of the old vagrant after his death, than at any time in his long life.

Initially, the embalmed, naked cadaver was placed in the studio window, in order to
see if passers-by became desensitised to the sight with the passage of time. Later on,
as a probable concession to local outrage and police warnings, the body was moved
upstairs to a library room taking its place beside other boxes of bones – both human
and animal – voodoo charms and the skeleton of a witch.

The witch skeleton came with an impressive provenance. In 1921, Charles Brooker,
a builder from the Essex village of St Osyth, bought a row of run-down cottages,
and while out digging for sand in one of the back gardens, came upon two skeletons lying side by side. Buried on a north–south axis, rather than the customary
east–west orientation of Christians, outside the limits of the parish graveyard, they
were discovered to have had iron rivets driven through their ankles, knees and wrists.
Though badly damaged in the initial excavation, the bodies were thought to be that
of Ursula Kemp and Elizabeth Bennet, denied a Christian burial and held down
with iron – the traditional metal for combating a witch's power.[29] The hatred and fear
these women had inspired, in this corner of Essex in 1582, manifested itself through
precisely the sort of outpouring of scorn, hatred and violence that Lenkiewicz had
sought to study.

Ursula Kemp was the example of a suspected witch who proved the exception to the rule – established by serious scholars since the late 1970s – in that she
was both a midwife and a healer who had fallen foul of the authorities on account
of her attempts to alleviate common ailments brought on by the dampness of the
marshlands. Unpopular with her neighbours on account of her ready temper and
grasping ways, she was warned by an erstwhile friend that 'thou hast a naughty name'
in the community. When misfortune repeatedly struck St Osyth – with plough
horses falling dead in their harnesses; milk becoming spotted with blood; a child
falling to its death from a cradle; a new mother suddenly sickening and dying; and
the local collector of the Poor Rate and his wife perishing in the throes of agony –
the villagers thought they knew exactly who to blame. Cross-examined by the lord
of the manor, imprisoned in Colchester Castle and tried at the Hilary Assizes,
Ursula Kemp's testimony shifted, just like that of Isobel Gowdie, dramatically, over
just four days.

In her first examination, she admitted that she had once sought relief from her
arthritis by travelling eight miles to a neighbouring parish, to see a cunning woman –
'Cock's wife of Weeley, now deceased' – and that, with her aid, she had learned to
'unwitch' the afflicted. Ursula made a clear distinction between 'white' and 'black'
magic, contending that she 'could not witch' and employed her counter-magic only
for the good of the community, lifting spells and easing the afflictions of others.
However – as with the case of Gowdie – by the time of her third, and final, tearful

confession, she had confessed to making a demonic pact and keeping a menagerie of familiar spirits at her door. There were two males, 'Titty and Jack', who took the form of grey and black cats, who killed upon her command; and two female spirits – 'Pigin' who appeared as a great black toad and 'Tyffin', who took the form of a white lamb – who could cause sickness, lame humans and animals, and cause cattle to die. Convicted, she was hanged at Chelmsford, her body dipped in pitch and left to swing upon the gallows pole four weeks, as a reminder of her transgressions against God and man.

Ursula Kemp's case had hinged upon the extraordinary levels of antipathy felt towards her by close neighbours and former friends, which led to relatively minor disputes over the refusal of charity; not providing sand with which to scour her pots and pans, or settling a debt through the gift of a cheese, escalating to the extent that their testimony claimed her life. Her 'naughtiness' – malice and general unpleasantness towards all who came in her way – was referred to again and again in the courtroom, and contributed to the extraordinary treatment of her body. One of her interrogators, Brian Darcy, the local magistrate, rushed into print to justify the convictions, while Reginald Scot was moved to write *The Discoverie of Witchcraft*, two years later, specifically in order to refute his claims about the handling of the trial. By then, Ursula Kemp had been cut down and returned for burial to her own parish.[30] The problem was that St Osyth did not want her. According to local custom, she was denied church burial by the minister and thrown into an unconsecrated pit, in sight of the church.

There she remained, for more than 300 years, until Brooker's spade scraped across her coffin lid and disturbed her remains. Initially, he believed that he had uncovered a crime scene but when the police and local archaeologists had revealed this not to be the case, he turned his thoughts to making money out of the discovery of a notorious witch. Brooker built a wooden frame around the skeleton, placed a grill and trapdoor on top and surrounded the body with iron railings. He then charged visitors to the neighbouring resort of Clacton-on-Sea to view the witch's body; charabanc trips were organised to see it and commemorative postcards sold. One tourist recorded in 1921, on the back of a souvenir card, 'there is a clamp through one hip – to prevent her from escaping, after she was buried ... it is evidently the skeleton of a *deformed* witch, as the bones are crooked', noting with interest that the witch had a 'perfect set of teeth'. Yet, Ursula Kemp's bones did not remain undisturbed for long. They were moved after a house fire in 1933 and bought for £100, in November 1963, by Cecil Williamson for his Museum of Witchcraft. Williamson – Gerald Gardiner's one-time business partner – had no doubt that these were the bones of Kemp. He had a coffin specially constructed for her, lined with purple silk, and proudly displayed the bones to the crowds

who flocked to his museum at Boscastle, in Cornwall. Among these was the young
Robert Lenkiewicz who was greatly impressed by the remains 'of the last witch [sic]
to be killed in England, nailed into the base of her coffin with iron nails', and – it
seems – was determined to possess it. 'He said he had gone in search of it in later
years', one of his friends recalled, but by then the bones had gone on their travels once
again. In 1982, on the occasion of the 400th anniversary of Ursula Kemp's execution,
the village that had shunned her in life wanted to reclaim her mortal remains long
after her death. However, Cecil Williamson was not minded to part with her, simply
to satisfy civic pride. 'I would never dream of going into the museum without having
a chat to her', he told one interviewer, and elsewhere wrote of 'lucky old Ursula. Done
to death in 1582, yet in 1982 she lies snug and warm, and well cared for with a deal of
affection from those who see and come to know her', adding that just 'maybe there is
a touch of magic somewhere in all this'.[31] Williamson seems to have rejected the offers
from St Osyth, largely out of a sense of understandable outrage at the manner that
both he, and Kemp, had suffered at the hands of the established church. Burying her
in the ground once denied to her did not sit easily with his conscience. An approach
from a wholly different quarter did, however, produce results.

Shortly before his death, Williamson was contacted by Lenkiewicz and agreed to
sell him Kemp's bones, for a figure supposed to have been in the region of £5,000.
They continued their journey across the south-west and formed one of the macabre
centrepieces of Lenkiewicz's new library building, situated in a previously derelict,
deconsecrated church, on Plymouth's Lambhay Hill. Lenkiewicz, having secured
modest civic funding for his latest project, intended to model his purpose-built
instillation, with its high-backed carrels and towering, gothic bookcases upon
Duke Humphrey's library at the Bodleian, and to add to the brooding atmosphere,
Ursula Kemp was, by all accounts, kept in an open coffin on the first floor.
Dr Philip Stokes, saw the body in 1999, shortly after its purchase, and recorded that:

> The skeleton was lying inside the coffin, which was lined with blue material ... [It
> was] laid out ... with nails laid beside it at the appropriate points. It was at the far
> end of the library ... where the indexer would work. There was nothing special about
> it, it was just dried out old bones. I was not surprised it was there because Robert has
> had major projects on death and was an authority on witches ... It was one way of
> representing the sociological conditions of an early period. Robert was very concerned
> about man's inhumanity to man. He had an affection for Ursula Kemp as someone
> who had suffered persecution. It is not in the least bit morbid.

If not a morbid soul, the artist certainly still liked to shock. In the spring of 2002, a
visiting journalist noted:

As casually as if he were flicking a piece of fluff from my shoulder, Robert Lenkiewicz let slip the disconcerting news that we were not alone in his library. Just behind me, in a long wooden box on top of a piano lay the skeleton of Ursula Kemp, a sixteenth-century midwife who was hanged for witchcraft and nailed into her coffin. 'She is here for safe-keeping at the moment', he said, quietly. 'The nails are still there.'[32]

He played the same trick on one of his friends, who asked him

if he ever found [the skeleton he had been searching for] and he told me I was leaning my head on it. I jumped up and saw he was right. My headrest had been the side of an open coffin and there were the bones, nailed inside to prevent their resurrection.[33]

Others reacted differently and the doctoral student, who had helped the artist with his Latin, reflected, 'the skeletal remains ... kept me company. The only sounds [heard in the library] were the muted cries that came from the seagulls that nested around the observation tower. This was my home from home.'[34]

Ursula, however, had other tricks to play. Whether Lenkiewicz noticed it, or not, 'her's' was not one skeleton but two. As Anthony Harris has noted, there were three hip joints in the coffin, 'one being placed below the right shoulder blade ... and Williamson, in his reconstruction [had] fitted the right femur back to front into what remains of the matching pelvis'. Furthermore, when he saw the bones in Lenkiewicz's library they were

in a very fragile state, many of them in a much worse condition than is indicated by the photographs from the 1920s. The upper set of teeth, which was near complete, has all but gone ... Both femurs are now fractured in several places and this is particularly unfortunate because in the early photographs one appears to be larger than the other.[35]

Thus, the deformity of the bones and the possibility that Ursula Kemp suffered from a progressively debilitating condition, such as arthritis, cannot be taken for granted. There remains a possibility that the jumble of bones, taken from different skeletons, accounts for an apparent deformity which bore no relation to any medical condition experienced in life. What seems to have occurred is that, in digging in the working-man's cottage garden, Charles Brooker disturbed two burials: one being that of Ursula Kemp, and the other that of her partner in crime, Elizabeth Bennet, who hanged beside her at Chelmsford. One of these skeletons was more degraded than the other and both were possibly incomplete. As a consequence and with an eye to the tourist market, he compiled a composite set of bones, taking the most dramatic nails from both burials, to create one complete and very dramatic image of death. Unfortunately, we are unable at present to test the hypothesis as they were not destined to remain in Lenkiewicz's possession for long.

Anxious for the return of its former exhibit, the Museum of Witchcraft at Boscastle reportedly offered the artist up to £30,000 for the return of the bones, but Lenkiewicz declined. He undoubtedly felt that 'Ursula's' remains sat well with his witchcraft library, which he now counted as the 'finest in Europe', and was understandably concerned not to begin to – literally – dismember his collection. It was the fate of that collection that now began to consume the artist's waking hours. His major exhibition at the NEC, in January 1994, and his one-man shows, in the spring of 1996, were specifically conceived in order to try to raise money to fund his book-buying sprees and plans were put forward to Plymouth Council for a public art gallery, studio and library complex to showcase his collections 'for the sole purpose of the provocation of thought'. It was hoped that a £1.5 million lottery grant would be secured to restore three buildings in the Barbican in order to house his archive and artworks, and to serve as an educational resource for both scholars and the general public. The artist's studio and the witchcraft mural on the Barbican were central to the bid, with Lenkiewicz envisaging a grandiose scheme for glazing the whole area and fronting it with an enormous stained-glass window of *The Last Judgment*.[36] Yet, the sad truth was that, by the turn of the century, both the mural and the artist's finances were on the verge of ruin.

IV

When Lenkiewicz had begun work, in 1971, the Barbican wall had been in a poor state of repair and it is doubtful how effective his own attempts at rendering the surface had been, with cracks soon emerging in the plaster. The paints used had been of variable quality and the image was beginning to fade by the beginning of the 1980s. These problems were far from insurmountable, had it not been for Lenkiewicz's neglect of his own work and the playing of an April Fool's joke that arose out of one of his habitual disputes with the local council. Several weeks after the city had destroyed another of his murals, in the redevelopment of the Hoe Theatre, Lenkiewicz – stung by his inability to achieve critical acclaim and by the repeated accusation that his work was inherently kitsch, 'Vettriano with porn' as one later critic put it – took matters into his own hands. He assembled a band of helpers and, in the space of one night, 30 March to 1 April 1981, whitewashed over his Barbican mural and replaced it with an expanse of gleaming white paint, onto which were mounted three ceramic flying ducks. The Elizabethan heritage of the city was, thus, erased to make way for the most mindless expression of suburban kitsch and consumerism. Art was recognised as being fully subordinate to the market. It was an effective enough comment and one which, if offered as performance by a less talented but more media-friendly conceptual artist, would have won recognition and featured in all the major textbooks. However, Lenkiewicz's talent as a figurative painter, and reputation as an eccentric practical joker, resulted in its impact being confined to a few raised eyebrows and wry smiles. Indeed, the artist was shocked and somewhat hurt by the discovery that many of the locals on the Barbican had not even registered the loss of his work. He badly miscalculated the amount of damage that the water-based white-wash would do to the images now buried beneath.[37] He had wrought destruction on the greatest of his public works, with no gain save for a few more local headlines that celebrated his lifestyle as opposed to his real talent.

Yet, by the late 1990s, Lenkiewicz began to reappraise the work. He had plans to restore it and had fixed a series of wooden battens to the wall to stabilise it in advance of repainting the images. Much later, Chris Parsonage, a local businessman who had bought the former studio on the Barbican, promised to fund the restoration and pro-jected that it would cost £60,000 and take three years to complete the restoration, based upon a staff of eight professional artists and up to 20 volunteers committing themselves full time to the project. Samples of the paint were sent to the University of Newcastle-Upon-Tyne for analysis to see if a match could be found, while art students at the University of Plymouth were approached to work on the damaged mural. Richard Clark, a local artist who had known and worked with Lenkiewicz, was chosen to oversee the project and described the task as immense:

> About 60 per cent of the paint is still on the wall ... It looks worse than it is ... The peeling paint will be stuck back on and we will then use photographic references to paint in bits that are missing. A plastic coat will then be placed over the paint to preserve it. It will never be exactly the same as it was originally but it will be fairly close. There will be some loss in pigment colour.

Viewed in this light, Lenkiewicz's original achievement in conceiving and executing the mural, with modest funds and only a handful of amateur helpers, appears all the more remarkable.

Throughout his life, Lenkiewicz had been possessed with prodigious energies and drive, enabling him to complete – if his own estimates are to be believed – anything up to 10,000 finished canvasses. He habitually worked long into the night to finish commissions, before recklessly hurling himself forward into fresh book-buying sprees. Increasingly, the fate of his great witchcraft library came to consume his every waking moment. In what amounted to an act of virtual blackmail, he told the City Council that he would close up his businesses and leave Plymouth, if funds were not found in order to safeguard the future of his witchcraft library.[38] Funds were indeed found and the tower and former ecclesiastical buildings that now formed the heart of his library complex, though now filled with witchcraft books, took on a decidedly monastic appearance that drew comment and comparison at the time. One interviewer reminded him of the film version of Umberto Eco's *The Name of the Rose*, and of the fate of the Dominican library, crammed with forbidden texts from the Classical world, which caught fire. He was asked which of his own volumes he would save in case of a disaster. Lenkiewicz thought: 'That [film scene] was an agony to watch!', but that

> it would have to be: the *Acts with Spirits*, John Dee; the *Occulta Philosophia*, Agrippa von Nettesheim; *The Malleus Maleficarum*, folio first edition, Kramer and Sprenger; a Ramon Lull and a couple of Renaissance manuscripts. That's one armful!'[39]

Lenkiewicz had always thought that death would come as a 'welcome oblivion', not to be feared, but a close friend was probably right when he observed that – in the event – Lenkiewicz would have regarded it as a 'dreadful inconvenience'. His health took a sudden turn for the worse as 2001 drew to its close and, while he continued to see the specialists in the preceding weeks, he succumbed to massive heart failure on 5 August 2002.[40] In the aftermath of his death many things went astray and, among them, the bones of Ursula Kemp. Peter Walmsley, the executor of the vast, disorderly estate, admitted that he had no idea where they were but that they might eventually come to light. The idea was briefly floated to incorporate Kemp's remains into a public exhibition of witchcraft artefacts at his library but it is impossible to say if one or more of the 'Quantity of bones' auctioned from the Lenkiewicz estate in April 2008, belonged to either Ursula Kemp or Elizabeth Bennet.[41] What was found, however, in his studio when it was searched on 15 August 2002, was the body of 'Diogenes' slipped into a 'large drawer within a cupboard'.[42]

On examination, Lenkiewicz's estate was worth far less than was thought when he died. He was effectively asset rich but cash poor, while the scale of his debts were staggering. Thus, while the true value of the assets – mainly located in his book collection, as opposed to his own artworks – shrank, the total debt increased in line with inflation and the continuing costs of storage for his library, legal fees and insurance. Worse still, some 200 claims were made on the estate, while the city council showed no interest in preserving his library, intact, once bids to the Heritage Lottery Fund and European Regional Development bids fell through. As a consequence, 343 of his most valuable witchcraft books were sold by Sotheby's in November 2003, realising just under £600,000. The first edition of the *Malleus Maleficarum* was sold for £78,000 – four times its guide price – alone. His copies of Hermes Trismegistus, Ramon Lull and Ulric Molitor went in the same way, together with his grimoires. The greatest purpose-built library of witchcraft texts ever seen in Britain was dispersed among private collectors and dealers across the globe.[43]

The loss of his books, the almost total dissolution of his own studio paintings, and the fact that his canvasses had never been acquired for public galleries, meant his work could easily be dismissed and he risked being almost entirely forgotten. Within days of his death, the anonymous obituary published in *The Times* described him as a painter whose 'gift for self-publicity considerably outran his skills with the brush or the pencil.'[44] When his grimoires were auctioned in 2007, a sixteenth-century love spell he had once owned caused considerable media interest, with Judy Finnegan managing – despite the presence of Christina Oakley Harrington, a leading expert on witchcraft beside her on the studio sofa – to mangle the artist's biography almost beyond recognition on prime-time TV. Lenkiewicz, she declared, was a 'very weird man ... aged 80 who died about five years ago [who had] this thing about tramps and vagrants, and used to befriend them and all the rest of it.'[45] It was obviously aberrant behaviour, in the post-Thatcher years, to have any sympathy – let alone liking – for the disadvantaged: an unwittingly revealed attitude that Lenkiewicz, himself, would certainly have treasured. As one friend remarked: 'He was loved by ordinary people, which is never a good thing if you want to be the next Damien Hurst.'[46] In his own fashion, he sought to better the lot of the dispossessed and was able to communicate directly with the great mass of working people, through his celebration of the beauty of the human form which contrasts strongly with Beryl Cook's work, now cluttering up the art galleries on the Barbican, which depicts the working class as simple, unthinking grotesques. Perhaps the greatest discrepancy lay between his public persona of exhibitionism and radicalism, and his output, which was conservative and traditional in terms of technique, if not content.

He was capable of truly great and innovative work. His *St Anthony Embracing Demon*, an oil on canvas dating from 1993, ranks foremost among these and shows the old hermit, naked and blanched, embracing the darkness: clutching a struggling, snarling, fiery-eyed little demon in an act of self-love.[47] Lenkiewicz himself, saw the study in the following manner:

The Temptation of St Anthony, according to the Athanasius biography, is usually presented as an old man assailed by horrible demons from below over whom he eventually triumphs. I was much more interested in the idea of him trying to hold on to the demons; that is, the demons were trying to get away from *him* rather than vice versa. The popular view is that St Anthony is hallucinating and the parallel view for me is that lovers, we in our relationships, are also hallucinating ... the other person in the relationship doesn't exist. I was ... interested in the fact that in many of the descriptions the demons are *heard* more than seen. I was interested in the mindless, meaningless chatter of the demons and of life itself and how it might relate to the way we communicate.[48]

He reorientated the business of witchcraft from an external force which struck at thrones and whole peoples, to a purely internal manifestation of love, desire and loss. In a rapidly de-Christianising West, it is the psychological malaise that fascinates us, rather than the theological imperative.

While the painting of St Anthony disappeared between the closed doors of a private collection, the witchcraft mural on the Barbican sits in an entirely public state of decay. As Chris Parsonage, who had led the restoration plans, explained: 'The mural ... deserves to be saved. Everyone agrees it needs to be restored but no one actually wants to do anything.'[49] Furthermore, with the estate still in administration, Anna Navas – representing the Lenkiewicz Foundation – thought, in spring 2006, that it was simply not 'realistic to expect [the property developer who owned Lenkiewicz's former studio] to preserve the mural. In fact I think it would be impossible to do so.'[50]

The face of Frances Howard – the witch on the Barbican – has become little more than a palimpsest, her face divided into two by a wooden slat: one eye remaining, now imploring our help rather than commanding our attention. She seems to know, as well as we do, that time is short before the summer sun blanches the last details from her courtly gown and the winter wind breaks off the remaining chips of paint that recall her expression, whipping them far out to sea and replacing her beauty with the brutal reality of jagged brick. In this manner, the aristocratic witch might be seen to have finally become one with the tens of thousands of her poor and anonymous sisters, hounded across Western Europe over the space of some 250 years, whose lives were fully submerged in the story of an imagined crime. It is a barely less savage indication of the blind workings of chance that Robert Lenkiewicz – portrait painter – devoted his latter years and the greater part of his fortune in collecting and preserving the relics of witches and witchcraft, only to have his own masterpiece consigned to oblivion. With hindsight, it is easy to see this prophesised by the mural, itself, as the ill-shod feet of Simon Forman trample not only the metaphysical pamphlets of Agrippa, Fludd and Dee into the gutter, but also the work of the artist, himself.

CHAPTER TEN

The Way Through the Woods

I

As so often in her long life, Mary Whitehouse was shocked and saddened by what she saw on the television screen. Often, she had railed against promiscuity, the deviancy (as she saw it) inherent in homosexuality, and the excessive violence that she read into teatime serials such as *Dr Who* and *The Man from Uncle*. In this case, what had drawn her wrath was the image of a threadbare shaman, the 'Lord of the Trees', wearing the antler horns and head of a deer, slipping through the forest to restore the balance of nature and to return the spirit of a dead young hero to life. Broadcast over the Easter holidays, the unfamiliar retelling of the Robin Hood story appeared to hang heavy with pagan overtones of a religion far older than Christianity.

Steeled by the politics of the Cold War and the watchfulness of the Moral Rearmament Movement, she had fashioned a successful niche for herself in British public life through her sheer combativeness, her knack for delivering a memorable and acerbic quote to waiting reporters, and a certain amount of organisational ability. Thus, it was hardly surprising that the attempt to produce 'a Robin for the 1980s', complete with necromancers, witches, respect for the Cabala and a nod towards racial diversity proved disturbing and, for her, largely inexplicable.

She was quick to track down the author of the hit serial, Richard 'Kip' Carpenter, and challenge him to a public debate. However, unlike many other artists and intellectuals who had fallen within her sights, Carpenter did not underestimate her intelligence or cunning. Confronted by Whitehouse and the hard-right-wing MP, Teddy Taylor, who had equated the show with 'devil worship' and 'objected to the [programme's] relentless slaughter and blasphemous religious elements', Carpenter ensured that he had a trick or two of his own to play.

'I'm a professional writer,' he said by way of introduction, 'and you're a professional what?' Without a blink from behind the steel-rimmed spectacles, she declared that she was 'not a professional anything'. 'Good,' Carpenter shot back. 'Now I'm dealing with an amateur!' The remark brought the house down.

This brief exchange saw two visions of postwar Britain collide. One was rooted in the social conservatism and political reaction of the 1950s, the other was charting a course that believed in progress, and which led naturally from the creation of the Welfare State, in the 1940s, to the beginnings of the Permissive Society, 20 years later. It also demonstrated the clash between a fundamentalist expression of faith, forced onto the back foot by the rapid secularisation of society, and one element of a particularly English expression of counterculture that had gathered strength since the late nineteenth century.

As a child growing up in King's Lynn in the 1930s, Richard Carpenter's first literary passion was for the tales from Classical Greek mythology and stories, reworked by Shakespeare for a younger audience. After studying at art school in Cambridge and a period of National Service – during which he acquired his nickname, 'Kip' – he won a scholarship to the Old Vic Theatre School and toured with various repertory companies, before landing roles in children's television series' and big-budget, British movies. The collapse of the British film industry over the following decade caused him to radically rethink his career and to turn his hand to scriptwriting instead.

A simple accident led to his first big success. Driving back from his brother-in-law's farm, he decided to take a scenic route home and promptly got lost. Pulling over to the side of the road to look at the map, he glanced about him and noticed the word 'Catweazle' scratched into an old, partially overgrown gatepost. The name stuck with him and he began to think about building a story and a personality around the name. However, it was only when he saw Hieronymus Bosch's painting of a humiliated Jesus crowned with thorns, with its portrayal (in the bottom left of the canvas) of 'a wizardy old man with [a] pointed beard', that the idea of a children's series about a time-travelling wizard was born.[1] 'I had always been interested in things concerning the manipulation of time,' Carpenter told an interviewer in 1990,

and I had never seen a show where someone came from the past into the present. I thought 'who could come from the past to the present and still retain their sanity, except somebody who could rationalise it?' And the only person who could make some sort of sense out of what they saw would be a magician who believed that he was in a world of new magic. So from that it began to build up.

For the writer, the interesting person was the one

who is outside society and, in fact, if you look at all my stuff from *Catweazle* onwards, it's all to do with loners and people who are outside society. In a sense, that is the hero; the heroic figure is the man who takes on the world alone. I suppose that's in a sense true of *Catweazle* because he has to take the world on alone because he's in a new world.

Finding refuge in the old buildings at the appropriately named *Hexwood Farm*, the hapless magician is taken for an old tramp, down on his luck, whose stories about witchcraft and being tumbled out of his cave and pursued through the forest by Norman soldiers, are assumed to be no more than deluded ramblings. Carpenter would go on to write all 26 episodes of *Catweazle*, which ran on ITV for two series from 1970 to 1971, and saw the eponymous eleventh-century witch – played to perfection by Geoffrey Bayldon – searching for the 13 symbols of a mystical zodiac that would finally permit him to return to his own time. The theme of Gardnerian witchcraft is particularly strong, with the grizzled old man bearing an uncanny resemblance to Gerald Gardner, the founder of modern witchcraft, himself. And indeed, in the opening episode, Catweazle – athame (ritual knife) in hand – performs a spell that appears to be very close in form to a Wiccan rite.[2]

As he struggled to comprehend twentieth-century society, Catweazle habitually equated new technologies with witchcraft, playing with language and distorting it, to the obvious amusement of an audience of under-tens. Thus, electricity is 'electrickery', the telephone is a 'telling bone', and a light bulb is seen as the sun caught up in a bottle. In this way, the mundane could once more become the magical and the rather dull, materialist world of science and technology could appear to be imaginative, creative and more than a little mystical.

However, while *Catweazle* won a number of awards, including the 1971 Writers' Guild Award for best children's drama script, a change of management at London Weekend Television (LWT) brought about the sudden cancellation of the series. Other projects followed, including the incredibly popular *Adventures of Black Beauty*, which led Carpenter to collaborate with Paul Knight, a gifted producer. The pair formed their own production company and began working on a treatment of the Robin Hood legends that would eventually become *Robin of Sherwood*. No one had attempted to put the outlaw on television since Richard Greene's *Adventures of Robin Hood* premiered more than 25 years before, and Carpenter was determined that he 'had to make it my story, and my Robin Hood'.[3]

Carpenter was well aware of the problems inherent in pursuing a historically accurate Robin. Longbows, favoured initially by the Welsh, had not been invented during the reigns of Richard 'the Lionheart' and King John; a 'friar' Tuck in this period pre-dated his order by at least six years; and Maid Marion did not enter into the legend until the sixteenth century, and then only via the May Games and the persona of the May 'Queen'. The omission of any, or all, of these facts would have bled much of the fun out of the tales and severely constrained a dramatist, but fortunately Carpenter intuitively understood the nature and power of myth. 'Mythology,' as he later wrote, is as intertwined with magic as mistletoe is with the oak. It is vitally important to all of us ... the mystery behind history. The archetypes of every aspect of human character and behaviour are to be found in myth, affecting each one of us to the very core of our being. Because they are truer than fact.[4]

'Every part of England,' he thought, 'every wood, every tree, every stream is connected to some aspect of history or legend in this country ... we trail history behind us like a peacock trails its tail; we carry it with us.'[5] Thus, his reimagining of *Robin of Sherwood* imparted a sense of nature – bordering upon animism – which fitted well with the growing environmental movement of the late 1970s and 1980s, and a popular culture that had seen youth as an unbridled revolutionary force. Consequently, though still present, his earlier, more overtly Socialistic themes – originating in Geoffrey Trease's *Bows Against the Barons* and tacitly apparent in the Richard Greene series – were supplemented with a feel for the emergent Green politics, characterised by a lighter touch. Thus, he framed *Robin of Sherwood* within a clash of cultures between the dominant, brutalised and brutalising Norman elites, and the native English who had lost everything – their language, their livelihoods, their homes and even their old gods – at the Conquest.[6] This was immediately apparent in his initial pitch to the commissioning editors at Harlech TV (HTV):

> We have to create a group of strongly individual young people whose belief in freedom and the English spirit is almost fanatical ... It is the instinctive physical need of the wild animal. They are nervous young wolves, watching and watchful. They are not at all hearty ... This Robin Hood isn't surface swash and buckle – it's kill or be killed and hit and run. It's the image of a man lying buried and bleeding within a suit of armour. It's panting for breath in the undergrowth with rain lashing down and the soldiers moving nearer.

For a generation of youngsters raised with *Dungeons and Dragons* games, *The Warlock of Firetop Mountain* and fantasy films like *Conan the Barbarian*, *Krull* and *Dragonslayer*, the addition of a 'sword and sorcery' element to Robin Hood was something new and instantly appealing. 'I've always been interested in magic,' Carpenter told Richard Marson, in 1985.

> All my work has either had magic or the supernatural in it because, basically, I'm writing for young people who are interested in that sort of thing. I don't think Robin Hood has ever had that slightly eerie, mystical element before.[7]

These qualities manifested themselves most clearly in the episodes featuring Simon de Bellême, the brooding necromancer played by Anthony Valentine, who is driven to madness and sadism by his experiences in the deserts of the Holy Land; and in those set around Ravenscar Abbey where, under the guise of religious conformity, the Abbess Morgwyn (Rula Lenska) leads a coven of former nuns dedicated to slipping the bonds that confined Lucifer to Hell.[8] Here, there is a clear duality of 'Light and Dark', where different branches of religion and magic contend. The Gardnerian Paganism of the Greenwood and the liberal Catholicism of Friar Tuck battle with demons and magicians whose use of ritual reflects the writings of Aleister Crowley. Yet, even here there is an ambiguity in the scripts as superstition and rationality collide. Thus, Robin is able to defeat the 'demons' who plague the village of Uffcombe, near Ravenscar, as he sees through their hideous disguises and reveals them to be no more than ordinary, and very frightened, men.

Similarly, in *The Witch of Elsdon*, Jennet – the woman tried for heresy – is far from being the worker of malign magic but is instead a village healer and herbalist, dedicated to helping her neighbours in the manner of a New Age archetype. She finds herself in court, not because of her spells and hedge magic, but simply as the result of Guy of Gisburne's spite after she rejects his crudely amorous, leering advances. The *crime* of witchcraft is something malicious, unfounded and completely irrational within the context of Carpenter's *Robin of Sherwood* but the same cannot be said for the paganic roots that underpin Jennet of Elsdon's healing art.

II

'The Witch' had become more or less a stock figure in children's historical fiction during its golden, postwar period.[9] In Rosemary Sutcliff's fiction, she appears as Ancret, the village wise woman, who lives in a house fashioned from a green mound and first appears under the shadow of an elder tree, still with a mystique of youth and with streaming hair and dark eyes the colour of the tree's ripened berries.[10] Gifted with prophecy, Ancret dreams (and tells) of the death of a red-haired man, fallen at the foot of an oak tree, with the barb of an arrow lodged in his heart so that 'his blood soaked down into the roots of the tree, and the tree strengthened and put out new leaves, so that he and the tree were one'.[11] Within the week, news comes to the startled villagers of the killing of the King, William Rufus, while out hunting in the New Forest, thus seeming to confirm her ability to see into the future. Christianity seems little more than a veneer, as the peasants still dance to mark the pagan festivals at the turning of the seasons, and continue to worship a Horned God, with little thought of the village priest and the ecclesiastical court. For, Sutcliff tells us,

Red William belonged to the Old Faith, scarcely paying even lip service to the faith of Christ, all men knew that; and he had red hair, even as the man under the oak tree of Ancret's dream. Red, the colour of fire, of blood, of sacrifice. Was it not always a red-haired man who died for the life of the people ... chosen to be the 'Dying God' for that particular time?[12]

Sutcliff was greatly influenced by Hugh Ross Williamson's 'essay in detection', *The Arrow and the Sword*, which sought to portray William Rufus as an overtly pagan King who met his mysterious death 'on the morrow of Lammas', in the depths of the forest, on a date and at a place imbued with 'a definite pagan significance'.[13] We are told, as though it were established fact, that 'red – the colour of blood – is and always has been all over the world pre-eminently the witch colour'. It is given that the death of William II – who had considered himself 'divine' – was consummated 'at sunset on the site of ... a pre-Christian holy place; [as] the King's slayer stands under an elder tree; the King partakes of a kind of last sacrament of herbs and flowers; ... [and] is slain by an arrow loosed by his intimate'.[14] This is powerful and attractive imagery, not least in the imagining of Rufus's body being loaded into a cart and jolting down the forest tracks on its route to Winchester Cathedral. On the way, the blood of the 'Divine King' trickles through the rough boards and sprinkles the dry earth, investing it with fertility and permitting the harvest to flourish and next year's flowers to bloom.[15] The miracle is witnessed, not by lords, courtiers or churchmen, but by the peasantry, who are still pagans, who understand fully the nature of the King's sacrifice and give thanks for it, forming a mute guard of honour for the cart as it passes. Viewed in such a light, William Rufus can appear as a singularly appealing anti- or counter-cultural hero – the brave soldier who showed no trace of religious bigotry in his dealings with the Jews, and who willingly gave his life – sacrificing all his talents and victories – in the selfless pursuit of both the good of his people and the demands of his own office and faith. The problem is that there is very little evidence on which to base Williamson's thesis, and the greatest modern authority on the King's life dismisses any suggestion that he might have been a pagan as 'clearly absurd'.[16] Williamson relied solely upon E.A. Freeman's study of *The Reign of William Rufus* (published in 1882) for his historical details and took all else, concerning the nature of witchcraft and the King's death, unquestioningly from the pen of Margaret Murray.[17] As a result, while his evocation of the ill-starred King had much to commend itself to novelists and screenwriters, it cut little ice in the world of professional historical research.

For Rosemary Sutcliff, however, the sacred murder of the King marked a sea-change in the religiosity of the English people. William Rufus had averted disaster by his actions, but once 'they felt that the shadow which had lain so dark across the land was slipping away behind them', and famine and plague had been prevented, the peasants

> were no longer afraid, and so they left the old gods, and went to church again; and because the clergy preached hell fire and their consciences were tender, they grew afraid as they had not been before, of those among them who still danced for the Horned One in the woods or smeared honey on an oak tree. So there were a few witch hunts, and folk looked askance at any old woman they passed gathering simples in the lane, and made the Horns with their fingers to avert evil. Even Ancret, going into Steyning to sell her spare honey, found that the folk were careful not to meet her gaze or step in her shadow, though on the Manor they had too many memories of warts charmed away and fevers cooled by her for any such folly.[18]

Prominent in all of Rosemary Sutcliff's stories is the interplay between physical weakness – through disability or disease – and moral courage. There is also a clear appreciation of those marginalised by society, through poverty or illness, or a combination of both. This comes through forcefully in *The Witch's Brat*, in which, upon his grandmother's death, the eponymous hero is driven from his village by neighbours who had feared her power. Although it is not explicitly stated, it is implied that the old woman is Ancret, who had prophesised that: 'You will be one of the menders of this world; not the makers, nor yet the breakers, just one of the menders.' The friendless, lamed boy is eventually taken in by the monks of a nearby monastery and he dedicates himself to healing the sick – an art that he appears to have inherited from his grandmother – and to the establishment of Rahere's new hospital of St Bartholomew's in Smithfield.[19] Consequently, the narrative rapidly turns away from its roots in an *a priori* popular (and, by extension, pagan) culture in order to celebrate the majesty and triumph of High Gothic art and the order inspired by the cloister. It is not, it has to be said, one of Sutcliff's most popular or satisfying novels. A sense of loss hangs heavy over its pages; its characters know full well that they will never be great, and the mystery woven around Ancret in *Knight's Fee* is squandered, and she rendered commonplace by the reprise. Most jarring of all is the stern sense of religious duty, which is largely absent from her other novels, and which does much to hem in any nascent sense of adventure or character development. Sutcliff seems to have been aware of this and once explained in the course of an interview that she had difficulty imagining, or empathising with the totality of Mediaeval Christian belief, telling Emma Fisher that: 'I can't accept a world which is quite so impregnated with religion; the terrific hold that the Church had in every facet of life ... After the late Norman times, I just don't understand the people.'[20]

As a consequence, the difference between the sense of joy and freedom of expression gifted to pagans, in *Knight's Fee*, and the harsh aestheticism and consequent narrowing of horizons inherent in the Christian pursuit of monasticism in *The Witch's Brat*, is both dramatic and profound.

Rosemary Sutcliff's reimagined witch certainly influenced the characterisation of Jennet of Elsdon, who nursed her neighbours' children through their fevers and had knowledge of 'plants and berries ... The poisons growing beside the cures.'[21] Yet, where the earlier stories had characterised the witch as invariably old – sometimes graceful, sometimes wizened – Jennet was 'young and beautiful with long flaxen hair', a maiden as opposed to a crone.[22] Such a dramatic refiguring can and does enable an object of pity, or contempt, to radically transform into a figure fit for admiration and emulation. The frustration felt by many adolescents, stems from their sense of powerlessness over their own destiny – a destiny which is still controlled by adults. Carpenter's stroke of genius was to cast his *Robin of Sherwood* outlaws as a predominantly youthful band, whose enemies are invariably staid, cynical adults such as the Sherriff and his brother, Abbot Hugo. Guy of Gisburne is the exception to the rule, but is played as spoiled, brutal and petulantly stupid foil to Robin. Consequently, it is the Sherriff's unvarnished materialism, coloured by the 'grown-up' need for compromise and jockeying for advantage, rather than just his cruelty, that makes him worthy of censure. He believes in nothing at all, and – unlike the credulous Gisburne – instantly sees through the lies spun about Jennet of Elsdon. If she is a witch, he jokes to Gisburne, then her true crime was to have been a 'very pretty' one. 'If she'd tried to bewitch me, I think I'd have been inclined to let her.'[23]

For Carpenter, building upon an idea of the Middle Ages made familiar through the works of authors like Rosemary Sutcliff, the characters needed to

> exist in a magical ambiance yet at the same time be very much more real than actors in costume – they must think Medieval. They must believe in superstition and magic. We must see it in their eyes ... It's the fear of the dark, of ghosts and gods and demons. It is belief in spells and curses, in the power of stones and the evil eye. It is the hope that the tree, blasted by winter, will live again. It is living as part of the landscape itself and sharing a forest pool with deer [that] the young wolves will hunt tomorrow.

In an interview for the *Electric Picture Show*, screened in 1983, he enlarged upon these themes, explaining, 'what really attracted me was [Robin Hood's] connection to nature, with the wild wood – the greenwood – and the pre-Christian religion of tree worship and fertility.' Sherwood is suddenly not just the backdrop, but the wellspring for the action that follows, as

The cycle of death and rebirth made whole areas into an impenetrable jungle where rotting skeletons of trees lay buried under a tangle of creepers and brambles. To most people, the forest was a place of evil, where demons called from the darkness and the howls of lost souls could be heard mingling with the cries of hunting owls.[24]

Yet, for Robin and his band, Sherwood was also the expression of 'the vivid and changeable English countryside ... [with its] crags and reed choked meres; sunlit forest paths and dripping caves.' The interdependence of the hunter and the hunted, ensures that the outlaws – or 'wolfsheads', as they are styled – do not fear, but become an integral part of, the forest, attuned to its rhythms and its ecology. Mediaeval England has, thus, become a ritual landscape, where burned-out Saxon villages are swallowed by encroaching woods, and where hoar-frosted trees press-in upon stone circles.[25]

In repeating the symbolism of 'the tree that is reborn in the spring', Carpenter was signalling the centrality of Paganism to the framework, and internal logic, of the series. The outlaws are bound to the land – and more specifically the forest – through the figure of Herne the Hunter, the shaman or 'medicine man', who at times took upon himself an aspect of the divine. It is Herne who provides the rationale for Robin's struggle, turning simple banditry into insurgency, and giving the robbers a theological imperative – in terms of the preservation of the green wood and the honouring of old gods – alongside their stated aim of (ultimately) overturning the Norman Conquest. Carpenter explained that:

> I'd always said that if we were going to make [the story] really legendary it had to have some element of fate in it ... I always saw Robin as a yeoman, a man of the people ... That's how they describe him in the ballads. He also had [to have] some sort of mentor or guide, and I'd read somewhere else that Robin was the people's Arthur, so I decided he needed a Merlin figure. I created Herne to fill that space, and I wanted a character who was a bit equivocal, in that you weren't sure whether he was human or whether he was divine, or indeed who he was at all.[26]

III

The origins of Herne the Hunter, assiduously harvested and comprehensively reworked by Carpenter, may not have seemed to other eyes immediately appealing or appropriate for incorporation into the Robin Hood legend. He first appears, in the spring of 1597, in the production of Shakespeare's new play, *The Merry Wives of Windsor*. The playwright has Mistress Page attest:

There is an old tale that Herne the Hunter,
Sometime a keeper here in Windsor Forest,
Doth all the winter-time, at still midnight,
Walk round about an oak, with great ragg'd horns;
And there he blasts the tree, and takes the cattle,
And makes milch-kine yield blood, and shakes a chain
In a most hideous and dreadful manner.
You have heard of such a spirit, and well you know
The superstitious idle-headed eld
Receiv'd, and did deliver to our age,
This tale of Herne the Hunter for a truth.[27]

In choosing Windsor and its parks, Shakespeare was setting a local folk tale, familiar to his audience within the landscape of the woodlands that stretched out from the castle's walls. Herne is portrayed as the dreadful spirit of a former huntsman, is linked to one particular, ravaged, oak tree and wears a horned headdress associated with his erstwhile profession. In the closing act, Falstaff's lecherous credulity is lampooned, as he dresses up as Herne and lies in wait underneath the supposedly haunted tree, only to be surprised and humiliated by the very women he had hoped to seduce. The huntsman's horns thus become those of the cuckold, as he is trumped at his own game by Mistress Page's daughter, her friends and allies, who ambush him disguised as fairies, satyrs and hobgoblins.[28] Shakespeare is, therefore, introducing Herne as an established character from folklore, only to then mercilessly ridicule that body of belief: contrasting popular country superstitions with elite urban systems of thought, to the amusement and entertainment of the latter. In the same manner as John Aubrey would later conceive of modernity pushing back the frontiers of imagination, folklore and tradition, Shakespeare was seeking to signal the end of an old order and a marked shift in cultural values. Ironically, in embodying the kernel of an old folktale within his satire, he unwittingly preserved precisely that essence of an *a priori* oral culture that he was ranged against and which was being lost across the English countryside, as more materialistic and individualistic values gained ground during the course of the late sixteenth and early seventeenth centuries. As a consequence, in terms of historicity, Shakespeare's account of 'Herne the Hunter' is all we have to go on for the existence and form of a legend, now otherwise unrecorded and simply unknowable to us.

By the eighteenth century, helped by the popularity of the play, one particular oak within Windsor's Little Park had come to be identified as 'Herne's Oak' – or 'Sir John Falstaff's Oak' – and became a popular tourist attraction, being the subject of two published engravings before its unwitting felling, on the orders of George III, in 1796.

Souvenir hunters and sellers harvested the timber for carving into tea caddies, chairs and stools, with Benjamin West – the President of the Royal Academy – securing one of the larger branches for his own private collection of curios.[29] An anonymous writer contributed verses 'Upon Herne's Oak being cut down' to the *Whitehall Evening Post* and lamented that:

> The hunter in his morning range,
> Would not the tree with lightness view;
> To him, Herne's legend, passing strange,
> In spite of scoffers, still seem'd true

And wondered:

> where were all the fairy crew
> Who revels kept in days remote,
> That round the oak no spell they drew,
> Before the axe its fibres smote?[30]

However, it was Harrison Ainsworth in his gothic novel *Windsor Castle*, published at the height of his success in 1843, who succeeded in weaving a narrative about the barebones of the tale that dominated the manner in which Herne's tale was framed, told and restaged for the next 130 years. The inclusion of Falstaff in *The Merry Wives of Windsor* suggested a chronology to Ainsworth; since Shakespeare's fictional character had flourished under Henry IV and Henry V, it seemed reasonable to locate the living Herne – who had appeared as a spirit *c.*1402–15 – within the previous reign of the ill-fated Richard II (1377–99). As King Richard's personal badge was a White Harte, the imagery of the stag probably re-enforced a connection in Ainsworth's mind between that particular sovereign and the legend. Consequently, Ainsworth's Herne appears as a young forester at Windsor who, on account of his incredible skill at hunting and affinity with the woods, becomes a favourite of the King. 'If a hart was to be chased,' we are told,

> if a wild boar was to be reared, a badger digged out, a fox unkennelled, a marten bayed or an otter vented, Herne was chosen for the task. No one could fly a falcon so well as Herne – no one could break up a deer so quickly or so skilfully as him. But in proportion as he grew in favour with the King, the young keeper was hated by his comrades, and they concerted together to ruin him.

Thrown from his horse during one particularly gruelling chase, Richard II is saved from being gored to death by Herne's bravery; he takes the blow aimed at the King and succeeds in killing the maddened stag. Distraught, King Richard promises to do anything within his power to return the dying Herne to life.[31] This proves to be something of a Faustian pact, as a mysterious rider, on a pitch-black steed, suddenly breaks through the trees, introduces himself as Philip Urswick and offers to heal the forester, provided he is given a free pardon by the King for his past crimes. Richard quickly consents and Urswick slices the antlers from the deer's head and has them fastened to Herne's brow, as the first part of a healing charm. The King is relieved as Urswick tells him that the boy will be back at work within the month, and watches as his other beaters and foresters fashion a makeshift stretcher and carry the bleeding and bruised Herne off through the woods to the sanctuary of Urswick's ram-shackled hut. It is here that the action takes a darker twist, as the foresters – whose jealousy had been aroused by Herne's talent and expertise – continue to plot against him. Overhearing their low conversation, Urswick asks them what they would give to him, were he to destroy the boy and his career. Though they have nothing with which to pay him, they readily agree to undertake the first thing that he asks of them. In effect, they are selling their souls.

Herne duly recovers and returns, as promised at the month's end, to serve the King. Richard is delighted to see him, showering him with gifts – including a golden chain and a silver hunting horn – and appointing him as his chief huntsman and keeper of Windsor Park. However, the nature of Urswick's magic soon becomes evident as Herne, though restored to health, has been cursed and stripped of his former abilities; 'all his skill as an archer – all his craft as a hunter.'[32] As the forests go to ruin and the game flees, the King is reluctantly forced to dismiss Herne for his incompetence. Broken-hearted, the youth straps the bloodied antlers back upon his head and rides off through the trees, swinging his chain of office around him to clear the way. As evening comes, a pedlar discovers Herne's body hanging from the branches of a great oak tree and rushes off to tell the keepers of his terrible discovery. However, by the time they return to the grove, the corpse has mysteriously vanished and no trace of Herne can be found. That night, a terrible storm breaks over Windsor Castle and the oak tree is split asunder by a lightning strike.

The murderous treachery of the foresters gains them little, as Herne's curse seems to follow them. Indeed, every huntsman who succeeds him in the post of Head Keeper at Windsor is stricken by the same fate, losing all their ability at the chase and their affinity with the natural world of the forest. In despair, they return to Urswick who now calls in his debt from their original bargain. They must seek out Herne's ghost, beside the blasted oak and consent to join in his wild ride as part of his own train of huntsmen. Together they wreak havoc upon the King's deer, each night butchering everything in sight and laying waste to the forest until, at last, the King is forced to act. Richard ventures out to the oak at midnight and finds Herne there, mounted upon a spectral steed. Herne explains the nature of the betrayal he suffered at the hands of his fellow keepers and says that his depredations will only come to an end once he is revenged and the King consents to hang his persecutors from the branches of his oak. This Richard does and Herne disappears, to trouble him and his deer no more.[33]

Just as Kipling would later use Shakespeare's Puck, Ainsworth employed Herne as an enduring figure and a constant in the midst of a narrative that quickly slips between different historical time periods. He reappears whenever there is a wrong committed, or the country becomes unsettled. Thus, the fall of Richard II and Henry IV's usurpation of the throne calls him forth again

> with a new band ... and again hunted the deer at night. His band was destroyed, but he defied all attempts at capture; and so it has continued to our own time, for not one of the seven monarchs who have held the castle since Richard's day have been able to drive him from the forest.[34]

The mainstay of the novel, wrapped around an historical account of – and guide to – the castle itself, concerns the rise and fall of Anne Boleyn and Henry VIII's love for her. Herne appears as a terrible and, at times, malicious spirit, who ambushes hunting parties, abducts young maidens and – finally – confronts King Henry to remind him of the wrong that he has done in condemning Queen Anne to death. As well as the haunted tree (which has inexplicably changed from an oak to a beech over the course of the novel), Ainsworth creates a mythic landscape for the parkland at Windsor, complete with marshes, foresters' cottages lost in dark woods, and a lakeside cave – home to Herne – complete with a secret entrance. Significantly, Richard Carpenter's Herne inhabits exactly the same type of cave system, complete with underground lakes, waterfalls and luminescent witch-fire, within Sherwood Forest, and it is there that Robin Hood visits him to pledge himself to the service of the Horned God.

Ainsworth's story proved to be extremely popular, selling tens of thousands of copies, constantly remaining in print until the late 1960s, and filling the shelves of the great Victorian public libraries.[35] Illustrated by specially commissioned engravings by George Cruikshank, the 1844 edition succeeded in imprinting an image of an antlered Herne – blowing a horn, urging his steed on through the tangled forest, and accompanied by two black hounds and a great night owl – upon the popular consciousness. The image became standard, and was frequently reworked, not least by the painters of pub signs across the home counties in the postwar period.[36] Susan Cooper's novel, *The Dark is Rising*, written for a teenage audience, operated within this framing of 'the Wild Hunt', with Herne's towering figure glimpsed in the wood by moonlight. Herne, half beast, half man, possesses 'strange tawny eyes, yellow-gold, unfathomable, like the eyes of some huge bird' and a quick smile that could spread in friendship but which also told of cruelty 'and a piti-less impulse to revenge.'[37] He is still tied to his Oak in Windsor Great Park and to Shakespeare's conception of his ride through the winter snows.

A radical break with this tradition was made, in 1947, with Mary Fairclough's exhi-bition of a large coloured pencil study of *Herne the Hunter*. Born in Bristol in 1913, Fairclough studied part-time at the West of England Art College, before embarking on a successful commercial career shortly before the outbreak of World War II. She worked as an illustrator for a number of children's books for Macmillan and Evan Brothers, as well as producing prints and woodcuts that focused upon peasant and indigenous cultures.[38] Her own affinity with conservation and the pre-industrial world suggested Herne to her as a fitting subject for her art and she seems to have taken Harrison Ainsworth's doomed hero as her model and point of departure. However, it is also possible that she had read – or at least knew about – the work of Margaret Murray and Christina Hole on witchcraft, which was gaining a wider currency in the immediate postwar period. In *The God of the Witches*, Murray had incorporated into her thesis Ainsworth's fictional tale of Herne meeting the Earl of Surrey at Windsor as though it were part of pre-existing folklore, and confidently stated that 'Cernunnos ... in English parlance was Herne, or more colloquially "Old Hornie"', despite the fact that there was no evidence for the worship of the god, either before or during the Roman occupation of Britain.[39] Mary Fairclough's rendering of Herne placed him, for the first time, within a definite ecology. Brooding and gaunt-leted, he is sketched crouching in a forest glade. Deer brush past him and disappear through the trees, unconcerned by the presence of a figure who now – crowned by a magnificent pair of antlers – seems only part human. He sits between two worlds; that of the animals who inhabit the forest, and that of the men who would copse the trees and hunt the game. Yet, through the curse that deprived him of his gifts, the hunter has become the hunted. And it is this sure and certain knowledge that has worn itself into the furrows of his face.

Mary Fairclough's sketch stands mid-point between Harrison Ainsworth's gothic tale of a doomed forester, transformed into a malignant spirit, and the later equa-tion of Herne with a specific god, or gods, the worship of whom – obliterated by the coming of Christianity – survived through a fragmentary and garbled folklore. The genesis of revived Paganism after the late 1940s, and the establishment of a recognis-able counterculture in the 1960s, led to a number of attempts to link the rudiments of Herne's tale to the religious practices of some of the earliest peoples to inhabit the British Isles. Thus, Herne became associated with the Horned God, Cernunnos or Pan, with the 'Wild Hunts' of Germanic and Norse folklore and, finally, with the god, Odin, himself. In a further twist, he also took on an aspect of the dying god, left to bleed to death on the forest floor in order that the natural order and – by extension – the crops, did not fail.[40] If we look again at the first section of Ainsworth's story, in which Herne's sacrifice prevents the death of the King, we can perceive echoes of the legends surrounding the sacrificial death of William Rufus. Indeed, Michael John Petry, writing in 1972 and Eric L. Fitch, writing in 1994, made these parallels explicit and significant, with the 'Red King' dying willingly under an oak tree, during the course of a stag hunt.[41] In this manner, Herne the simple – if skilled – forester now became both a sacrifice and a god.

The transformation was given potent expression in a cycle of poems written between the mid-1970s and beginning of the 1980s, and privately published by Eric Mottram in 1981. Herne is now evoked as one 'expert beyond us in woodcraft', for whom

Holly thickness projected impervious,
A yard before him pleasurable difficulties,
A blue stream from bushes footed twisted snakes between
roots leapt a wild spectral humanity;
deer skins around tawny gaunt limbs,
he, his skull helmet antlered,
phosphoric fire cut in links
rusted from his left arm chain,
on his right wrist a horned owl
dilated talon erect
red balled, feathers angered
in full cauldrons the moons.[42]

In Mottram's poem, Herne transcends Ainsworth's gothic vision and becomes the point for poetic departure, a symbol of a wider paganic past and a fragile and threatened ecology in the present, that finds its most terrible expression in the dropping of cluster bombs and the spraying of Agent Orange upon the forest floors of Vietnam.[43] For the first time, he is radicalised – part Orpheus, part Actaeon, part John Barleycorn – the critic of Western Capitalism since its inception, the patron of poets, but also 'the savage man', the forester who knows that 'you can't hunt and be half-hunter'.[44] Above all though, he avows that 'happiness itself is a forest in which/we are bewildered, run wild or dwell, like Robin Hood, outlawd and at home'.

It is tempting to suggest that Richard Carpenter was cognisant of Eric Mottram's work. Indeed, if we look at his central evocations of Herne, 'forest and forest floor', the interdependence of their vision – and the similarities between Carpenter's original treatment of *Robin of Sherwood* and Mottram's poetics become clear. These are tales in which one can perceive Herne's 'green world/place/the stag/now part of the earth can elevate the winter tree/in pure leaf unclustered/outbranching play'.[45] Here, the dying god is again referenced 'in a game whose laws include death and chords/a new kind of flower out of blood'.[46] At times, the metre and word-play serve almost to evoke the developing ritual language of the Pagan revival, as Herne's message is carried on a 'wind made visible by scents/from enclaved turfs/paths recognisable through/time and space … notched hill lines/words in mouth as nut/or water flow/under heated branches'.[47] Here, in the remaining primordial forests, Herne remains 'a wild spectral object/slightly human in deer skins'.[48]

Far from Cruikshank spirited engraving of the huntsman, Herne – as viewed by Eric Mottram – has now become a link between the animal world and that of man, a denizen of the forest. This particular development, branching away from Ainsworth's original story, is forcefully suggested by Chesca Potter's anthropomorphic portrayal of a half-stag, half-human god, to be claimed now not by Norse, Germanic or English folklore, but by Celtic belief systems of standing stones, Druidic groves, the taking of skulls, and the works of Green Men at the threshold between life and death.[49] These innovations appear to have directly influenced Richard Carpenter when he went in search of his 'Merlin figure' to tie Robin to the forest. Herne was less threatening than an explicit Horned God with its overtones of Satanism, and more robust than the Victorian and Edwardian reimagining of Pan or Puck. Herne offered a vision of Paganism – tied to place and nature – that imbued Carpenter's Robin Hood series with a sense of spirituality hitherto absent from previous versions. He was quick to stress

> There is no magic in the original ballads and almost no reference to the popular idea of Robin fighting against oppression. But the story has been snowballing for over 700 years and has grown with each retelling. That's what has kept it alive. I hope that my version remains true to the spirit of Robin Hood, while at the same time providing a few new ideas of my own.[50]

These 'new ideas' of his breathed fresh life into the story of Herne. First, he relocated the geographic setting of the legend from Windsor Little Park in Berkshire, to Sherwood Forest in Nottinghamshire.[51] Second, he backdated the tale from the reign of Richard II to that of Richard I, 'the Lionheart'. Third, he dispensed with the idea of Herne as a spirit and, instead, transformed him into a shaman, gifted with second sight and possessed at particular times with an aspect of divinity. Indeed, if we look at the seminal image of a Tungus shaman – engraved in 1705 for Nicolaes Witsen's early anthropological study, *Nord en Ost Tartarye* – we see a figure wrapped in a deerskin, wearing a horned headdress and falling into a trance-like state through the beating of a drum. The image is really not that dissimilar to the portrayal of Herne in *Robin of Sherwood* by the actor John Abineri. Lastly, the reconceptualisation of Herne laid emphasis on the co-dependency of humanity and the environment. Written at a time when environmental politics and, by extension, the Green Party, Friends of the Earth and Green Peace, were all still gaining ground, Carpenter lent his outlaws a currency and a voice that was strikingly modern. Moreover, in equating Herne with a re-engagement with neo-shamanic practices which were increasingly common across the Pagan movement, he was pre-empting developments in the New Age, traveller and rave culture that would come to the fore a decade or more later.[52]

Supporting this vision was an ethereal soundtrack, written and performed by the Irish folk-rock band, Clannad. Significantly, for a series that was so grounded in a sense of 'Englishness' – in terms of a national resistance conducted against the invading Normans and an appreciation of the very earth as being mystical – the cross-fertilisation with Gaelic culture provided a lighter touch and one which helped to avoid the pitfalls of a narrow sense of nationalism, or even of jingoism. The resulting album – the appropriately entitled *Legend* – provided a soundtrack that set the mood for the greenwood and drove the action forward, through its echoes of battle and sense that this England was, after all, a 'strange land' where both Saxon and Norman were eventually subsumed by a far older ritual landscape. One track specifically references Herne as both a dying god left prone on the forest floor and as a solitary figure patiently waiting in Sherwood for 'twenty years' in expectation of the coming of Robin Hood, and a fresh Saxon rebellion. With gold discs, BAFTA awards and album sales of over a million, *Legend* brought the paganised figure of Herne to a worldwide audience that Harrison Ainsworth could only have dreamed about.[53]

IV

The Pagan theme that underpinned the entire series was expressed most effectively and forcefully in an episode entitled 'The Lord of the Trees', first screened in March 1985. It places Herne and the religious practices of the outlaws centre stage. The scene is set for Midsummer's Eve in Sherwood, when the neighbouring villagers slip away to join the outlaws in the heart of the forest in order to celebrate the solstice in a clearing sacred to Herne, and to receive a 'blessing' which will ensure the success of their harvests and well-being over the coming year, binding the people once more to the land. Their festivities are marked by the raising of bonfires, by feasting, drinking and dancing in a spontaneous and joyous expression of their ancient, pagan faith. The only prohibition is that blood cannot be spilled in the days prior to the granting of Herne's blessing: if anything, whether human or animal is harmed during that time, then the ritual is spoiled and the harvest jeopardised. This taboo serves to effectively disarm Robin and his band of 'wolfsheads', and permits Gisburne to ride deep into the forest and to hunt the outlaws with an impunity – and freedom from the flight of arrows – that he had not enjoyed before.

With no Sheriff to hold him back or counsel caution – for de Rainault, we are told, is away in London on business – Gisburne recruits a band of Brabançon mercenaries, 'land pirates' of the worst kind, and thoroughly enjoys himself cutting a bloody swathe through the countryside in his desire to root out heresy. Here, his desire to be seen as a great crusader is starkly contrasted with the desire of his men, under his old friend Bertrand de Nivelle, to rape and pillage. Furthermore, as he sets about destroying the altars he finds raised to Herne in the villages that lie in his path, his religious ardour comes to look faintly ridiculous in the eyes of the mercenaries. When he cannot either shake the peasantry out of their attachment to their god, or find explicit evidence of their poaching, he takes an axe to an oak tree held sacred to Herne. His impotent rage and ineffectual blows raise mocking laughs from de Nivelle's hardened veterans, who consider that 'the hero' is now making war upon trees; but the tears of the villagers at the destruction of their sacred shrine confirm a curse upon him. Herne is begged by his people to exact a vengeance, as 'Lord of the Trees' so that he might 'know your power'.[54]

Unfortunately, Gisburne does not know when to stop, determining to wreck the blessing and to kill 'their god', Herne, before their very eyes, at the height of the celebrations. However, amid the chaos of battle, Gisburne's plans suddenly miscarry. Herne's antlered head rises again above the throng and, separated from the mercenaries, Gisburne sets off to pursue him through the forest. Thorns, branches and briars tear at the young knight's cloak as Herne leads him deeper and deeper into the heart of Sherwood and the very trees seem to be calling out to him, repeating his whispered name as admonition and curse. Thoroughly lost, Gisburne turns in panicked flight, attempting to slash his way through a forest that seems to be closing in around him.

The denouement of the tale follows quickly: it transpires that it is Robin, disguised in the antlers, who has led Gisburne through the woods and – after ensuring that he is in no position to return to the fray – Robin doubles back to find the wounded

Herne, who is quick to tell the outlaws that the blessing has been given for the year. The villagers, their animals and crops have been made fruitful and the bond between the forest and the settlements, the outlaws and the oppressed, has been renewed. Paradoxically, though they have 'seen their god become a man'; Robin, the outlaws and the villagers, seem actually to have become more devoted to Herne and his fertility cult. They have rigorously observed the taboos of their faith, triumphed against an enemy that would have destroyed them and their ways, and gained a powerful insight into Herne's own role as a shamanic intermediary with the gods of the forest. Moreover, in his dying and rebirth – albeit with Robin's assistance – Herne has fulfilled his own religious duty in becoming one with the land. The harvest has been secured and the balance of nature restored.

There can have been few so uncompromisingly sympathetic and overt portrayals of Pagan religious practice shown on prime-time television, and Richard Carpenter's rendering of the Craft, complete with its festivals, hints of liberated – or at least guiltless – sexuality and individual freedom, forcefully demonstrated just how far the modern revival of witchcraft had come, towards the societal mainstream, since its un-banning a little more than 30 years before. Unsurprisingly, Carpenter's work served to create a prominent place for the figure of Herne within the new Pagan pantheon of gods, and – particularly in the USA – where enthusiastic fanzine writers expanded upon his creation, adding fresh layers of stories based around the forest god to the tales of Robin Hood, in evocatively entitled publications like *Herne's Son*, *Darkmere*, *Sherwood Legacy* and *Under the Greenwood Tree*.[55] In each, there is an acceptance of a definite Pagan cosmology underpinning the stories and verses, woven with varying skill around themes and events suggested by the television series. In this manner, it is acknowledged that: 'Only dying God and Summer King/Can slay the cold, renew the Spring', while:

> ... jagged thorns,
> Part for he who wears the Horns.
> Blooming flower, seed and fern,
> Bow before the feet of Herne,
> And dappled deer swiftly run,
> Before the Hunter and his Son.[56]

Alongside the fanzines, at one point a cottage industry had sprung up around *Robin of Sherwood*, which dovetailed with its resurgent popularity as it was repeated on US cable channels, enabling the internet-buyer to purchase incense burners shaped like John Abineri's image of Herne, or a set of ceramic figures that recreated the marriage of Robin and Marion in the greenwood, with the antlered god centre stage, bestowing his blessing.[57] By 1993, a study by John Matthews of Robin Hood – *Green Lord of the Wildwood* – could appear in which the outlaw was linked directly to the Green Man and to Robin Goodfellow, as a fertility spirit. At this point, helped decisively by a television series aimed for an early, or pre-teen market, Herne the Hunter had become an integral part of Robin's story and, fittingly, Carpenter provided a glowing foreword to the book, suggesting that

> England's most famous rebel should now appear ... as the very spirit behind today's Green movement; the embodiment not only of freedom but of the power of Nature and a potent symbol of our disillusion with a dulling, wasteful and poisonous technocracy.

Unsurprisingly, given John Matthew's creative and groundbreaking work on shamanism, Herne was now portrayed as an echo of Odin, leading out the Wild Hunt and 'associated with Robin as a guardian of the forest, whose rights involved 'Hodening'. The wearing of horns ... associated with fertility and the hunt.'[58] This provided an internal clarity and coherence that the Herne story had previously always lacked and, in an example of life mirroring art, put his character within the framework of modern-day Paganism.[59] In precisely this way, John Matthews joined with Mark Ryan – the actor who had played Nasir, Robin's Saracen ally in the television series – to create a Wildwood set of tarot cards that built explicitly upon Carpenter's vision of the Pagan gods of Sherwood; and which showcased Herne, in various guises, across every deck. Significantly, Herne – costumed in a tattered cloak and antlered headdress, just as he appeared in the series – now also carried a shaman's drum, as used by the Sami people. Form and function united, in order to suggest the manner in which Herne worked his magic, even though more than 1,000 miles separated Sherwood Forest from the tundra and Lake Inari. However, the mixing of different cultural expressions was far less important than the message imparted by this striking new imagery: that Herne now sat at the centre of a significant development within the revived Pagan religion.

Carpenter had, after all, suggested in his initial pitch to the commissioning executives at HTV that the outlaws should be a small, close-knit group, so that 'we can get to know [them], so that everyone is a character ... if we have Robin and twelve and Marion: we have a Coven.'[60] It was no surprise, therefore, that when Robin and his outlaws join the forest to the village, under a sacred oak, in a libation and a chorus affirming 'Blessed be', they are consciously referencing the remarkable growth of Pagan witchcraft, since the 1940s. Behind the obvious creative stream – which had taken a figure from Shakespearean farce, via a Ricardian suicide, to the status of god-head – the outlines of certain powerful cultural and religious developments remained to give the foundations of what was effectively a new cycle of myth, a durability and a coherence that they would, otherwise, have lacked.

This sense of a promise of a return to an age of rain-swept freshness, before guilt and the abasement of the individual self took hold, lies at the foundation of much of the modern-day Pagan revival. It is implicit in Gerald Gardner's love of the English countryside, its mysterious woods, hoar frost and darkened pools. It is there, in Margaret Murray's evocation of the dying king become fertility god, as William Rufus' blood forges a sacred compact between the people and the land, permitting the harvest to ripen again. It stands alongside Herne, the Horned God, as he watches both the hunter and the hunted from the thickets of the forest floor. It is there in Apuleius' world of flaking murals, recording glorious actions and of desolate temples, their statues broken and their garden sanctuaries overgrown with weeds. Yet their stories are not forlorn or without a larger purpose within this mythic retelling. That these stories have survived, and with them the 'hope for a new sun and another day, born of time's mystery and man's love of light' is, therefore, victory enough.[61] The witch, so long reviled, is the vehicle for this transformation. Freed from her rags, cleaned of centuries of dirt and grime, she is Isis and Marion, Michelet's peasant creation and Isobel Gowdie's freedom to dream. For those who value the human spirit, or for those who would revive the old gods in our own time, her story is not so much about the need to embrace the darkness of witchcraft, but to make the winter turn once more into spring.

Notes

1. The Figure at the Window

1   A. Lang (ed.), *Perrault's Popular Tales* (Oxford: Clarendon Press, 1888), pp. vii–viii & xvii–xxxvi; C. Perrault, *Memoirs of My Life*, ed. & trans. J.M. Zarucchi (Columbia: University of Missouri Press, 1989), pp. 16–9; M. Soriano, *Les Contes de Perrault, Culture Savante et Traditions Populaires* (Paris: Editions Gallimard, 1968), pp. 75–87, 95–8, 111–2 & 176–9; M. Tatar, *The Hard Facts of the Grimms' Fairy Tales* (Princeton, NJ: Princeton University Press, 1987), pp. 106 & 108–11.

2   B. Stoker, *Famous Impostors* (London: Sidgwick & Jackson Ltd., 1910, rpt. 1967), p. 188.

3   D. Purkiss, *The Witch in History. Early Modern and Twentieth Century Representations* (London & New York: Routledge, 1996), pp. 163 & 189.

4   J. Caulfield, *Portraits, Memoirs and Characters of Remarkable Persons* (London: J. Caulfield & I. Herbert, 1794), vol. I, p. 25.

5   Ibid., pp. 25–6.

6   See S. Stevenson, D. Thomson & J. Dick, *John Michael Wright. The King's Painter* (Edinburgh: Trustees of the National Galleries of Scotland, 1982), p. 86.

7   See, for the most satisfying and compelling examples, M. Adler, *Drawing Down the Moon. Witches, Druids, Goddess-Worshippers and Other Pagans in America Today* (New York: Penguin Compass, 1979, rpt. 1986); O. Davies, *America Bewitched. The Story of Witchcraft after Salem* (Oxford: Oxford University Press, 2013); R. Hutton, *The Triumph of the Moon. A History of Modern Pagan Witchcraft* (Oxford: Oxford University Press, 1999); Purkiss, *The Witch in History*; L. Roper, *Oedipus and the Devil. Witchcraft, Sexuality and Religion in Early Modern Europe* (London & New York: Routledge, 1994); M. Warner, *From the Beast to the Blonde, on Fairy Tales and their Tellers* (London: Chatto & Windus, 1994).

8   R. Briggs, *Witches & Neighbours. The Social and Cultural Context of European Witchcraft* (New York & London: Penguin Books, 1996, rpt. 1998), p. 11.

9   P. Aughton, *North Meols and Southport. A History* (Preston: Carnegie Press, 1988, rpt. 1989), pp. 79–80, 84, 88, 91, 148, 166 & 185–6; J. Cotterall, *Churchtown. The Village That Gave Birth to Southport* (Southport Christian Book Centre, 2014), pp. 72–5, 85, 143, 217–25 & 229–34; P.F. Lynch, *North Meols, Southport. A Parish and its People Before 1820*, foreword Rev. W. Pick (Kempsey, Worcestershire: Hughes & Company, 2009), pp. 81, 138, 229–31, 237–8, 253, 258 & 264–5.

10 A. Runeberg, *Witches, Demons and Fertility Magic* (Helsinki: Fennica, 1947), pp. 135–6.

11 E.E. Evans-Pritchard (ed.), *Man and Woman Among the Azande* (London: Faber & Faber, 1974), pp. 13, 78–81 & 167–8; E.E. Evans-Pritchard, *Witchcraft, Oracles, and Magic Among the Azande* (Oxford: Oxford University Press, 1976), pp. 2–3, 10–14, 18–30, 33–4, 51–4, 56–63, 187–95, 217–18 & 227.

12 See K. Thomas, *Religion and the Decline of Magic. Studies in Popular Beliefs in Sixteenth- and Seventeenth-Century England* (London: Penguin Books, 1971, rpt. 1991), pp. 402–3, 551–4, 675–7; A. Macfarlane, *Witchcraft in Tudor and Stuart England. A Regional and Comparative Study*, 2nd edn, intro. J. Sharpe (London: Routledge, 1999), pp. xv, xvii–xviii, xxvii–xxix, 198 fn. 11, 211–16, 218, 221–2, 226–8, 232, 234, 240–5, 250 & 310–12.

13 O. Davies, *Popular Magic. Cunning Men in English History* (London: Hambledon Continuum, 2003, rpt. 2007), pp. 9, 21, 29–32, 67–9, 71–2, 76–7, 83, 87, 104–6 & 111; O. Davies, *Grimoires. A History of Magic Books* (Oxford: Oxford University Press, 2009, rpt. 2010), pp. 67–70.

14 C. Larner, *Enemies of God. The Witch-Hunt in Scotland* (Oxford: Basil Blackwell, 1981, rpt. 1983), pp. 144–5.

15 See, for example, the very different approaches adopted by A.L. Barstow, *Witchcraze. A New History of the European Witch Hunts* (San Francisco & London: Pandora, HarperCollins, 1994, rpt. 1995); Briggs, *Witches & Neighbours*; S. Clark, *Thinking with Demons. The Idea of Witchcraft in Early Modern Europe* (Oxford: Oxford University Press, 1997, rpt. 1999); S. Federici, *Caliban and the Witch. Women, the Body and Primitive Accumulation* (Brooklyn, NY: Autonomedia, 2004, rpt. 2009); C. Ginzburg, *Ecstasies. Deciphering the Witches' Sabbath*, trans. R. Rosenthal (London: Penguin Books, 1991, rpt. 1992); Scarre & Callow, *Witchcraft and Magic*; Thomas, *Religion and the Decline of Magic*; H.R. Trevor-Roper, *The European Witch-Craze of the 16th and 17th Centuries* (Harmondsworth: Penguin Books, 1967, rpt. 1978).

16 Voltaire, quoted in Scarre & Callow, *Witchcraft and Magic*, p. 3.

17 Barstow, *Witchcraze*, pp. 16, 23–6, 29, 55, 63–4, 97–102, 105–7, 111–17, 127, 133–8, 141–5, 148–50, 159–60 & 165; M. Daly, *Gyn/Ecology. The Metaethics of Radical Feminism* (London: The Women's Press, 1978), pp. 183–6, 192–3, 196, 201–2, 216–17 & 221; A. Dworkin, *Woman Hating* (New York: E.P. Dutton & Co., 1974), pp. 34–5, 48, 129–30, 136, 139–42, 147, 149; Federici, *Caliban and the Witch*, pp. 11, 14, 16, 92, 94–5, 97–100, 103, 144, 146, 164–5, 174 & 183–4; M.J. Gage, *Woman, Church and State* (New York: Humanity Books, 1893, rpt. 2002), pp. 230–4, 236, 239–42, 244, 246, 255, 275 & 278.

18 G. Lachman, *Madame Blavatsky. The Mother of Modern Spirituality* (New York: Jeremy P. Tarcher/Penguin, 2012), pp. x–xii; H. Murphet, *When Daylight Comes. Biography of Helena Petrovna Blavatsky* (Wheaton, IL, Madras, India & London: Theosophical Publishing House, 1975, rpt. 1988), pp. xvii, xxx–xxxi & 258–60; R. Pearsall, *The Table-Rappers. The Victorians and the Occult* (Thrupp, Stroud: Sutton Publishing, 1972, rpt. 2004), pp. 211–17; P. Washington, *Madame Blavatsky's Baboon. Theosophy and the Emergence of the Western Guru* (London: Secker & Warburg, 1993), pp. 2–4, 32–3, 53–5, 57–65, 84–5, 152, 172, 383, 386–93 & 396–401.

19 D. Pears, *Wittgenstein* (Fontana/Collins, London, 1971), pp. 13–14, 79–82, 128–33, 142–5, 147–8, 150, 152–3 & 183.

20 Hutton, *Triumph of the Moon*, pp. 398–9 & 413–16.

21 R. Hutton, 'Foreword' in P. Heselton, *Wiccan Roots. Gerald Gardner and the Modern Witchcraft Revival* (Chieveley, Berkshire: Capall Bann Publishing, 2000), p. 1.

2. The Witch House of Bamberg

1 1 Kings ix, 7–9.
    See also L. Apps & A. Gow, *Male Witches in Early Modern Europe* (Manchester & New York: Manchester University Press, 2003), pp. 74–5 & 165; G. de Givry, *Witchcraft, Magic and Alchemy* (New York: Dover Publications, 1931, rpt. 1971), pp. 202–4; J.B. Russell, *A History of Witchcraft. Sorcerers, Heretics, and Pagans* (London: Thames & Hudson, 1981, rpt. 1997), p. 87.

2 W. Behringer, *Hexen und Hexenprozesse in Deutschland* (Munich: Deutscher Taschenbuch-Verlag dtv, 1988), pp. 245–6; W. Behringer, *Witchcraft Persecutions in Bavaria. Popular Magic, Religious Zealotry and Reasons of State in Early Modern Europe* (Cambridge: Cambridge University Press, 1997), p. 156; A. Stickler, *Eine Stadt im Hexenfieber. Aus dem Tagebuch des Zeiler Burgermeister Johann Langhans, 1611–1628* (Berlin Centaurus – Verlags Gesellschaft, 1994),

pp. 74–5; R. Walinski-Kiehl, 'Prince Bishopric of Bamberg' in R.M. Golden (ed.), *Encyclopedia of Witchcraft. The Western Tradition* (Santa Barbara & Oxford: ABC-Clio, 2006), vol. I, p. 87.

For the origins of witch-hunting in the region, see G. Loeffler, 'Dz sie dem Boesen feindt ihr seel verheissen. Hexenprozesse in Kulmbach und Bamberg', in *Historicher Verein Bamberg*, vol. 140 (Bamberg: Selbst-Verlag des Historischen Vereins, 2004), pp. 61–98.

3 S. Clark, *Thinking with Demons. The Idea of Witchcraft in Early Modern Europe* (Oxford: Oxford University Press, 1997, rpt. 1999), pp. 324, 439, 453–4, 560 & 579; G. Schormann, *Hexenprozesse in Deutschland* (Gottingen: Vandenhoeck & Ruprecht, 1993, rpt. 1996), p. 51; Stickler, *Eine Stadt im Hexenfieber*, p. 44.

4 W. Behringer, *Witches and Witch-Hunts. A Global History* (Cambridge: Polity Press, 2004), p. 114.

See also R. Walinski-Kiehl, 'Witch-Hunting and State-Building in the Bishoprics of Bamberg and Würzburg, c.1570–1630', in J. Dillinger, J.M. Schmidt & D.R. Bauer (eds), *Hexenprozess und Staatsbildung/Witch-Trials and State-Building* (Bielefeld: Verlag fur Regionalgeschichte, 2008), p. 258.

5 H. Sebald, *Witch-Children from Salem Witch-Hunts to Modern Courtrooms* (Amherst, NY: Prometheus Books, 1995), p. 150.

6 Sebald, *Witch-Children*, p. 115.

7 Ibid., pp. 128–30 & 133–4.

8 H.G. Haile (ed.), *The History of Doctor Johann Faustus* (Urbana: University of Illinois Press, 1965), pp. 1, 13 & 15; E.M. Butler, *The Fortunes of Faust* (Thrupp nr. Stroud: Sutton Publishing, 1952, rpt. 1998), pp. 3, 12–13 & 21.

9 Walinski-Kiehl, 'Witch-hunting and State-Building', p. 254.

10 Behringer, *Witches and Witch-Hunts*, p. 112; Walinski-Kiehl, 'Witch-hunting and State-Building', p. 255.

11 H.R. Trevor-Roper, *The European Witch-Craze of the 16th and 17th Centuries* (Harmondsworth: Penguin Books, 1967, rpt. 1969), p. 88.

12 W.B. Smith, *Reformation and the German Territorial State: Upper Franconia, 1300–1630* (Rochester, NY: University of Rochester Press, 2008), p. 174; Stickler, *Eine Stadt im Hexenfieber*, p. 60.

13 Smith, *Reformation and the German Territorial State*, p. 175; Stickler, *Eine Stadt im Hexenfieber*, pp. 62–9.

14 H.C.E. Midelfort, *Witch Hunting in Southwestern Germany, 1562–1684. The Social and Intellectual Foundations* (Stanford, CA: Stanford University Press, 1972), pp. 139 & 145.

15 B. Levack (ed.), *The Witchcraft Source Book* (New York & London: Routledge, 2004, rpt. 2005), p. 199; Apps & Gow, *Male Witches*, pp. 159–60.

16 Apps & Gow, *Male Witches*, pp. 160–1.

See also Behringer, *Hexen und Hexenprozesse*, pp. 305–10, for the account in the original German.

17 Ibid., p. 162. See also Levack (ed.), *Witchcraft Source Book*, pp. 199–200.

18 Apps & Gow, *Male Witches*, p. 163.

19 Behringer, *Witches and Witch-Hunts*, p. 112; Smith, *Reformation and the German Territorial State*, pp. 174–5.

20 Apps & Gow, *Male Witches*, p. 159.

It seems likely that Junius's body would have been burned following the headsman's stroke.

21 Apps & Gow, *Male Witches*, p. 77.

22 H. Boguet, *An Examen of Witches*, ed. M. Summers (Bungay, Suffolk: John Rodker, 1929), p. xxxiii.

23 G. Scarre & J. Callow, *Witchcraft and Magic in Sixteenth and Seventeenth Century Europe*, 2nd edn (Houndmills, Basingstoke: Palgrave Macmillan, 2001), pp. 23–4; P. Morton (ed.), *The Trial of Tempel Anneke. Records of a Witchcraft Trial in Brunswick, Germany, 1663*, trans. B. Dahms (Peterborough, Ontario, Canada: Broadview Press, 2006), p. xxix.

24 L. Bauer, 'Die Bamberger Weihbischofe Johann Schoner und Friedrich Förner' in *Historicher Verein Bamberg*, vol. 101 (Bamberg: Selbst-Verlag des Historischen Vereins, 1965), p. 471; W.B. Smith, 'Friedrich Förner, the Catholic Reformation and Witch Hunting in Bamberg', *Sixteenth Century Journal*, vol. 36 (2005), p. 116.

25 M. Del Rio, *Investigations into Magic*, ed. & trans. P.G. Maxwell-Stuart (Manchester & New York: Manchester University Press, 2000), p. 73.

26 Smith, 'Förner', pp. 123–4.

27 G.L. Burr (ed.), *The Witch Persecutions* (Charleston, SC: BiblioBazaar, 1896, rpt. 2008), pp. 42–3.

28 Smith, *Reformation and the German Territorial State*, pp. 178–81.

29 Schormann, *Hexenprozesse in Deutschland*, pp. 37–9 & 44–5.

3. The Widow, the Fish and the Enchanted Goatskins

1   Even the otherwise excellent studies – H.H. Hofstatter, *Art of the Late Middle Ages* (London & New York: Harry N. Abrams, 1968); H. Landolt, *German Painting. The Late Middle Ages, 1350–1500* (Ohio & Geneva: Skira, 1968) – fall into this category.

2   K. Thomas, *Religion and the Decline of Magic* (London: Penguin Books, 1971, rpt. 1991).
    It is worth noting that in one recent study, the author mistook the address of the museum in which the painting was housed – the former Georgi Dimitrov Platz – with the name of the artist, himself. See R. Muchembled, *Damned. An Illustrated History of the Devil* (San Francisco, CA: Seuil/Chronicle, 2004), p. 96.

3   Thus, for example, the otherwise comprehensive study by Jane P. Davidson – *The Witch in Northern European Art, 1470–1750* (Dusseldorf: Luca Verlag Freren, 1987) – omits it entirely. The notable exception to this trend is to be found in the work of Lyle Dennis Dechant, who presented his paper on 'Nudity, Privacy and the Female Body: A New Look at the Leipzig "Love Magic" Panel', at the *Visions of Enchantment* conference, held at the University of Cambridge, 17–18 March 2014. Foremost among his insights, is the sense that the anonymous artist fashioned his vision of *Der Liebeszauber* from well-established archetypes of female beauty, that had acted as staples for artists working in the Lower Rhine region.

4   R. Hutton, 'A Modest Look at Ritual Nudity', in R. Hutton, *Witches, Druids and King Arthur* (London & New York: Hambledon Continuum, 2003), pp. 193–214.

5   L. Apuleius, *The Apologia and Florida of Apuleius of Madaura*, trans. & ed. H.E. Butler (Oxford: Clarendon Press, 1909), p. 54; S.J. Harrison, *Apuleius. A Latin Sophist* (Oxford: Oxford University Press, 2000), pp. 1, 3, 5, 7 & 38–9.

6   K. Bradley, *Apuleius and Antonine Rome: Historical Essays* (Toronto: University of Toronto Press, 2012), pp. 5–6.

7   Apuleius, *Apologia*, pp. 19–20, 27, 58–9, 60 & 113–14.

8   Ibid., pp. 24–5, 30 & 51.

9   Ibid., pp. 5–7 & 186–99.

10 Bradley, *Apuleius and Antonine Rome*, pp. 6, 15–16 & 19–20.

11 Apuleius, *Apologia*, pp. 59 & 80.

12 Ibid., pp. 59–60 & 77.

13 Ibid., pp. 60–1.

14 Ibid., pp. 62–3.

15 Ibid., p. 63; Bradley, *Apuleius and Antonine Rome*, pp. 8, 10–12, 21 & 187.

16 Apuleius, *Apologia*, p. 23.

17 Ibid., p. 56.

18 Ibid., p. 84.

19 L. Apuleius, *The Transformation of Lucius, Otherwise known as The Golden Ass*, trans. R. Graves (Harmondsworth: Penguin Books, 1950), pp. 31 & 86; E.H. Haight, *Apuleius and His Influence* (London, Calcutta & Sydney: George G. Harrap & Co. Ltd., 1927), pp. 25, 29, 43, 96, 100 & 183; P. Ward, *Apuleius on Trial at Sabratha* (Cambridge: The Oleander Press, 1968, rpt. 1969), pp. 3 & 5–6.

20 Apuleius, *Golden Ass*, pp. 29–32 & 266.

21 Ibid., pp. 31, 83–4 & 225.

22 Ibid., pp. 85–6.

23 Ibid., pp. 72 & 84–5.

24 Ibid., pp. 49–51.

25 Ibid., p. 88; Ovid, *Fasti*, trans. & ed. A.J. Boyle & R.D. Woodard (London: Penguin Books, 2000, rpt. 2004), p. 141; A. Scobie, 'Strigiform Witches in Roman and Other Cultures', *Fabula*, vol. 19 (1978), p. 74.

26 Apuleius, *Golden Ass*, pp. 90–3, 95–6, 174, 205 & 257.

27 Ibid., pp. 12–14.

28 Bradley, *Apuleius and Antonine Rome*, pp. 28–9.

29 Apuleius, *Golden Ass*, pp. 213–14.

It is possible, as Elizabeth Hazelton Haight pointed out, that Apuleius was mocking the Christians in more than one way: for, in graffiti daubed on the walls of Rome by pagans, the figure of Jesus was often depicted as half-ass, half-man. Apuleius' little ass would, therefore, have been in exalted company and the miller's wife would have been tormenting the symbol of her own faith.

See Haight, *Apuleius and his Influence*, p. 26.

30 Apuleius, *Golden Ass*, p. 225.

31 Ibid., p. 214.

32 G. de la Bedoyere, *Gods with Thunderbolts. Religion in Roman Britain* (Stroud, Gloucestershire: Tempus, 2002), pp. 182–3.

33 Ben Perry quoted in Carver, *The Protean Ass*, p. 3.

34 S. Tilg, *Apuleius' Metamorphoses* (Oxford: Oxford University Press, 2014), pp. 39–40, 50–2, 55 & 79.

35 Apuleius, *Golden Ass*, pp. 270–1.

36 Ibid., p. 277. See also Bradley, *Apuleius and Antonine Rome*, pp. 38–40.

This in stark contrast to the view of one modern authority, who sees 'Apuleius … content merely to tack on at the end a piece of solemn pageantry as ballast to offset the prevailing levity of the preceding ten books'.

B.E. Perry, *The Ancient Romances* (Berkeley & Los Angeles, CA: University of California Press, 1967), pp. 244–5. This view is echoed in Harrison, *Apuleius. A Latin Sophist*, pp. 248 & 259.

37 Apuleius, *Golden Ass*, p. 279.

See also R.E. Witt, *Isis in the Graeco-Roman World* (London & Southampton: Thames & Hudson, 1971), pp. 126–9.

38 Tilg, *Apuleius' Metamorphoses*, pp. 1–3, 6–7, 12, 15 & 19–20.

39 Bradley, *Apuleius and Antonine Rome*, pp. 24–5, 28 & 31–5.

40 Carver, *The Protean Ass*, pp. 15 & 17.

41 De la Bedoyere, *Gods with Thunderbolts*, pp. 191–3, 197, 199 & 202–3; F. Cumont, *The Oriental Religions in Roman Paganism*, intro. G. Showerman (London: Kegan Paul, Trench & Trubner, 1911), pp. 108–11 & 133–5; J. Godwin, *Mystery Religions in the Ancient World* (London: Thames & Hudson, 1981), pp. 7, 38–9, 70, 98–9 & 164–5; R. Hutton, *Pagan Britain* (New Haven & London: Yale University Press, 2013), pp. 236–47, 273 & 280–3; R. MacMullen, *Paganism in the Roman Empire* (New Haven & London: Yale University Press, 1981), pp. 97, 113–15, 119, 122, 124–7, 129–30 & 132–7. See also R. Lambert, *Beloved and God: The Story of Hadrian and Antinous* (London: Weidenfeld & Nicolson, 1984). For a more dated, and altogether more idiosyncratic, version of the impact of Mithras – where the imaginative impact of Michelet and Frazer looms large – there is: E. Wynne-Tyson, *Mithras. The Fellow in the Cap* (London: Rider & Company, 1958), pp. 25, 28, 179 & 182–3.

42 M. Dillon, *Girls and Women in Classical Greek Religion* (London & New York: Routledge, 2002, rpt. 2003), p. 77.

43 Bradley, *Apuleius and Antonine Rome*, pp. 7, 63–7, 69–70, 73–8, 168 & 179–80.

44 Apuleius, *Golden Ass*, p. 286.
    See also W. Burkert, *Ancient Mystery Cults* (Cambridge, MA & London: Cambridge University Press, 1987), pp. 90–1.

45 Carver, *The Protean Ass*, pp. 24 & 28–9 & Bradley, *Apuleius and Antonine Rome*, pp. 183–6, 188 & 202.

46 MacMullen, *Christianizing the Roman Empire*, p. 54.

47 Harrison, *Apuleius. A Latin Sophist*, p. 226; N. Lenski (ed.), *The Cambridge Companion to the Age of Constantine* (Cambridge & New York: Cambridge University Press, 2006), pp. 112, 131–2 & 174; R. MacMullen, *Christianizing the Roman Empire, AD 100–400* (Cumberland, Rhode Island: Yale University Press, 1986), p. 53; R. Rees, *Diocletian and the Tetrarchy* (Edinburgh: Edinburgh University Press, 2004), pp. 57–8; E. Sauer, *The Archaeology of Religious Hatred in the Roman and Early Medieval World* (Stroud, Gloucestershire: The History Press, 2003), p. 173. As Harrison makes clear, the Isis Cult was an expensive, and highly exclusive, one to join.

48 Godwin, *Mystery Religions*, pp. 22–4.

49 M.R. Lefkowitz, *Women in Greek Myth* (London: Duckworth, 1986), p. 108; A.B. Burn, *The Penguin History of Greece. From the Neolithic Pioneers to the Closing of Athens's Philosophical Schools* (London: Penguin Books, 1965, rpt. 1990), p. 393.

50 E. Gibbon, *The History of the Decline and Fall of the Roman Empire*, ed. J.B. Bury (London: Methuen & Co. Ltd., 1898, rpt. 1911), vol. V, pp. 109–10; A. Amenabar (director), *Agora* (MOD Producciones, Spain & Paramount Pictures, USA, 2010).

51 Lefkowitz, *Women in Greek Myth*, pp. 107–10 & 131.

52 Carver, *The Protean Ass*, p. 19.

53 E.R. Dodds, *Pagan and Christian in an Age of Anxiety* (Cambridge: Cambridge University Press, 1965, rpt. 2000), p. 125; Carver, *Protean Ass*, p. 18; A. Kofsky, *Eusebius of Caesarea Against Paganism* (Boston & Leiden: Brill Academic Publishers, 2000), pp. 27 & 214.

54 St Augustine, *Concerning the City of God against the Pagans*, trans. H. Bettenson, intro. G.R. Evans (London: Penguin Books, 1972, rpt. 2003), p. 324.

55 St Augustine, *City of God*, p. 28.

56 T. Taylor, *Apuleius on the God Socrates* (Washington, DC: Holmes Publishing Group, Sequim, 1822, rpt. 2001), pp. 12–13; Harrison, *Apuleius. A Latin Sophist*, pp. 8, 137, 172–3 & 208–9.

57 Taylor, *Apuleius on the God Socrates*, p. 13.

58 Dodds, *Pagan and Christian in an Age of Anxiety*, pp. 16–17; M. Grant, *The Emperor Constantine* (London: Weidenfeld & Nicolson, 1993), p. 127; MacMullen, *Christianizing the Roman Empire*,

p. 13; Rees, *Diocletian and the Tetrarchy*, p. 60; P. Stanford, *The Devil. A Biography* (London: Mandarin, 1996, rpt. 1998), pp. 72–3.

59 St Augustine, *City of God*, pp. 354 & 386–7.

60 Ibid., pp. 363 & 5.

61 MacMullen, *Christianizing the Roman Empire*, p. 28.

62 St Augustine, *City of God*, p. 325.

63 Ward, *Apuleius on Trial*, p. 20.

64 A. Marcellinus, *History*, trans. J.C. Rolfe (London: Loeb Classical Library, 1950), vol. I, pp. 534–41.

65 Ibid., pp. 536–9. See also J.W. Drijvers & D. Hunt (eds), *The Late Roman World and its Historian. Interpreting Ammianus Marcellinus* (London & New York: Routledge, 1999), pp. 55, 60–1, 178, 181 & 183–7.

66 Apuleius, *Apologia*, pp. 10–11, 14 & 25; St Augustine, *City of God*, pp. 318–26, 329, 345, 352–3 & 356–7.

67 *City of God*, pp. 359–61 & 364.

68 Ibid., pp. 319, 323 & 345.

69 Ibid., pp. 329–30.

70 St Augustine, *Confessions*, pp. 38 & 177.

71 J. Bodin, *On the Demon-Mania of Witches*, trans. R.A. Scott (Toronto: Centre for Reformation & Centre for Renaissance Studies, 2001), pp. 57 & 68–9; M. Del Rio, *Investigations into Magic*, trans. & ed. P.G. Maxwell-Stuart (Manchester: Manchester University Press, 2009), pp. 73, 80, 86, 95 & 156; C.S. Mackay (ed.), *The Hammer of Witches* (Cambridge: Cambridge University Press, 2009), pp. 100, 105–6 & 112.

72 Del Rio, *Investigations into Magic*, pp. 33, 73 & 156.

73 Mackay (ed.), *Hammer of Witches*, p. 112.

74 R. Kieckhefer, *Magic in the Middle Ages* (Cambridge: Cambridge University Press, 1990), pp. 28–9 & 32. See also Harrison, *Apuleius and his Influence*, pp. 25–6.

75 Carver, *Protean Ass*, pp. 59, 71, 111–12 & 153.

76 J. Sharpe, *Instruments of Darkness. Witchcraft in England, 1550–1750* (London: Penguin Books, 1996, rpt. 1997), p. 24; K.H. Vickers, *Humphrey Duke of Gloucester* (London: Archibald Constable & Company Ltd., 1907), pp. 270–9 & 289.

77 Carver, *Protean Ass*, pp. 158–9; Vickers, *Duke Humphrey*, pp. 275, 363, 365, 367–8 & 403–7.

78 Carver, *Protean Ass*, pp. 163–5; Wind, *Pagan Mysteries in the Renaissance*, pp. 42 & 242.

79 Carver, *Protean Ass*, pp. 172 & 261.

4. A Nightmare Given Form

1 W.M. Conway (ed.), *Literary Remains of Albrecht Dürer* (Cambridge: Cambridge University Press, 1889), p. 145; M. Kloss, *Albrecht Dürer. Bild- und Leseheft fur die Kunstbetrachtung* (Berlin, DDR: Volk und Wissen, 1967), p. 30; C. White, *Dürer. The Artist and his Drawings* (Oxford: Phaidon Press, 1971, rpt. 1981), pp. 214–15.

2 J. Bialostocki, *Dürer and his Critics, 1500–1971. Chapters in the History of Ideas including a Collection of Texts* (Baden-Baden: Koerner, 1986), p. 27; Conway (ed.), *Literary Remains*, p. 144: & White, *Dürer*, pp. 186 & 214.

3 Conway (ed.), *Literary Remains*, p. 143.

4 See J.P. Filedt Kok (ed.), *Livelier than Life. The Master of the Amsterdam Cabinet or the Housebook Master, c.1470–1500* (Amsterdam: Rijksprentenkabinet & Rijksmuseum, 1985).

5   G. Bartum, G. Grass, J.L. Koerner & U. Kuhlemann, *Albrecht Dürer and his Legacy. The Graphic Work of a Renaissance Artist* (London: British Museum Press, 2002), p. 227; E.J. Dwyer, 'The Subject of Dürer's Four Witches', *Art Quarterly*, vol. 34 (1971), pp. 456 & 470; J. Poesch, 'Sources for Two Dürer Enigmas. The Four Naked Women or the Choice of Paris', *The Art Bulletin*, vol. 64 (1964), p. 82.

6   J. Updike, *The Witches of Eastwick* (London: Andre Deutsch, 1984); T.M. Luhrmann, *Persuasions of the Witch's Craft* (London & Basingstoke: Picador, 1989, rpt. 1994), Plate 1.

7   F. Anzelewsky, *Dürer. His Life and Art*, trans. H. Grieve (London: Alpine Fine Arts Collection, 1980, rpt. 1982), pp. 58–9; White, *Dürer*, pp. 66–7.

8   White, *Dürer*, p. 67.

9   J. Campbell Hutchison, *Albrecht Dürer. A Biography* (Princeton, NJ: Princeton University Press, 1990), pp. 31 & 34–7.

10 Campbell Hutchinson, *Albrecht Dürer*, p. 34.

11 L.W. Spitz, *Conrad Celtis: The German Arch-Humanist* (Cambridge, MA: Harvard University Press, 1957), p. 65.

12 Spitz, *Conrad Celtis*, pp. 84–5; L. Forster (ed.), *Selections from Conrad Celtis, 1459–1508* (London: Cambridge University Press, 1948), pp. 9 & 12.

13 Bartrum et al., *Albrecht Dürer*, p. 227; Dwyer, 'Dürer's Four Witches', pp. 456 & 70; Poesch, 'Two Dürer Enigmas', p. 82; M. Thausing, *Albrecht Dürer. His Life and Works*, trans. F.A. Eaton (London: John Murray, 1882), vol. I, pp. 214–15.

14 M. Summers (trans. & ed.), *The Malleus Maleficarum of Heinrich Kramer and James Sprenger* (London: Dover Publications, 1928, rpt. New York, 1971), p. 140.

    P.G. Maxwell-Stuart in his modern translation, does not reproduce this passage. See P.G. Maxwell-Stuart (trans. & ed.), *The Malleus Maleficarum* (Manchester & New York: Manchester University Press, 2007), p. 166.

15 Bartrum et al., *Albrecht Dürer*, p. 227.

16 M.A. Sullivan, 'The Witches of Dürer and Hans Baldung Grien', *Renaissance Quarterly*, vol. 53 (2000), p. 352.

17 H.M. von Aufsess et al., *Willibald Pirkheimer, Feldobrist und Humanist* (Nuremberg: Glock und Lutz, 1969), pp. 8–10; E. Panofsky, *The Life and Art of Albrecht Dürer* (Princeton, NJ: Princeton University Press, 1955) p. 7; W. Pirckheimer, *Der Schweizerkrieg* (Berlin Militarverlag der Deutschen Demokratischen Republik, 1988), passim; White, *Dürer*, p. 88.

18 Spitz, *Conrad Celtis*, p. 84.

19 T. Brehm, A. Fries, M. Hamann, C. Jahn & J. Tschoeke (eds), *The Dürer Tour. Discovering Dürer in Nuremberg* (Nuremberg: Verlag W. Tummels, 2004), pp. 53–5.

20 Theocritus, *Idylls*, trans. A. Verity & intro. R. Hunter (Oxford: Oxford University Press, 2002), pp. 7–10 & 88.

    See also R. Muchembled, *Damned. An Illustrated History of the Devil* (San Francisco, CA: Seuil/Chronicle, 2004), p. 96.

21 Bartrum et al., *Albrecht Dürer and his Legacy*, pp. 107–8; Panofsky, *Life and Art of Albrecht Dürer*, p. 31; White, *Dürer*, pp. 54–5; E. Wind, *Pagan Mysteries in the Renaissance* (Harmondsworth: Penguin, 1958, rpt. 1967), fn. 30, p. 122.

22 Panofsky, *Life and Art of Albrecht Dürer*, p. 33.

    See also R. Hutton, *Witches, Druids and King Arthur* (London & New York: Hambledon Continuum, 2003), pp. 193–4 & 202–3.

23 Hutton, *Witches, Druids and King Arthur*, p. 203.

24 Bartrum et al., *Albrecht Dürer and his Legacy*, p. 27; C. Zika, 'Dürer's Witch, Riding Women and Moral Order', in D. Eichberger & C. Zika (eds), *Dürer and his Culture* (Cambridge: Cambridge University Press, 1998, rpt. 2005), pp. 118 & 120.

25 Zika, 'Dürer's Witch', pp. 120–1.

26 Ibid., pp. 124–5.

27 Ibid., p. 126.

28 See Bartrum et al., *Albrecht Dürer and his Legacy*, pp. 19, 27, 51–2, 54–7, 182–3, 227–9 & 306–11; E. Schickler, *Geniestreiche des Wetkunstlers Albrecht Dürer/The Genius of a Cosmopolitan Artist* (Nuremberg: Tummels Verlag, 2005), pp. 96–7.

29 Bartrum et al., *Albrecht Dürer and his Legacy*, pp. 228–9.

30 M. Pfister-Burkhalter, *Urs Graf. Federzeichnungen* (Leipzig: Insel-Verlag, 1960), plates 2–4, 13, 22 & 30.

31 E. & J. Lehner, *Devils, Demons, Death and Damnation* (New York: Dover, 1971), plates 90 & 95.

32 D. Hoak, 'Witch-Hunting and Women in the Art of the Renaissance', *History Today*, vol. 31 (February 1981), p. 22; Zika, 'Dürer's Witch', p. 134.

33 Bartrum et al., *Albrecht Dürer and his Legacy*, p. 188; C.R. Dodwell (ed.), *Essays on Dürer* (Manchester & Toronto: Manchester University Press & University of Toronto Press, 1973), pp. 21, 68, 82, 128, 130, 134 & 143–4; Panofsky, *Life and Art of Albrecht Dürer*, pp. 157–71; Schickler, *Albrecht Dürer*, pp. 73–4; Thausing, *Albrecht Dürer*, vol. II, pp. 222–3.

34 Hoak, 'Witch-Hunting and Women', p. 23.

35 Anzelewsky, *Dürer*, p. 85; Bartrum et al., *Albrecht Dürer and his Legacy*, p. 187; Panofsky, *Life and Art of Albrecht Dürer*, p. 151; Waetzoldt, *Dürer and his Times*, plate 100.

36 Panofsky, *Life and Art of Albrecht Dürer*, p. 152.

37 Bialostocki, *Dürer and his Critics*, p. 35; White, *Dürer*, p. 40.

5. The Brutalised Witch

1 C.E. Bowen, *Battle and Victory; or the Story of a Painter's Life* (London & New York: Griffith, Farran, Okeden and Welsh, c.1882), pp. 6–7, 89–91, 98–9, 101–2, 163 & 177; J.S. Patty, *Salvator Rosa in French Literature. From the Bizarre to the Sublime* (Kentucky: Lexington, 2005), pp. vii, 2, 17–18, 70, 72–3, 77–81, 86, 101 & 114; R.W. Wallace, *The Etchings of Salvator Rosa* (Princeton, NJ: Princeton University Press, 1979), pp. 12–13.

In addition, there is the less than funny, 'comic' melodrama: Prof. Deinhardstein, 'Salvator Rosa, or, The Portrait of Danae' in J.D. Haas (ed.), *Gleanings from Germany* (London, 1839), pp. 291–320; and a Continental attempt to translate Rosa's form of satire into a modern idiom: F.T. Fougas, *Satire Contre La Musique, imitee Salvator Rosa* (Geneva, 1866).

2 K. Owenson (subsequently Lady Morgan), *The Life and Times of Salvator Rosa*, 2 vols. (London & Paris: A. & W. Galignani, 1824).

3 See, in particular: J. Scott, *Salvator Rosa. His Life and Times* (New Haven & London: Yale University Press, 1995); H. Langdon, with X.F. Salomon & C. Volpi, *Salvator Rosa* (London: Dulwich Picture Gallery & Kimbell Art Museum, in association with Paul Holberton Publishing, 2010).

4 M. Kitson, *Salvator Rosa* (London & Harlow: Arts Council, 1973), p. 16: J.S. Patty, *Salvator Rosa in French Literature. From the Bizarre to the Sublime* (Lexington, KT: University Press of Kentucky, 2005). p. vii; Wallace, *Etchings of Salvator Rosa*, p. 82.

5 L.C. Hults, *The Witch as Muse: Art, Gender and Power in Early Modern Europe* (Philadelphia, PA: University of Pennsylvania Press, 2011), p. 201.

6   Kitson, *Salvator Rosa*, p. 12; Scott, *Salvator Rosa*, p. 51.

7   Langdon et al., *Salvator Rosa*, pp. 170–1, 178 & 180.

8   Ibid., p. 170.

9   This was evidenced on a visit organised by Treadwell's, London's foremost esoteric bookshop, to view the canvas at the National Gallery, in November 2004.

10 Langdon et al., *Salvator Rosa*, p. 178.

11 M. Mahoney, *The Drawings of Salvator Rosa* (New York & London: Garland Publishing, 1977), vol. II, nos. 28.1–28.9.

12 Horace, Book I Satire 8, lines 21–33.
       See Horace, *Satires and Epistles*, intro. & trans. N. Rudd (London: Penguin Books, revised edition, 1979, rpt. 1987), pp. 73–4.

13 Horace, Book I Satire 8, lines 40–4.

14 Lucan, *Civil War*, trans. S.H. Braund (New York: Oxford University Press, 2000), pp. 120–1.

15 Ibid., p. 120.

16 Ibid., pp. 118–19.

17 Langdon et al., *Salvator Rosa*, p. 180.

18 Scott, *Salvator Rosa*, pp. 47, 49 & 54.

19 B. Brinkmann, *Witches' Lust and the Fall of Man: The Strange Fantasies of Hans Baldung Grien* (Frankfurt am Main Michael Imhof Verlag, 2007), p. 19; Hults, *The Witch as Muse*, p. 75.

20 Scott, *Salvator Rosa*, pp. 49 & 97–8.

21 See K. Oettinger & K.A. Knappe, *Hans Baldung Grien und Albrecht Dürer in Nurenberg* (Nuremberg: Hans Carl Verlag, 1963), plates 23–63.

22 Brinkmann, *Witches' Lust*, pp. 20–1.

23 R.A. Koch, *Hans Baldung Grien. Eve, the Serpent, and Death* (Ottowa: National Gallery of Canada, 1974), p. 8; Brinkmann, *Witches Lust*, p. 96.

24 Hartlaub, *Hans Baldung – Hexenbilder*, plate 10 & pp. 17–18.

25 Brinkmann, *Witches' Lust*, pp. 31–5.

26 Ibid., pp. 31, 34–5 & 145; Hults, *The Witch as Muse*, p. 84; J.P. Davidson, *The Witch in Northern European Art, 1470–1750* (Dusseldorf: Luca Verlag, 1987), pp. 20–1.

27 Gert von der Olsen, writing in 1983, quoted in Brinkmann, *Witches' Lust*, p. 35.

28 Brinkmann, *Witches' Lust*, pp. 32–3.

29 J.H. Marrow & A. Shestack (eds), *Hans Baldung Grien. Prints & Drawings* (Washington & New Haven: National Gallery of Art & Yale University Art Gallery, 1981), pp. 114–16.

30 C. Zika, *The Appearance of Witchcraft. Print and Visual Culture in Sixteenth-Century Europe* (Abingdon, Oxfordshire & New York: Routledge, 2007), p. 13.

31 Zika, *The Appearance of Witchcraft*, pp. 65–6, 72–98 & 233–4; B. Ankarloo & G. Henningsen (eds), *Early Modern European Witchcraft. Centres and Peripheries* (Oxford: Clarendon Press, 1990, rpt. 2001), pp. 122–3; B.P. Levack, *The Witch-Hunt in Early Modern Europe*, 2nd edn (London & New York: Longman, 1987, rpt. 1995), pp. 41, 51 218 & 228–9.
       It may well be that in conceiving his witches stoking a cooking pot, Baldung Grien was adapting an earlier image of *Two Witches* by Filippino Lippi, by stripping away the obvious Classical illusions and planting the action firmly within Teutonic culture.

32 Hults, *The Witch as Muse*, p. 94.

33 Ibid., fig. 3.9, p. 88.

34 Zika, *The Appearance of Witchcraft*, pp. 156, 160–2, 179, 182 & 185; L. Roper, *Witch Craze. Terror and Fantasy in Baroque Germany* (New Haven & London: Yale University Press, 2004), pp. 141–2 & 144–50; H.R. Trevor-Roper, *The European Witch-Craze of the 16th and 17th*

Centuries (Harmondsworth: Penguin Books, 1969, rpt. 1978), pp. 116–19; H.C. Midelfort, *Witch Hunting in Southwestern Germany, 1562–1684* (Stanford, CA: Stanford University Press, 1972), pp. 30–1 & 65–7.

35 Brinkmann, *Witches' Lust*, pp. 118–19. See also Koch (ed.), *Ausstelling Hans Baldung Grien*, plates 22a & 22b; Hartlaub, *Hans Baldung – Hexenbilder*, pp. 20–1.

36 Brinkmann, *Witches' Lust*, p. 145.

37 Ibid., pp. 133–4, 137 & 145–6.

38 Marrow & Shestack (eds), *Hans Baldung Grien. Prints & Drawings*, pp. 270–1.

39 M.A. Sullivan, 'The Witches of Dürer and Hans Baldung Grien', *Renaissance Quarterly*, vol. 53 (2000), p. 386.

40 W. Schulz, *Cornelis Saftleven, 1607–1681. Leben und Werke* (Berlin & New York: Walter de Gruyter, 1978), plate 2 & p. 182.

41 Schulz, *Cornelis Saftleven*, plate 20 & p. 188; Davidson, *The Witch in Northern Art*, p. 67.

42 Davidson, *The Witch in Northern Art*, plates 23, 25 & 29.

43 The painting is now, sadly, lost. See Wallace, *Etchings of Salvator Rosa*, p. 15.

44 O.G. Boetzkes, *Salvator Rosa: Seventeenth-Century Italian Painter, Poet, and Patriot* (New York, Washington & Hollywood: Vantage Press, 1960), p. 92; Petty, *Salvator Rosa*, pp. 156–7; Owenson (Lady Morgan), *Life and Times of Salvator Rosa*, vol. I, p. 328.

45 U. Limentani, *Poesie e Lettre Inedite di Salvator Rosa* (Florence: L.S. Olschki, 1950), p. 17; Owenson (Lady Morgan), *Life and Times of Salvator Rosa*, vol. I, fn. 2 p. 328; F. Walker, 'Salvatore Rosa and Music', *Monthly Musical Record*, vol. 79 (1949), pp. 199–209 & vol. 80 (1950), pp. 13–18; A. Bruers, N. Pirrotta, F. Schlitzer & P. Capponi, *La Scuola Romana – G. Carissimi, A. Cesti e M. Marazzoli* (Sienna: Nello Ticci, 1953), pp. 56–79.

It has been suggested that Cesti's darkly atmospheric score provided the inspiration for Purcell's *By the Croaking of the Toad*.

46 Limentani, *Poesie e Lettere*, p. 49.

47 Ibid., p. 50.

48 R. Martin, *Witchcraft and Inquisition in Venice, 1550–1650* (Oxford: Basil Blackwell, 1989), pp. 106–7.

49 L. Salerno, 'Four Witchcraft Scenes by Salvator Rosa', *The Bulletin of the Cleveland Museum of Art* (Cleveland Museum of Art, September, 1978), p. 230; Langdon et al., *Salvator Rosa*, p. 165; Hults, *The Witch as Muse*, p. 202.

50 Hults, *The Witch as Muse*, pp. 205–6.

6. Little Sister Jeanne of the Angels

1 M. de Certeau, *The Possession at Loudun*, trans. M.B. Smith (Chicago & London: University of Chicago Press, 1970, English edition 1996, rpt. 2000), pp. 184–9. See also S. Cordier, *Balthazar de Monconys* (Paris: Andre de Rache, 1967), pp. 17–18.

2 Sister Jeanne, quoted in de Certeau, *Possession at Loudun*, pp. 219–20.

3 As Aldous Huxley pointed out, the lettering of the stigmatas only appeared on Sister Jeanne's left hand. Had they been on her right, she might have found scratching, or painting, the letters far more difficult to manufacture. See de Certeau, *Possession at Loudun*, p. 221; Cordier, *Balthazar de Monconys*, pp. 17–18; Y. le Hir, 'L'Expression Mystique dans l'Autobiographie de Soeur Jeanne des Anges', *Revue d' Histoire et de Philosophie Religieuses*, vol. 60, no. 4 (October–December 1980), pp. 453–6.

4   de Certeau, *Possession at Loudun*, p. 222.

5   Ibid., pp. 224–5.

6   Ibid., p. 15.

7   Ibid., p. 16.

8   Like almost all of those thought to be possessed at Loudun, Marthe de Sainte Monique came from a wealthy background. Her father was a prosperous 'bourgeois of Loudun'. However, unlike the five leading nuns in the case, she could not claim high nobility. This social factor may, in part, explain why her testimony was less prominent than it should have been.

9   de Certeau, *Possession at Loudun*, p. 16.

10 Ibid., pp. 16–17.

11 A. Harbage, *Thomas Killigrew, Cavalier Dramatist, 1612–83* (New York: Benjamin Brown, 1930, rpt. 1967), pp. 59–61; A. Huxley, *The Devils of Loudun* (London: Chatto & Windus, 1954), p. 291; T. Killigrew, 'Letter', *European Magazine* (1803), pp. 102–6.

12 Huxley, *Devils of Loudun*, p. 292.

13 Harbage, *Thomas Killigrew*, pp. 61–2; Huxley, *Devils of Loudun*, p. 292. See also P. Major (ed.), *Thomas Killigrew and the Seventeenth Century English Stage. New Perspectives* (Farnham, Surrey & Burlington, VT: Ashgate, 2013), p. 192.

14 R. Rapley, *A Case of Witchcraft. The Trial of Urbain Grandier* (Manchester: Manchester University Press, 1998), p. 90; de Certeau, *Possession at Loudun*, pp. 19–20 & 31–4.

15 Nicolas Aubin, a Protestant pastor in Loudun, who knew Grandier and whose own account of the trial was to form a cornerstone of Aldous Huxley's later novel, recalled that the priest

> was tall and good-looking, with a mind both firm and subtle, always … well dressed, never walking except in long robes. That external politeness was accompanied by that of the mind. He expressed himself with great ease and elegance. He preached rather frequently. He acquitted himself of that function incomparably better than most monks who climb up to the pulpit … He was sweet and civil to his friends, but proud and haughty to his enemies. He was jealous of his rank and never relinquished his own interests, repelling affronts with such rigour that he turned people against him whom he could have won over by taking a different tack.

Aubin quoted in de Certeau, *Possession at Loudun*, p. 53.
    See also E. Goldsmid (ed.), *The History of the Devils of Loudun. The Alleged Possession of the Ursuline Nuns, and the Trial and Execution of Urbain Grandier* (Edinburgh: Privately Printed, 1887), vol. I, pp. 21–3 & 26–7.

16 Rapley, *A Case of Witchcraft*, p. 91.

17 Ibid., p. 91.

18 Ibid., pp. 112 & 118.

19 In the end, no less than three copies of the demonic pact were brought before the attention of the court; one written in Latin; the other two in French. The original covenant, the judges revealed, was kept by the Devil, himself, locked away in Hell. According to this, Grandier had abjured God, Jesus and all the saints, renouncing his humanity, and promising 'never to do good, to do all the evil I can, and would wish not at all to be a man but that my nature be changed into a devil the better to serve you'.
    See de Certeau, *Possession at Loudun*, p. 98; Goldsmid (ed.), *The History of the Devils of Loudun*, vol. III, pp. 6–7.

20 J. des Anges, *Ich War die Teufelin von Loudun. Die Memoiren einer Besessenen* (Vienna: Tosa, 2008), pp. 88–9.

21 This version of events, with black demons circling above Grandier's pyre, was later illustrated as the woodcut that accompanied: R. Allain, *Pourtraict Representant au Vif l'Execution Faicte a Loudun en la Personne de Urban Grandier* (Poitiers, 1634).

22 de Certeau, *Possession at Loudun*, pp. 184–7 & 195.

23 Ibid., p. 214.

24 R. Clark, *Strangers & Sojourners at Port Royal. Being an Account of the Connections between the British Isles and the Jansenists of France and Holland* (New York: Octagon Books, 1972), pp. 55–6, 64 & 106.

25 Rev. Fr. Tranquille, *Veritable Relation des Justes Procedures Observees au fait de la Possession des Ursulines de Loudun, et au Proces de Grandier* (Poitiers, 1634); M. de Hedelin, Abbé d'Aubignac, *Relation de M. Hedelin, Abbé d'Aubignac, touchant les Possedees de Loudun* (Paris, 1637); N. Aubin, *Histoire des Diables de Loudun* (Amsterdam, 1693).

26 J. des Anges, *Autobiographie d'une Hysterique Possedee*, eds. G. Legue & G. de la Tourette (Paris: Editions Millon, 1886, rpt. 1985).

27 Y. le Hir, 'L'Expression Mystique dans l'Autobiographie de Soeur Jeanne des Anges', pp. 453–9.

28 Michelet, *Satanism and Witchcraft*; A. Dumas, *Celebrated Crimes. Volume IV. Karl-Ludwig Sand, Urbain Grandier and Nisida* (Doylestown, PA: Wildside Press, n.d. c.2010).

29 Dumas, *Celebrated Crimes*, vol. IV, p. 136.

30 Ibid., p. 153.

31 Ibid., p. 156.

32 Ibid., p. 170.

33 Ibid., p. 185.

34 Michelet, *Satanism and Witchcraft*, p. 144.

35 Ibid., p. 142.

36 Ibid., p. 144.
     It is worth noting that, again, it is Nicolas Aubin who provides Michelet with his source for Grandier and the events surrounding the trial.

37 Michelet, *Satanism and Witchcraft*, pp. 148–9.

38 Huxley, *The Devils of Loudun*, pp. 81, 94–5 & 98.

39 Ibid., p. 77.

40 Ibid., p. 128.

41 Ibid., pp. 110–11.

42 Ibid., pp. 121–2.

43 Ibid., p. 131.

44 Ibid., pp. 131–2.

45 R. Crouse, *Raising Hell. Ken Russell and the Unmaking of the Devils* (Toronto: ECW Press, 2012), p. 42; E. Salmon, *The Dark Journey. John Whiting as Dramatist* (London: Barrie & Jenkins Ltd., 1979), p. 38.

46 J. Whiting, *The Devils* (London: Heinemann, 1961), p. 21. See also Salmon, *Dark Journey*, pp. 236, 239, 241–2 & 249–51.

47 Whiting, *The Devils*, p. 119.

48 J. Iwaszkiewicz, *Mère Jeanne des Anges*, trans. G. Lisowski (Paris: Robert Laffont, 1943, rpt. 1959); J. Kawalerowicz (director), *Mother Joan of the Angels* (London: Second Run, DVD, 1961 re-issued 2005).

49 Jerzy Kawalerowicz, interview with Ray Privett, liner notes to *Mother Joan of the Angels*, DVD booklet, p. 4.

50 J. Baxter, *An Appalling Talent/Ken Russell* (London: Michael Joseph Ltd., 1973), pp. 13 & 33.

51 J. Lanza, *Phallic Frenzy. Ken Russell and His Films* (London: Aurum, Press Ltd., 2008), p. 123; Crouse, *Raising Hell*, p. 157; G. Goodwin, *Evil Spirits. The Life of Oliver Reed* (London: Virgin Books, 2000,

rpt. 2005), p. 149. Vanessa Redgrave, who played Sister Jeanne in *The Devils*, barely namechecks the film in her autobiography, see V. Redgrave, *An Autobiography* (London: Hutchinson, 1991), p. 150.

52   Crouse, *Raising Hell*, pp. 153–4; Lanza, *Phallic Frenzy*, pp. 121–2.

53   Only recently has a version of *The Devils* been re-issued through the British Film Institute; see *The Devils*, directed K. Russell (BFI Video, 2012).

54   For a fuller discussion, see *Phallic Frenzy*, p. 122; Crouse, *Raising Hell*, pp. 120, 126 & 129–30; Goodwin, *Evil Spirits*, pp. 142–3.

55   Baxter, *An Appalling Talent*, p. 202; *Phallic Frenzy*, p. 105; J. Gomez, *Ken Russell* (London: Frederick Muller Ltd., 1976), p. 137. Russell reinforced this position when discussing Whiting's adaptation of the novel: 'I thought the play was rather sentimental … It was very good dialogue, but I thought it evaded the central issue. I thought it soft-centred; it wasn't hard enough.'

56   Dumas, *Celebrated Crimes*, vol. IV, pp. 79–80; Michelet, *Satanism and Witchcraft*, p. 145.

57   T. Peake, *Derek Jarman* (London: Little, Brown & Company, 1999), p. 155.

58   Crouse, *Raising Hell*, p. 72.

59   Peake, *Derek Jarman*, pp. 155–7; R. Wollen, *Derek Jarman: A Portrait* (London: Thames & Hudson, 1996), pp. 15, 85–6 & 96.

60   Crouse, *Raising Hell*, p. 71.

61   Here, the intervening years tend to vindicate Russell's depiction of the witch hunter as pop-culture superstar. It was not quite so clear when Joseph Gomez wrote his seminal critique of the film: see, Gomez, *Ken Russell*, pp. 149–50.

62   *The Devils*, BFI DVD.

63   Whiting, *The Devils*, p. 111.
     For Reed's own reaction, see Goodwin, *Evil Spirits*, p. 146. What Reed had the studio insure against, was the permanent loss of his eyebrows.

64   H. Boguet, *An Examen of Witches*, ed. M. Summers (Bungay, Suffolk: John Rodker, 1929), pp. 4–5.

65   Baxter, *An Appalling Talent*, p. 201.

7. I Shall Go Unto a Hare

1   R. Pitcairn (ed.), *Criminal Trials in Scotland*, vol. III, Part II (Edinburgh: William Tait, 1833), pp. 602–16. See also J. Callow, entry for 'Isobel Gowdie' in the *Oxford Dictionary of National Biography*. Available at www.oxforddnb.com.

2   H. Pryce, *The Great Marquis of Montrose* (London: Everett & Co. Ltd., 1912), pp. 255–8; B. Robertson, *Lordship and Power in the North of Scotland. The Noble House of Huntly, 1603–1690* (Edinburgh: John Donald, 2011), pp. 132–4; S. Reid, *The Campaigns of Montrose. A Military History of the Civil War in Scotland, 1639 to 1646* (Edinburgh: The Mercat Press, 1990), pp. 103–19; R. Williams, *Montrose. Cavalier in Mourning* (London: Barrie & Jenkins, 1975), pp. 237, 240 & 244–5.

3   Pitcairn (ed.), *Criminal Trials in Scotland*, vol. III, pp. 603 & 610.

4   Ibid., pp. 603–4 & 610–11.

5   Ibid., pp. 606–7.

6   Ibid., p. 604. See also D. Purkiss, *At the Bottom of the Garden. A Dark History of Fairies, Hobgoblins, and Other Troublesome Things* (New York: New York University Press, 2000, rpt. 2001), pp. 88 & 113.

7   Pitcairn (ed.), *Criminal Trials in Scotland*, vol. III, p. 615.

8 Ibid., pp. 610 & 612.

9 Ibid., pp. 613–14.

10 Ibid., p. 618 fn. 15. See also L. Linton, *Witch Stories* (London: Chapman & Hall, 1861), p. 77.

11 P.H. Brown (ed.), *The Register of the Privy Council of Scotland*, 3rd Series, vol. I (Edinburgh: General Register House, 1908), p. 243.

12 Brown (ed.), *The Register of the Privy Council of Scotland*, 3rd Series, vol. I, p. 243.

13 B.P. Levack, *Witch-Hunting in Scotland. Law, Politics and Religion* (New York & London: Routledge, 2008), pp. 81–97.

14 W. Scott, *Letters on Demonology and Witchcraft*, intro. P.G. Maxwell-Stuart (London: Wordsworth Editions/Folklore Society, 2001), pp. 6–7 & 9.

15 Scott, *Letters on Demonology and Witchcraft*, p. 163; R. Hutton, *The Triumph of the Moon. A History of Modern Pagan Witchcraft* (Oxford & New York: Oxford University Press, 1999), pp. 100; Purkiss, *At the Bottom of the Garden*, p. 88.

16 Scott, *Letters on Demonology and Witchcraft*, p. 170.
    See also A. Campbell (ed.), *Scottish Tales of Terror* (London & Glasgow: Collins/Fontana Books, 1972), pp. 155–6.

17 Scott, *Letters on Demonology and Magic*, pp. 170–1.

18 J.W. Brodie-Innes, *The Devil's Mistress*, intro. D. Wheatley (London: Sphere Books Ltd., 1915, rpt. 1974), pp. 16–17.

19 Ibid., p. 17.

20 Ibid., pp. 19 & 30–1.

21 Ibid., pp. 139–40.

22 Ibid., p. 258.

23 Ibid., pp. 271–6.

24 M. Murray, *My First Hundred Years* (London: William Kimber, 1963), p. 104.

25 M. Murray, *The Witch-Cult in Western Europe. A Study in Anthropology* (Oxford: The Clarendon Press, 1921), pp. 29, 37–8, 65–7, 70, 78, 84–5, 99–100, 105–6, 111, 114–16, 129, 142, 153, 164, 166, 171, 180–1, 187–8, 190, 193, 196, 199, 201, 229–30, 235 & 244–5.

26 Murray, *Witch-Cult*, pp. 114 & 120.

27 R. Hutton, *The Pagan Religions of the Ancient British Isles. Their Nature and Legacy* (Oxford: Blackwell Publishing, 1991, rpt. 1993), p. 303.

28 Pitcairn (ed.), *Criminal Trials in Scotland*, vol. III, p. 603.

29 E. Rose, *A Razor for a Goat. Problems in the History of Witchcraft and Diabolism* (Toronto, Canada: University of Toronto Press, 1962, rpt. 2003), pp. 194–5 & 206; N. Cohn, *Europe's Inner Demons. The Demonization of Christians in Medieval Christendom* (London: Pimlico, 1975, rpt. and revised 1993), p. 161.

30 C. Ginzburg, *Ecstasies. Deciphering the Witches' Sabbath* (London: Penguin Books, 1989, rpt. 1992), pp. 8 & 112 fn. 26. See also Cohn, *Europe's Inner Demons*, pp. 153–60; R. Hutton, *The Stations of the Sun. A History of the Ritual Year in Britain* (Oxford & New York: Oxford University Press, 1996), pp. 422–4; R. Hutton, *The Triumph of the Moon. A History of Modern Pagan Witchcraft* (Oxford & New York: Oxford University Press, 1999), pp. 276–8 & 377–8; R. Hutton, 'The Great Debate', *The Cauldron* (May 2003), pp. 9–16; Purkiss, *At the Bottom of the Garden*, pp. 88 & 112–13.

31 D. Valiente, *An ABC of Witchcraft. Past and Present* (London: Robert Hale Ltd., 1973, rpt. 1994), pp. xv, xvii, 50 & 72.

32 Ibid., p. 142.

33 Ibid., pp. 50 & 141–2.

34 Pitcairn, vol. III, pp. 604, 607–9, 611 & 614–16.

35 D. Wheatley, intro. to Brodie-Innes, *The Devil's Mistress*, pp. 7–8.

36 Wheatley, intro. to Brodie-Innes, *The Devil's Mistress*, p. 8.

37 G. Masterton, *Graham Masterton Omnibus: The Hymn and Night Plague* (London: Time Warner Paperbacks, 1991, rpt. 2003), p. 269.

38 C. Forde, *The Drowning Pond* (Harlow, Essex: Pearson/Longman, 2005, rpt. 2006), pp. 92 & 160.

39 G. Lachman, *It Must be Witchcraft* (BBC Radio 3, 21 August 2006).

40 J. McNair, inner notes to: The Sensational Alex Harvey Band, *Framed & Next*, CD (Mercury Records, 1972 & 1973, re-released 2002).

41 J.N. Munro, *The Sensational Alex Harvey* (Edinburgh: Polygon, 2002), pp. 97 & 110–11.

42 Maddy Prior, 'The Fabled Hare' on *Year* (Park Records, 1993).

43 Inkubus Sukkubus, 'Woman to Hare' on *Vampyre Erotica* (Resurrection Records, 1997).

44 S. Johnson, sleeve notes to J. MacMillan, *Symphony no.3 'Silence' & the Confession of Isobel Gowdie* (Chandos Records Ltd., 2005).

45 E. Wilby, *The Visions of Isobel Gowdie. Magic, Witchcraft and Dark Shamanism in Seventeenth-Century Scotland* (Brighton: Sussex Academic Press, 2010).

46 E. Wilby, *Cunning Folk and Familiar Spirits. Shamanistic Visionary Traditions in Early Modern British Witchcraft and Magic* (Brighton: Sussex Academic Press, 2005), pp. 174, 178 & 185.

47 R. Hutton, *The Shamans of Siberia* (Glastonbury: The Isle of Avalon Press, 1993), passim; J. Pentikainen, T. Jaatinen, I. Lehtinen &. M.-R. Saloniemi (eds), *Shamans* (Tampere: Tampere Museums' Publications, 1998), pp. 9, 11, 13–14, 16–17, 19–26, 45–9 & 53–4; R.J. Wallis, *Shamans/Neo-Shamans. Ecstasy, Alternative Archaeologies and Contemporary Pagans* (London & New York: Routledge, 2003), pp. 137–9.

48 J. Goodacre (ed.), *The Scottish Witch-Hunt in Context* (Manchester & New York: Manchester University Press, 2002), pp. 31–2.

8. The Flight of the Witch

1 J. Aubrey, *Remaines of Gentilisme and Judaisme*, ed. J. Britten (London: Folk-Lore Society, 1881), pp. 67–8.

2 Aubrey, *Remaines of Gentilisme*, pp. 27, 104 & 131–2; J. Aubrey, *Miscellanies upon Various Subjects* (London & Salisbury: W. Ottridge & E. Easton, 1784), pp. 186, 196–7 & 243. See also P. Anderson, *A Midsummer Tempest* (Aylesbury: Futura Publishers, 1974, rpt. 1975). Poul Anderson takes this vision, of a vanishing arcadia, to its logical extremes, with a Cromwellian army destroyed by the force of nature under Glastonbury Tor; with Puck and Prince Rupert saving Oberon, Titania and the faerie from the iron heel of industry, and the cancer of pollution.

3 Aubrey, *Remaines of Gentilisme*, pp. vii & 26; J. Collier (ed.), *The Scandal and Credulities of John Aubrey* (London: Peter Davies, 1931), pp. xviii–xix.

4 Aubrey, *Remaines of Gentilisme*, pp. 18 & 126; Aubrey, *Miscellanies*, pp. 51 & 188–9.

5 A. Powell, *John Aubrey and his Friends* (London: Mercury Books, 1948, rpt. 1963), p. 38; M. Hunter, *John Aubrey and the Realm of Learning* (London: Duckworth, 1975), p. 102.

6 Trevor-Roper, *European Witch-Craze*, p. 111. See also N. Hampson, *The Enlightenment. An Evaluation of its Assumptions, Attitudes and Values* (London: Penguin Books, 1968, rpt. 1990), pp. 24–5, 27 & 35–8.

7 See D. Jesseph, 'Mechanism, Skepticism and Witchcraft. More and Glanvill on the failures of Cartesian philosophy', in T.M. Schmaltz (ed.), *Receptions of Descartes. Cartesianism and*

Anti-Cartesianism in Early Modern Europe (London & New York: Routledge, 2005), pp. 199–217; J. Cottingham, *Descartes. Descartes' Philosophy of the Mind* (London: Phoenix, 1997), pp. 4–5.

8   C. Pythian-Adams, 'Rural Culture', in G.E. Mingay (ed.), *The Victorian Countryside* (London: Routledge, 1981), vol. 2, p. 624.

9   M. Gijswijt-Hofstra, B.P. Levack & R. Porter, *Witchcraft and Magic in Europe: The Eighteenth and Nineteenth Centuries* (London: The Athlone Press, 1999), p. 208.

10 F. Thompson, *Lark Rise to Candleford* (London: Penguin Books, 1945, rpt. 1989), p. 252.

11 J. Barry, *Witchcraft and Demonology in South-West England, 1640–1789*, (Basingstoke: Palgrave Macmillan, 2012), p. 72; Gijswijt-Hofstra, Levack & Porter, *Witchcraft and Magic*, p. 173; O. Davies, 'Witchcraft. The Spell that didn't Break', *History Today*, vol. 49, no. 8 (August 1999), pp. 7–13; R. North, *The Life of Francis North, Lord Keeper of the Great Seal under Charles II and James II*, ed. E.E. Reynolds (London: Thomas Nelson & Sons Ltd., n.d., c.1938), p. 109.

    For a late account of English witchcraft, from 1804 to 1805, see C. Hole (ed.), *Witchcraft at Toner's Puddle, 19th C. From the Diary of the Rev. William Ettrick* (Dorchester: Dorset Record Society, 1964).

12 Sharpe, *Instruments of Darkness*, pp. 290–1; Hutton, *Triumph of the Moon*, pp. 107–8; O. Davies, *Witchcraft, Magic and Culture, 1736–1951* (Manchester: Manchester University Press, 1999), pp. 1–7.

13 Davies, 'Witchcraft. The Spell that didn't Break', pp. 7–8.

14 W.E.H. Lecky, *History of the Rise and Influence of the Spirit of Rationalism in Europe* (London: Longmans, Green & Co., 1910), p. 10. See also p. 12 for a fuller exposition of the same theme.

15 Hampson, *The Enlightenment*, pp. 128–41 & 146–61.

16 C. Hill, *Some Intellectual Consequences of the English Revolution* (Wisconsin University of Wisconsin Press, 1980), p. 64. For the growing literature which emphasises the survival of beliefs in witchcraft, see Davies, *Witchcraft, Magic and Culture*, passim; Gijswijt-Hofstra, Levack & Porter, *Witchcraft and Magic*, pp. 99–100, 116–17, 121–3, 146–50, 153–6, 159, 162, 173–4 & 208–9; O. Davies, *America Bewitched. The Story of Witchcraft after Salem* (Oxford: Oxford University Press, 2013), passim.

17 Voltaire quoted in Gijswijt-Hofstra, Levack & Porter, *Witchcraft and Magic*, pp. 219–22.

18 J.R.R. Tolkien, 'On Fairy Stories', in *Tree and Leaf* (London: Unwin Hyman Ltd., 1964, rpt. 1988), p. 34.

19 H. Middleton, *Grimms' Last Fairytale. A Novel* (London: Abacus, 1999).

    Other influences can be detected in Ridley Scott's *The Duellists*; and in Neil Jordan's filming of Angela Carter's re-telling of Little Red Riding Hood, *The Company of Wolves*. Stylistic debts can also be found in Tim Burton's *Sleepy Hollow*; and in Christophe Gans' *Brotherhood of the Wolf/ Le Pacte des Loups*.

20 J.C.F. von Schiller quoted in B. Bettelheim, *The Uses of Enchantment. The Meaning and Importance of Fairy Tales* (London: Penguin Books, 1975, rpt. 1991), p. 5.

21 C. Kamenetsky, *The Brothers Grimm and their Critics. Folktales and the Quest for Meaning* (Athens, GA: Ohio University Press, 1992), p. 27.

22 The Third Reich had hailed the Grimms' *Nursery and Household Tales* as a 'sacred book' and had institutionalised the teaching of their fairy stories. See M. Tatar, *The Hard Facts of the Grimms' Fairy Tales* (Princeton, NJ: Princeton University Press, 1987), p. 15; J. Zipes, *The Enchanted Screen: The Unknown History of Fairy Tale Films* (London: Taylor & Francis, 2011), p. 341; J. Zipes, *The Brothers Grimm. From Enchanted Forests to the Modern World* (New York & Houndmills, Basingstoke: Palgrave Macmillan, 2002), pp. 231–2.

    Ironically, the stories had also been banned almost a century earlier in the Austro-Hungarian Empire, where it was feared that they would foster superstition and threaten the progress of the Enlightenment. See M.E. Hammond, *Jacob and Wilhelm Grimm. The Fairy Tale Brothers* (London: Dennis Dobson, 1968), p. 101.

23 Ironically, Disney contains its own subliminal undercurrent of violence. British audiences of the 1930s were quick to notice Mickey Mouse's penchant for carrying firearms and Donald Duck's hair-trigger temper and love of fisty-cuffs. See A. Dorfman & A. Mattelart, *How to Read Donald Duck: Imperialist Ideology in the Disney Comic* (New York: International General, 1975).

24 Thus, even though the children in the audience at the BFI sponsored screenings of *The Singing Ringing Tree*, in the early 1990s, were enthralled by – and even 'liked' – the figure of the malevolent dwarf, their parents 'questioned whether a contemporary adaptation would have chosen to attribute such potently wicked characteristics to a person of restricted growth'. See D. Petrie (ed.), *Cinema and the Realms of Enchantment. Lectures, Seminars and Essays by Marina Warner and Others* (London: British Film Institute, 1993), pp. 81, 120 & 122.

25 Tatar, *Hard Facts of the Grimms' Fairy Tales*, p. 15.

26 See, for example Kamenetsky, *The Brothers Grimm and their Critics*, pp. 92–3.

27 Jacob and Wilhelm Grimm. *The Fairy Tale Brothers*, pp. 18–19.

28 Zipes, *The Brothers Grimm*, pp. 71–5 & 79–80. See also P. Taylor & H. Rebel, 'Hessian Peasant Women, their Families and the Draft', *Journal of Family History*, vol. 6 (Winter 1981), pp. 347–78.

29 Bloch, quoted in Zipes, *The Brothers Grimm*, pp. 114–15 & 122.

30 P. Miller, *A Wife for the Pretender* (London: George Allen & Unwin Ltd., 1965); P. Miller, *James* (London: George Allen & Unwin Ltd., 1971).

31 BBC Written Archives Centre, Reading: G. del Strother to C.F.G. Max-Muller (5 December 1955); J.H. Mewett to C.F.G. Max-Muller (21 December 1955); C.F.G. Max-Muller to J.H. Mewett (23 December 1955).

32 Alongside *Tales from Europe*, Lotte Reiniger's beautiful, silhouette renderings of world-wide folk tales – also brought to be the BBC via Peggy Miller – and Jim Henson's *The Storyteller*, made for HBO in the USA and broadcast on Channel 4 in the UK, in 1987, which showcased many of the Grimms darker and lesser known stories, sit as companion pieces and deserve a wider recognition.

    DEFA, itself, turned away from the production of fairy tale films, as the 1960s wore on, preferring children's films that explored more contemporary issues; although elements of the fantastical remained right until the end, as in the case of *Der Drache Daniel* (released in 1990). The innovative tradition of fairy tale films, pioneered by DEFA, was further developed by Czechoslovak studios. In point of fact, *Three Wishes for Cinderella* was a German–Czech co-production. This was part of a last flourish, which culminated in the spine-tingling *Panna a Netvor/Beauty and the Beast*, directed by Juraj Herz in 1978. See I. Konig, D. Wiedemann & L. Wolf (eds), *Alltagsgeschichten. Arbeiten mit DEFA-Kinderfilmen* (Munich: KoPad, 1998), pp. 117–23; J. Zipes, *The Enchanted Screen. The Unknown History of Fairy-Tale Films* (New York & London: Routledge, 2011), pp. 237–8.

33 S. Allan & J. Sandford (eds), *DEFA. East German Cinema, 1946–1992* (New York & Oxford: Berghahn Books, 1999), pp. 3–4, 23–4 & 31–3; Petrie (ed.), *Cinema and the Realms of Enchantment*, pp. 129–30 & 133–4.

34 Peggy Miller quoted in Petrie (ed.), *Cinema and the Realms of Enchantment*, p. 121.

35 F. Munz, *Die DEFA Marchenfilme* (Frankfurt am Main DEFA-Stiftung und Zweitausendeins, 2012), pp. 76–9 & 92–5: Petrie (ed.), *Cinema and the Realms of Enchantment*, p. 122; A. Graham, 'The Truth is Out There', *Radio Times* (10–16 May 2008), p. 136. See also A. Smith, 'Fast Forward to Fear', *The Scotsman* (24 May 1999), for an article that entirely missed the point, and thoroughly trivialised the genre.

36 H. Christian Andersen, *Hans Andersen's Fairy Tales* (London, Melbourne & Cape Town: Ward & Lock Ltd., n.d., c.1930), pp. 78–85; Munz, *Die DEFA Marchenfilme*, pp. 56–9; J. Zipes, *Fairy*

Tales and the Art of Subversion. The Classical Genre for Children and the Process of Civilization (London: Heinemann, 1983), pp. 81–2. See also the splendid re-issue of the *Tinderbox* in DVD format by Ice Storm in *Tales from Europe – The Singing Ringing Tree and the Tinderbox* (Box Set 7952096, Ice Storm/Network, 1957 & 1959, reissued 2003).

37 J. Andersen, *Hans Christian Andersen, A New Life*, trans. T. Nunnally (New York, Woodstock & London: Overlook Duckworth, 2005), pp. 243–4 & 246–7. Significantly, when an author of teenage fiction attempted a novelisation of *The Tinderbox*, he divorced the story entirely from Christian Andersen's imagination and claimed that it was based upon an, earthier, Grimms' tale instead. See J. Reeves, *The Cold Flame* (Harmondsworth: Penguin Books, 1967, rpt. 1970).

38 Anon., 'Das Singende, Klingende Baumchen', *Film Spiegel*, vol. IV, no. 13 (1957), p. 12; A. Geelhaar & K.-H. Appelmann, *Das Singende Klingende Baumchen* (Berlin & Leipzig: Kiro-Verlag, 1993), passim. Selina Hastings has tracked-down other sources drawn from Slavic folklore and Sorbian stories. She notes that:

> A Story called *The Little Singing Ringing Tree* was published in 1801 in a book of fairy tales collected in Braunschweig, a city in Lower Saxony. A reference to the story and the collection appears in the 1812 edition of Jacob and Wilhelm Grimm's book *Kinder- und Hausmarchen* (*Children's and Household Tales*) in a note to the tale 'Hurleburlebutz'.

See S. Hastings & L. Brierley, *The Singing Ringing Tree* (New York: Henry Holt & Company, 1988), p. ii.

39 S. Heiduschke, *East German Cinema. DEFA and Film History* (New York: Palgrave Macmillan, 2013), pp. 53–4; Munz, *Die DEFA Marchenfilme*, pp. 24–9; I. Konig, D. Wiedemann & L. Wolf, *Marchen. Arbeiten mit DEFA-Kinderfilmen* (Munich: KoPad, 1998), pp. 21–7.

40 Anon., 'Das Singende, Klingende Baumchen', p. 12.

41 A. Geelhaar (ed.), *Fortunat und Seine Sohne* (Berlin Kinderbuchverlag, 1963); A. Geelhaar, *Der Brief aus Odessa* (Berlin Kinderbuchverlag, 1971); A. Geelhaar & G. Zucker, *Der Kleine Kommandeur* (Berlin Kinderbuchverlag, 1976); A. Geelhaar, *Der Prinz von Hovinka* (Berlin Kinderbuchverlag, 1977).

42 See A. Geelhaar, *Das Singende, Klingende Baumchen* (Berlin Eulenspiegel Verlag, 2003).

43 Warner, *From the Beast to the Blonde*, p. 297; Petrie (ed.), *Cinema and the Realms of Enchantment*, pp. 9–10.

44 A more pronounced example of Peggy Miller's skill as a film and script editor can be seen in her treatment of *Three Wishes for Cinderella*, which was also broken into three parts by the BBC. She cut scenes that impeded the flow of the narrative, and which showed the suffering of a fox caught by the huntsmen's hounds. This turned an ambiguous statement by the Czech director, into a forceful example of Cinderella's humanity and concern for the rights of animals; as an earlier scene in which she prevents the prince and his laddish companions from killing a young deer was retained, by Miss Miller, and celebrated.

See also M. Hudson, 'Return of the Teatime Terror', *The Daily Telegraph* (30 March 2002), Arts & Books Supplement. The long term impact made by *The Singing Ringing Tree* was registered, in 1988, by the production of a children's book by a British author and illustrator that reproduced the script of Geelhaar and Miller; and also in the course of a Christmas radio phone-in about 'Lost Children's Film', in 2014. See Hastings & Brierley, *The Singing Ringing Tree*; *The Paul O'Grady Show*, BBC Radio 2 (28 December 2014).

45 Bettelheim, *The Uses of Enchantment*, pp. 12 & 150; Tolkien, 'On Fairy Tales', p. 44.

46 J. Grimm, *Teutonic Mythology*, trans. from the 4th edn by J.S. Stallybrass (London: George Bell & Sons, 1883), vol. III, p. xv.

47 Hammond, *Jacob & Wilhelm Grimm. The Fairy Tale Brothers*, pp. 85–7 & 89; M.B. Peppard, *Paths through the Forest. A Biography of the Brothers Grimm* (New York, Chicago & San Francisco: Holt, Rinehart & Winston, 1971), pp. 50–3; Tartar, *Hard Facts of the Grimms' Fairy Tales*, pp. 47–8; Zipes, *The Brothers Grimm*, pp. 28–9 & 84.

48 Grimm, *Teutonic Mythology*, vol. III, p.xiii; Hammond, *Jacob and Wilhelm Grimm. The Fairy Tale Brothers*, p. 101; Zipes, *The Brothers Grimm*, pp. 28–9; Kamenetsky, *The Brothers Grimm and their Critics*, pp. 105–106, 113–14.

49 J. Grimm, *Teutonic Mythology*, vol. III, trans. J.S. Stallybrass (Cambridge: Cambridge University Press, 2012), pp. 1039, 1044 & 1075.

50 Ibid., p. 1075.

51 Ibid., pp. 1057 & 1061.

52 Ibid., p. 1040.

53 Ibid., pp. 1072, 1074 & 1099.

54 Ibid., pp. 1073, 1088–9.

55 Ibid., pp. 1072–3, 1078 & 1081.

56 J. Michelet, *Satanism and Witchcraft. A Study in Medieval Superstition* (London: Tandem Books, 1965), p. 9.

57 E.K. Kaplan (ed.), *Mother Death. The Journal of Jules Michelet, 1815–1830* (Amherst, MA: University of Massachusetts Press, 1984), pp. 108 & 128.

58 R. Barthes, *Michelet*, trans. R. Howard (Berkeley & Los Angeles, CA: University of California Press, 1992), p. 213.

59 See, respectively E. Wilson, *To the Finland Station. A Study in the Writing and Acting of History* (London & Glasgow: Fontana/Collins, 1960, rpt. 1970), pp. 9–40; Barthes, *Michelet*, passim.

60 Kaplan (ed.), *Mother Death*, p. 108.

61 These found swift English translations as: J. Michelet, *Love*, trans. J.W. Palmer (New York: Rudd & Carleton, 1859); J. Michelet, *Woman*, trans. J.W. Palmer (New York: Rudd & Carleton, 1860).

62 Michelet quoted in Barthes, *Michelet*, pp. 164 & 166.

63 Michelet writing on 24 July 1839, in Kaplan (ed.), *Mother Death*, p. 74.

64 Kaplan (ed.), *Mother Death*, pp. 98, 113, 115, 120 & 124; A.R. Pugh, *Michelet and his Ideas on Social Reform* (New York: Columbia University Press, 1923), p. xix; O.A. Haac, *Jules Michelet* (Boston: Twayne Publishers, 1982), pp. 86–8. For a less charitable vision of Athenais Michelet – as a 'professional' widow – and a much more limited view of her influence upon her husband, see A. Mitzman, *Michelet, Historian. Rebirth and Romanticism in Nineteenth-Century France* (New Haven & London: Yale University Press, 1990), pp. 284–5.

65 Kaplan (ed.), *Mother Death*, pp. 55 & 133.

66 Mitzman, *Michelet, Historian*, pp. 38–9; Wilson, *To the Finland Station*, pp. 26 & 30; Bathes, *Michelet*, pp. 136–7. See also A. Somerset, *The Affair of the Poisons. Murder, Infanticide and Satanism at the Court of Louis XIV* (London: Weidenfeld & Nicolson, 2003).

67 P. Viallaneix, 'Preface' to J. Michelet, *La Sorcière* (Paris: Garnier-Flammarion, 1966), p. 15.

68 Ibid., p. 17.

69 Michelet, *Satanism and Witchcraft*, p. 168.

70 Viallaneix, 'Preface', p. 17.

71 N. Cohn, *Europe's Inner Demons. The Demonization of Christians in Medieval Christendom*, revised edition (London: Pimlico, 1975, rpt. 1993), pp. 151–2; Hutton, *Triumph of the Moon*, p. 138.

72 Viallaneix, 'Preface', pp. 18–19.

73 Michelet, *Satanism and Witchcraft*, op. cit.; J. Michelet, *Magic, Sorcery, and Superstition* (New York & Toronto: Citadel Press, 1995).

74 Quoted in Viallaneix, 'Preface', p. 19.

75 Michelet, *Satanism and Witchcraft*, p. 15.

76 Ibid., p. 9.

77 Ibid., pp. 33–4.

78 Ibid., pp. 19 & 34.

79 Ibid., p. 94.

80 See, for example S. Ravenwolf, *Teen Witch: Wicca for a New Generation* (St Paul, MA: Llewellyn Productions, 1998); F. Horne, *Witchin': A Handbook for Teen Witches* (London: Element, 2002).

81 Michelet, *Satanism and Witchcraft*, pp. 218–19.

82 J. Pilkington Jr, *Francis Marion Crawford* (New Haven, CT: College & University Press, 1964), pp. 17–19.

83 Ibid., pp. 35–6; M.H. Elliott, *My Cousin F. Marion Crawford* (London: The Macmillan Co., 1934), pp. 67–70.

84 Pilkington, *Francis Marion Crawford*, pp. 37, 90, 98–100 & 182–3.

85 P. Demetz, *Prague in Black and Gold. The History of a City* (London: Penguin Books, 1997 rpt. 1998), p. 321; J.H. Pearse, *Romance Novels, Romantic Novelist. Francis Marion Crawford* (Bloomington, IL: Author House, 2011), pp. 69–70; Pilkington, *Francis Marion Crawford*, pp. 93–4; Elliott, *My Cousin F. Marion Crawford*, pp. 231, 248–9.

86 D. Sayer, *The Coasts of Bohemia. A Czech History* (Princeton, NJ: Princeton University Press, 1998), pp. 115–17.

87 A.M. Ripellino, *Magic Prague*, trans. M.H. Heim (London: Picador, 1994, rpt. 1995), p. 55.

88 F. Marion Crawford, *The Witch of Prague. A Fantastic Tale* (London & New York: Macmillan and Co., 1890, rpt. 1892), p. 13

89 Ibid., pp. 10 & 12.

90 Ibid., pp. 17–18.

91 Ibid., pp. 66–7.

92 See Anon., *The Prague Golem. Jewish Stories of the Ghetto* (Cesky Tesin Vitalis, 2005); C. Bloch, *The Golem. Legends of the Ghetto of Prague*, trans. H. Schneiderman (Vienna: John N. Vernay, 1925); A.L. Goldsmith, *The Golem Remembered, 1909–1980. Variations of a Jewish Legend* (Detroit, MI: Wayne State University Press, 1981).

93 By way of coincidence, the real Franz Kafka, then a seven-year-old, was living within a few hundred yards of the houses, churches, synagogues and monuments that feature in *The Witch of Prague*. Crawford seems to have lighted upon the choice of surname as being representative among Prague's Jewry. The use of 'Israel' simply underscored his unambiguous use of characterisation. The story of Simon Abeles stems from one pamphlet, published to support the Jesuit proselytising campaign directed against the Jews of Prague, at the close of the seventeenth century. It may, or may not, have a basis in reality and the figure of Simon Abeles, himself, may owe more to polemical fiction – in both 1694 and 1890 – than to the tragedies of a boy who once lived. Rather, it seems that the sudden death of a child – through natural causes – was used by the Jesuit Order to reactivate Mediaeval blood libels and to whip-up a frenzy of popular hatred against the ghetto.

94 Crawford, *The Witch of Prague*, p. 219.

95 Ibid., pp. 217, 221–2, 225 & 230.

96 Ibid., p. 305.

97 Ibid., pp. 125–8.

98 Ibid., p. 127.

99 Ibid., pp. 136 & 138.

100 Ibid., pp. 34, 93 & 123. See also R. Pearsall, *The Table-Rappers. The Victorians and the Occult* (Thrupp, Stroud: Sutton Publishing, 1972, rpt. 2004), pp. 16–28; 92–100.

101 Crawford, *The Witch of Prague*, pp. 25, 109 & 187–8.

102 Ibid., pp. 263–4.

103 Ibid., p. 264.

104 Ibid., p. 275.

105 A. Owen, *The Darkened Room. Women, Power and Spiritualism in Late Victorian England* (Chicago & London: University of Chicago Press, 1989, rpt. 2004), pp. 1–2, 4–7, 9, 15–17, 206–12, 239–40 & 242; Pearsall, *Table-Rappers*, pp. 57–66.

9. *The Witch on the Barbican*

1 B. Mooney, 'Light, Shade ... and Obscurity', *The Daily Telegraph Magazine* (13 July 1973), p. 38.

2 Philip Callow, quoted in E. Gunnell, *The Barbican* (Bodmin St Teath, 1977), pp. 33–4.

3 Museum of Witchcraft, Boscastle, refs. 1197, 469 & 411 respectively.

4 R.O. Lenkiewicz, *Notes on the Barbican Mural* (Devon: Ashburton, 1972), p. 5.

5 Anon., 'A Citizen's Diary', *Western Evening Herald* (14 August 1971), p. 4.

6 Lenkiewicz, *Notes on the Barbican Mural*, pp. 5 & 23.

7 A. Somerset, *Unnatural Murder. Poison at the Court of James I* (London: Weidenfeld & Nicolson, 1997), pp. 116–17, 126–7, 132, 270–1, 294–6, 321 & 323; D. Lindley, *The Trials of Frances Howard. Fact and Fiction at the Court of King James* (London & New York: Routledge, 1993, rpt. 1996), pp. 49–51, 54, 96, 99, 104 & 193.

8 Lenkiewicz, *Notes on the Barbican Mural*, p. 15.

9 Bearne's Auctioneers of Fine Art, *Lenkiewicz 2008* (Exeter, April 2008), p. 130.

10 Lenkiewicz, *Notes on the Barbican Mural*, p. 15.

11 Ibid., pp. 10 & 19.

12 Ibid., p. 6.

13 Ibid., p. 23; White Lane Press, *R.O. Lenkiewicz* (Plymouth, Devon: Fearns Publishing, 1997), pp. 34 & 44–45. Sheer bad luck has continued to dog Lenkiewicz's work, even after the artist's death. In 2012, a fire at Chilford Hall, outside Cambridge, destroyed many of his major canvasses including *The Burial of John Kynance*.

14 Stokes, *Portrait of Robert Lenkiewicz*, p. xi.

15 F. Mallett, 'The Story of Robert Lenkiewicz', *Western Evening Herald* (15 August 2002); F. Mallett (ed.), *Robert Lenkiewicz. Paintings & Projects* (Plymouth: White Lane Press, 2006), p. 12; P. Stokes, *A Portrait of Robert Lenkiewicz* (Plymouth: White Lane Press, 2005), p. viii. In some ways Lenkiewicz pre-empted the themes explored by Frances Yates in *The Occult Philosophy in the Elizabethan Age* (London & New York: Routledge, 1979, rpt. 2001).

16 Lenkiewicz, *Notes on the Barbican Mural*, p. 24.

17 'Robert Lenkiewicz' interview by Ashley Peters in the unpaginated A. Peters (ed.), *Eighty from the Eighties. The Peninsula Voice Interviews* (Penzance: Rainyday Publications, 1993); L. Ramskold, 'The Myth of the 10,000' in *Lenkiewicz Foundation Newsletter*, No. 9 (December 2012), p. 4.

18 White Lane Press, *R.O. Lenkiewicz*, pp. 98 & 118.

19 Ibid., pp. 118–19.

20 Ibid., p. 118.

21 J. Semmens, 'Lenkiewicz: The Book Collector'. Available at http://robertlenkiewicz.org/lenkiewicz-book-collector.

22 L. Hull, 'How a Dead Frog could help you Woo a Lover', *Daily Mail* (25 June 2007); S. Mansfield, 'A Room Full of Strange Tails', *The Scotsman* (7 May 2007).

23 Freudenheim et al., *Lenkiewicz, Self-Portraits*, p. 80; Nichols, *Robert Lenkiewicz*, p. 57.

24 For instance, one of Lenkiewicz's books, now owned by the present author – Lisa Jardine's *Ingenious Pursuits. Building the Scientific Revolution* (London: Abacus, 1999) – bought new by the artist, seems never to have been read by the artist and bears no more than the pencil marks designating its catalogue mark in the 'Metaphysics' Room.

25 Nicols, *Robert Lenkiewicz*, p. 55.

26 'Hans' and 'James' in the unpaginated: Jojo, *Remembering Robert*.

27 Freudenheim et al., *Lenkiewicz, Self-Portraits*, p. 76.

28 Nichols, *Robert Lenkiewicz*, p. 79.

29 A. Harris, *Witch-Hunt: the Great Essex Witch Scare of 1582* (Essex: Ian Henry, 2001), pp. 82–3.

30 Harris, *Witch-Hunt*, pp. 12–13, 20, 23, 28 & 70–2; Sharpe, *Instruments of Darkness*, p. 98.

31 Cecil Williamson, quoted in Harris, *Witch-hunt*, p. 88.

32 E. Grice, 'He's just Sex Mad and paints Women', *The Daily Telegraph* (7 August 2002).

33 'James' in Jojo, *Remembering Lenkiewicz*.

34 N.J. Fox in Freudenheim et al., *Lenkiewicz, Self-Portraits*, p. 78.

35 Harris, *Witch-hunt*, pp. 90–1.

36 Palmer, *Lenkiewicz beyond the Grave*.

37 T.L. Freudenheim et al., *Robert Lenkiewicz, Self-Portraits* (Plymouth: White Lane Press, 2008).

38 Anon., 'Surprise move by Lenkiewicz', *Plymouth Extra* (2 December 1993); Anon., 'Lenkiewicz Barbican Gallery Plan Welcomed', *Western Evening Herald* (1 March 1995); Anon., 'Lenkiewicz's First Day Sales Top £120,000', *Sunday Independent* (9 January 1994); D. Macaulay, 'Hit Show means Robert can really Paint Town', *Western Morning News* (15 January, 1994); J. Mildren, 'Lenkiewicz Museum and Library Boost', *Western Evening Herald* (12 December 1994).

39 *R.O. Lenkiewicz*, p. 119.

40 Palmer, *Lenkiewicz beyond the Grave*, DVD; A. Blood, 'Devil or Deity?', *Plymouth Evening Herald* (20 April 1996), p. 3; Mike Palmer in Nichols, *Robert Lenkiewicz*, p. 159.

41 Mallet (ed.), *Robert Lenkiewicz*, p. 17; J. Garnett, 'Mystery of Lenkiewicz Skeleton' & 'Lenkiewicz kept Witch in his City Library', *Western Evening Herald* (21 November 2002), pp. 1–2; J. Garnett, 'Location of Bones Unknown', *Western Evening Herald* (22 November 2002); Bearne's Auctioneers & Valuers of Fine Art, Lenkiewicz 2008 (Exeter, 12 April 2008), Lot 294, p. 105.

42 Anon., 'Diogenes Mystery is Finally Solved', *Plymouth Evening Herald* (11 October 2002), p. 3; J. Garnett, *The Story of Robert Lenkiewicz*, *Plymouth Evening Herald* (16 August 2002); Kirby, 'Respectability at Last', p. 9.

43 Anon., 'Lenkiewicz Occult Book Collection auctioned off', *Plymouth Evening Herald* (21 November 2003); Anon., 'Local Artist's Occult Books fetch £600k', *Western Morning News* (21 November 2003); M. Fleming, 'The Last Picture Show as Paintings moved out: End of an Era for Lenkiewicz Studio', *Plymouth Evening Herald* (19 April 2005); J. Garnett, 'Lenkiewicz Will Dispute', *Plymouth Evening Herald* (1 April 2003), pp. 1 & 9; J. Garnett, 'Library of Occult is to be Sold', *Plymouth Evening Herald* (30 October 2003); T. Kirby, 'Respectability at Last for the Artist who Embalmed a Tramp', *The Independent* (19 September 2003), p. 9; T. Nichols, 'A Last Sad Look: It's the End of an Era as Lenkiewicz's Paintings Taken Away to be Sold', *Plymouth Evening Herald* (27 June 2003), p. 1.

Initial valuations put the estate at £6.5 million – the bulk of the worth lying with the books – while his debts stood at approximately £1.7 million. However, when London experts looked at the books, the valuation of the Library dwindled to a mere £1 million. A succession sales of the prime paintings and books raised over £2 million but £800,000 of outstanding debts still remained.

   See also E. Shaw, 'Fighting to Save the Artist's Legacy', *Western Morning News* (15 August 2002); & M. Freeman, 'On the Eve of the Final Sale to settle the debts of the Lenkiewicz Estate'. Available at http://www.thisisplymouth.co.uk.

44 Anon., 'Robert Lenkiewicz', *The Times* (7 August 2002), p. 29.
   Rather than being 80, at the time of his death, Lenkiewicz was only 61.

45 Channel 4's *Richard & Judy Show* (broadcast 29 June 2007).

46 See H. Ptasiewicz, 'The Art of Robert Lenkiewicz'. Available at http://www.robertlenkiewicz. org/art-robert-lenkiewicz.

47 Mallett (ed.), *Robert Lenkiewicz*, plate 66.

48 White Lane Press, *R.O. Lenkiewicz*, p. 110.

49 T. Nicholls, 'I'll Save Mural from Decay', *Plymouth Evening Herald* (5 December 2003).

50 A. Navas in an email to the present author (20 March 2006).

10. The Way Through the Woods

1 S. Farquhar, 'Kip Carpenter – Obituary', *The Independent* (10 March 2012).

2 See A. Fennett, *Catweazle Annual* (Manchester: World Distributors, 1980), pp. 6–7.

3 R. Carpenter quoted on: *The Electric Picture Show* (Grampian TV, 1983).

4 R. Carpenter in J. Matthews, *Robin Hood. Green Lord of the Wildwood* (Glastonbury: Gothic Image Publications, 1993), p. ix.

5 Carpenter quoted on: *The Electric Picture Show*.
   His vision was succinctly captured by Simon Farquhar, in his obituary for Carpenter, published in *The Independent* (10 March 2012):

   He was forever romantic without sentimentality, melancholic yet optimistic, mystical yet believable; his love of the English landscape and fascination with its folklore enchanted much of his work. A childlike sense of wonder without a hint of childishness made him for 20 years the master of that most tricky of genres: family drama.

6 See G. Trease, *Bows Against the Barons* (Moscow: Co-operative Publishing Society for Foreign Workers, 1934). Later, revised editions, shed the more obvious Communist parallels. Richard Greene's *The Adventures of Robin Hood* had been produced by Hannah Weinstein, a significant figure in the American Left and the Civil Rights Movement, who employed a number of writers on the series – including Waldo Salt, Robert Lees and Ring Lardner junior – who had been blacklisted and forbidden from working during the McCarthyite terror in the USA.

7 R. Marsden, 'Exploring the Legend – An Interview with Richard Carpenter', *Starburst*, no. 83 (July 1985), p. 36.

8 Simon de Bellême was based upon the scarcely more pleasant historical figure of Robert de Bellême, 3rd Earl of Shrewsbury, a major landowner and political figure during the reigns of William Rufus and Henry I. Reviled by monastic chroniclers, de Bellême was recast as 'Sir Isenbart de Baleme' in Henry Gilbert's *Robin Hood and the Men of the Greenwood* (London: T.C. & E.C. Jack, 1912), and in E. Charles Vivian's *The Adventures of Robin Hood* (London: Ward Lock, 1927). Both of these works influenced Carpenter and gave him the

idea of de Bellême's murderous intent towards Maid Marion. The Prioress, who poisons Robin at the end of the cycle of traditional tales, clearly prefigures Morgwyn of Ravenscar; though the twist here is that she acts out of a devotion to demonic as opposed to Christian tradition.

   For the historical Robert de Bellême, see F. Barlow, *William Rufus* (London: Methuen, 1983, rpt. 1990), pp. 24–5, 267–71, 274–6, 286–8, 332–3, 379, 381–5 & 402–3.

9   R. Welch, *The Gauntlet* (London: Oxford University Press, 1951, rpt. 1964), pp. 102–5.

10 R. Sutcliff, *Knight's Fee* (London: Oxford University Press, 1960, rpt. 1966), p. 67.

11 Ibid., pp. 132–3.

12 Ibid., pp. 133 & 240.

13 H.R. Williamson, *The Arrow and the Sword* (London: Faber and Faber Ltd., 1947), pp. 106–7.

14 Ibid., pp. 110 & 117.

15 Ibid., pp. 110–11.

16 Barlow, *William Rufus*, p. 113.

17 E.A. Freeman, *The Reign of William Rufus* (Oxford: The Clarendon Press, 1882); M.A. Murray, *The Divine King in England. A Study in Anthropology* (London: Faber & Faber, n.d., 1956), pp. 11–15, 17, 28–30, 56 & 59–60; Murray, *God of the Witches*, pp. 160–8. Murray was in no doubt that 'Rufus was so clearly a pagan [that] he could not receive any kind of recognition from the Christian Church'. See Murray, *The Divine King*, pp. 56 & 60.

18 Sutcliff, *Knight's Fee*, p. 134.

19 R. Sutcliff, *The Witch's Brat* (London: Oxford University Press, 1970), pp. 2, 4 & 6–7.

20 Quoted in B.L. Talcroft, *Death of the Corn King. King and Goddess in Rosemary Sutcliff's Historical Fiction for Young Adults* (Metuchen, NJ, & London: Scarecrow Press, Metuchen, 1995), p. 109.

21 R. Carpenter, *Robin of Sherwood* (Harmondsworth: Puffin Books, 1984, rpt. 1985), p. 79.

22 Ibid., p. 69.

23 Ibid., p. 71.

24 Ibid., p. 9.

25 This imaginative re-paganisation of Saxon England reached its height with Julian Rathbone's novel, *The Last English King* (London: Little, Brown & Company, 1997), pp. xvi–xvii, 118–21 & 305; where the vibrant, highly sexed, patriotic and overtly pagan Godwins are contrasted with the effete, treacherous and devoutly Christian Edward 'the Confessor'.

26 Marston, 'Exploring the Legend', p. 37.

27 W. Shakespeare, *The Merry Wives of Windsor*, Act IV Scene 4.

28 *Merry Wives of Windsor*, Act V Scenes 1–5. It is worth noting that prior to assuming the role of Herne the Hunter, Falstaff had already been persuaded by the women to dress up 'like the witch of Brainford', and had been beaten, humiliated, and threatened with hanging for begging at the door. See Act IV Scene 2. See also K.M. Briggs, *the Anatomy of Puck. An Examination of Fairy Beliefs among Shakespeare's Contemporaries and Successors* (London: Routledge & Kegan Paul Ltd., 1959), pp. 51 & 128.

29 E.L. Fitch, *In Search of Herne the Hunter* (Chieveley, Berkshire: Capall Bann Publishing, 1994), pp. 23–4.

30 Ibid., p. 147.

31 W. Harrison Ainsworth, *Windsor Castle. An Historical Romance*, New Edition (London: Henry Colburn Publisher, 1844), pp. 202–3.

32 Ibid., p. 205.

33 Ibid., pp. 206–11.

34 Ibid., p. 211.

35   J. Richards, 'The 'Lancashire Novelist' and the Lancashire Witches', in R. Poole (ed.), *The Lancashire Witches. Histories and Stories* (Manchester & New York: Manchester University Press, 2002), pp. 166–8.

36   See plate IX in J.M. Petry, *Herne the Hunter. A Berkshire Legend* (Reading, Berkshire: William Smith Ltd., 1972); Fitch, *In Search of Herne the Hunter*, p. 55. For the description on which Cruikshank's engraving was based, see Harrison Ainsworth, *Windsor Castle*, p. 77.

37   S. Cooper, *The Dark is Rising* (Harmondsworth: Puffin Books, 1973, rpt. 1979), pp. 244–5.

38   Grey Owl, *Tales of an Empty Cabin* (London: Lovat Dickson Ltd., 1936); G. Hutchinson, *Grey Owl. The Incredible Story of Archie Belaney, 1888–1938* (Hastings: Self-published, 1985, rpt. 2014), pp. 29–32; L. Dickson (ed.), *The Green Leaf. A Tribute to Grey Owl* (London: Lovat Dickson Publishers, 1938), pp. 13–33 & 35–48.

39   C. Hole, *Witchcraft in England*, illus. M. Peake (London: B.T. Batsford, 1945), pp. 22–5; Murray, *God of the Witches*, pp. 27 & 32; Hutton, *Pagan Religions*, pp. 217 & 233.

40   D. Valiente, *An ABC of Witchcraft. Past and Present* (London: Robert Hale Ltd., 1973), p. 184; J. & S. Farrar, *The Witches' Way. Principles, Rituals and Beliefs of Modern Witchcraft* (London: Robert Hale, 1984, rpt. 1990), pp. 14–15. Appropriately enough, Janet and Stewart Farrar named their home 'Herne's Cottage'.

41   Petry, *Herne the Hunter*, pp. 83 & 97; Fitch, *In Search of Herne the Hunter*, pp. 112–14 & 159.

42   E. Mottram, *A Book of Herne* (Colne: Arrowspire Press, 1981), p. 1.

43   Ibid., pp. 34–5.

44   Ibid., pp. 79, 83 & 88.

45   Ibid., p. 8.

46   Ibid., p. 17.

47   Ibid., p. 79.

48   Ibid., p. 77.

49   See T.M. Luhrmann, *Persuasions of the Witch's Craft. Ritual Magic in Contemporary England* (London: Picador, 1989, rpt. 1994), plate 10; Fitch, *In Search of Herne the Hunter*, p. vi.

50   Carpenter, *Robin of Sherwood*, p. 5.

51   Pennethorne Hughes had already introduced the idea that:

> The legend of Robin Hood was never entirely localised in Sherwood Forest. It appears up and down the country, sometimes with episodes attached to parallel heroes such as Rob Roy or Herne the Hunter (an obvious incarnation of Cernunnos, horns and all) but usually under the name of Robin

She also states that Robin and his outlaw band 'met, as did witches and fairies, round a great oak or oaks. They opposed particularly the Christian Church'. See P. Hughes, *Witchcraft* (London: Longman, 1952, rpt. 1972), p. 67.

52   See R.J. Wallis, *Shamans/Neo-Shamans. Ecstasy, Alternative Archaeologies and Contemporary Pagans* (Routledge, London & New York, 2003); R. Hutton, *Shamans. Siberian Spirituality and the Western Imagination* (London & New York: Hambledon & London, 2001), pp. 50–8; M. Eliade, *Shamanism. Archaic Techniques of Ecstasy*, trans. W.R. Task (London: Penguin Books, 1964, rpt. 1989), pp. 168–71.

53   B. Bennett, *Clannad. Moments in a Lifetime* (Belfast: Appletree Press, 2008), pp. 9, 25, 35, 39, 43, 59 & 63.

54   R. Carpenter & R. May, *Robin of Sherwood and the Hounds of Lucifer* (Harmondsworth: Puffin Books, 1985), p. 60.

55 This development was necessitated, in part, by the cancellation of the *Robin of Sherwood* series, after Goldcrest Productions went into liquidation, in 1986, following the vast losses incured by the Al Pacino movie, *Revolution*. It was also made possible by the advent of the home computer, which made private publication – for the enjoyment of friends and fellow fans – financially viable and aesthetically appealing. Many of the early fanzines were hand-coloured and all were lovingly and profusely, if at times amateurly, illustrated. For overtly Pagan themes, see for example L. Patterson, 'Herne' in *Herne's Son*, vol. I (Spring 1988), pp. 53–7; D. Linn & D. Locher, 'Herne II' in *Herne's Son*, vol. 1 (Spring 1988), pp. 62–57; D. Linn, 'Ladies of the Shadows' & 'Herne's Sons' in *Herne's Son*, vol. II (Fall 1988–9), pp. 36–47; K. Turner, 'Shadows of the Mind' in *Darkmere*, vol. I (September 1986), pp. 29–35.

56 *Herne's Son*, vol. II, pp. 113 & 35, respectively.

57 Appropriately enough, the North American company concerned was called *Herne's Child Wares*.

58 Matthews, *Robin Hood*, pp. 47–54.

What is more surprising is that Fitch's *In Search of Herne the Hunter*, published in 1994, while recording a vast amount of material relating to Herne – including a series of cowboy novels with little obvious relationship to the god-head – remains entirely silent about Richard Carpenter's creation, save for a single footnote on p. 97.

59 See J. & S. Farrar, *The Witches' Way*, pp. 69 & 79, for the manner in which Herne was now evoked, alongside Pan, in major Pagan rituals such as that for the 'Drawing Down of the Moon'. In 2010, a metal band named after *Herne*, released an album themed around the woodland god, with an image of John Abineri in *Robin of Sherwood* on the cover. The lyrics of the first track echoed Harrison Ainsworth's account of the huntsman saving the King; but otherwise the album references Herne within the tradition of the Wild Ride and is deeply influenced by *Beowulf*, Saxon epic poetry and the Asartu path to modern Paganism. Musically, it is influenced by the Nordic black metal bands of the 1990s. See Herne, *Face of the Hunter* (King Penda Records, 2010).

60 In essence, Carpenter is again taking a lead from Pennethorne Hughes, who described of Robin 'twelve chief companions – thirteen of the witch coven'. Hughes, *Witchcraft*, p. 67; from Margaret Murray who wrote of Robin Hood belonging 'essentially to the people, not to the nobles. He was always accompanied by a band of twelve companions, very suggestive of a Grandmaster and his coven'. Moreover, she thought that Robin, himself, acted as 'the incarnate God'. Carpenter put the two ideas together and replaced Robin with Herne as the god-head. See Murray, *God of the Witches*, pp. 36–7.

61 G. Vidal, *Julian* (London: Abacus, 1964 rpt. 1997), p. 532.

Select Bibliography

Adler, M., *Drawing Down the Moon. Witches, Druids, Goddess-Worshippers, and Other Pagans in America Today* (New York & London: Penguin Compass, 1979, rpt. 1986).

Anglo, S. (ed.), *The Damned Art. Essays in the Literature of Witchcraft* (London, Henley and Boston, MA: Routledge & Kegan Paul, 1977, rpt. 1985).

Ankarloo, B., and Henningsen, G. (eds), *Early Modern European Witchcraft. Centres and Peripheries* (Oxford: Clarendon Press, 1990, rpt. 2001).

Apps, L., and Gow, A., *Male Witches in Early Modern Europe* (Manchester & New York: Manchester University Press, 2003).

Apuleius, L., *The Transformation of Lucius, Otherwise Known as The Golden Ass*, trans. R. Graves (Harmondsworth: Penguin Books, 1950).

Barry, J., and Davies, O. (eds), *Witchcraft Historiography* (Basingstoke: Palgrave Macmillan, Houndmills, 2007).

Barstow, A.L., *Witchcraze. A New History of the European Witch Hunts* (San Francisco & London: Pandora, HarperCollins, 1994, rpt. 1995).

Behringer, W., *Witchcraft Persecutions in Bavaria. Popular Magic, Religious Zealotry and Reasons of State in Early Modern Europe* (Cambridge: Cambridge University Press, 1997).

Bettelheim, B., *The Uses of Enchantment. The Meaning and Importance of Fairy Tales* (London: Penguin Books, 1975, rpt. 1991).

Bialostocki, J., *Dürer and His Critics, 1500–1971. Chapters in the History of Ideas Including a Collection of Texts* (Baden-Baden: Koerner, 1986).

Bodin, J. *On the Demon-Mania of Witches*, trans. R.A. Scott (Toronto: Centre for Reformation Studies & Renaissance Studies, 2001).

Boguet, H., *An Examen of Witches*, ed. M. Summers (Bungay, Suffolk: John Rodker, 1929).

Bracelin, J. (I. Shah), *Gerald Gardner: Witch* (Thame: I-H-O Books, 1960, rpt. 1999).

Brauner, S., *Fearless Wives and Frightened Shrews. The Construction of the Witch in Early Modern Germany*, intro. R.H. Brown (Amherst, MA: University of Massachusetts Press, 1995).

Briggs, K.M., *Pale Hecate's Team. An Examination of the Beliefs on Witchcraft and Magic Among Shakespeare's Contemporaries and His Immediate Successors* (London: Routledge & Kegan Paul, 1962).

Briggs, R., *Witches and Neighbours. The Social and Cultural Context of European Witchcraft* (New York & London: Penguin Books, 1996, rpt. 1998).

———, *The Witches of Lorraine* (Oxford: Oxford University Press, 2007).

Brinkmann, B., *Witches' Lust and the Fall of Man: The Strange Fantasies of Hans Baldung Grien* (Frankfurt am Main: Michael Imhof Verlag, 2007).

Carver, R.H.F., *The Protean Ass. The Metamorphoses of Apuleius from Antiquity to the Renaissance* (Oxford: Oxford University Press, 2007).

Certeau, M. de, *The Possession at Loudun*, trans. M.B. Smith (Chicago & London: University of Chicago Press, 1970, English edition 1996, rpt. 2000).

Clark, S., *Thinking with Demons. The Idea of Witchcraft in Early Modern Europe* (Oxford: Oxford University Press, 1997, rpt. 1999).

Cohn, N., *Europe's Inner Demons. The Demonization of Christians in Medieval Christendom*, revised edition (London: Pimlico, 1975, rpt. 1993).

Crawford, H.M., *The Witch of Prague. A Fantastic Tale* (London & New York: Macmillan & Co., 1892).

Daly, M., *Gyn/Ecology. The Metaethics of Radical Feminism* (London: The Women's Press, 1978, rpt. 1979).

Davidson, J.P., *The Witch in Northern European Art, 1470–1750* (Dusseldorf: Luca Verlag Freren, 1987).

Davies, O., *Witchcraft, Magic and Culture, 1736–1951* (Manchester: Manchester University Press, 1999).

———, *Popular Magic. Cunning Folk in English History* (London: Hambledon Continuum, 2003, rpt. 2007).

———, *Grimoires. A History of Magic Books* (Oxford: Oxford University Press, 2009, rpt. 2010).

———, *America Bewitched. The Story of Witchcraft After Salem* (Oxford: Oxford University Press, 2013).

Dillinger, J., Schmidt, J.M., and Bauer, D.R. (eds), *Hexenprozess und Staatsbildung/Witch-Trials and State-Building* (Bielefeld: Verlag fur Regionalgeschichte, 2008).

Dillon, M., *Girls and Women in Classical Greek Religion* (London & New York: Routledge, 2002, rpt. 2003).

Dworkin, A., *Woman Hating* (New York: E. P. Dutton & Co., 1974).

Eichberger, D., and Zika, C. (eds), *Dürer and His Culture* (Cambridge: Cambridge University Press, 1998, rpt. 2005).

Estrange Ewen, C. l' (ed.), *Witch Hunting and Witch Trials. The Indictments for Witchcraft from the Records of 1373 Assizes Held for the Home Circuit A.D. 1559–1736* (London: Kegan Paul, Trench, Trubner & Co. Ltd., 1929).

Evans-Pritchard, E.E. (ed.). *Man and Woman Among the Azande* (London: Faber & Faber, 1974).

Evans-Pritchard, E.E., *Witchcraft, Oracles, and Magic Among the Azande* (Oxford: Clarendon Press, 1976).

Federici, S., *Caliban and the Witch. Women, the Body and Primitive Accumulation* (New York: Autonomedia, Brooklyn, 2004, rpt. 2009).

Flint, V., Gordon, R., Luck, G., and Ogden, D., *Witchcraft and Magic in Europe: Volume 2. Ancient Greece and Rome*, eds. B. Ankarloo & S. Clark (London: The Athlone Press, 1999).

Frazer, J.G., *The Golden Bough. A Study in Magic and Religion*, abridged edition (London & Basingstoke: Papermac/Macmillan Publishers Ltd., 1922, rpt. 1988).

Gage, J.M., *Woman, Church and State* (New York: Humanity Books, 1893, rpt. 2002).

Gardner, G.B., *Witchcraft Today*, intro. M. Murray (London: Jarrolds, 1954, rpt. 1968).

———, *The Meaning of Witchcraft* (Boston, MA: Weiser Books, 1959, rpt. 2004).

Gay, P., *The Enlightenment: An Interpretation. Vol. 1 – The Rise of Modern Paganism* (London: Wildwood House, 1970, rpt. 1973).

———, *The Enlightenment: An Interpretation. Vol. 2 – The Science of Freedom* (London: Wildwood House, 1970, rpt. 1973).

Geis, G., and Bunn, I., *A Trial of Witches. A Seventeenth Century Prosecution* (London & New York: Routledge, 1997, rpt. 1998).

Geyl, P., *Debates with Historians* (London & Glasgow: Fontana/Collins, 1955, rpt. 1970).

Gibson, M., *Reading Witchcraft. Stories of Early English Witches* (London & New York: Routledge, 1999).

Gibson, M. (ed.), *Witchcraft and Society in England and America, 1550–1750* (London: Continuum, 2003).

Gijswijt-Hofstra, M., Levack, B.P., and Porter, R., *Witchcraft and Magic in Europe. Vol. 5 The Eighteenth and Nineteenth Centuries* (London: Athlone Press, 1999).

Ginzburg, C., *The Cheese and the Worms: The Cosmos of a Sixteenth-Century Miller* (London: Penguin, 1980, rpt. 1988).

———, *Ecstasies. Deciphering the Witches' Sabbath*, trans. R. Rosenthal (London: Penguin Books, 1991, rpt. 1992).

Grimm, J., *Teutonic Mythology*, Vol. III, trans. J.S. Stallybrass (Cambridge: Cambridge University Press, 2012).

Henningsen, G., *The Witches' Advocate. Basque Witchcraft and the Spanish Inquisition* (Reno, Nevada: University of Nevada Press, 1980).

Heselton, P., *Witchfather. A Life of Gerald Gardner, Vol. 1 Into the Witch Cult* (Loughborough: Thoth Publications, 2012).

———, *Witchfather. A Life of Gerald Gardner, Vol. 2 From Witch Cult to Wicca* (Loughborough: Thoth Publications, 2012).

Hults, L.C., *The Witch as Muse: Art, Gender, and Power in Early Modern Europe* (Philadelphia, PA: University of Pennsylvania Press, 2011).

Hutton, R., *The Pagan Religions of the Ancient British Isles. Their Nature and Legacy* (Oxford: Blackwell Publishing, 1991, rpt. 1993).

———, *The Triumph of the Moon. A History of Modern Pagan Witchcraft* (Oxford: Oxford University Press, 1999).

———, *Witches, Druids and King Arthur* (London & New York: Hambledon Continuum, 2003).

———, *Pagan Britain* (New Haven & London: Yale University Press, 2013).

Huxley, A., *The Devils of Loudun* (London: Readers Union, Chatto & Windus, 1954).

Juschka, D.M. (ed.), *Feminism in the Study of Religion. A Reader* (London & New York: Continuum, 2001).

Kamenetsky, C., *The Brothers Grimm and their Critics. Folktales and the Quest for Meaning* (Athens, GA: Ohio University Press, 1992).

Kelly, A., *Crafting the Art of Magic. Book I. A History of Modern Witchcraft, 1939–1964* (St Paul, MA: Llewellyn Publications, 1991).

Kittredge, G.L., *Witchcraft in Old and New England* (Cambridge, MA: Harvard University Press, 1929).

Kunze, M., *Highroad to the Stake. A Tale of Witchcraft*, trans. W.E. Yuill (Chicago & London: University of Chicago Press, 1987).

Ladurie, E. le Roy, *Jasmin's Witch. An Investigation into Witchcraft and Magic in South-West France During the Seventeenth Century*, trans. B. Pearce (London: Penguin Books, 1983, rpt. 1987).

Larner, C., *Enemies of God. The Witch-Hunt in Scotland* (Oxford: Basil Blackwell, 1981, rpt. 1983).

Lecky, W.E.H., *History of the Rise and Influence of the Spirit of Rationalism in Europe* (London, Bombay & Calcutta: Longmans, Green & Co., 1910).

Leland, C.G., *Aradia, or the Gospel of the Witches*, trans. M. & D. Pazzaglini (Blaine, Washington, DC: Phoenix Publishing, 1998).

Lenkiewicz, R.O., *Notes on the Barbican Mural* (Ashburton, Devon: Fearns Publishing Company, 1972).

Levack, B.P., *The Witch-Hunt in Early Modern Europe*, 2nd edn (London & New York: Longman, 1987, rpt. 1995).

Levack, B.P. (ed.), *New Perspectives on Witchcraft, Magic and Demonology. Volume 4: Gender and Witchcraft* (New York & London: Routledge, 2001).

———, *The Witchcraft Sourcebook* (New York & London: Routledge, 2004, rpt. 2006).

Lindley, D., *The Trials of Frances Howard. Fact and Fiction at the Court of James I* (London and New York: Routledge, 1993, rpt. 1996).

Luhrmann, T.M., *Persuasions of the Witch's Craft. Ritual Magic in Contemporary England* (London: Picador, 1989, rpt. 1994).

Macfarlane, A., *Witchcraft in Tudor and Stuart England. A Regional and Comparative Study*, 2nd edn, intro. J. Sharpe (London: Routledge, 1970, rpt. 1999).

Mallett, F. (ed.), *Robert Lenkiewicz. Paintings and Projects* (Plymouth: White Lane Press, 2006).

Marwick, M. (ed.), *Witchcraft and Sorcery. Selected Readings* (Harmondsworth: Penguin Books, 1970).

Michelet, J., *Satanism and Witchcraft. A Study in Medieval Superstition*, trans. A.R. Allinson (London: Tandem Books, 1965).

Midelfort, H.C.E., *Witch Hunting in Southwestern Germany, 1562–1684. The Social and Intellectual Foundation* (Stanford, CA: Stanford University Press, 1972).

Monter, E.W., *Witchcraft in France and Switzerland. The Borderlands during the Reformation* (Ithaca & London: Cornell University Press, 1976).

Morton, P.A., *The Trial of Tempel Anneke. Records of a Witchcraft Trial in Brunswick, Germany, 1663*, trans. B. Dahms (Peterborough, Ontario, Canada: Broadview Press, 2006).

Murray, M.A., *The Witch-Cult in Western Europe. A Study in Anthropology* (Oxford: Clarendon Press, 1921).

———, *The God of the Witches* (London: Sampson Low, Marston & Co. Ltd., n/d, orig. 1931).

Newall, V. (ed.), *The Witch Figure. Folklore Essays by a Group of Scholars in England Honouring the 75th Birthday of Katharine M. Briggs* (London & Boston: Routledge & Kegan Paul, 1973).

Notestein, W., *History of Witchcraft in England, from 1558 to 1718* (Washington, DC: American Historical Association, 1911).

O'Keefe, D.L., *Stolen Lightening. The Social Theory of Magic* (Oxford: Martin Robertson, 1982).

Owen, A., *The Darkened Room. Women, Power, and Spiritualism in Late Victorian England* (Chicago & London: University of Chicago Press, 1989, rpt. 2004).

Pearson, J., Roberts, R.H., and Samuel, G. (eds), *Nature Religion Today. Paganism in the Modern World* (Edinburgh: Edinburgh University Press, 1998).

Petherbridge, D., *Witches and Wicked Bodies* (Edinburgh: National Galleries of Scotland in association with the British Museum, 2013).

Purkiss, D., *The Witch in History. Early Modern and Twentieth Century Representations* (London: Routledge, 1996, rpt. 2003).

———, *At the Bottom of the Garden. A Dark History of Fairies, Hobgoblins, and Other Troublesome Things* (New York: New York University Press, 2000, rpt. 2001).

Rapley, R., *A Case of Witchcraft. The Trial of Urbain Grandier* (Manchester: Manchester University Press, 1998).

Ripellino, A.M., *Magic Prague*, trans. D.N. Marinelli (Basingstoke & Oxford: Picador, 1973, rpt. 1994).

Roper, J. (ed.), *Charms and Charming in Europe* (Houndmills, Basingstoke: Palgrave/Macmillan, 2004).

Roper, L., *Oedipus and the Devil. Witchcraft, Sexuality and Religion in Early Modern Europe* (London & New York: Routledge, 1994).

———, *Witch Craze. Terror and Fantasy in Baroque Germany* (New Haven & London: Yale University Press, 2004).

Rose, E., *A Razor for a Goat. Problems in the History of Witchcraft and Diabolism* (Toronto: University of Toronto Press, 1975, rpt. Revised 1993).

Rosen, B. (ed.), *Witchcraft in England, 1558–1618* (Amherst, MA: University of Massachusetts Press, 1969, rpt. 1991).

Runeberg, A., *Witches, Demons and Fertility Magic. Analysis of their Significance and Mutual Relations in West-European Folk Religion* (Helsingfors: Societas Scientiarum Fennica, 1947).

Savage, C., *Witch. The Wild Ride from Wicked to Wicca* (London: The British Museum Press, 2000).

Scarre, G., and Callow, J., *Witchcraft and Magic in Sixteenth- and Seventeenth-Century Europe*, 2nd edn (Houndmills, Basingstoke: Palgrave Macmillan, 2001).

Scholz Williams, G., *Defining Dominion. The Discourses of Magic and Witchcraft in Early Modern France and Germany* (Ann Arbor, MI: University of Michigan Press, 1995, rpt. 1999).

Scot, R., *The Discoverie of Witchcraft*, intro. M. Summers (New York: Dover Publications, 1930, rpt. 1972).

Scott, J., *Salvator Rosa. His Life and Times* (New Haven & London: Yale University Press, 1995).

Sebald, H., *Witch-Children from Salem Witch-Hunts to Modern Courtrooms* (Amherst, NY: Prometheus Books, 1995).

Sharpe, J., *Witchcraft in Seventeenth-Century Yorkshire: Accusations and Counter Measures*, Borthwick Paper No. 81 (York: University of York, 1992).

———, *Instruments of Darkness. Witchcraft in England, 1550–1750* (London: Penguin Books, 1996, rpt. 1997).

———, *Witchcraft in Early Modern England* (Harlow: Pearson Education, 2001).

Smith, W.B., *Reformation and the German Territorial State: Upper Franconia, 1300–1630* (New York: Rochester University Press, Rochester, 2008).

Stephens, W., *Demon Lovers. Witchcraft, Sex, and the Crisis of Belief* (Chicago & London: University of Chicago Press, 2002, rpt. 2003).

Thomas, K., *Religion and the Decline of Magic. Studies in Popular Beliefs in Sixteenth- and Seventeenth-Century England* (London: Penguin Books, 1971, rpt. 1991).

Thompson, E.P., *Customs in Common* (London & New York: Penguin Books, 1991, rpt. 1993).

Trevor-Roper, H., *The European Witch-Craze of the 16th and 17th Centuries* (Harmondsworth: Penguin Books, 1967, rpt. 1978).

Valiente, D., *The Rebirth of Witchcraft* (London: Robert Hale, 1989, rpt. 2007).

Wallis, R.J., *Shamans/Neo-Shamans. Ecstasy, Alternative Archaeologies and Contemporary Pagans* (London & New York: Routledge, 2003).

Warner, M., *From the Beast to the Blonde, on Fairytales and their Tellers* (London: Chatto & Windus, 1994).

Whiting, J., *The Devils. A Play Based on a Book by Aldous Huxley* (London: Heinemann, 1961).

Wilson, E., *To the Finland Station. A Study in the Writing and Acting of History* (London & Glasgow: Fontana/Collins, 1960, rpt. 1970).

Yates, F.A., *The Occult Philosophy in the Elizabethan Age* (London & New York: Routledge, 1979, rpt. 2010).

Zika, C., *The Appearance of Witchcraft. Print and Visual Culture in Sixteenth-Century Europe* (Abingdon, Oxfordshire & New York: Routledge, 2007).

Zipes, J., *The Enchanted Screen. The Unknown History of Fairy Tale Films* (London: Taylor & Francis Ltd., 2011).

———, *The Irresistible Fairy Tale. The Cultural and Social History of a Genre* (Princeton & Oxford: Princeton University Press, 2012).

Index

References in **bold** refer to plate illustrations.